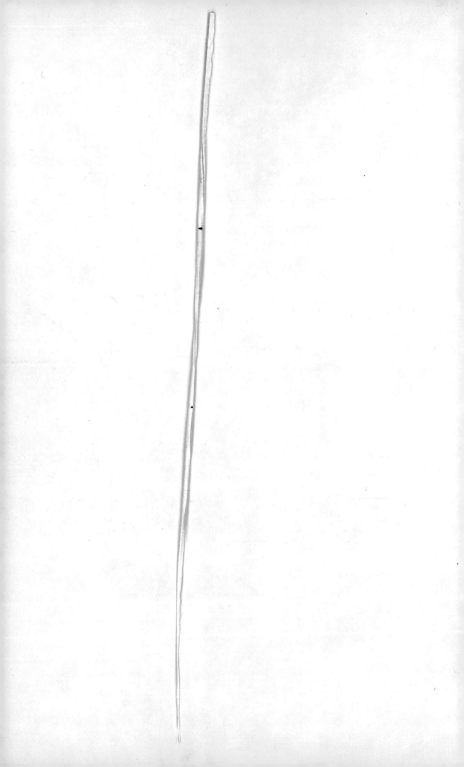

A COMMENTARY

ON THE GENERAL PROLOGUE TO

THE CANTERBURY TALES

THE MACMILLAN COMPANY
NEW YORK · BOSTON · CHICAGO
DALLAS · ATLANTA · SAN FRANCISCO

MACMILLAN AND CO., LIMITED
LONDON · BOMBAY · CALCUTTA
MADRAS · MELBOURNE

THE MACMILLAN COMPANY
OF CANADA, LIMITED
TORONTO

THE CHAUCER MINIATURE

FROM THE ELLESMERE MS.

A COMMENTARY
on the General Prologue
to the Canterbury Tales

BY

MURIEL BOWDEN

NEW YORK

THE MACMILLAN COMPANY

1949

For permission to use the copyrighted material in this volume, acknowledgment is made to the followin
lishers and authors: American Philological Association for an article by J. M. Manly, *Transactions*, XX:
1907; Ernest Benn Ltd. and G. P. Putnam & Sons for passages from J. J. Jusserand's *English Wayfari*
in the Middle Ages, transl. Lucy Toulmin Smith, 1890; Basil Blackwell & Mott Ltd. for passage
Le Livre de Seyntz Medicines ed. E. J. Arnould, (Anglo-Norman Text Society, II, 1940); Chatto & \
for passages from *The Rule of Saint Benedict* transl. Cardinal Gasquet, 1936; Columbia University Pr
passages from Lynn Thorndike's *History of Magic and Experimental Science* and from an article by
Emerson in *Romanic Review*, XIII, 1922; Constable & Company for a passage from *Fifteenth Century*
and Verse ed. A. W. Pollard, 1903, and for material from Vol. CIV of *Nineteenth Century*, 1928; Co
of His Britannic Majesty's Stationery Office for passages from *Political Poems and Songs* ed. Thomas
(Rolls Series 14) and from Walsingham's *Historia Anglicana* ed. Henry Thomas Riley (Rolls Serie
J. M. Dent & Sons Ltd. and E. P. Dutton for passages from Arthur Penrhyn Stanley's *Historical Me*
of Canterbury, 1906, and *Le Roman de la Rose* transl. F. S. Ellis, 1900; The Gilmary Society for p
from the Catholic Encyclopedia; Ginn & Company for passages from A. S. Cook's *A Literary Middle*
Reader, 1915; Henry Holt & Company for passages from J. M. Manly's *Canterbury Tales*, 1928, an
New Light on Chaucer, 1926; Houghton Mifflin Company for passages from John Livingston Lowes' \
tion and Revolt in Poetry, 1922; Houghton Mifflin Company and Oxford University Press for passag
the *Complete Works of Geoffrey Chaucer* ed. F. N. Robinson, 1933; The Johns Hopkins Press for \
from *Modern Language Notes*, XII, 1897, LIV, 1939, LVI, 1941; Lea & Febiger for passages from Henry
Lea's *A History of Auricular Confession and Indulgences in the Latin Church*, 1896; Longmans, G
Company for passages from Dorothy Hughes' *Illustrations of Chaucer's England*, 1918, *The Golden Le*
Jacobus De Voragine transl. Granger Ryan and Helmut Ripperger, 1941, and *Walter of Henley's Hu*
ed. and transl. Elizabeth Lamond, 1890; for passages from Grove: *Dictionary of Music and Musician*
right 1904, 1927, and 1932 by The Macmillan Company and used with their permission; The Macmilla
pany and the Society for Promoting Christian Knowledge for passages from H. F. Westlake's *Parish* \
Mediaeval England, 1919; The Macmillan Company and the Cambridge University Press for passage
E. Power's *Medieval English Nunneries*, 1922, G. R. Owst's *Preaching in Medieval England*, 1926,
Owst's *Literature and Pulpit in Medieval England*, 1933, G. G. Coulton's *Social Life in Britain*
G. G. Coulton's *Medieval Panorama*, 1939, G. G. Coulton's *Life in the Middle Ages*, 1928; The M
Academy of America for passages from an article by Pauline Aiken in *Speculum*, X, and from G
Columnis's *Historia Destructionis Troiae* ed. Nathaniel Edward Griffin, 1936; Methuen & Compa
passages from G. G. Coulton's *Chaucer and His England*, 1937, Abbot Gasquet's *English Monastic Lif*
George Unwin's *The Gilds and Companies of London*, 1938; Modern Language Association for passag
PMLA; New York University Press for passages from *Essays in Honor of Carleton Brown*, 1940;
University Press for passages from Walter Clyde Curry's *Chaucer and the Medieval Sciences*, 1926;
University Press and Clarendon Press for the following: H. P. Cholmeley's *John of Gaddesden and t*
Medicinae, 1912, John Gower's *Complete Works* (ed. G. C. Macaulay), 1901 and 1902, R. L. Greene
English Carols, 1935, *Chronicle of Makhairas* (ed. and transl. R. M. Dawkins) 1932, Langland's *Pier*
man (ed. Skeat), 1886, Chaucer's *Complete Works* (ed. Skeat), 1894, Rashdall's *Universities of Europ*
Middle Ages (ed. Powicke and Emden), 1936, Stow's *Survey of London* (ed. Kingsford), 1906; Oxfo
versity Press and Early English Text Society for the following: Arderne's *Treatises* (ed. D'A.
O.S.139, *The Prologue and Tale of Beryn* (ed. Furnivall and Stone) E.S.105, *The Brut* (ed. Brie) \
136, *Life and Death of Sir Thomas Moore* (ed. R. W. Chambers) O.S.186, *Fifteenth Century Courte*
(ed. R. W. Chambers) O.S.148, *Book of Knight of La Tour Landry* (ed. Thomas Wright) O.S.33
Coventriae (ed. K. S. Block) E.S.120, *Mandeville's Travels* (ed. Hamelius) O.S.153, 154, *English W*
Wyclif (ed. F. D. Matthew) O.S.74, Myrc's *Instructions for Parish Priests* (ed. Peacock) O.S.31, (
Chyualry (ed. A. T. P. Byles) O.S.168, *Secreta Secretorum* (ed. R. Steele) O.S.74, *Two 15th Cent.*
Books (ed. T. Austin) O.S.91; Routledge & Sons Ltd. for passages from *Chivalry* ed. Edgar Prestag
Charles Scribner's Sons and John Murray for passages from *The Book of Ser Marco Polo* ed. and tra
Henry Yule, 1903; The Society of Antiquaries of London for passage from Hilary Jenkinson's \
Archaeologia, Vol. LXXIV, 1925; Staples Press Limited for passages from James Galloway's *The*
and Chapel of Saint Mary Roncevall, 1914; University of Chicago Press for passages from *Modern P*
an article by O. F. Emerson, I, 1903, article by E. Rickert, XXIV, 1926, article by E. P. M. Die
XXVI, 1929; University of Illinois Press for passages from an article by A. S. Cook, *Journal of Eng*
Germanic Philology, XIV, 1915; Paul Alonzo Brown for passages from *The Development of the L*
Thomas Becket published by the University of Pennsylvania Press, 1930; Wisconsin Academy of
Arts, and Letters for passages from an article by E. P. Kuhl in *Transactions*, XVIII, 1916.

FOR

R. S. L. AND H. L. G.

IN ADMIRATION AND AFFECTION

42152

PREFACE

THIS BOOK is intended for three classes of readers. First, for those schooled in Chaucerian criticism I have attempted to collect and arrange the outstanding latest critical opinions on the *General Prologue* to the *Canterbury Tales*, and to point out the best of the known parallels between Chaucer's words and ideas and those of authors prior to or contemporaneous with him. Second, for the college students I have expanded the more important notes to be found in good editions of the *Canterbury Tales* with the hopes that the late fourteenth century will take on the colours of actuality, and that a reference which may suggest fields for further investigation will thus be provided. And third, for the general reader who would like to become better acquainted with Chaucer I have striven to make clear what is obscure in the language, or in the ideas, customs, and institutions of Chaucer's England, so that the great poet will speak meaningfully and provocatively to him. I ask that the scholar and the specialist excuse what may seem to them unnecessarily elementary in the following pages, such as translations of medieval Latin, Old French,* and difficult Middle English excerpts, and the glossing ** of many of Chaucer's lines; and that Chaucer's newer friends be not irked by the highly technical and specialized character of some of the Notes. In quotations I have adjusted the letters *u* and *v* to modern practice, and substituted modern sound symbols for the Middle English þ and ʒ. Quotations from the *General Prologue* are cited by line number in the text; all other Chaucer references are given with other references in the Notes.

* Occasionally, where the words of the Old French are in themselves important to a discussion (as in Chapter III), a passage is quoted in the original French.

** I have based the glossing on the needs I have observed among students who are reading Chaucer for the first time. But occasionally all of us must be reminded of the exact meanings of words. Even such a scholar as Sir Israel Gollancz has mistranslated (*Chivalry*, ed. Edgar Prestage [London, 1928], p. 173) Chaucer's "His hors were goode . . ." as "His horse was good."

As far as I am aware, the *General Prologue* has never before been treated in such a manner, and, as a teacher and student of Chaucer, I feel that such a study is essential for the fuller comprehension of "worthie Chaucer glorious." Only in great University libraries can teachers and students find the materials alluded to in the best editions of Chaucer, or the research articles which have added so largely to the knowledge of the poet himself and of his times. I have tried therefore to make available in one book much that has for many been "unknowe . . . and lost" because necessarily it has been "unsought."

My work has perforce been limited in scope. Foreign manuscripts and many modern foreign publications have been unavailable during the last six years, and I have been obliged to rely on whatever source material I could obtain in this country; and because of the secondary nature of much of this material, I have found it difficult (sometimes impossible) to gather adequate criteria for weighing evidence—frequently conclusions have had to be suggested rather than stated. But if the book illumines the understanding of a few, or opens even a small window upon new vistas for the majority of those who read it, I am satified that it has not failed in its purpose.

As a basic Chaucer text I have used Professor F. N. Robinson's edition of *The Complete Works of Geoffrey Chaucer* (Cambridge, Mass., 1933) ; and I am much indebted throughout to the writings of W. W. Skeat, J. M. Manly, G. G. Coulton, and G. R. Owst, to all of whom due acknowledgments are made. Many acknowledgments of debt and expressions of gratitude cannot appear in the text, however; and it gives me great pleasure to speak of them here. My book could scarcely have been undertaken, nor could the joy I have had in living with Chaucer's masterpiece been so profoundly satisfying, without the untiring encouragement and constructive, scholarly criticism of Professor Roger Sherman Loomis, "myn owene maister deere." I am also deeply grateful to a number of other members of the faculty of Columbia University for their interest and help, particularly to Professor Elliott Van Kirk Dobbie for his unsparing pains in criticizing the manuscript and for his valuable detailed suggestions, and to Professor Adriaan J. Barnouw for his scholarly opinion and criticism. I should like also to express my appreciation to the staff of the Columbia University Library, particularly to Miss Jean Macalister and to Miss Jacqueline Castles for their efficient and willing aid in procuring books and finding references for me; and to Mrs. Adele B. Mendelsohn for her kindness in smoothing my path in many ways during the last six years.

Finally I am most happy to acknowledge here my very great debt to two friends: first, to Mrs. Laura Hibbard Loomis, scholar in the medieval period, and formerly Professor of English at Wellesley College, for her encouragement and her readiness to give me exceptionally detailed criticism; and second, to Mr. Howard Goodhart, distinguished bibliophile and book-collector, for his generosity in opening his library to me, and for the heartening and sustained interest he has shown in my work in the Chaucer field.

M. B.

Columbia University
May, 1948

CONTENTS

CONTENTS

CHAPTER I

"THIS WORLD SO VARIABLE,"

1380–1387

IT IS A truism that a great poet speaks always to the heart and to the imagination in words that bear a universal meaning. Nevertheless, to comprehend fully the poet, we must also behold his limited world of actuality and the poet himself as living in that world. Geoffrey Chaucer, whom Lydgate called "the first that ever elumined our language with flowers of rethorick eloquence," [1] can of course give us some measure of delight whenever and however we read him, but our pleasure is the more profound the more confidently we are able to hold the mirror of his art up to a nature that is peculiarly that of the fourteenth century. We shall attempt in this book, therefore, to look at the happy company of Canterbury pilgrims gathered together at the Tabard Inn nearly six hundred years ago with the eyes and understanding of that bygone age, and to hear what the poet's own contemporaries had to say about the social types the company represent and the social scene to which they belong.

In what sort of world, under what circumstances of personal fortune or misfortune did the poet conceive his great masterpiece? What is known about the activities, the comings and goings, of Geoffrey Chaucer during the period from 1380 to 1387 when the ideas for the *Canterbury Tales* took root in his mind and germinated? The social, political, and economic conditions of life in England, the habits of thought and the institutions of this period, present a problem to anyone who investigates them unless he realizes that the time was not so much one of transition as of paradox. These years were strongly medieval and amazingly "modern," yet nearly everything in them that pointed towards today was, in the following centuries, inexplicably arrested. We often find 1387 strangely nearer to us in spirit than 1487, or 1587, or even 1887. In retrospect the late fourteenth century does not appear to bridge any gap, but to stand alone, with old and new in constant contradiction.

These years from 1380 to 1387, and even, indeed, to 1400, were extraordinarily modern in that they heard Englishmen freely voicing the theory that all men are created equal,[2] and saw labour resisting employer in concerted action;[3] yet these were years so thoroughly imbued with traditional beliefs that he who preached the brotherhood of man in one sentence, reminded his audience in the next that the tiller of the soil was ordained by God to be inferior, and that the peasant was guilty of actual sin if he rebelled against his lot.[4] This was a period when the "commons" in Parliament had become in many essentials what they are today: they constituted the junction between the government and the people, and they were one of the two necessary elements in a valid parliament;[5] yet this was a period when the commons were only beginning to assert legislative power,[6] and when, in the modern sense, they in no way "represented" the common people.[7] This was a period when widespread interest prevailed among the upper classes in learning and the arts, in education for the sons of the gentry,[8] and in furthering the use of English as a respectable language in which to write and to conduct the affairs of state; yet this was still a period of dark illiteracy for the poor, and a period when Wyclifite insistence upon popular reading of a vernacular Bible was construed as grounds for religious persecution.[9] The world of the late fourteenth century was wholly medieval in that it was still harassed by combat with monstrously powerful and inimical forces: the cold and the darkness, the storm and the sea, the unfriendly mysteries waiting beyond the horizon, disease and sudden death, and an avid Satan ever ready to lay hold of the soul. It was still a local world, untroubled by the smoke and noise of machines, or by the bewilderments of modern science, or by global problems, yet a world so ill-equipped psychologically to meet change that its problems were as overwhelming as if they had encircled the earth. It was a world weighed down by a crushing load of religious and feudal traditions and a stubborn reverence for outmoded formulae. But this sharply paradoxical world, in which Chaucer lived and wrote, was peopled with men and women, human beings whose loves and hates, sins and virtues, were very much the same as they had been "withinne a thousand yeer," or as they are today, or as they probably will be for a thousand years to come.

The immensely complicated political scene in England during the years 1380 to 1387 centered in London. Although the seat of government was located in Westminster, a municipality adjacent to London proper,[10] London shared in sophisticated court life. Even more important, London was the center of trade and finance and the home of intellectuality, setting the standards for English fashions, English customs, and English ideas: "what London thought was also what England thought."[11] It had been Londoners who eagerly listened to, and openly sympathized with, Wyclif's first bold protests against Church practices.[12] It was a group of disgruntled Londoners who admitted Wat Tyler's men to the city in the Peasants' Revolt of 1381; it was the London mob who swelled the rebel band in sacking the Duke of Lancaster's palace, the Temple, and the priory of St. John's Clerkenwell, and it was with the connivance of London soldiers that Tyler and his men were able to enter the Tower and murder the inoffensive Archbishop Simon of Sudbury and the Treasurer Hales.[13] Again it was Londoners who, sickened by wholesale murder and destruction, finally rallied to the defence of the King and the loyalists, and changed what might have been a nightmare revolution into an uprising which ended in complete lack of success for the peasants.[14]

It was in London that the great trade rivalries, often resulting in armed attacks, were nourished, and became political issues, so that the packed parliament became a matter of course; in London, exporter fought importer, native business men quarrelled with foreign, merchant-princes forced small dealers to the wall, the heavily armed retainers of the powerful victuallers' gilds warred against those of the equally powerful non-victuallers,' even journeymen within the gilds united against their own master-craftsmen.[15] Moreover, London politics, which were essentially English politics during this period, were distorted by a national crisis of great magnitude: the Hundred Years' War had reached a phase of disheartening stalemate when the *Canterbury Tales* was conceived and born,[16] and Englishmen were bitterly divided over allegiance to the King.

Dissatisfaction with the conduct of the war with France and with the domestic policy of the Crown was rife. It combined with the would-be usurpers of power to bring about most of the difficulties of the ill-starred Richard II. The year 1385 saw the breach between the King and Parliament formally acknowledged; the strength of ordered justice could not now even be hoped for in the State. The magnetic personality of Richard had won him ardent supporters, bent on keeping him on the throne at all costs; but he had as many, if not more, determined adversaries who would no longer overlook, or declared they would not, his consistent preferment of court favourites, his wanton extravagance, and his arrogant wilfulness. In this year men learned to walk warily through sullen crowds, or in ominously empty streets. Who could now be trusted, who now was friend and who foe? These were days when the sword or the gallows might be anyone's fate.

In 1386 Richard's cause suffered two further misfortunes. The first of these was the remarkable impetus which the rising popularity of the Duke of Gloucester, Richard's uncle and strongest enemy at this time, received through the capture by forces under Gloucester's command of the Flemish fleet. To understand how momentous this naval victory seemed to the English, we must remember that no major battle in the war had been won by the English since the spectacular success of Richard's father, the Black Prince, at Poitiers thirty long years before. On the continent only Calais and a narrow strip of land in distant Aquitaine remained in English hands. English command of the seas had been lost, and the French and Spanish were repeatedly raiding English coastal towns. Rumours were everywhere afoot that the French were assembling an enormous force to invade England.

This fear of invasion was especially real. The chronicler Walsingham, from the security of his monastery and his later knowledge that invasion was not to occur, wrote of the Londoners of 1386 as follows:

When it was understood for certain that the King of France had collected his ships and made ready his army, and was of purpose to invade England, the Londoners, timid as hares and nervous as mice, sought conflicting counsel on all sides, peered into dark places, and began to mistrust their own strength, and despair of resistance as though the city were on the point of being taken. Those who in peace had arrogantly boasted that they would drive all Frenchmen out of England, now when they heard the rumour, albeit unfounded, of the enemy's approach, thought that all England could scarcely protect them. And so, as though drunken with wine, they rushed to the city walls, breaking and tearing down all the adjacent houses, and timorously doing everything they were wont to do in the greatest extremity.[17]

For anyone who has in recent years admired the magnificent courage of Londoners facing a vastly greater danger, it is difficult to picture their ancestors as being "timid as hares and nervous as mice," but undoubtedly there must have been some fire of panic to have produced the smoke of Walsingham's account. Furthermore, since this was a period of unprecedented uncertainty and stress, we can well believe that many Englishmen were then in great fear, and were ready to turn to any leader who appeared to promise success in the war.

The second misfortune to Richard's cause in 1386 was the departure of John of Gaunt for Spain. This uncle of the King's was no more liked than his nephew, and hence, for Richard, he was negligible as a potential enemy. But when he left England, his place was taken by his son, Henry Bolingbroke, the future Henry IV, whose popularity at that period made him a foe with whom Richard really had to reckon. When Bolingbroke joined with Gloucester, the combination against the King was formidable.[18]

Both Richard and Gloucester and all England with them spent 1387 in preparing for armed conflict. Misfortune dogged the King and his supporters to such an extent, however, that Gloucester was able to seize control of the government; in December he marched against London, confined his nephew temporarily in the Tower, and succeeded in having himself appointed at the head of a commission of regency. He then summoned a parliament which he stipulated should be free of Richard's adherents; [19] it was this parliament which history was to dub the Merciless because of its wholesale decrees of death or exile for so many of Richard's friends, men who must all have been known to Chaucer. Gloucester's triumph was brief, to be sure; nevertheless, the disasters and terrors of his short regime must have had far-reaching effects on all who witnessed them.

And what of Geoffrey Chaucer during this period of national and local unrest and calamity? The records do not tell us a great deal about the poet, but there is enough to enable us to reconstruct his life from 1380 to 1387 with a fair degree of certainty.[20]

Chaucer's personal circumstances from 1380 to 1384 appear to have been thoroughly comfortable. He and his wife Philippa were living in Chaucer's rent-free house over Aldgate, where they had been in pleasant and convenient residence since 1374, and both were much in favour at court. Chaucer was receiving a substantial pension and other grants from the Crown; Philippa, as a former member of John of Gaunt's household, was receiving a pension [21] and occasional costly gifts [22] from the Duke. Philippa, it will be remembered, was the sister of Katherine Swynford, who became the mistress and later the third wife of John of Gaunt. Chaucer also had held from 1374 the important public office of Controller of the Customs on Wool, Hides, and Sheepskins; furthermore, he was made Controller of the Petty Customs in 1382. That Chaucer was involved in a case of abduction in 1380 could scarcely have ruffled the calm of his material prosperity, for he was quickly cleared of the charge, and had the honour of being vouched for by such important men as Sir William de Beauchamp, brother of the Earl of Warwick and captain of the town of Calais, a man for whom Chaucer had served as mainpernor in 1378; [23] by Sir William Neville, a relative of both Sir Lewis Clifford [24] and Beauchamp, and a member of the King's Council; by Sir John Clanvowe, another member of the King's Council, and a great diplomat and soldier; and by the only slightly less important John Philipot, a power in London politics and an associate of Chaucer's in the Customs.[25] Towards the latter part of this five-year period of success Chaucer had attained sufficient importance in his position to be granted, for four months in 1383 and one month in 1384, a temporary deputy in the Wool Customs so that he might absent himself from London to attend to private business. These years, in spite of the general conditions of political and social upheaval, were indeed a time when material Fortune smiled on the poet.

But the records tell us only bare facts, and the thought of the period and events which Chaucer may have observed without actually participating in them must have had their influence on the sensitive poet: like Ulysses, Geoffrey Chaucer was a part of all that he had met. How, then, did his environment and the large events of the period affect him? How did he spend his time when he was not employed in the busy Custom House, so near to Aldgate?

The unfinished *House of Fame,* composed in the Aldgate house, gives us a humorous, although probably none the less true, picture of Chaucer's leisure in these years; the inimitable eagle of the poem, as he bears "Geffrey" aloft, informs his understandably nervous burden that, as Jupiter's friend, he is aware of the poet's habits:

> . . . thou wolt make
> A-nyght ful ofte thyn hed to ake
> In thy studye, so thou writest—
>
> .   .   .   .
>
> For when thy labour doon al ys,
> And hast mad alle thy rekenynges,
> In stede of reste and newe thynges,
> Thou goost hom to thy hous anoon;
> And, also domb as any stoon,
> Thou sittest at another book
> Tyl fully daswed ys thy look,
> And lyvest thus as an heremyte,
> Although thyn abstynence ys lyte.[26]

Thus we see Chaucer coming home from his day at the Custom House, eagerly reaching for a book or his pen after his bountiful supper (no "heremyte" given to "abstynence" is this portly gentleman!). He is perhaps putting the finishing touches to, or reading over, the lately completed *Parliament of Fowls,* that most delightful of love-vision poems. He may be writing the *House of Fame,* or translating Boethius's *De Consolatione Philosophiae*, or possibly he may be beginning the *Troilus and Criseyde,* for which he easily borrows scenes to be observed from the Aldgate windows: busy London from one, and the approach to the city, along the ribbon-like road stretching across the marshes, from another.[27] For no matter how much of a menace London may have seemed to Chaucer at times, the city was in his blood, its sights and sounds and smells always an influence upon him. To know Chaucer's London, then, is as important for us in our understanding of the poet as to know, as far as we can, how national events affected him.

Chaucer's London was, like the times, a study in contrasts. The poet must have been as used to looking upon the splendour and extravagance of palace surroundings [28] as upon the meanness of small dwellings crowded together in narrow lanes. The intricacies, excitements, and conflicts of a thriving commerce must have been as familiar to Chaucer as the squalor and desperate uncertainty of the London poor. Many writers on medieval London have ignored the miseries, either because of contemporary pride, or of later conviction that the past, because it was the past, was golden; we find examples of these two points of view in the fifteenth-century panegyric "London thou art of townes A *per se*," which speaks only of happy gayety and wealth,[29] and in William Morris's romantic description of fourteenth-century London, which speaks of the city as "small and white and clean." [30] Chaucer's London was indeed "small" in area, but its population was relatively large;[31] to a certain extent the city was "white," for many of the closely built, gabled houses, with their overhanging bay windows, were lime-washed; but since the city was without proper sanitation, London could not possibly be called "clean." The number of Ordinances passed in the fourteenth century stipulating better disposal of garbage and sewage indicates clearly the ineffectuality of such measures.[32] Moreover, the general sense of orderly peace conveyed by William Morris's phrase, and that of uniform stately prosperity conveyed by the fifteenth-century poem, are both denied by the din and smells of a London in which brewers, wine merchants, bakers, cooks, fishmongers, butchers, poulterers, grocers, weavers, clothiers, furriers, shoemakers, tanners, glovers, makers of small wares, armourers, spurriers, blacksmiths, and many others,[33] all plied their busy trades within the city walls. Indeed, as Besant writes, "there was no noisier city in the whole world," and he adds a graphic description of the odours which inevitably would arise from the making of soap, tallow, and glue, from the breweries, cook-shops, and slaughter-houses—all of which would mingle with the smell of decaying food and worse refuse thrown into the streets or floating in the open ditches.[34] But uproar and smell were an intrinsic part of the city, and an exiled Londoner in the Middle Ages undoubtedly had the same nostalgic longing to return to his discordant and unclean city as has his urban descendant today when he is transplanted. Chaucer could not have been really happy long away from London.

So much for the substantial public official during the years 1380 to 1384, and for the Londoner keenly aware of the life at his threshold. But what can be said of the Geoffrey Chaucer who was the trusted friend of King and court during the same period? How did he feel when Wat Tyler's men surged into London? Did he ever support the stern and impassioned Wyclif? What was his opinion of the scandalous Flemish Crusade of 1383?

Chaucer's only reference to the Peasants' Revolt, as such, is meagre: in the *Nun's Priest's Tale,* written probably more than ten years after the rising, he says—

> Certes, he Jakke Straw and his meynee
> Ne made nevere shoutes half so shrille,
> Whan that they wolden any Flemyng kille,
> As thilke day was maad upon the fox.[35]

But these few light words cannot be any indication of Chaucer's feeling in 1381 when blood was running in the streets and fire was burning the possessions of his friends; when the unfortunate Flemings were being massacred by Tyler's rebels, aided by the savagely resentful native workmen of London; [36] when the "good and kind" Sudbury was outrageously struck down before the altar and dragged with Hales to Tower Hill and there cruelly murdered.[37] Could Chaucer, the friend of justice and true "gentilesse," have looked upon the heads of Sudbury and Hales, mounted on London Bridge for the satisfaction of the blood-lust of ruffians and criminals, without being horrified? Would he not have been in sympathy with his intimate friend Gower, who wrote in appalled condemnation of the drunken excesses of the violent mob? [38] Yet one outcome of the rebellion must have pleased Chaucer, for three of his friends were knighted by Richard for their gallant services during the revolt, and all three of these friends had served at one time or another as Collector of Customs while Chaucer was Controller: William Walworth (mayor of London in 1381), John Philipot, and Nicholas Brembre.

There can be little doubt that Chaucer was influenced during the years 1380 to 1384, to say nothing of later years, by the teachings of Wyclif and his followers, the Lollards.[39] The great reformer had entered the King's service some years before,[40] while Chaucer was still a member of the Royal Household, and the impressionable poet may well have been moved by Wyclif's sincerity and eloquence. Chaucer, however, never became an avowed Lollard as did some of his friends. The so-called Lollard Knights are listed by Walsingham as Sir William Neville, Sir Lewis Clifford, Sir John Clanvowe, Sir Richard Stury, Sir Thomas Latimer, and Sir John Montague; [41] of these men, the first four named are known to have been intimately connected with Chaucer. A number of other prominent members of the gentry class and a few of the higher nobility embraced Wyclif's teaching; and although their motives were mixed, as Dr. Workman points out, some accepting Lollardy as "a revolt against the tyranny of clericalism, a desire to obtain more freedom, or a hankering after Wyclif's schemes of disendowment," others being motivated by a genuine belief that the Church stood in need of reform,[42] Chaucer could hardly have been unaffected by such widespread interest among his friends in Wyclif's ideas. Certainly Chaucer shows clearly in the *Canterbury Tales* that his religious sympathies were with the Lollards to this extent: in general, he recognizes frankly and denounces by implication Church abuses of his time; and in particular, he invests his Parson, one of the most highly idealized of the company at the Tabard, with many of the characteristics of the Wyclifites.[43]

Apart from Wyclif's attack on Church doctrine, the questioning of religious beliefs was very much in the air in Chaucer's day. The Crusades had taught Christians that the infidel was often a man of great virtue; was it logical that such a man was to be eternally damned? [44] And why was so much of other Church teachings at odds with common sense or with the conduct of many of the teachers? Furthermore, the educated religious thinker of the time had access to the writings of the Moslem philosophers through thirteenth-century translations made by Jewish scholars; the influence on Christian free-thought of the great Moslem philosopher Ibn-Roschid (Averroës) was especially strong.[45] It seems unlikely that Chaucer could have been unaware of the scepticism prevalent in his world, and although he omits from his great work explicit reference to such questioning, we do find there what is very probably implicit reference.[46]

The Flemish Crusade of 1383 may also have had some influence on Chaucer's thinking. This English expedition against the French claimant for the position of Christ's Vicar on earth, at the time of the Papal Schism, was fathered by four groups: first, the papalist party backing the cause of Urban VI, the Pope in Rome, opposed to the French Clement in Avignon; second, the English wool merchants, who, for commercial reasons alone, wished to aid the Flemings against the French; third, the enemies of Wyclif, for Wyclif preached vehemently against such an unseemly "crusade"; and fourth, the enemies of John of Gaunt, for the Duke was then seeking to send English armies elsewhere. The launching of the expedition made a great stir in England; the supporters of the "holy" war were wildly enthusiastic, the denunciators bitter in their opposition. The crusade, too quickly entered upon and soon over, ended in the ignominious defeat of the English.[47] Again Chaucer omits personal comment. Could the poet, however, as a man and as a public official, have been untouched by this scandalous and ill-conducted affair?

During the years 1385 to 1387, Chaucer's personal life seems to have continued to be fairly untroubled. Early in 1385 Richard granted Chaucer a permanent deputy in the Wool Customs, which suggests that the poet had already left London. Also, the payment on Chaucer's pension made two months later was not stated to have been made to him personally; later in the year his name was included in the list of persons to be given mourning for the King's mother, whose residence was in Kent; and shortly after that Chaucer was commissioned as justice of the peace for Kent. All of these facts indicate Chaucer's loyalty to Richard at this time, and point to Chaucer's move to Kent on either the King's business or his own.

In 1386 Chaucer's house over Aldgate was his no longer, although his lease of 1374 read "to have and to hold . . . for the whole life of him, the same Geoffrey," [48] and both his controllerships had come to an end. Did Gloucester's possible animosity bring about Chaucer's relinquishment of the Aldgate house and the controllerships, or did Chaucer voluntarily wind up all his London affairs because he now lived more or less permanently in Kent? [49] In any case, Chaucer was commissioned again in 1386 as justice of the peace for Kent; more significant still, he was elected as one of the two "knights of the shire," that is, as one of the two members of the Commons,[50] for Kent, this being almost conclusive evidence that Chaucer was now a resident of that county. Chaucer seems to have had a house in Greenwich at this time, also—probably on Crown land.[51] Additional evidence that the poet was now living in Kent is found in the fact that he was named in a commission of 1386 with Sir Simon Burley and Chief Justice Tresilian to investigate a Kentish legal matter. Furthermore, as Miss Margaret Galway observes, Chaucer's later appointment to the important post of Chief Clerk of the King's Works, a post so important that it was once held by the famous Bishop of Winchester, William of Wykeham, points to the necessity for his having had previous experience in some smaller, but similar, position. Most logically and easily this would have been in the royal residence at Eltham, not far from Greenwich.[52]

But it cannot be supposed that Chaucer did not occasionally leave his headquarters in Kent. In 1386 Philippa was admitted into the fraternity of Lincoln Cathedral with Henry Bolingbroke and several members of John of Gaunt's household. It is possible that Chaucer attended this ceremony by which his wife became entitled to the special prayers of the cathedral body. We do know that the poet was in London that year to give testimony at the Scrope-Grosvenor trial,[53] and since he was knight of the shire in 1386, he may have attended some parliamentary sessions in Westminster. Moreover, in 1387 Chaucer was granted safe-conduct to go to Calais with Sir William de Beauchamp, although there is no record of Chaucer's having actually left England; if he did so, his absence was probably brief. This was the year apparently that Philippa died, and whether or not Chaucer grieved for her, he must have felt the financial loss of her annuity in which, it may be presumed, he had shared. The journey to Calais would be expensive; then, too, political dissension at home was reaching serious proportions.

The question may be raised as to why Chaucer, as Richard's friend, was left unmolested in Kent when so many of the King's adherents were either banished or executed. Perhaps Bolingbroke, who later on as Henry IV was to show much the same favour to the poet as had Richard, interceded for Chaucer, or perhaps two of Gloucester's followers, Cobham and Devereux, as Kentish neighbours, were instrumental in saving Chaucer from Gloucester's enmity.[54] The most probable explanation, however, is that Chaucer was too unimportant politically to warrant his removal from his position as trusted friend in the Royal Household. Obviously Chaucer was permitted to live in safety during difficult and dangerous months.

Although Chaucer was afterwards in the mood to refer humorously to his life in Greenwich as "dul as deed" and as in a "solytarie wildernesse," [55] the comparative peace and security of his residence there when Gloucester was in power made it possible from a practical standpoint for him to begin his great masterpiece. As to why Chaucer felt impelled to write as he did at this time, the reasons are not far to seek. His hours were more his own; and his productive powers as an artist were fully ripe, and were even acknowledged abroad. By 1386 Eustache Deschamps, one of the most prominent poets of France, expressed the admiration and friendship which he felt for Chaucer in a ballade addressed to the "grant translateur, noble Geffroy Chaucier." For one of the leading French poets of the day to compare Chaucer to Socrates in wisdom, to Seneca in morals, and to "Auglux," the renowned Aulus Gellius of the second century famous for his success both as an author and as a judge, in practical matters, and to say that Chaucer has attained Ovid's greatness in the art of poetry is all very far from faint praise; Chaucer is also hailed in this ballade as the earthly god of love in England, and as the worthy translator of the *Roman de la Rose*.[56] Thus we know that Chaucer's genius had now received generous recognition in France.

Chaucer had at this time completed his great psychological story, the *Troilus and Criseyde*, and in this work, his imagination fired by Boccaccio's narrative, Chaucer reached the pinnacle of dramatic realism. Rich in plot and character study, embellished with subtle humour and philosophic background, the *Troilus and Criseyde* is companion, from the point of view of artistry, to the very different *Canterbury Tales:* the poet who had created lovely, unhappy Criseyde and the witty, flesh-and-blood Pandarus could not now have ceased to write unless he had also ceased to breathe; and since the *Legend of Good Women* had been set aside as perhaps too narrow and too monotonous in theme, the composition of the *Canterbury Tales* may be said to have been now inevitable.

But why was Chaucer so silent about political realities when he wrote of men and women with such deep intuitive insight? Was it only discretion that prompted him to omit so much of the externals of life? Certainly we are obliged to admit that caution must have played some part in Chaucer's avoidance of such matters, for to be too bold in one's utterance in the Middle Ages was to gamble with death, and Chaucer's temperament was not a martyr's; but caution could not have been the most weighty deterrent. The most important reason for Chaucer's silence about political affairs and national events undoubtedly lies in the very nature of his genius: the poet's magnificent Human Comedy is the more human—it is "drenched in life," as John Livingston Lowes has said—in that it is without the immediate, and is concerned with the universal and the timeless. Furthermore, Chaucer the artist must have realized that personal worries and griefs also had no place in a perfect comedy of men and manners: there is no hint in Chaucer's poetry of what it meant to him when such men as Nicholas Brembre, the chivalric Simon Burley, Chief Justice Tresilian, and the writer Thomas Usk were sent to their deaths.

Let us picture Chaucer, therefore, as beginning the *General Prologue* when he is safe in Kent. He has not forgotten the world of events, but he is able to transcend whatever is of the calamitous moment. He is in Kent in body, but in London much of the time in spirit; in mind he is lodged at the Tabard, just beyond the city limits, fully ready for his pilgrimage to Canterbury with those immortal "sondry folk" whose company he joins.

NOTES

(The abbreviations used to designate books and articles mentioned in the Notes will be found listed alphabetically in the Bibliography, opposite the full reference. References to lines in the *Canterbury Tales* are given by fragment and line numbers only.)

For the general historical facts of this chapter I am indebted to articles in the *Encyclopaedia Britannica* and the *Dictionary of National Biography*, and to Oman's *History of England (1377–1485)*, Trevelyan's *England in the Age of Wycliffe*, Workman's *John Wyclif*, Coulton's *Chaucer and his England*, Steel's *Richard II*, and Miss Margaret Galway's article, "Geoffrey Chaucer, J.P. and M.P." (*MLR*, XXXVI, pp. 1–36).

1. Spurgeon, I, 14. Quoted from Lydgate's *Serpent of Devision*.

2. John Ball, the "mad priest of Kent," preached this theory as early as 1360. More aristocratic proponents of the idea were not lacking, however. Owst writes (*Lit. and Pulpit*, pp. 291 ff.) that the theory was used as a "favourite homiletic argument" by fourteenth-century preachers "in support of their innocent diatribes upon the Pride of Life and emptiness of human boasting." Even the learned Bromyard employs the argument. The aristocratic and orthodox Gower is sometimes "extreme in his theoretical socialism" (Coulton, *Med. Village*, p. 236; Gower, *Mirour*, ll. 23,389 ff.).

3. The Peasants' Revolt of 1381 was brought about by many causes, themselves indicative of a not unmodern attitude on the part of the labourer. There had been a rapid increase in the number of free labourers, who were no longer obliged to toil for the lord of the manor even though they might be bound to make him payments, and who hired out their services to whomever they wished. As wages were steadily mounting, the labourer was in a position to pick and choose, and to join with his fellows in demanding "rights" in a way that would have been impossible in England at an earlier date.

4. Owst, *Lit. and Pulpit*, pp. 361–370.

5. Pollard, p. 107.

6. *Ibid.*, p. 127.

7. Pollard points out (pp. 108 f.) that *commons* here means "communes," not "common people"; the communes were the shires or counties of England, and the county courts in which the "knights of the shire" were chosen did not include the "common people."

8. Coulton, *Ch. and his Eng.*, Chap. II *passim; Med. Pan.*, Chap. XXXI *passim*.

If a boy had not a private tutor, there were at least three grammar schools in Chaucer's London; after attending one of these schools, a boy who was intended for a worldly career might become a page and later a squire in the household of a nobleman, as a necessary preliminary to a military career, or as a good preparation for civilian public service; or (perhaps as well) he might attend one of the Inns of Court, the "law schools," which were filled not only with future lawyers, but also with those who needed some legal training for big-business careers or government posts. The future prelate, of course, and surprisingly, the future physician (see Chap. XIII below), attended one of the already great universities in England at Oxford or at Cambridge, or studied on the continent.

9. Trevelyan, pp. 342, 370.

10. The city of London was surrounded in Chaucer's day by "a constellation of villages" (Coulton, *Ch. and his Eng.*, p. 117), so that the busy, noisy city appeared to be set in acres of rose gardens and green orchards, with flower-sprinkled meadows and cool forests beyond.

Some of the more important settlements without the walls of the city were the municipality of Westminster, on the way to which lay the village of Charing, where the Hospital and Chapel of St. Mary Rouncivalle, the headquarters of Chaucer's Pardoner, was located; Lambeth across the Thames from Westminster, where was the Manor of the Archbishop of Canterbury; and the borough of Southwark, east of Lambeth and south of London Bridge, where stood the Augustinian Priory of St. Mary Overy, the Tabard Inn and many other hostelries, and the notorious Marshalsea prison. There were also numerous small settlements clustering around such centers as the Temple, St. Bartholomew's, the Charter House, and the Priory of St. John's Clerkenwell (Wheatley, Chap. XII and *passim*).

11. Coulton, *Ch. and his Eng.*, p. 135.

12. Workman, I, 275–324 *passim*.

13. Oman, pp. 39 ff.

14. Trevelyan writes (p. 253) that although the Peasants' Revolt was the cause of doing away with certain labour troubles in the fifteenth century, "the demand for personal freedom, which had been the chief cause for revolt, was for the moment crushed."

Oman states (p. 64) that "the manorial records of the years 1382 and 1383 show instances which prove that the first result of the suppression of the rebellion was to encourage many lords to reassert old rights, and to tighten the relaxed bonds of serfdom." Oman also points out that serfdom "was not killed once and for all by the armed force of rebellion," but that it disappeared slowly from economic causes.

15. Unwin. pp. 127 ff.

16. Skeat (III, 372–379) reasons that the real or imagined journey to Canterbury could take place only in 1387; he considers no date after 1390 or before 1386. The years 1388, 1389, and 1390 would include a Sunday in

the pilgrimage. In the *Introduction to the Man of Law's Tale*, April 18 is given as the day of the month, and this *Tale* is usually accepted as being told on the second day of the journey: if a Sunday occurred on the pilgrimage, a careful, realistic writer like Chaucer would have at least mentioned that the pilgrims heard Mass before setting out on that day. In 1386 the whole journey would have taken place in Holy Week, a highly improbable situation. "But in 1387 everything comes right; they [the pilgrims] assembled at the Tabard on Tuesday, April 16, and had four clear days before them. And when we consider how particular our author is as to dates, we shall do well to consider the probability that this result is correct" (p. 374). Also, 1387 fits the scheme of days mentioned in the *Knight's Tale*.

17. Translated by Miss Dorothy Hughes in *Illustrations of Chaucer's England* (p. 142) from Walsingham's *Hist. Ang.*, Notices of 1386.

18. Trevelyan, Chap. VII *passim*.

19. *CR*, 1385–9, p. 457. Miss Galway (*MLR*, XXXVI, 32) calls my attention to this reference.

20. Miss Galway (*loc. cit.*, pp. 1 ff.) collects all the documented biographical facts concerning Chaucer from 1385 to 1389. She takes her material from the *Life Records of Chaucer* (Chaucer Society) and from letters of Miss Rickert's to the *Times Literary Supplement*. I make use of the facts collected by Miss Galway. For the facts before 1385 I use the material in Robinson (pp. xv ff.) and in Manly (*Cant. Tales*, pp. 17 ff.).

21. Chaucer also received a pension from John of Gaunt, but it is not known how long the pension continued.

22. Philippa received a silver-gilt cup from John of Gaunt on New Year's Day in each of the years 1380, 1381, and 1382. Coulton says (*Ch. and his Eng.*, p. 96) that the first of these cups cost about three pounds, and that the other two were even more valuable.

We may think of the three pounds in 1380 as having about the same value, psychologically speaking, as $600 in modern money (see n. 13 in Notes to Chap. II below).

23. A *mainpernor* was one who gave surety for another (*NED*).

Sir William de Beauchamp was responsible to the king for 400 *l.* a year, which in turn made Chaucer responsible for the same large sum amounting roughly to $83,000 in modern money (see n. 13 in Notes to Chap. II below).

24. Sir Lewis Clifford was a particularly intimate friend of Chaucer's. See n. 56 below.

25. Richard Morel, a "rich neighbour at Aldgate" (Manly, *Cant. Tales*, p. 21), was the fifth witness, but I have been unable to learn anything more about him.

26. *House of Fame*, ll. 631–633, 652–660.

27. Chaucer's descriptive touches within the walls of Troy, the street scenes and those in Criseyde's and Pandarus's respective houses are obviously taken from the London of his own day; and what Troilus sees and hears as he waits in vain for his lady at the walls of Troy (V, ll. 1142 ff.) must be what Chaucer saw and heard whenever he looked eastward, away from London, on an Aldgate summer evening.

28. Besant, p. 110.

29. This poem was formerly ascribed to Dunbar. There is no real evidence, however, that Dunbar was the author (see Bühler, *Rev. Eng. St.*, XIII, 5).

30. William Morris, *Earthly Paradise*, Prologue: The Wanderers.

31. The part of present-day London designated as the "City" covers the same territory as that covered by the whole of Chaucer's London—that is, the walled town. The modern City is the smallest of the twenty-nine divisions which make up Greater London today: it is roughly rectangular in shape, and has an area of about one and one-half square miles.

The population of the walled London in Chaucer's time is estimated at 40,000 (Coulton, *Ch. and his Eng.*, p. 115), a number which certainly must have made for crowded conditions in such a small area. York, the next largest city in England then, had a population of only about 7,000 (Wheatley, p. 47).

32. Riley in *Liber Albus, Mun. Gild. Lond.*, pp. xl ff.

33. *Ibid.*, pp. lix–xciii.

34. Besant, pp. 148 f.

35. VII 3394–3397 (B² 4584–4587).

36. Chaucer is known to have been in London during the Peasants' Revolt. Manly reminds us (*Cant. Tales*, p. 21) that Chaucer "during this very time . . . quit-claimed his father's house in Thames Street."

37. Trevelyan, p. 236.

38. Gower, *Vox. Clam.*, Lib. I.

39. The word lollard comes from the popular O. Dut. name given to a member of a lay order of mendicants, founded about 1300 to care for the sick and to dispose of corpses. These mendicants were first called Alexiani after their patron saint, but because of the way they sang their prayers, the term *lollaert*, or *lolbroether*, developed. [*lollen, lullen* = mussare, musitare, mutire, numeros non verba canere, sonum imitari; lollaerd, mussitator, mussitabundus . . .] The clergy looked upon these men with disfavour: first, they would not join any of the established orders; second, many of them were free-thinkers, so that *lollaert* and "heretic" often possessed the same meaning; and third, their conduct was frequently disorderly. In England, the transfer of the name to the followers of Wyclif probably stemmed from the identification of *lollard* and *heretic*. (*Middelnederlandsch Woordenboek*, "Lollaert.")

40. Workman, I, 210.

41. Walsingham, *Hist. Ang.*, II, 159.

42. Workman, II, 376.

43. See the chapters below on the clerical members of the company of Chaucer's Canterbury pilgrims.

44. Coulton, *Med. Pan.*, p. 460.

45. *Ibid.*, pp. 460 f.

46. See I (A) 1303 ff., for example, or V (F) 877 ff. In both these passages Chaucer shows clearly that he is *aware* of questioning.

47. Oman, pp. 82 ff.

48. Riley, *London*, p. 377.

49. That Chaucer of his own accord gave up the Aldgate house seems

more likely than that he was forced to do so because of Gloucester's animosity, since Chaucer's friend Brembre, then Mayor of London, at once leased the house to Richard Forester (or Forster), another of Chaucer's friends and, presumably, one of the King's adherents.

50. A "knight of the shire" was originally one of the two gentlemen from each shire of the rank of knight, elected to the Commons by the shire courts. As time passed, the shire representation lost any distinctive features, and "knight of the shire" in Chaucer's day merely meant one of the gentry elected to the Commons. (*NED*, "Knight.")

Chaucer speaks of the Franklin as "ful ofte tyme . . . knyght of the shire," and the Franklin is not a knight.

51. Galway, *loc. cit.*, pp. 29 f.

52. *Ibid.*, pp. 15 f.

53. This is the famous lawsuit about a coat of arms—each family claimed the right to the same insignia. At this trial in 1386 Chaucer's age was recorded as forty "and more" (*et plus*), which furnishes us with our principal "evidence" as to the date of Chaucer's birth. Chaucer's testimony, in favour of the Scrope family, is of course positive proof that he was then in London.

54. Galway, *loc. cit.*, pp. 29 f.

55. *Lenvoy de Chaucer a Scogan,* ll. 45 f.

56. See Manly (*Cant. Tales*, pp. 22 ff.) and Jenkins (*MLN*, XXXIII, 266–278) for the reference to and interpretation of Deschamps's ballade. Both writers quote the ballade in full. The ballade was taken to Chaucer by Sir Lewis Clifford, then just returning from France: "Mais pran en gré les euvres d'escolier / Que par Clifford de moy avoir pourras   "

CHAPTER II

"THANNE LONGEN FOLK TO GOON ON PILGRIMAGES"

Whan that Aprille with his shoures soote
The droghte of March hath perced to the roote,
And bathed every veyne in swich licour
Of which vertu engendred is the flour;
Whan Zephirus eek with his sweete breeth
Inspired hath in every holt and heeth *
The tendre croppes, and the yonge sonne
Hath in the Ram his halve cours yronne,
And smale foweles maken melodye,
That slepen al the nyght with open ye
(So priketh hem nature in hir corages) . . .

(ll. 1–11)

EACH TIME we read the opening lines of the *General Prologue* the familiar words conjure up April's sun-caressed and rain-washed skies, the bright and delicate green of young leaves, the joyous rediscovery of love and new life. Chaucer gives us the feeling, as we read, that he is the first poet ever to have put this picture into words, yet of course we are aware of the sober fact that all poets, from earliest antiquity to the present day, have celebrated the coming of spring, and what is more, that the very phrases employed by medieval poets in particular were often set in conventional patterns.[1] As Professor Tatlock remarks:

. . . Literature was currently conceived not as a sheer creation of the imagination, but rather as an adapting and re-telling of what had been told before. The medieval reader, and writer, felt vividly the impressiveness and charm of authority, precedent and associations, and in general did not find inventiveness and originality a thing to be striven for or claimed.[2]

* holt: "wood," or "grove" ("plantation" in the English, but not the American, sense).

Chaucer uses an opening for the *Prologue* that, while it may have had charm for some of his contemporaries because of its zest and elusive freshness of style, had a special fourteenth-century appeal in "precedent and associations." What more natural than for Chaucer to use as a model a passage from Guido delle Colonne's *Historia Destructionis Troiae*? For Guido was an author Chaucer much admired,[3] and the *Historia* was one of the sources of Chaucer's recently completed *Troilus and Criseyde*; certainly Chaucer's lines show striking parallels with this passage, a translation of which follows:

It was the season when the sun, hastening under the turning circle of the zodiac, had now entered its course under the sign of the Ram, in which the equinox is celebrated, when the days of the beginning of spring are equal in length to the nights; then when the season begins to soothe eager mortals in its clear air; then when as the snows melt, gently blowing zephyrs wrinkle up the waters; then when fountains gush out into slender jars; then when moistures breathing out from the earth's bosom are raised up within trees and branches to their tops, wherefore, seeds leap forth, crops grow, fields become green brightened by flowers of various colours; then when trees put on renewed foliage everywhere; then when the earth is decked with grass, and birds sing, sounding like the cithara in the euphony of sweet harmony.[4]

Here are nearly all the actual expressions Chaucer uses; the time is in the Ram, when moisture ("licour") flows through every sap-vessel ("veyne") after the drought of March;[5] the sweet zephyrs have quickened ("inspired") the tender tops of the branches ("croppes"); the young sun is now beyond the spring equinox and the second half of Aries;[6] the birds sing in melody; even the very repetition of the word *when* seems to be borrowed from Guido. Chaucer adds one detail to Guido's conventional picture: the little birds, incited by nature in their desires ("so priketh hem nature in hir corages"), sleep all the night with open eye! The poet uses this same idea again, as we shall see, in describing his young Squire, who loved so hotly that he slept no more "than dooth a nyghtyngale." Medieval natural history taught that nightingales did not sleep in the mating season.[7]

But the medieval Chaucer is also the timeless Chaucer, and realism comes as naturally to him as the acceptance of a literary convention: the traditional spring picture is not followed by the usual

romantic or heroic events, but by a freshly matter-of-fact statement:

> Thanne longen folk to goon on pilgrimages,
> And palmeres [8] for to seken straunge strondes,
> To ferne halwes, kowthe in sondry londes.

(ll. 12–14)

Undoubtedly, in this season of wanderlust, every one of Chaucer's
audience, quite as much as his poorer and less well-born contemporaries, did long to go on that form of medieval popular excursion
known as a pilgrimage. Lords and ladies, burgesses and their wives,
rich and poor, cleric and lay, all yearned when the bleak winter was
past to take to the road, to become pilgrims and to visit distant shrines
in various lands. Later on in the *Prologue* the poet names some of
those shrines specifically,[9] but now he speaks only of England's most
famous place of pilgrimage, the shrine of St. Thomas à Becket at
Canterbury:

> . . . from every shires ende
> Of Engeland to Caunterbury they wende,
> The hooly blisful martir for to seke,
> That hem hath holpen whan that they were seeke.[10]

(ll. 15–18)

We cannot know who was the first holy and humble man of
heart who, in his simple desire to tread the hallowed ground upon
which the footsteps of Jesus had fallen, journeyed from afar to
accomplish his sacred memorial visit, but we do know that by the
second century there were many pilgrims actuated solely by devotion
to their beloved Master. In the third and fourth centuries, according
to the works of Eusebius and others, men had begun to travel to
the Holy Land for the special purpose of prayer. This purpose, implying "acceptance of the theory of sanctuaries which it is an act of
piety to visit," created the pilgrimage as later generations were to
understand it: "a journey undertaken, from religious motives, to a
place held to be sacred."[11] But prayer alone, even before the holy
shrines of Bethlehem and Jerusalem, could not long satisfy man,
ever seeking to bolster up his faith with the tangible. This piece of
wood found near Calvary—was it not, perhaps, a part of the true
Cross? This nail and this thorn—might they not have once pierced

the only-begotten Son of God? Surely such objects, made sacred by an earthly contact with Heaven, would possess a virtue which would enable sinful, puny man to plead his cause the more readily? The intense urge to believe swept away all doubts, both as to the authenticity and as to the efficacy of the relics, and thus the veneration of relics became an essential part of pilgrimage. ✓

Although many devout Christians of Western Europe were always able to find their perilous way to the remote Holy Land, many more were unable to manage that long, difficult journey, and it was imperative that the Church should find for these latter an alternative. Care for the tombs of saints had long been a pious custom: to extend the custom into a religious act through which divine aid would be obtained was but a step, and from that step soon developed the belief in miracles performed at the grave. Medieval man, searching always in desperate hope for assurance in his extraordinarily complicated and hazardous world, came to be even more deeply convinced than his ancestor of the Dark Ages that intercessory powers and miraculous manifestations were attached to the bodies of saints and their relics, and the number of pilgrimages to the graves of local martyrs, and of the treasures left there in propitiation, saw steady increase throughout the Middle Ages. Indeed, the honour paid to some of the venerated saints at times exceeded that paid to God. At Canterbury "we find at the altar of God no oblation, at the Virgin's only 4 *l.* 1 *s.* 8 *d.*, at Becket's 954 *l.* 6 *s.* 3*d.*!" [12] In the year 1220, when St. Thomas's body was translated from the crypt to Trinity Chapel, the receipts were immense, amounting to between one-fifth and one-quarter of a million dollars in modern currency in the anniversary year of 1420, the monetary receipts were less (about half as much as in 1220),[13] but other gifts—rings, brooches, jewels, gold, spices, tapers, cups, and statues—continued to be donated with unabated enthusiasm.[14] And it was as much the relic as the tomb of the martyred archbishop which drew peasant and prince to Canterbury.

Owing to the great veneration of relics, the securing of them became one of the important objectives of pilgrimage, and Western Europe set about collecting relics at an early date from what was believed to be the inexhaustible supply of the Holy Land, Constantinople, and Rome. Dean Stanley, in an interesting account of pilgrimage in his *Historical Memorials of Canterbury,* says that the collection of relics "became a mania, such as never was witnessed before or since"; and he adds:

Hence the strange practice of dismembering the bodies of saints—a bone here, a heart there, a head here—which painfully neutralises the religious and historical effect of even the most authentic and the most sacred graves in Christendom. Hence the still stranger practice of the invention and sale of relics, which throws such doubt on the genuineness of all. Hence the monstrous incongruities, often repeated, of the same relics in different shrines. Hence the rivalry, the thefts, the commerce of these articles of sacred merchandise . . .[15]

Chaucer's Pardoner, with his pillow-case which he says is the veil of "Oure Lady," his fragment of St. Peter's "seyl," and his "pigges bones" that are to be sold as the hallowed remains of some saint, is no unusual figure.

Pilgrimages were also undertaken very frequently as a form of penance. King Alla, in Chaucer's *Man of Law's Tale,* travels to Rome for this purpose as a matter of course.

> Kyng Alla, which that hadde his mooder slayn,
> Upon a day fil in swich repentance
> That, if I shortly tellen shal and playn,
> To Rome he comth to receyven his penance;
> And putte hym in the popes ordinance
> In heigh and logh, and Jhesu Crist bisoghte
> Foryeve his wikked werkes that he wroghte.[16]

In fact, the whole theory of indulgences had entered into pilgrimage, and, as Skeat points out, "Rome abounded with shrines at which several thousand years of remission from purgatory could be obtained." [17] We know that the Pardoner of the *Canterbury Tales,* who "streit was comen from the court of Rome" with a wallet brimful of dubious "pardoun," will pass them all off on the gullible, eventually, as plenary indulgences! [18]

But all the pilgrimages of the later Middle Ages possessed a striking characteristic which was quite apart from religious motive, and which had been entirely lacking in the preceding centuries: the journey itself had become an occasion for pleasure. Even the long expeditions to foreign shrines were thoroughly enjoyed by nearly everyone who made them, no matter how serious and devout was the intent of the undertaking. Two factors had brought about this "excursion" attitude towards pilgrimage. First, the ever increasing number of pilgrims made for better roads and more comfortable inns, and for greater safety along the now no longer lonely ways; and second, when everybody was making a pilgrimage, the vast crowds were not composed of burning zealots, but of ordinary human beings, who turned naturally to mirth and jollity, who relished their food and drink, who enjoyed the company of their fellows, and who found, particularly if they were Englishmen, delight in travel. By the fourteenth century, then, the perilous journey of extreme hardship taken in austere ardour by the sternly pious had almost vanished from the world, leaving in its stead a journey similar in difficulty to the nineteenth-century "trip abroad," an undertaking which, even as late as 1900, still had some hazards and required serious preparation, yet was safe enough, sufficiently romantic and exciting to provide a never ending topic of interest for later conversations with the stay-at-homes.

It was inevitable, of course, that the popularization of pilgrimage should bring with it many ills. The insincere found a far too easy "penance," the light-minded were given fatal opportunity for dalliance, the profligate and the thief had broad, new fields for wickedness, and it was to hold back the rising sea of these evils that Walter Hilton, a fourteenth-century Augustinian Canon, wrote a parable of the ideal wayfarer and exhorted the would-be pilgrim as follows:

> What so thou heres or sees or felis that sculde lette the in thi wey, abide not with it wilfully, tary not for it restfully, behold it not, like it not, drede it not; bot ay go forth in thi wey and thinke that thu woldes be at Ierusalem. . . . And if men robbe the and dispoile the, bete the, scorne the, and dispise the . . . go forth as noght were. . . . And also if men wil tary the with tales and fede the with lesynges, for to drawe the to mirthes . . . make def ere and answer not ageyn.[19]

It was admonitions like Walter Hilton's, however, which fell on deaf ears, for the pilgrims continued to listen avidly to the "lesynges" which drew them to pleasures, and tarried "restfully" whenever they could!

The pietistical and self-adulatory Margery Kempe, in her vigorous and amazing book, protests much about the wickedness of pilgrimages. She writes in detail of her journey to the Holy Land which took place in the opening years of the fifteenth century. By the time her group of travellers had reached Holland, Margery had begun her floods of contrite tears, her fasting, her glum silences, broken only by her relentless quotations from Scripture. The company shamefully reproved her, for they wished to feast and make merry as was the custom (they said) of pilgrims; in fact, they were sufficiently indignant over Margery's unconventional behaviour to expel her from their number, although they later permitted her to return with the proviso, "Ye shall not speak of the Gospel where we are, but shall sit still and make merry as we do at meat and supper!" So Margery (who did know, after all, on which side her bread was buttered) conformed as was necessary; and she made no objection at all, in her inimitably inconsistent fashion, when it came to taking precaution against danger, nor did she hesitate to avail herself of the various conveniences provided for the wayfarer. She even rode a donkey, as did the other and more frankly sybaritic pilgrims, when Jerusalem was reached, instead of walking barefoot along the stony paths! [20]

That even journeys to the Holy Land were in part "merry" is an indication of how much greater was the opportunity for festivity and carnival on a visit to a neighbouring shrine, and it is not surprising that the followers of Wyclif, in their seeming determination to exclude nearly everything from life which was not of a sternly religious nature, should flatly condemn all pilgrimage. Man should confine himself to "merytory werkes," cry the Lollards in sermon after sermon, then he will have no time for vanity and "leccherie" of the pilgrimage.[21] One preacher of the fourteenth century says in his hard anger:

For men that may not haunt her leccherie at home as they wolden for drede of lordis, of maystris and for clamour of negheboris, thei casten many dayes byfore and gederen what thei may . . . to go out of the cuntrey in pilgrimage . . ., and lyven in the goinge in leccherye, in gloutenie, in drunkennesse, and mayntenen falsenesse of osteleris, of kokis, of taverners, and veynly spended hore good . . . ; bostyng of her glotenie whan thei comen home that thei never drank but wyn in al the iourney. . . . And somme men don it of her owne grett wille, rather to see faire cuntreys than for ony swete devocioun in her soule to God, or to the seynt that thei seken.[22]

Although the Wyclifites were alone in their censure of pilgrimages *per se*, many of the more orthodox churchmen condemned the behaviour of pilgrims. In *Les Lamentations de Matheolus*, the French translation of a widely known Latin poem of the fourteenth century, a Flanders cleric, who wrote as a warning to young men, also points out the follies in which women indulge in making so-called pilgrimages. These women do not visit shrines for proper purposes, but only to make the church a *maison de rendez-vous*: they invent new miracles so that they will have an excuse to visit monasteries far from their homes, and there they pay court to Venus instead of to a saint! [23]

The Knight of La Tour Landry writes in like vein in edifying his daughters with the "ensaumple of a yong lady that had her herte moche on the worlde." The lady was in love with a handsome squire, and that she might have "beter leiser" to speak with him, "she made her husbonde to understond that she had vowed in diverse pilgrimages." The unsuspecting husband then permitted his wife to go on her pilgrimage, but the lady enjoyed laughter with her lover rather than her prayers. So, at the mass, in the midst of her flirtation, she was taken with sickness; this sinful lady lay in a swoon for three days, during which time she had a ghastly vision of all the horrors of hell. When she recovered from her swoon, the lady repented, and vowed she would amend her ways, which she did so successfuly that her virtue became renowned. "And therefor here is an exsaumple that no body shulde go in holy pilgrimages for to fulfell no foly, plesaunce, nor the worlde, nor flesshely delite. But thei shulde go enterly with herte to serve God . . ." [24]

Although the twentieth-century reader may smile at the punishments which are meted out in the *exempla* to impious pilgrims, there can be no question that the behaviour of such pilgrims in the later Middle Ages was a serious and real problem of which Chaucer was fully aware; but Chaucer shows us both sides of the picture, the "falsnesse," the "leccherye," the "gloutenie" and "drunkennesse" of some of the pilgrims, together with the dignity and genuine devoutness of others. These men and women are presented as they actually were on that April day in 1387, and the censure, when it is due, is left for the most part to Chaucer's audience. The bleak, dark winter has passed and of course folk long "to goon on pilgrimages"! The company is gay and hearts are young, the horses prance and curvet in the joyful return of spring, the inns along the way are excellent, and at journey's end will be the excitement of Canterbury crowds, the wonders of the celebrated Cathedral, and sincere gladness and satisfaction in praying at the shrine of "the hooly blisful martir." If this were not in essence a religious journey, we should readily excuse the noisy good spirits, the venial over-indulgence in food and drink, and the inevitable quarrels, all of which now appear so unseemly.

Chaucer's pilgrims display every frailty and absurdity of human nature. The forthright Wife of Bath loves pleasure intensely; she will never stay at home with a dull husband when the excitement of a merry jaunt presents itself, and she speaks in good-humored contempt of her fifth husband, who, when he would keep his wife by his side, tiresomely quoted an "olde sawe" (that it was an "old" saw has significance)—

> "Whoso that buyldeth his hous al of salwes,
>   And priketh his blynde hors over the falwes,
>   And suffreth his wyf to go seken halwes,
>   Is worthy to been hanged on the galwes!" [25]

The wife also tells with glee of how she availed herself of the golden opportunities which she had when her fourth husband went to London:

> Myn housbonde was at Londoun al that Lente;
>   I hadde the bettre leyser for to pleye,
>   And for to se, and eek for to be seye
>   Of lusty folk. What wiste I wher my grace
>   Was shapen for to be, or in what place?
>   Therfore I made my visitaciouns
>   To vigilies and to processiouns,
>   To prechyng eek, and to thise pilgrimages,
>   To pleyes of myracles, and to mariages,
>   And wered upon my gaye scarlet gytes.* [26]

Unquestionably the Wife of Bath enjoyed the noisy jollity of pilgrimages! And her candid desire to see and be seen should be compared with Deschamps's heading to one of the chapters of the contemporary *Miroir de Mariage*; "How wives seek indulgences, not for the devotion which they have, but to see and be seen." [27] And, in the same work, two husbands (who might be brothers to Alisoun's five) exchange views upon the conduct of their wives. "A woman is

* *gyte*: "dress," or "gown" or "mantle."

always noble," one says with heavy sarcasm. "My wife always does the exact opposite of what I wish and command!" The other replies that when he asks for peas or herring he is given beans or mackerel, and if he begs that his wife stay at home, off she goes on a pilgrimage to St. Denis. Later the mother-in-law, in league with her daughter (the joke is venerable), scolds the daughter's husband, telling him that he must allow his wife—if he expects a family—to "confide" in the saints, and that he must encourage her to visit a great number of these saints, whose shrines are in different parts of the country, whenever the fancy takes her.[28]

The "tall stories" which helped to make pilgrimages so attractive to those who took them, and to those who heard about them from the returned travelers, were another characteristic feature of pilgrimage frowned upon by the Wyclifites and spoken of by everyone. Some time before the *Canterbury Tales,* Chaucer mentions in the *House of Fame* the noise and confusion of Rumour's dwelling, a house full at all times of "shipmen and pilgrimes";

> And, Lord, this hous in alle tymes,
> Was ful of shipmen and pilgrimes,
> With scrippes bret-ful of lesinges,
> Entremedled with tydynges,
> And eke allone be hemselve.[29]

And Langland writes:

> Pylgrimis and palmers . plyghten hem to-gederes,
> To seche seint Iame . and seyntys of rome,
> Wenten forth in hure way . with meny un-wyse tales,
> And haven leve to lye . al hure lyf-time.[30]

As would be expected, the Lollard William Thorpe also has much to say concerning the proclivity of pilgrims towards story-telling; he talks, too, at great length about all the evils connected with pilgrimage. Master Willam himself furnishes us with the account of his own "Examination of heresy" in 1407, and gives us a detailed picture of the proceedings, which were conducted by Arundel, the Archbishop of Canterbury, with every sign of that prelate's irritated distaste. What is particularly interesting to us, however, in Thorpe's long defence, is the vivid picture we receive of contemporary pilgrimage. Master William says in part:

For (as I well know, since I have full oft assayed) examine, whosoever will, twenty of these pilgrims! and he shall not find three men or
women that know surely a commandment of God, nor can say their
Pater noster and *Ave Maria*! nor their *Credo*, readily in any manner of
language. And as I have learned, and also know somewhat by experience of these same pilgrims, telling the cause why that many men and
women go hither and thither now on pilgrimages, it is more for the
health of their bodies, than of their souls! more for to have richesse and
prosperity of this world, than for to be enriched with virtues in their
souls! more to have here worldly and fleshly friendship, than for to have
friendship of God and of His saints in heaven. . . .

For with my Protestation, I say now, . . . 'though they have fleshly
wills, travel for their bodies, and spend mickle money to seek and to
visit the bones or images, as they say they do, of this saint and of that:
such pilgrimage-going is neither praisable nor thankful to God, nor to
any Saint of God. . . .'

Wherefore, Sir, I have preached and taught openly, and so I purpose all my lifetime to do, with God's help, saying that 'such fond people waste blamefully God's goods in their vain pilgrimages, spending
their goods upon vicious hostelars, which are oft unclean women of their
bodies; and at the least those goods with the which, they should do
works of mercy, after God's bidding, to poor needy men and women.'

These poor men's goods and their livelihood, these runners about
offer to rich priests! . . . Yea, and over this folly, ofttimes divers of
these men and women of these runners thus madly hither and thither
into pilgrimage, borrow hereto other men's goods (yea, and sometimes
they steal men's goods hereto), and they pay them never again.

Also, Sir, I know well, that when divers men and women will go
thus after their own wills, and finding out one pilgrimage, they will
ordain with them before to have with them both men and women that
can well sing wanton songs; and some other pilgrims will have with them
bagpipes: so that every town that they come through, what with the
noise of their singing, and the sound of their piping, and with the jang-
ling of their Canterbury bells, and with the barking out of the dogs
after them, they make more noise than if the King came there away,
with all his clarions and many other minstrels. And if these men and
women be a month out in their pilgrimage, many of them shall be, a
half year after, great janglers, tale-tellers, and liars.[31]

Master William courted disaster, of course, by his bold utter-
ances, and it is somewhat surprising that his punishment was not
more serious than imprisonment. For not only did Thorpe give voice

to heretical [32] opinions, but he ran a grave risk in impugning the veneration of St. Thomas, however indirect his attack may have been. Thomas à Becket, the sacrosanct healer of all true believers, had now long been a national hero who drew to Canterbury king and commoner from all over Europe. Dean Stanley points out that there is "no country in Europe which does not exhibit traces of Becket," [33] and that to ascertain the saint's "churches and memorials through the British dominions would be an endless labour." [34] Pilgrimage to Canterbury was England's most cherished pride until the Reformation. And how had this come about? The story of Becket out-fictions fiction, yet is starkly real, and yet makes as exciting reading today as any tale ever told.

The year 1170 marked a precarious reconciliation between the fiery, arrogant Henry II of England (then in France) and the recalcitrant Thomas à Becket, former Chancellor and now Archbishop of Canterbury. The ten-year struggle had been long and bitter, and was fated from the start never to be resolved in peace and amity. Becket returned to England in December with the adamantine determination that he would continue his fight for what he conceived to be the rights of the Church and of his office. The journey to Canterbury was accomplished in great pomp, after an absence of six years, but for the most part, Becket was met with hostility. Among his enemies were the de Broc family, who occupied Saltwood, an archiepiscopal castle granted them by the king. Ranulf de Broc and his brother lost no opportunity to insult and harry the Primate, and all hope of accord between Church and State was definitely lost. On Christmas Day, Becket preached his sermon in the Cathedral on the Vulgate text, "On earth, peace to men of good will," pointing out all too clearly that there could be no peace between himself and those who opposed him. Whereupon, "in a voice of thunder," [35] he excommunicated the two de Brocs, two priests, and the Bishops of York, London, and Salisbury, who, Becket claimed, had encroached upon his prescriptive rights. The three bishops went at once to France to complain to the King, who was seized with one of his paroxysms of fury, and cried out:

"A fellow that has eaten my bread has lifted up his heel against me —a fellow that I loaded with benefit dares insult the King and the whole royal family, and tramples on the whole kingdom—a fellow that came to court on a sumpter-mule sits without hindrance on the throne itself. What sluggard wretches, what cowards have I brought up in my court, who care nothing for their allegiance to their master! not one will deliver me from this low-born priest!" [36]

The words of the King fanned to white heat the enmity of four of the listening knights. Reginald Fitzurse ("son of the Bear," sometimes called "Beyrson"), Hugh de Moreville, William de Tracy, and Richard le Bret (or "le Brez") set out immediately for England, where they were joined by Robert de Broc and a band of armed men. With these companions they rode, still in their furious rage, to Canterbury, where they arrived on Tuesday, the twenty-ninth of December. The murder of Becket followed their arrival by a matter of minutes.

The world is in possession of twenty-five contemporary accounts of that deed of heavy violence; four of the accounts are written by men who claim to have been eye-witnesses.[37] There is remarkable agreement between one account and another, and the story of the murder itself was repeated in successive generations with little variation. A fourteenth-century manuscript contains a homily, which reads in part like a translation of one of the eye-witness reports of Becket's murder, and an excerpt, which Chaucer himself might have once heard, follows:

. . . Ther were iiii knyghtes in this lond, of cursid lyvyng; and for to have a rewarde and a thanke of the king of yngelonde, they made an othe upon the halydam that with one consent thei shuld sle and distroy holy Thomas, one hight Reynalde beyrson, an other William Trasy, the third Sir Richard Bryton, the iiiith Sir hew morvile. So, upon childremasse day in Cristemas weke, al-moste at nyght, these iiii knyghtes cam to Caunterbery in to the hall of the bisshoppes paleis. Then Sir Reynolde Beyrson, for he was most cursid of kinde, without any salutyng reverens he said thus un to seint Thomas, "The King that is be-yonde the see send us to the, commaunding and bidding the that thou assoyle all the bissopis that thu haste do acursid." "Syrres," quod seint Thomas, "I do you to wille thei be acursid be auctoryte and power of our holy fader the pope, but in no wise bi me, and I may not assoile them that our holy ffadir the pope hath acursid with-oute auctorite of hym." "Well," quod Reynolde, "then we see thou woll not do the kynges commaundementes. By God thou shalt dye!" Then cried the other knyghtes, "Sle, sle!" And then thei yede oute of the halle and toke their counselle, and concluded for to sle hym. So thei armyd theim in alle haste, and in the mene tyme prestes and clerkes and other that were with hym drowghe holy Thomas in to the chirch and lokkid the dore and barrid it fast to hym. But whan seint Thomas perceyved that the iiii knyghtes were sparrid oute and wolde have cum in, and myght not, he went to the dore and unbarrid it. Then he toke a knyght by the hand and seid, "It is not semyng for [to] make holy cherche as a castell or a place of defence. Cum in my childre in goddes name." Than it was so derk that thei myght not wele se nor knowe seynt Thomas from a nother man, but cried and seide, "Ubi est proditor?"—"Where is this traytour?" "Nay," quod seint Thomas, "no traitour but Archbissop is here. I cum not to fle but to abide and take my dethe for goddes sake and holy chirche right." Then sir Reynolde beyrson stroke at hym and smote of half his croun. Then an other knyght stroke in the same place and smote of the sculle. Then fell down holy Thomas on his knees and seid thus—"Commendo deo, beate marie et sancto dionisio meipsum et ecclesie causam." "I commende to god, to oure lady seint marye, and to seint dionyse my cause and the ryght of holy chirche"; and so he dyed. Then the thrid knyght stroke at hym, and halfe the stroke felle up on a clerkes arme that helde up seint Thomas, and so down unto seint Thomas hand. Then the fourth knyght smote his swerd up on the paviment and brake the poynte of his swerde, and seid, "He is dede. Go we hens!" But when thei were at the dore outeward, one of hem, Robert broke, went ageyn and sette his fote in his nek, and with his swerde shed oute the braynes on the pament. Thus toke holy Thomas of Cauntebery his dethe full mekely, for right of holy chirche and the welfare of yngelonde.[38]

We can picture the scene which followed the murder of the great archbishop: the portentous darkness of the vast Cathedral, the armed knights rushing in savage triumph from the church they had desecrated in order to ransack and plunder the palace of the man they had slain, thunder and torrents of rain without, the ghoulish, relic-seeking crowd within surging towards the dead Becket, attempting either to dip their garments in the widening pools of blood and brains, or to despoil the corpse. For although no one as yet thought of the archbishop as a true saint, through his murder in the Cathedral, the holy sanctuary, he had become a martyr for the cause of the Church, and his remains were, therefore, of value. Eventually the monks, the timid monks who so strangely failed to come to the assistance of their superior, were successful in clearing the Cathedral, but not before at least one citizen of Canterbury had managed to wet his coat with the martyr's blood. He later gave this mixed with water to his sick wife, who was miraculously cured of her ailment.

By the time the news of the healing properties of Thomas à Becket's blood was told abroad, however, the martyr had become a saint, and all of Canterbury, and soon the whole world, was ready to believe any miracle. For the monks who had disrobed the body for decent burial had discovered what was to them (indeed, to everyone in the Middle Ages) proof positive of the sainthood of the man that some of them had deemed worldly and arrogant. Underneath the elaborate vestments which Becket had worn was a haircloth encasing the body, and the whole haircloth, the greatest proof of sanctity of all, "boiled over" with vermin "like a simmering cauldron"! [39] After such a revelation, there was nothing strange to anyone's mind that the cry "SAINT THOMAS!" should echo through the Cathedral, or that that cry should be heard and honoured throughout the world. The miracle of the curative powers of the sacred blood was accepted unquestioningly, and the ambitious statesman, who had so lately been either hated or ignored, became in a short time the most celebrated and venerated saint of all Europe. The hot violence which had surrounded Becket in life was transmuted into an equally intense passion of adoration of "St. Thomas," a passion the very intensity of which was soon to debase faith for many into preposterous credulity. By the fourteenth century, great numbers of pilgrims from "every shires ende" were wending their way to Canterbury, but the piety of the devout among them was vitiated, at least on the journey itself, by the thoughtless irreverence of the pleasure-seekers and by the deliberate evil of the scoundrels.

Of the miracles wrought by the "Waters of St. Thomas," the diluted blood of the martyr, the most celebrated were those of healing, and these are the only miracles of which Chaucer speaks directly: [40] the pilgrims, he says, visit the holy, sainted martyr who had helped them "whan that they were seeke." The monk Benedict a contemporary of Becket and one of our two principal sources for the first miracles of Thomas à Becket, writes:

By his merit the blind see, the lame walk, lepers are cleansed, the deaf hear, the dead are raised, the mute speak, the poor have the gospel preached to them, paralytics are healed, those afflicted with dropsy recover, the mad are restored to reason, epileptics are cured, those having a fever are raised up, and to conclude briefly, all manner of infirmity is cured: and almost all the gospel miracles have been reproduced in many ways by his merit.[41]

Although he gives the healing miracles greatest prominence, Benedict lists many [42] others, as, for example, the lost articles recovered through prayers to St. Thomas, the animals of all kinds restored to health and usefulness (and often, to praise the saint, given the speech of man), the tempests stilled, and severe punishments supernaturally visited upon those who failed to make promised Canterbury pilgrimages and upon those who tried to deter others from visiting the shrine of St. Thomas. Even as late as Chaucer's day, Archbishop Sudbury's death by mob violence was ascribed by many to Sudbury's having rebuked eleven years before, as Bishop of London, a typically noisy group of pilgrims on their way to Canterbury,[43] a group, it is to be feared, very similar in behaviour to the company of the *Canterbury Tales*.

In giving an April background to the *Canterbury Tales,* Chaucer shows that he did not intend that his pilgrims should arrive in Canterbury at the time of one of the great festivals, which were held in December and July; nor does he suggest that the pilgrimage was connected with any jubilee celebration. In 1420, for instance, a jubilee year, "no less than a hundred thousand" Englishmen, Irish- and Welshmen, Scots, Frenchmen, and Normans, swept into Canterbury,[44] kings, nobles, ministers of state, gentry, and the lowly, priests and people, all seeking the shrine of Becket. Chaucer's pilgrims, on the other hand, give no indication whatsoever that they are anticipating any exceptional scene in Canterbury. The author of the fifteenth-century *Prologue and Tale of Beryn,* in his plan to continue Chaucer's *Canterbury Tales,* begins his work consistently, therefore, when he places the pilgrims in a scene that is characteristic of the activities of an occasional group of pilgrims at an ordinary season.

Chaucer's pilgrims as pictured in the *Tale of Beryn*—and they are still Chaucer's, even though guided by a less sure hand—arrive in a quiet season. Canterbury is always busy and gay, but in April, 1387, it is only normally crowded. The doors of the Cheker stand hospitably wide, and the visitors from Southwark find no difficulty in securing excellent accommodations within the massive walls; perhaps the pilgrims even pause, before they go to the Cathedral, to admire the extensive courtyard about which their inn is built in a quadrangle, or to gape at the impressive pillars which support the first floor and form a colonnade running the full length of *Le Mer-ceria,* or Mercery Lane.[45] But no one wishes to tarry long when St. Thomas's shrine is still unvisited and only a few yards away, so the pilgrims hasten very shortly to the great Cathedral.

Both the exterior and interior of the Cathedral in the fourteenth century presented quite different aspects from those which they present today. As regards the exterior, there was no central tower, although there seems to have been a steeple of sorts, and at the northwest corner of the nave stood the old Norman tower, topped by a spire, a tower which lasted into the nineteenth century.[46] The present southwest tower did not exist in Chaucer's time. As regards the interior, Dean Stanley writes: "Bright colours on the roof, on the windows, on the monuments; hangings suspended from the rods . . . running from pillar to pillar; chapels, and altars, and chantries intercepting the view, where now all is clear . . ."[47] The Cathedral itself was thus clearly one of the marvels of Canterbury, and the author of the *Tale of Beryn* imbues his company with an urgency to behold it.

At the door of the wonderful Cathedral, the Knight marshals the pilgrims in their proper order:

> Then atte Chirche dorr the curtesy gan to ryse,
> Tyl the knyght, of gentilnes, that knewe righte wele the guyse,
> Put forth the Prelatis, the Person, & his fere.[48]

A monk sprinkles the pilgrims with holy water, and prevents the Friar, who characteristically would see the nun's face from a more intimate range, from taking the sprinkler from him. The Knight then goes with "his compers toward the holy shryne," while the Pardoner, Miller, and "othir lewde sotes" stand open-mouthed before the stained glass, and, "countirfeting gentilmen," try to make out the subjects of the pictures, their guesses, of course, being incorrect. The Host reproves them for their levity; then they, too, move towards the shrine, where they kneel and pray "in such wise as they couth," unseemly mirth at last subdued by the solemnity of the scene and the occasion.[49]

The picture of St. Thomas's shrine drawn by Erasmus in one of his *Colloquies*, only a century after Chaucer, must be very much like what the poet's contemporaries saw. Erasmus's description is in part as follows:

. . . The first prospect upon entering the church is only the largeness and the majesty of the body of it, which is free to everyone. . . . [All that is then seen is] the bulk of the structure, and the gospel of Nicodemus; with some other books that are hung up to the pillars; and here and there a monument. . . . The quire is shut up with iron gates, so that there's no entrance; but the view is still open from one end of the church to the other. There's an ascent to the quire of many steps, under which there is a certain vault, that opens a passage to the north-side, where we saw a wooden altar that is dedicated to the Holy Virgin. . . . From hence we passed down into a vault underground, . . . [and then] returned to the quire. . . . From hence we went to see the table and the ornaments of the altar; and after that, the treasure that was hidden under it. If you had seen the gold and silver that we saw, you would have looked upon Midas and Croesus as little better than beggars. . . . Our next remove was into the vestry; good God! what a pomp of rich vestments, what a provision of golden candlesticks did we see there! . . . From hence we are carried yet farther; for beyond the high altar, there is still another ascent, as if it were into a new church. . . . [At the summit of this ascent] there stood a wooden box upon a golden one; and upon the craning up of that with ropes, bless me, what a treasure was there discovered! . . . The basest part of it was gold; everything sparkled and flamed with inestimable gems, some of them as big or bigger than a goose egg. There stood about with great veneration some of the monks: upon the taking off of the cover, we all worshipped; the Prior with a white wand touched every stone one by one, telling us the name of it, the prices, and the benefactor. The richest of them were given by princes.[50]

After the blazing splendour of the shrine, pilgrims, now quiet and awestruck, would be shown the relics, including the rusty fragment of Le Bret's sword, part of St. Thomas's skull encased in silver, the very much soiled linen of the saint, and the relics of a few less famous personages, over four hundred items in all.[51] Some of these sacred remains were presented to pilgrims to kiss—"ech man with his mowith"—and in the *Tale of Beryn* the pilgrims, not possessed of any modern hygienic squeamishness, readily comply with the custom. Not very much later, however, one of the pilgrims described by Erasmus made a "wry mouth" at these relics instead of kissing them, and was outspoken in his opinions about the veneration of unclean objects.[52]

Upon securing their memorials of small leaden bottles, or *ampulles,* which were filled by the monks with the diluted blood (miraculously inexhaustible) of the martyred Becket, and which were given to all visitors to the shrine, the pilgrims from Southwark "drowgh to dynerward, as it drew to noon." On the way, they stop in Mercery Lane to buy secular tokens of their visit to Canterbury. Every shop and stall is well filled with brooches stamped with the head of St. Thomas or with representations of the *ampulles.* By this time, the awe engendered by the Cathedral has vanished, and the Miller and the Pardoner, themselves again, steal as many brooches as they can. They know the more brooches they have to stick in their caps, the more impressive they will be when they reach home. The Summoner observes the thieving, and greedily cries "halff part!" but as all three fear the Friar, who is watching them for no friendly purpose, they stop, and nonchalantly pretend to be doing something else. So, at last, after many pauses, the entire company arrive once more at the Cheker, and, after washing, they sit down to a convivial feast.[53] When they have eaten and drunk their fill, the Host, who is still master of ceremonies, suggests how the day is to be ended:

> "Then al this aftir-mete I hold it for the best
> To sport & pley us," quod the hoost, "eche man as hym lest,
> And go by tyme to soper, & [thanne] to bed also;
> So mowe wee erly rysen, our journey for to do." [54]

Each pilgrim follows the advice of the Host as to amusing himself in the way that appeals to him. The Knight and his son change their clothes, and go to see the walls and defences of the town, where the Knight discourses wisely on military tactics. The Monk, Parson, and Friar set out to visit an acquaintance in Canterbury, the Prioress and the Wife of Bath walk happily together in the beautiful herb garden of the Cheker, and most of the "lewed sotes" go off to make a night of it at the taverns.[55] The author of the *Tale of Beryn* has not Chaucer's genius; yet he does give us, with many realistic touches, a late fourteenth-century picture of a group of pilgrims in Canterbury, and for that we are grateful.

In his own incomparable lines, Chaucer represents himself as meetings the pilgrims at the Tabard Inn in Southwark:

> Bifil that in that seson on a day,
> In Southwerk at the Tabard as I lay
> Redy to wenden on my pilgrymage
> To Caunterbury with ful devout corage,
> At nyght was come into that hostelrye
> Wel nyne and twenty in a compaignye,
> Of sondry folk, by aventure yfalle
> In felaweshipe, and pilgrimes were they alle,
> That toward Caunterbury wolden ryde.
> The chambres and the stables weren wyde,
> And wel we weren esed atte beste.
> And shortly, whan the sonne was to reste,
> So hadde I spoken with hem everichon
> That I was of hir felaweshipe anon,
> And made forward erly for to ryse,
> To take oure wey ther as I yow devyse.
> But nathelees, whil I have tyme and space,
> Er that I ferther in this tale pace,
> Me thynketh it accordaunt to resoun
> To telle yow al the condicioun
> Of ech of hem, so as it semed me,
> And whiche they weren, and of what degree,
> And eek in what array that they were inne—
>
> (ll. 19–41)

Southwark, in Chaucer's time, was a small suburb of London, totally unlike the congested city district which bears the name today. The old Southwark spread its orchards and gardens and widely spaced dwellings south and east of the curving Thames, and was the "chief thoroughfare to and from London and the southern counties and towns, and the cities of the Continent." [56] For that reason and for the fact that its inns could not be made subject to the restrictive regulations of London,[57] Southwark was noted for its hostelries, and the Tabard was one of the most comfortable, the rooms and stables being so ample that fully "nyne and twenty" [58] sundry folk could be accommodated in the best possible manner.

Medieval inns were named for their distinguishing signs. The signs outside the Tabard must have pictured a "tabard," or coat embroidered with armorial bearings, sleeveless and open at the sides.[59] The original property of the old inn consisted of two holdings deeded in 1306 to the Abbey of Hyde-by-Winchester, whose abbot maintained a town lodging within the inn yard until the dissolution of the monasteries.[60] The holdings adjoined each other and fronted on what is now the Borough High Street, forming a wedge-shaped lot over 300 ft. deep, with a frontage of about 75 ft. and a rear width of about 125 ft.[61] The inn buildings were completely destroyed by the great Southwark fire of 1676, and, as far as can be ascertained, no contemporary drawing of the Tabard exists. The well known drawing which appears in Urry's *Chaucer* of 1721 may have been copied from an earlier picture, or it may have been sketched from memory or hearsay. It shows a swinging sign suspended over the road leading out to the country, and stone steps that extend outside the building to the galleries—"good evidence of a medieval inn." [62] A sixteenth-century inventory of the interior of the Tabard is in existence, and Mr. Philip Norman, who has edited this inventory, writes that the rooms and fixtures mentioned probably "represent the inn very much as seen by Chaucer." [63] Since the rooms are not described, however, and since the fixtures listed are principally locks and keys, the inventory does not add very much to our picture of the Tabard, but merely confirms our impression of commodiousness.[64]

At the spacious Tabard Inn, then, the pilgrims accept the poet as one of themselves, and make an agreement to rise early the next morning to set off in one company for Canterbury. And now, explains Chaucer in his intimate fashion, while he has the time and space, he will introduce the pilgrims to us; for that seems to him the orderly thing to do, to tell us at the start the character, degree, and array of each of these men and women.

Thus Chaucer begins his great masterpiece, and gives us actuality: his world as in his time.

NOTES

(The abbreviations used to designate books and articles mentioned in the Notes will be found listed alphabetically in the Bibliography, opposite the full reference. References to lines in the *Canterbury Tales* are given by fragment and line numbers only.)

1. Miss Rosemond Tuve (*MLN*, LII, pp. 9–16) shows that Chaucer includes all the elements which make up the long and elaborate tradition of the spring setting.

2. Tatlock, *Anglia*, XXXVII, pp. 85 f.

3. Guido is cited by Chaucer as his "authority" in the *House of Fame* (l. 1469) and in the *Legend of Good Women* (ll. 1396, 1464).

4. Tempus erat quod sol maturans sub obliquo zodiaci circulo cursum suum sub signo iam intraverat arietis, in quo noctium spatio equato diebus celebratur equinoctium primi veris, tunc cum incipit tempus blandiri mortalibus in aeris serenitate intentis, tunc cum dissolutis nivibus molliter flantes zephiri crispant aquas, tunc cum fontes in ampullulas tenues scaturizant, tunc cum ad summitates arborum et ramorum humiditates ex terre gremio exhalantes extollunter in eis, quare insultant semina, crescunt segetes, virent prata variorum colorum floribus illustrata, tunc cum induuntur renovatis frondibus arbores circumquaque, tunc cum ornatur terra graminibus, cantant volucres et in dulcis armonie modulamine citarizant. . . . (*Hist. Destr. Troiae*, Lib. IIII)

Skeat says (V, 1 f.) that "Chaucer seems to have had in his mind" the passage quoted above; but he also calls attention to a passage similar in tone from Vincent of Beauvais's *Speculum Naturale,* lib. xv. c. 66, entitled *De Vere.*

Several scholars have made other suggestions as to Chaucer's source for the first eleven lines of the *Prologue.* Miss Tuve suggests (*loc. cit.*) that Chaucer may have used *Secreta Secretorum,* although she inclines more strongly to the belief that Chaucer used a number of sources; John E. Hankins (*MLN,* XLIX, pp. 80–83) makes out a case for Chaucer's use of the second-century poem, *Pervigilium Veneris,* giving a line by line comparison; and a number of scholars have pointed out the resemblance between Chaucer's spring picture and *Boethius,* Bk. I, Met. v, ll. 18–22, and Bk. II, Met. iii, ll. 5–8. The weight of the evidence, however, seems to be on the side of the Guido passage.

5. In a thirteenth-century book on husbandry (Cripps-Day, p. 69), the "dry" season of March is mentioned.

6. The *zodiac* is a zone of the celestial sphere bounded by two circles equidistant from the ecliptic (i.e., the great circle which forms the apparent yearly path of the sun on the surface of the celestial sphere) and about 18 degrees apart. The paths of the moon and of the principal planets also apparently lie in the zodiac; the heavenly bodies in the zodiac were grouped in ancient times into twelve "constellations" each corresponding to the sun's progress each month. In the late fourteenth century the sun entered the first sign, Aries (i.e., "Ram"), on March 12, and left the sign on April 11. The calendar month of April therefore saw the sun running half his course in Aries and half in the next sign. Chaucer speaks of the sun as "yonge," because the second sign has only just been entered—the second half of the Ram (since it is April) having been completed. (*Ency. Brit.,* "Aries," "Zodiac"; Skeat, V, 2 f.)

7. The Knight of La Tour Landry writes (p. 156): ". . . the nightyngales, as longe as they be amerouses, they synge pleasauntly day and night." Manly notes (*Cant. Tales,* p. 495) that Pliny makes a similar statement.

Cf. *The Romaunce of the Sowdone of Babylone,* ll. 41–48, lines which were probably imitated from Chaucer.

8. Palmers were originally so-called because as pilgrims who had visited Palestine they brought back palm-branches as a token of the journey; later the term was used for any pilgrim. (*NED,* "Palmer.")

9. See below, pp. 221 ff.

10. " 'Identical rime,' as in *seke: seeke* was permitted, or even sought in Old French and Middle English." (Robinson, p. 753.) "Identical rime" is also found in modern French.

11. *Ency. Brit.*, "Pilgrimage."

12. Henry Todd, *Illustrations*, p. 355. The figures quoted by Todd belong to the reign of Henry II, according to P. A. Brown in his *Development of the Legend of Thomas Becket* (p. 19). Todd gives no date, and misleadingly mentions Henry VIII in the same sentence.

13. W. A. Scott Robertson (*Arch. Cant.*, XIII, 510) gives the figure for 1220 as approximately 1071 pounds, and for 1420 as 570 pounds. The problem is to translate these sums into something comparable to our modern values.

*   *   *   *   *

As Coulton shows (*Hist. Assoc. Leaflet # 95*) no index for medieval moneys which will satisfy the economists can be arrived at scientifically, but we can approach the problem from a "metaphorical" or "psychological" point of view by comparing a sum of money producing a certain mental attitude in the Middle Ages with the sum of money producing the same mental attitude today. Now willingness-to-work may be considered, for our purposes, as an "invariant" attitude during the last six centuries, and it can in a sense be measured by wages; and because the farm labourer's occupation has suffered the least drastic change since the late fourteenth century, his wages seem the best to use to discover our psychological index.

In an account rendered by Chaucer himself in 1391 as Clerk of the King's Works, ditchers and unskilled workmen each received 4 *d.* a day (Manly, *Cant. Tales*, p. 66); the Statistical Abstract of the United States for 1944–45 reports the farm labourer's daily wage to be $3.46 (p. 153—I have taken the figure given for "with board" as better for this purpose than the $3.93 "without board"). Hence, using the par value of the modern pound sterling in terms of United States money (4 *d.* = 8 cents), we have a ratio of 8:346, or, approximately, 1:43.

It is not intended that such a multiplier as 43 will do anything more than give the most general idea of "equivalence" to the average American, or that such a number can be defended mathematically or economically. I have borrowed Dr. Coulton's method (not his figures) to obtain an index which will convey only an *idea* to the non-specialist reader; such an index cannot be used, of course, for discovering the "value" of any specific commodity.

14. Stanley, p. 230.

15. *Ibid.*, p. 187.

16. II (B), 988–994.

17. *Piers Plow.*, II, p. 7.

18. The *Cath. Ency.* ("Indulgences") defines *indulgence* as follows: "An indulgence is the extra-sacramental remission of the temporal remission due, in God's justice, to sin that has been forgiven, which remission is granted by the Church." A "plenary" indulgence is a remission of all the debt due.

19. R. W. Chambers (E.E.T.S., v. 186), p. civ.

20. *Margery Kempe* (Butler-Bowdon), pp. 50–66.

21. Owst, *Lit. and Pulpit*, pp. 555 f.—but see all references to "pilgrims."

22. *Ibid.*, p. 333. Quotation taken from MS. Add. 24202, fol. 27b.

23. Van Hamel, Bk. II, ll. 947 ff.

24. La Tour Landry, Chap. 34.

25. III (D) 655–658.

26. III (D) 550–559.

27. Deschamps, *Miroir de Mariage*, Chap. XLIII. This work was probably begun in 1381 and completed in 1389 (see *Oeuvres Complètes,* IX, 166).

28. *Ibid.*, Chap. XI (ll. 800–809), Chap. XXXVI (ll. 3500–3509, 3526–3531).

29. *House of Fame*, 2121–2125.

30. *Piers Plow.*, C. Passus I. 47–50.

31. *15th Cent. Prose and Verse*, pp. 139–141.

32. *Acad.*, XXIV, 331. William Dynet, a Lollard, in an oath of recantation of heresy in 1395, swore before the Archbishop of York "that fro this day forthwarde I shall worshipe ymages, with praying and offering vn-to hem in the worschepe of the seintes that they be made after; and also I shal neuermor despyse py[l]gremage, ne states of holy chyrche in no degree."

33. Stanley, p. 190.

34. *Ibid.*, p. 192.

35. *Ibid.*, p. 60.

36. *Ibid.*, p. 63.

37. *Ibid.*, p. 53.

38. Owst, *Lit. and Pulpit*, pp. 132 f. Quotation taken from MS. Harl. 2247, fol. 23b.

39. Stanley, p. 98.

40. Chaucer implies, perhaps, that the Knight is making the journey as a thanksgiving for success in his campaigns. It is possible that others of the pilgrims have motives that have nothing to do with sickness.

41. Brown, *Dev. Leg. Thomas Becket*, pp. 166 f. Translated from *Materials for the History of Thomas Becket*, ed. J. C. Robertson, Rolls Series #67 (1875–1885), II, 26.

42. *Ibid.*, pp. 156–183.

43. Wharton, *Anglia Sacra*, I, 49. Coulton speaks of this event (*Ch. and his Eng.*, p. 142) in the same way: "many simple souls were rather pained than surprised when Wat Tyler's mob, eleven years later, hacked off the head of so free-thinking an Archbishop on Tower Hill."

44. Stanley, p. 215, taken from Somner's *Canterbury*, part i, app. no. xliv.

45. *Pilgrim's Guide*, p. 20.

46. Gostling, Chap. XVII, Cf. *Chron. Hist. Cant. Cath.*, plate opp. p. 320; and *Illust. Views Met. Cath. Ch.*, plate opp. p. 5.

47. Stanley, p. 220.

48. *Beryn*, ll. 135–137.

49. *Ibid.*, ll. 138–165.

50. Erasmus, pp. 39 ff.

51. Stanley, p. 223.

52. Erasmus, p. 46.

53. *Beryn,* ll. 171 ff.

54. *Ibid.,* ll. 227–230.

55. *Ibid.,* ll. 231 ff.

56. Wheatley, p. 376.

57. See, for example, an ordinance of 1365 from Letter-Book G, fol. cxxxv, translated by Riley (in *London,* p. 323), forbidding hostelers to bake bread; and a proclamation from the same source (fol. cclv—Riley pp. 347 f.) which deals with fourteenth-century "ceiling prices"affecting hostelers.

58. Robinson (p. 756) accounts in the traditional way for the discrepancy between this number and the actual number of pilgrims: in line 164 of the *Prologue,* the phrase "and prestes thre" is a late addition to the manuscripts to fill out an unfinished line; if Chaucer had lived to complete the *Canterbury Tales,* he very probably would have here described the Second Nun and the *one* priest accompanying the Prioress—one priest makes the total number of pilgrims exactly right. Manly (*Cant. Tales,* pp. 507 f.) agrees with Robinson.

59. Stow writes (II, 62): "From thence towards London bridge on the same side, be many fayre Innes, for receipt of travellers . . . Amongst the which, the most auncient is the Tabard, so called of the signe, which as we now tearme it, is of a Iacquit, or sleevelesse coat, whole before, open on both sides, with a square coller, winged at the shoulders: a stately garment of old time, commonly worne of Noble men and others, both at home and abroad in the warres, but then (to wit in the warres) their Armes embrodered, or otherwise depict upon them, that every man by his coate of Armes might be knowne from others . . ."

60. Rendle and Norman, p. 182.

61. Manly, *Cant. Tales,* p. 498.

62. Rendle and Norman, p. 190.

63. Norman, *Surrey Arch.,* XIII, 32.

64. *Ibid.*

CHAPTER III

THE PERFECT KNIGHT

And at a knyght than wol I first bigynne.
(l. 42)

THUS Chaucer introduces his *dramatis personae* with the character who was then, and who is still, the most important, the most romantic, and—in one sense—the most enduring. Throughout the years, we have listened as children to stories of King Arthur, and our imaginations have been stirred by the drama, the colour, and the lofty ideals of days "when knighthood was in flower"; we do not wholly lose the magic of those tales of chivalry as adults, and our mature acceptance of the principles of the chivalric code as a part of our ethical associations and aspirations has kept alive a strong belief that "knightly" behaviour is synonymous with decent moral conduct. But not many of us stop to question whether this long-familiar code is based on a way of life which was generally practised, or on a theory of conduct. Was there ever a Golden Age of Chivalry when the true *chevalier sans peur et sans reproche* was exemplified by all knights, or even by the majority? Certainly in every era there have been individuals whose bright and noble virtue has guided and inspired mankind, but the very fact that we can single out such knights is an indication that they are exceptional. An examination of the history of chivalry proves that the magnificent strength of the Order of Knighthood never lay in numbers who followed the Rule, but in the widespread acceptance of ideals in which medieval man had a belief as profound as in Christianity itself, and which he bequeathed to succeeding generations. Chaucer's Knight is the personification of those ideals, yet he is far more than the lay figure he would be were he that alone; like the other pilgrims taking this April journey to Canterbury, he is flesh and blood. He is one of those exceptional heroes who strive to live according to a great ideal yet who are at the same time understandably and understandingly human.

A Knyght ther was, and that a worthy man,
That fro the tyme that he first bigan
To riden out, he loved chivalrie.

(ll. 43–45)

Before the close of the eleventh century, chivalry as we understand it today did not exist as an institution. It was not until 1095,
when Urban II, in proclaiming the First Crusade, welded together
the Cross and the sword, that the Christian ideal of the Order of
Knighthood was created and took such high position in man's aspira-
tion.[1] "Now let those who have been in the habit of wastefully wag-
ing private wars, even against believers, proceed against the infidel
in worthy battle," the Pope exhorted the crusaders. "Now let those
who lived not long ago as plunderers be soldiers of Christ; now let
those who formerly contended against brothers and kinsfolk rightly
fight against the barbarians; now let those who were wont to be
mercenaries for a small sum, obtain eternal rewards!"[2] Urban commanded that the members of Christ's army should be "wise, provi-
dent, temperate, learned, peace-making, truth-seeking, pious, just,
equitable, pure,"[3]—a formidable order to be addressed to men very
few of whom, up to this moment, had been in the habit of exercis-
ing any of those virtues. It was inevitable, of course, that few would
ever attain, either then or in the centuries to follow, the exalted
standard set by Urban II. As Professor Hearnshaw points out, "the
decadence of chivalry can be discovered in its very idea"; "mediaeval religion was too irrational, mediaeval warfare too cruel," for the
institution of chivalry ever to have realized its ideal "even approximately."[4] What had the greatest importance for the world, however, was the extraordinary fact that all Christendom seized so gladly
and so immediately upon Urban's standards, and used them as the
measure of an ideal "parfit gentil knyght"; the knight was henceforth to be the champion of the Church, the righteous and impla-
cable enemy of the infidel, the compassionate protector of the weak
and oppressed, the defender of all Right and Justice. Almost at
once, rules for the Order of Knighthood were formulated,[5] all much
alike, varying only in degree of elaboration. By the fourteenth century, such codes had become commonplaces: everyone knew how
the true knight should conduct himself, and everyone knew how
seldom he was encountered in the world of actuality. Bromyard,
the fourteenth-century Dominican, bewails the fact that few knights

now take the Cross, "either in the letter or in the spirit," but choose rather to remain at home "in delights and sins." [6] As soon as these men are

. . . decorated with the belt of knighthood, they rise up against their fellow Christians, rage violently against the Patrimony of Christ, plunder and spoil the poor subject to them, afflict the wretched pitiably and pitilessly, and fulfil their extravagant wills and lusts.[7]

On the other hand, when knighthood is eulogized, and the absence of chivalric behaviour in the workaday world served to entrench the chivalric ideal in manners, morals, and literature, the praise is bestowed either on the glories of an imagined past or on the particular qualities of some beloved, actual figure.

From where, then, comes the creation of Chaucer's Knight? Did the poet draw upon general knowledge of what a knight should be, or did he use a living model, or did he go to some literary source? Probably those questions can never be answered definitely, for the Knight is too much himself—a brave and seasoned soldier, who from the time that he first "rode out"

> . . . loved chivalrie,
> Trouthe and honour, fredom and curteisie.
>
> .   .   .   .
>
> And everemoore he hadde a sovereyn prys;
> And though that he were worthy, he was wys,
> And of his port as meeke as is a mayde,
> He nevere yet no vileynye ne sayde
> In al his lyf unto no maner wight.
> He was a verray, parfit gentil knyght.
>
> (ll. 45–46, 67–72)

Schofield points out in detail that we can find for these lines an excellent literary parallel and a possible source in the pages of Watriquet de Couvin, who describes his knightly patron, Gauchier de Chatillon, in terms very nearly identical with those employed by Chaucer.[8] As Watriquet was one of the most notable poets of Hainault, the home of Queen Philippa, it seems reasonable to suppose that in his young days Geoffrey Chaucer, then dwelling in a royal household, would have become familiar with the writings of the older man, and that he might perhaps later have paid him the medieval compliment of borrowing his words. In the *Dit du Connestable de France,* an elegy of some three hundred lines, Watriquet speaks of his hero and patron as follows:

> Prouesce faisoit esveillier
> Courtoisie, honneur, et largesce
> Et loiauté, qui de noblesce
> Toutes les autres vertus passe.
>
> .   .   .   .
>
> Tant fust plains de courouz ne d'ire
> Onques n'issi hors de sa bouche
> Vilains mos; maniere avoit douche,
> Plus que dame ne damoisele.[9]

Thus Watriquet tells us that the prowess of his knight awakened the supreme virtues of "courtesy," "honour," "liberality," and "loyalty," while Chaucer describes his "gentil knyght" as possessing the same virtues and a love of "chivalrie." Also, Watriquet's hero was "never so filled with anger that there would come from his mouth a word of 'villainy'; he had a manner gentler than that of a lady or a 'maid'", while Chaucer's Knight "in al his lyf" has never yet said "vileynye" to anyone, and in his bearing he is "as meeke as is a mayde."

The correspondence between the descriptions of Watriquet and Chaucer, however, becomes even more striking when the words Chaucer uses are analyzed for meaning. If we are to understand the Knight as the fourteenth century knew him, such an analysis must be made.

In the later Middle Ages, "chivalry" usually connoted as it does today the whole knightly system with its religious, social, and moral code,[10] but occasionally the word was employed in more specialized senses, and there are instances of its use to express "prowess." This, indeed, had been one of the most frequent meanings of the word in earlier times.[11] We are justified, therefore, in interpreting Chaucer's "chivalrie" as having a double meaning here: the poet uses it both in the modern sense and in the sense of Watriquet's "proesce." The presence of other parallels suggests that Chaucer so intended the word to be understood.

French *courtoisie* and English *curteisie* are, of course, one, but chivalry gave the word much more significance than modern *cour-*

tesy. The ideal knight was to possess a consideration for others far surpassing "politeness," and instruction in this sort of courtesy was one of the first lessons in his long education.[12] Dr. Will Héraucourt, in his exhaustive study of Chaucer's *Wertwelt,* says that the mature Chaucer set aside any superficial meaning *curteisie* had acquired, and used the word to mean "helpful, tender, charitable, generous deportment." [13]

Watriquet's *preud'omme* and Chaucer's Knight both prize "honour" : that is, both have a fine awareness of and strict allegiance to righteousness. Dr. Héraucourt, again in *Die Wertwelt Chaucers,* calls attention to the change which is manifest in the poet's use of the word *honour* after he had translated Boethius;[14] after Chaucer had written: "And therfore it is thus that honour . . . cometh to dignyte for cause of vertu," [15] he unquestionably employed *honour* to mean much more than "distinction" or "reputation." "Honour" in such high moral sense would obviously be a *sine qua non* of true knighthood, and both Watriquet and Chaucer stress this quality in their respective heroes.

Watriquet's *largesce* corresponds to Chaucer's *fredom.* The word *largesce* was commonly used in Old French to denote our modern "liberality"; the companion word in Middle English was either *largesse* or *fredom,* both of which Chaucer uses. In the translation of Boethius, Chaucer writes:

What is most worth of rychesses? . . . Certes thilke gold and thilke moneye schyneth and yeveth bettre renoun to hem that dispenden it than to thilke folk that mokeren * it; for avaryce maketh alwey mokereres to ben hated, and largesse maketh folk cleer of renoun.[16]

Alexander, who is so full of "leonyn corage," is praised by Chaucer as being "of knyghthod and of fredom flour," [17] and in the *Parson's Tale* one of the designated "generale signes of gentilesse" is liberality.[18] The objection may be raised, however, that Chaucer sometimes uses the word *fredom* in other senses. But here Chaucer is describing a knight, and one of the virtues which are emphasized as necessary in nearly every medieval book of instruction for knights is material generosity. Jacobus de Cessolis, a Dominican of the late thirteenth century, writes, for example, in his *Chess-Book,* a widely popular allegory of the various social classes:

* *mokeren*: "hoard."

Also the knyghtes shold be large & liberall For whan a knyght hath regarde unto his singuler prouffit by his covetyse/ he dispoylleth his peple . . . Than late every knyght take heede to be liberall in suche wyse that he wene not ne suppose that his scarcete be to hym a grete wynnynge or gayn/ And for thys cause he be the lasse lovyd of his peple/ [19]

Surely Chaucer would not have omitted such an important chivalric virtue from the description of the Knight, and we must therefore be correct in saying that Chaucer's *fredom* is one with Watriquet's *largesce*.

Watriquet praises his patron for having possessed "loiaute"; Chaucer uses the word *trouthe*. In his writings Chaucer employs this word in three different senses, one of which is "fidelity" or "loyalty." [20] Since fidelity is obviously of paramount importance in such an Order as Knighthood, Chaucer would be obliged to include this quality in any true portrait of a "parfit" knight.

But all the close similarities between the words of Watriquet and those of Chaucer only suggest, it must be noted once more, that Chaucer may have borrowed from the poet of Hainault. He may, equally, have been using the same common medieval conception of an ideal. It is at least certain that Chaucer has much to say about his Knight for which there is no parallel in Watriquet's poem.

Chaucer uses the word *worthy* in connection with the Knight, in antithesis to the word *wys*, and we are therefore led to translate *worthy* as modern "brave." The idea that a hero should be both brave and "wise" (that is, "prudent") antedates the institution of chivalry. Beowulf is described as "courageous and wise," [21] for example, and Roland and Oliver illustrate the need for the blending of these two qualities.[22] By Chaucer's time, the combination had become a commonplace,[23] and it would be difficult to find any hero of romance who disappoints either writer or reader through failure to embody both bravery and prudence. Even without the word *wys*, Chaucer sometimes uses *worthy* to mean "brave", as in *Boece*, where "worthynesse" translates the Latin *valentiam*,[24] which is equivalent to the Latin *virtus*, or "bravery." [25]

The appearance of Chaucer's Knight is entirely in keeping with his virtues:

His hors were goode, but he was nat gay.
Of fustian he wered a gypon
Al bismotered with his habergeon,
For he was late ycome from his viage,
And wente for to doon his pilgrymage.

(ll. 74–78)

It is very much to the credit of the Knight that he is not over-dressed, not too "gay," for according to the sermon literature of the fourteenth century, the upper classes are continually censured for their "synful costlewe array of clothynge." [26] The homilists often coupled "the synne of aornement or of apparaille" with the posses-sion of "to manye delicat horses that been hoolden for delit," [27] so that Chaucer's *but* in line 74 has added force. The Knight's horses [28] are good, but since their owner is soberly clad, we realize at once that he has not an excessive number and that they are maintained solely because a knight must be fittingly mounted. Caxton's transla-tion of a thirteenth-century book on chivalry says:

To a knyght is gyven an horse / and also a Coursour for the sygnefye noblesse of courage / And by cause that he be wel horsed and hyhe / is by cause he may be sene fro ferre / and that is the sygnefyaunce that he oughte to be made redy to doo al that whiche behoveth to thordre of chyvalrye more / than another man/ [29]

Chaucer does not describe in detail his Knight's dress, for to do so would be as absurd as for a twentieth-century writer to de-scribe the conventional attire of today's well-to-do male citizen. Con-sequently, if we wish to see the Knight with fourteenth-century eyes, we must here go beyond Chaucer's text and supply for ourselves the details of costume which are now unfamiliar.

Since the Knight is "late ycome from his viage" * and is hasten-ing immediately with devout heart to St. Thomas's shrine, it is pos-sible, although hardly probable, that in spite of the peaceful nature of his journey, he is still wearing some of his battledress.[30] Chaucer may have visualized him, for example, in the habergeon with which the gypon has been "al bismotered." A habergeon was a sleeveless coat of mail, reaching half-way to the knee, and having a straight edged skirt. The gypon was a tight-fitting, also sleeveless, tunic, laced

* *viage:* "military expedition."

up at the side, and was worn over the habergeon when the knight was armed. The gypon was always made of some stout material; its hem was usually escalloped and reached to within an inch or so above the hem of the habergeon.[31] Chaucer's Knight wears a gypon of "fustian," a coarse material of cotton and flax, probably unbleached.[32] Even though the Knight is in haste to "doon his pilgrymage," he must have discarded, before the pilgrimage begins, the plate armour with which his arms and legs would be protected in battle. The artist of the Ellesmere MS. depicts the Knight without armour; the Knight wears a voluminous, wide-sleeved gown, and a hood or tippet draped about the head to give the effect of a hat.

But whether we see the Knight as partially armed, or as a civilian gentleman, we are aware always that he bears the honourable stains of long service. For the Knight has not played at war: he has shared valiantly in many battles.

> Ful worthy was he in his lordes werre,
> And therto hadde he riden, no man ferre,
> As wel in cristendom as in hethenesse,
> And evere honoured for his worthynesse.
>
> (ll. 47–50)

Some of the richness of colour in the Knight's portrait is to be found, as Manly has indicated,[33] in the list of "many a noble armee" in which the Knight has taken part. To many of Chaucer's contemporaries, this list was no mere catalogue of expeditions, as it is to us today, but a chapter of romance. "Cristendom" was small when Chaucer lived, and the lands beyond its boundaries were thrillingly mysterious. The chronicles and tales, the travel books, and the encyclopaedias all made for exciting reading, as is shown by the popularity of the works of Froissart, Machaut, Benoit de Sainte-More, Vincent of Beauvais, and many others. They all, like the supposed author, Sir John Mandevelle, who wrote the travel book *par excellence,* encouraged the even then escapist belief that extraordinary magnificence and wonder lay outside the humdrum world of everyday existence. Even the cold, dark, marshy regions of Lithuania and Russia, peopled by barbarians, possessed glamour because of their difference, but it was the realms of the East and the Southeast which held the greatest magic. For these were lands where flowered silks, pearls and gold and rubies, frankincense and myrrh and sandalwood, "ivory and apes and peacocks," were ever present in splendid profusion, and where golden warmth and light called forth exotic fruits of the earth as if by supernatural force. These were the lands which betrayed the returned traveller into fantastic "eyewitness" accounts of marvels and legends: the golden breasted phoenix outshining the sun, the monstrously born Medusa head that made the sea engulf the land at Satalye,[34] the "lady of fayrye" who dwelt in a castle beyond Layays with her mysterious "sparrehawk," [35] the incubators and leafless fig trees of Egypt.[36] Chaucer's Knight has been to these strange and wonderful countries. Who can read of him without vicarious savouring of extraordinary adventure?

Manly divides the campaigns of the Knight into three groups arranged in probable order of time.[37] The first group is made up of the events which are referred to in the following lines:

> In Gernade at the seege eek hadde he be
> Of Algezir, and riden in Belmarye.
>
> .   .   .   .
>
> And foughten for oure feith at Tramyssene
> In lystes thries, and ay slayn his foo.
>
> (ll. 56–57; 62–63)

In speaking generally of this group, Manly states that "these . . . are events in the long struggle to drive the Moors out of Spain and punish their piratical raids from northern Africa upon Christians and Christian commerce." [38] It is, therefore, impossible to put a definite date to any of the Knight's campaigns of this period with the exception of the siege of Algezir.

Algezir, since the eighth century, had been the most important stronghold of the Moors on the Iberian peninsula.[39] Situated in Granada on the west coast of the Bay of Algeciras, where modern Algeciras stands, Algezir served as the Moorish gateway to Europe. It is not surprising that the Moorish forces under Abo-l-Hassan did their utmost in the fourteenth century to retain possession of this strategic citadel, or that Alfonso of Castile spent nearly two years in besieging it, aided by "earls and barons and men-at-arms from the whole Christian world." [40] Algezir was finally starved into surrender in March, 1344, amid great rejoicing throughout Europe, although the victors had suffered severely from heavy losses inflicted by the expert archers and engineers of the enemy, from dissensions among themselves, and from the same terrible hunger and thirst which had assailed the vanquished.[41] But any sacrifice seemed worth the prize, and the letter of delighted congratulation sent by Edward III of England to Alfonso may be said to have been typical of the general exultation of Christendom.[42] "That Englishmen took part in the siege and were present at the surrender we know to be a fact and not one of Chaucer's poetic fictions," writes Manly; [43] and he cites an extant letter of credence dated August, 1343, and addressed to Alfonso, which was in favour of Henry, Earl of Derby, the father of Duchess Blanche of Lancaster, and of William de Montacute, Earl of Salisbury. Although no letters of protection for the men accompanying Derby and Salisbury are in existence, we may suppose that "the train of each consisted of about thirty men." Surely we can picture Chaucer's Knight as one of those gallant sixty, and imagine what grandeurs he may have seen in Algezir, for Granada was then the home of Moorish art and science, where the intricate beauties of palaces and mosques surpassed the Christian architecture of Europe, where jewelled and finely etched armour ("So unkouth and so riche, and wroght so weel / Of goldsmythrye . . ." [44]), carved ivories, and pottery shining with iridescent gold and copper lustre were in the possession of every noble.

So far as the campaigns against the African kingdom of Belmarye and the fighting for "oure feith" in the lists at Tramyssene (the modern Tlemcen in Algeria) are concerned, we have no way of knowing whether Chaucer had definite expeditions in mind, or whether he was thinking of the general warfare against the Moors which was carried on intermittently over a period of years in northern Africa. A letter, again from Edward III to Alfonso, dated June, 1341, congratulating the king of Castile upon his victory over the sovereign of "Benermeren" has been preserved,[45] and Froissart mentions a number of expeditions against the kingdoms of "Bellemarine" and "Tramesainnes," [46] describing in one chapter a challenge given by the Saracens to ten Christian nobles to combat bodily in the lists an equal number of Saracens "of name in arms." [47] Although the date, 1390, of this challenge is too late for Chaucer's Knight, the description indicates that such challenges were not unusual. "When the news of this combat was spread through the [Christian] army," Froissart writes, "and the names of the ten were told, the knights and squires said,—'they are lucky fellows, thus to have such a gallant feat of arms fall to their lot.' 'Would to Heaven,' added many, 'that we were of the ten.' "

The second group mentioned by Manly of the campaigns of Chaucer's Knight is made up of the events which are referred to in the following lines:

> At Alisaundre he was whan it was wonne.
>
> . . . .
>
> At Lyeys was he and at Satalye,
> Whan they were wonne; and in the Grete See
> At many a noble armee * hadde he be.
>
> . . . .
>
> This ilke worthy knyght hadde been also
> Somtyme with the lord of Palatye
> Agayn another hethen in Turkye.
>
> (ll. 51, 58–60, 64–66)

This is the most important group of the Knight's expeditions, and there is far more contemporary evidence than for the other two groups. Dates are definite: Satalye, 1361; Alisaundre, 1365; Lyeys, 1367. The service under the lord of Palatye is obviously less definite, but probably, as will be later indicated, this took place in the late 1360's.

The East changes slowly, and Satalye [48] exists today somewhat —in its physical aspects, at least—as it did six hundred years ago; but time has stripped it of importance and of its medieval splendour. Situated in Asia Minor, where the land curves to the southeast cupping the blue waters of the Mediterranean, Satalye, which is identical with the frequently mentioned "Adalia," was famous in the Middle Ages as the customary port of reembarkation for many of the Crusaders on their way to Palestine, especially since the Christian quarter of the city was close to the harbour on the Gulf of Adalia. [49] The Turkish, or principal, part of the city was built within

---

* *armee* appears in seventeen manuscripts, *aryve* in five—one manuscript is ambiguous. Robinson points out (p. 754, n. 60) that *armee* can be translated into modern "armed expedition" or "armada," from Latin *armata*, whereas "the reading *aryve*, . . . 'arrival or disembarkation,' is more difficult since the word is not found elsewhere in English."

high walls on the lofty fertile plateau which tops the steep, rocky cliffs rising abruptly from the sea. Flowers still bloom in the gardens of Satalye, and groves of orange and of olive trees still bear fruit, but gone are the wealthy nobles and many men of affairs who, in Chaucer's time, lived so lavishly and so intensely in busy palaces that were built in keeping with the lavish surroundings of nature.

It can be easily understood why all the rulers in the Middle Ages would covet rich Satalye, and perhaps Peter I of Cyprus may have had his genuine, crusading spirit mixed with a touch of human greed when he set out to regain the wealthy city and convenient harbour which had, in former times, belonged to the Cypriotes, and which had now been in Saracen hands for nearly two hundred years.

Peter I was born in 1329. His family, the de Lusignans, originally from Poitou, had ruled Cyprus as kings for nearly three hundred years; their court was brilliant, and Cyprus shared almost all the institutions of Western European civilization. We owe the legend surrounding Peter's birth and young manhood to his enthusiastic biographer, Guillaume de Machaut, who devotes about four-fifths of his long poem, *La Prise d'Alexandrie*, to the celebration of the life and virtues of *li bons roys & très vaillant homme*. We learn how all the gods of mythology blessed the newly born prince; how at a very early age he was trained in arms, in the honour belonging to a true *chevalier*, and in the service due to God; and how, when he was only twenty, he received inspiration from a vision of Christ on the Cross, and founded an order of chivalry, the Order of the Sword, which knights from all over Europe hastened to join.[50]

Machaut's poem is in the nature of a chronicle. Although he had never been in the Orient, he was well acquainted with many who knew the country, officers and knights of Europe who were attached to Peter I's Order of the Sword, and it is entirely possible that Machaut had an audience with Peter himself at Rheims or at Paris; so the eulogy, at least, may be based on first-hand observation.[51] In any event, Machaut's laudatory account of his hero and of his hero's exploits is not far removed from personal experience: in his poem, Machaut speaks of a squire of Champagne, Jehan de Reins, who was a veteran of Peter's crusades and who was well acquainted with Machaut, as the principal "source" of his *matière*.[52] As a courtly poet, Machaut was not, of course, concerned with a dispassionate estimate of Peter's generalship founded on cold accomplishment, but

in this he is like almost any writer of his time, including the chroni-
clers. Pierre de Lusignan was for Froissart, too, "the good king of
Cyprus"; [53] for Petrarch, a man of "glorious work"; [54] for Chaucer,
"worthy" Peter slain because of his great "chivalrie." [55] Froissart
quotes the epitaph of Peter I as follows:

And syr Phelyp of Maysyeres, chauncellour to Peter of Liesiegnen,
kynge of Cypres, wrote on his tombe as it foloweth, the copy wherof is
in the chapytre house of the freer Celestynes, in Paris: Peter of Liesiegnen, the vi kyng Latyne of Iherusalem, after Godfrey of Boloyne,
and kynge of Cypres, who by his grete prowes and hyghe empryse toke
by batayle at his cost these cytees, Alexandrie in Egypte, Triple in
Surie, Layas in Armony, Satalie in Turkye, and dyvers other cytees and
castelles of the infydelles and enemyes of the lawe of Ihesu Cryst . . . [56]

Such, then, was Pierre de Lusignan, who reigned as Peter I of
Cyprus, and went in 1361 upon his first crusade against the Saracens
in Asia Minor. By his own persuasive efforts, Peter was successful in
securing aid from the Hospitallers of Rhodes, who added four gal-
leys to the fleet of forty-six from Cyprus; from the Pope, who provided two ships; and from various lords and barons, among them a
number of Englishmen led by the Earl of Hereford,[57] who brought
the total number of vessels up to one hundred and nineteen.[58]
Machaut writes of the taking of Satalye as follows:

Peter I and his men sailed the high seas until they came to Satalie,
a great, powerful, strongly fortified city in Turkey; and there was
neither wall, nor gate, nor men that could prevent "li bons rois" from
capturing this city, or from destroying it and putting it to the sword;
and so the whole was consumed in flames. There was burnt much silk
—and many a beautiful lady, many damsels and children, Saracens
and Turks, perished by fire and sword.[59]

The chronicler Makhairas, who flourished in Cyprus in the late
fourteenth and early fifteenth centuries, and who also admired King
Peter, writes a more sober account of these same events.[60] He follows this with a description of the surrender of Alaya, a smaller city
nearby, which is not mentioned at this time by Machaut. Makhairas
says:

When . . . the Lord of Alaya learned that King Peter had taken
Adalia, great fear came into . . . [his heart and he was] . . . full of

bitterness. And at once . . . [the Lord of Alaya and another prince]
. . . sent their envoys to Adalia to the king, begging him to be good
friends with them, and they promised to pay him every year a fixed
amount, and he should set up his flags in their towns, and they would
be his men. When he saw the fair promises which they made to him,
the king was pleased and he sent some of his banners and they flew
them higher than their own. And on the eighth of September 1361
after Christ the king went out from Adalia, and brought with him the
rest of his army and came to Alaya.

The emir came out at once with a few followers and did homage
to him, and gave him (the keys of the castle, and gave him) also a
lordly present. By the king's command they accepted the presents, and
the keys the king handed back to him, and made an agreement between
them; and he swore to the king that he would be his servant to serve
him. . . .[61]

The bloodless and, as it proved to be, short-lived surrender of
Alaya is not to be confused with the winning of the more important
Alayas, or Layas (Chaucer's "Lyeys," modern Ayas), which was
the chief port of Armenia.[62] This city, situated on the Gulf of
Alexandretta, some three hundred miles from Satalye, had become,
as early as the thirteenth century, the shipping center for all Asiatic
wares arriving from Tabriz.[63] Marco Polo writes of Layas as follows:

There are two Hermenias, the Greater and the Less. The Lesser
Hermenia . . . [has] a city upon the sea which is called Layas, at which
there is a great trade. For you must know that all the spicery, and the
cloths of silk and gold, and the other valuable wares that come from
the interior, are brought to that city. And the merchants of Venice and
Genoa, and other countries, come thither to sell their goods, and to
buy what they lack. And whatsoever persons would travel to the interior
(of the East), merchants or others, they take their way by this city of
Layas.[64]

Layas was, therefore, another prize for Christians to win back
from the infidels, into whose hands it had fallen. Consequently
when the king of Armenia asked for Peter I's aid in regaining Layas,
Peter, always ready to do battle for the glory of God, at once prepared to restore the city to Christian rule. But this was in 1367, only
two years after the fall of Alexandria when Peter had gained the
bitter knowledge that most contemporary crusaders were actuated

solely by greed, and that may account for the fact that the strength and zest which characterized Peter's earlier campaigns are now lacking. Even Machaut writes less brightly of this last campaign of Peter's along the coast of Asia Minor, and although "beautiful Alayas" is won and the city burned and destroyed, *li bons roys* is soon forced to return to Cyprus and to leave what remains of Alayas to *les Sarrazins*.[65]

Not all Saracens were unfriendly to the Christians, however, and the service of Chaucer's Knight with "the lord of Palatye,/ Agayn another hethen in Turkye" may possibly refer to such an upright ruler as the heathen prince who was bound by treaty in 1365 to the kingdom of Cyprus;[66] or possibly to a Christian lord paying homage to a Turkish overlord.[67] Palatye, modern Palatia, or Balat, lying just north of the site of ancient Miletus, carried on a brisk trade with the merchants of Cyprus, Rhodes, Genoa, and Venice.[68] And although Chaucer and his English contemporaries may have known little about any actual military engagements of a late fourteenth-century "lord of Palatye," they could hardly have been unaware of the friendly relations which existed for twenty or more years between certain chivalric Christians and Turks. Chaucer would think it fitting that his own hero should give knightly service to Palatye during this period of concord, which began about 1365.

The Knight's expeditions in the "Grete See," that is, the Mediterranean,[69] are obviously vague, also; but again because we can connect the expeditions of Chaucer's Knight with those of Peter of Cyprus, we tend to assume that the "many a noble armee" was headed by that great Crusader.

The most spectacular event, for the fourteenth century, of all Peter I's crusades was the assault on Alexandria in 1365. In preparation for this huge undertaking, upon which he entered with such high hope, Peter visited in 1363 nearly every country of Central and Western Europe. His object, in this thoroughly modern publicity campaign, was twofold: to arouse interest and enthusiastic moral support, and to secure, on a vast scale, men, supplies, and ships. Except in England, where his experiences were not altogether happy,[70] Peter was rewarded by extraordinary success. Machaut merely lists *Engleterre* as one of the many places visited by the king, but devotes over six hundred lines of *La Prise d'Alexandrie* to an account of the lavishly triumphant progress through Europe of *cils roys* who had only to be seen to be extravagantly admired for his knightly bearing.[71]

Froissart writes of Peter's English visit as follows:

When the King of Cyprus had a favourable wind, he crossed the Straits, and arrived at Dover. He remained there two days to recover himself, whilst they unloaded his vessel and disembarked his horses. The king then continued his route by easy day-journeys, until he arrived at the good city of London. He was honourably received on his arrival, as well by the barons of France, who were there as hostages, as by the English lords, who rode out to meet him; for king Edward had ordered some of his knights, viz. the early of Hereford, sir Walter Manny, the lord Despencer, the lord Ralph de Ferrers, sir Richard Pembridge, sir Richard Stafford, and others [72] to meet him, who accompanied and conducted him to the lodgings which were prepared for him in the city of London.

It would take me a day were I to attempt relating to you the grand dinners, suppers, and other feasts and entertainments that were made, and the magnificent presents, gifts and jewels which were given, especially by Queen Philippa, to the accomplished king of Cyprus. In truth he was deserving of them, for he had come a long way and at great expense, to visit them, to exhort the king to put on the red cross, and assist in regaining countries now occupied by the enemies of God. But the king of England politely and wisely excused himself, by saying: "Certainly, my good cousin, I have every inclination to undertake this expedition; but I am growing too old, and shall leave it to my children. I make no doubt, that when it shall have been begun, you will not be alone, but will be followed most willingly by my knights and squires." "Sir," replied the king of Cyprus, "what you say satisfies me. I verily believe they will come, in order to serve God, and do good to them selves; but you must grant them permission so to do; for the knights of your country are eager in such expeditions." "Yes," answered the king of England; "I will never oppose such a work, unless some things should happen to me or to my kingdom which I do not at this moment foresee." The king of Cyprus could never obtain any thing more from king Edward is respect to this croisade; but, as long as he remained, he was politely and honourably feasted with a variety of grand suppers. . . . At the last of these, the king of Cyprus took his leave of the king and queen of England, who made him very magnificent presents: king Edward gave him also a ship called the Catharine, which was very beautiful and well built. The king of England had had her constructed, by his orders, to make the voyage to Jerusalem. She was valued at twelve thousand francs, and lay in the harbour of Sandwich.

The king of Cyprus was much pleased with this gift, and returned many thanks for it. . . . I do not know how it was, nor for what reason, but he left the ship in the harbour of Sandwich; for two years afterwards, I saw it there at anchor.[73]

We have no way of knowing whether or not the young Chaucer was present at any of the entertainments which the English king arranged for the royal visitor, but he could hardly have been ignorant of the arrival in England of such a much heralded embodiment of "gentilesse" as that "worthy Petro" of "heigh maistrie" whom the poet was later to celebrate in *The Monk's Tale*.

Peter I's qualities as a *prudome* were pronounced; but it is a question whether or not Peter's personality alone could have secured the enthusiastic backing of the European monarchs, most of whom were hard-headed men of affairs. Peter had powerful and worldly friends, as well as the idealists, who were interested in furthering an attack on the rich city of Alexandria, and through their championship preparations for the expedition were successfully completed by September, 1365. Peter thus set sail accompanied by a large and impressive force, knights and squires from everywhere in Christendom; and by two men of unquestionably noble motives who acted as trusted advisers to the king: Pierre de Thomas, the successor of Cardinal Talleyrand de Périgord and a great promoter of war against the infidel, and Philippe de Mézières, chancellor of the kingdom of Cyprus, and as true a *chevalier* as Peter I himself. The fleet which had been assembled to carry these numbers had grown to one hundred and sixty-five vessels. Among these vessels of various sorts were the remarkable "taforesses," [74] which Mézières describes as large, flat-bottomed ships, drawing but little water, built with a "great door" in the stern so that mounted cavalry, ready for battle, could be landed and taken off again after the fight [75]—for all the world like the landing craft of World War II! Indeed, the Egyptian "invasion" of 1365 was now ready to be launched.

Alexandria was one of the most beautiful strongholds of the Sultan, and certainly the most wealthy. Its houses of white stone extended over the entire width of the shore between the two ports. High walls surrounded the city, the towers of which were two hundred feet high, constructed with twenty-foot platforms for soldiers.

These walls were defended by large ditches, by battering rams and catapults, and the soldiers who manned them were picked archers and engineers; Alexandria was considered impregnable, and its fabulously rich stores completely safe. The merchandise of India, Nubia, and Egypt was amassed there, gold, rubies, naptha, cloth and silk, oil, honey, tallow, perfume, and spices.[76] This was a city of which to dream, and the fact that Alexandria was "wonne" must be partially ascribed to the driving force bred by greed in the majority of Peter's company.

Machaut's account of the taking of Alexandria is, of course, coloured by his love for his hero and by his profound belief in Peter's ideals; nevertheless, the account, though it omits too much,[77] is accurate as far as it goes. It is the kind of version which Chaucer would have most readily accepted and may even have known. A condensed translation of this account follows:

Sometime between October 5th and 9th, 1365, when far from the shores of Asia Minor, the king announced that Alexandria was to be attacked. He encouraged his people, who were aghast at such an ambitious undertaking, by telling them that God would surely further their noble cause and give them honour and victory. And the good king spoke truth for the days were beautiful, the sea quiet, and the winds gentle and favourable, so that by October 9th—which was the feast of St. Denis and also the king's birthday—they were able to anchor in the old harbour of Alexandria. The next day, the king commanded his men to disembark, and they, who were only eight thousand, met twenty thousand Saracens in the sea, which was like a calm lake. These Saracens fought ferociously, and they wounded many Christians before they were repulsed by the valour of our knights. The king himself entered the battle, sword in hand, and conducted himself with incredible bravery. The fighting continued with unabated fury until our men had pushed the Saracens to the shore; these enemies then retreated to the city and barricaded themselves within, doing much injury to our knights from the ramparts. In the meantime, the Hospitallers, who had disembarked to the east, engaged the Saracens on the opposite side and pursued them to one of the gates, where many were killed in their desperate frenzy to gain an entrance safe from the Christians. But when all the gates were finally closed, in spite of the valiant efforts of our men, there was nothing to do except sound the retreat. The king then ordered the horses to be landed, and he commanded a rest, after which a council was called.

One knight advised that they should give up the assault upon the impregnable city, but the king finally ordained that the offensive should be continued at all costs, for the Christians were the instruments of God against the infidel. The crusaders then promised to follow the king, and they attacked at another gate, hitherto untried. The continued fierce resistance of the Saracens, however, was again too much for the knights, and again they were obliged to withdraw. But at this moment, a sailor and a squire reached the ramparts by a narrow, secret passage through the conduits, of which they had just learned, and by the very bravery of their feat and their joyous cries to their comrades outside the walls, they so astounded and affrighted the Saracens that the latter fled from their posts. Then the king and the attackers at the gate, who had just succeeded in firing it, rushed triumphantly into the city. After many savage combats in the streets and at the gates, the city was finally ours, and the king retired to a great tower for the night. It was a scene of vast carnage—more than twenty thousand inhabitants of Alexandria were slain—"a massacre unequalled since the time of Pharaoh."

The king failed in securing rest. In the darkness of the night, a large band of Saracens gained re-entrance to the city, and the king was obliged to encourage and lead his knights against these invaders. After heroic battle, the Christians were again victorious, and now Alexandria was truly in our hands.

The king convoked his knights later, and addressed them as follows: "By the grace of God we have conquered our enemies, and this city is ours to keep and defend!" In this the king was supported by Pierre de Thomas and Philippe de Mézières, but the alien knights, who were now wickedly eager to return to their homes with their rich booty, murmured among themselves, and said it was impossible to guard and retain the city, and they made their shameful way to the ships. And since those knights who remained loyal to the king and their noble cause were too few in number to hold the city against the return of the Saracens, the king was obliged to sail away in deep sorrow and bitter disappointment. But divine wrath was visited upon those who forsook their sacred vows, for terrible tempests raged, and only the presence of the good king (whom God would not destroy) saved them all from death in the angry sea.[78]

The news of the capture of Alexandria, brief though the victory had been, brought great rejoicing in most of the courts of Europe, and the reputation of Peter as a perfect knight was again confirmed. It was thus natural enough that such a figure as Chaucer's "parfit knyght" should be pictured as having been "at Alisaundre." But Venice, "which cared little for the holy cause and much for its trade interests in the Sultan's dominions," [79] was angered by Peter's exploit, and immediately and effectively set about the repair of the damage to commercial relationships through subtle discrediting of the king of Cyprus. Largely because of Venetian influence, Peter was never again to have great success, although is name as a *prudome* was to last for many centuries.

The third group mentioned by Manly of the campaigns of Chaucer's Knight is made up of the events which are referred to in the following lines:

> Ful ofte tyme he hadde the bord bigonne
> Aboven alle nacions in Pruce;
> In Lettow hadde he reysed and in Ruce,
> No Christen man so ofte of his degree.

(ll. 52-55).

Chaucer is speaking here of the warfare which had been waged almost continuously since the early thirteenth century by the Teutonic Knights against the barbarians of Prussia ("Pruce"), Lithuania ("Lettow"), and Russia ("Ruce"). These peoples were cruel and savage fighters, who consistently resisted the culture and religion of Western Europe. Nevertheless, by the latter half of the fourteenth century, the Teutonic Knights had succeeded in taking possession of the land as far east as Königsberg on the Baltic Sea, and their crusades had become sufficiently prominent to attract the service of knights from all over Europe. Chaucer's Knight, then, is not unusual in that he has "reysed" * in Prussian campaigns, but the placing of him more than once at the Teutonic table of honour ("Ful ofte tyme he hadde the bord bigonne / Aboven alle nacions in Pruce . . .") indicates his exceptional nature.

The fact that there are only five occasions on record of the Teutonic table of honour (in 1377, 1385, 1391, 1392, and 1400), as Cook notes,[80] does not in any way preclude the probability that this particular ceremonial took place much more frequently, and Chaucer and his contemporaries may well have heard of the custom from knights who had been in Prussia and from the busy merchants who traded between that country and England. We cannot, there-

* *reysed:* "made a raid or military expedition"

fore, be definite as to the dates when the Knight "began the board," but perhaps he has just come from that honour. Manly places the Knight's expedition to Prussia in the 1385 campaign. He says:

In support of this, we may note in the first place, that Chaucer says that in Prussia the Knight was often given the highest seat at the table . . . in recognition of his distinguished character and services. He was, therefore, probably not a young knight at the time in question. If he fought first in 1344 at Algezir, he was probably in 1387, the supposed date of the Canterbury Tales, between sixty and sixty-five. Obviously he was not so old as to be ready to retire, for, says Chaucer, "he was late ycome from his viage"—the technical term for a military expedition. And this suggests the second reason for dating his career in Pruce, Lettow, and Ruce, or at least one of his campaigns there, immediately before his pilgrimage to Canterbury, namely that, inasmuch as he joined the pilgrimage in London, he had not landed at Dover or any port in Kent, but perhaps at some northern port lying nearer to Prussia. This is, of course, not conclusive, for, had he been returning from the Orient, he would perhaps have landed at Dartmouth or some other west of England port, as ships from the Orient usually did.[81]

Chaucer's immediate audience, however, would probably not have been too troubled as to the exact date of the Knight's Prussian campaign; instead, they would have been primarily interested in picturing the hero's experiences. Fortunately for twentieth-century imaginations, there are several contemporary descriptions of expeditions of the Teutonic Order. A long poem by a Peter Suchenwirt, herald or king-of-arms and wandering minstrel, who lived in the late fourteenth century, and who took part in the expedition of 1377, gives a notable description of the table of honour. The selections that follow are from Cook's excellent condensed translation.

In the year 1377, Duke Albert of Austria set out to achieve knighthood. With him rode many a noble knight and squire, besides fifty picked men of lower degree, all bound for Prussia. . . . [They encamped at Vienna, at Breslau, at Thorn, and at Marienburg, enjoying lavish hospitality wherever they went.] . . . Thence they made their way to Königsberg, where each nobleman emptied his sack in feasting the others. But the Duke's banquet excelled all the rest. Before each course was heard the sound of trumpets and pipes. Of viands there was no lack; for one course alone were served baked meats and roast, spiced and gilded. With these went wine of Italy, of Hungary, and of Istria, served in vessels of gold, silver, and precious stones. Before the meal was ended, the Duke, of his bounty, had gold and silver borne in and bestowed upon two knights and one squire, each the best of his own land according to the law of arms, and one whom reproach had never sullied. . . . Nor were heralds and minstrels without some taste of the lord's bounty. "Largesse!" they joyfully cried; and—truth to tell —my share still rejoices my heart.

After ten days more of feasting, the Grand Master [of the Teutonic Knights] gave a banquet, according to ancient custom, in the hall at Königsberg. When they sat down at the table of honour, Conrad of Krey began the board with the approval of everyone, for this he had well deserved by his deeds as a noble knight in many a land. Often had he spilt his blood, and borne hardships in his knightly order.

Thereupon an inroad into Lithuania was proclaimed, for to this end the band had come thither from their far country. The marshal and his counselors ordained that they should load horses and boats with provisions for three weeks. The retainers laid hands to the work, and brought supplies of all kinds in double measure, sparing neither gold nor silver. . . . The host marched through Samland . . . to the Szeszuppe, a stream nearly a spear's length deep. Over the river four bridges were thrown, and across these they pressed in swarms. From here they passed to the Memel, where the water is an arrow-flight broad. Then they came to the boats, and the sailors laid hold with a will, and between noon and vespers ferried more than thirty thousand over the river, in no fewer than six hundred and ten vessels, losing but three horses and one squire [squires were evidently "expendable"!].

The army was eager to reach the heathen land; thousands of men might be seen roaming among the sloughs in the wilderness. They feared neither ditch nor field, deep water, marsh, nor cliff. The moorland afflicted us sore. Across the desert pushed the army, now up, now down, now here, now there; leaping, slipping, and bending over. The branches caught many a one by the neck. Where the wind had blown down great trees, we must force our way over, whether it were hard or easy. In the press one heard many a cry that the Prussians bore hard upon us. Horses laden with food and drink were pulled along. Now and again men would fall ill; knee and leg would fail them, when they were pressed too hard. Such scolding and laughing as this caused! The horses were so kicked that many a one had need to limp. As the day drew to a close and night began to fall, we looked about for quarters, but good lodging was hard to find. The horses were turned out to pasture for the night.

Early in the morning we joyfully hastened into the heathen land, leaping and running as we went. . . . Bright of hue were the pearls great and small, the garlands and jewels on the helmets, reflecting the rays of the sun. The army brought many a worthy guest to a land called Samogitia. Merry was the bridal to which these guests came unbidden, and merry the dance of the heathen, where sixty of them lay dead. Merry, too, the red fire over the hamlet, springing high in the air. . . .

The army began to wander up and down in the land. God gave the Christians the good fortune to come unannounced, to the sorrow of many a heathen. The knights hunted them down, and brought them to a standstill with thrust and stroke. Woe was it for them, but well for us. The land was full of people and goods, so that we held revel with them, for what was loss to the heathen was gain to the Christians, as the scales of battle inclined; merry in truth was the day. . . . At night the heathen ceased not to make grim onslaughts on the army with sharp weapons, shooting, piercing, and smiting. The Christians, taking this in ill part, kept driving them back, so that their rest was small. Screaming aloud like wild beasts, the heathen struck through men, shot horses, and fled again to the moors; and thus they did the whole night. . . .[82]

We can indeed picture Chaucer's Knight, like Conrad of Krey, conducting himself with unusual valour in this savage fighting in the Prussia, Lithuania, and Russia of his day. And here one is again tempted to inquire whether or not the Knight represents an actual person.

Manly has been the greatest proponent of the theory that many of the pilgrims of the *Canterbury Tales* could be identified with men and women Chaucer knew, had we sufficient evidence. The evidence, however, is so scanty that the linking of literary figures to living prototypes must remain almost entirely conjectural. As concerns the Knight, Manly says:

Chance has provided us with an interesting set of documents which suggest that, though Chaucer may not have given us in the Knight a portrait of one of his own friends, he at least knew men of the exact type he has drawn with such affectionate skill.[83]

Manly then cites some of the testimony taken at the famous dispute between the Scrope and Grosvenor families, a dispute which arose over their respective rights to bear certain arms. Most of the witnesses testified when they had seen the arms borne publicly, and thus military careers were sketched. Manly points out that we find in the careers of three members of the Scrope family, Sir Stephen, Sir Geoffrey, and Sir William, hints as to "an approximate model" for the Knight. We know that Chaucer was acquainted with the Scropes.

Sir Stephen Scrope was said to be " 'in the assemblage from all Christian countries at the instance of the King of Cyprus, when he meditated his expedition to Alexandria.' " This same knight was also " 'armed in Prussia . . . and in Spain.' " [84]

Sir Geoffrey Scrope was said to have gone " 'with other knights, into Prussia, and there, in an affair at the siege of Wellon in Lithuania, he died . . .' " [85]

Sir William Scrope was said to have been seen " 'beyond the great sea in the company of the Earl of Hereford at Satalia in Turkey, at a treaty which was concluded between the King of Cyprus and . . . [the] Lord of Satalia . . .' " [86]

Thus we have "unmistakable evidence," Manly states, that Chaucer's Knight is "a figure at once realistic and typical of the noble and adventurous idealists of his day." [87]

Evidence of the "ideal" nature of the Knight is perhaps found in what his portrait reveals to us of the attitude of certain writers of the Middle Ages towards war, although Christian opinion was almost undivided in approving holy wars. (Gower, who, in the *Confessio Amantis,* condemns all war, is a notable exception.) Wyclif opposed all wars of aggression: in the *De Officio Regis,* the eighth book of his *Summa,* he uses the final chapter to thunder forth his thesis that such war is contrary to the law of Christ, of nature, and of reason, and is utterly evil—sin and war are one, as Christ and peace are one; [88] yet Wyclif admits that wars waged for the love of God are right. [89] The orthodox Bromyard, as would be expected, bewails the fourteenth-century unpopularity of crusades, [90] and "denounces those who have suffered no 'imprisonment' in God's cause against the Saracens." [91] Bromyard seems too much of a Jeremiah, however, for although the behaviour of some knights might warrant his denunciation, many more upheld the chivalric tradition of fighting the infidel. This may in large part explain why Chaucer lays stress only on those expeditions of the Knight which were against the infidel. Chaucer does mention that the Knight has distinguished himself in "his lordes werre," a war which may not have been of a religious nature; but so little emphasis is placed upon that part of the Knight's military career that the matter has little significance. On the other hand, the Knight's campaigns against the heathen are for the most part specifically named, and they fill more than one-third of the lines devoted to the Knight's full portrait. Even if this emphasis on crusades is not an indication of Chaucer's own attitude towards war, the poet seems to be making an implied reference to a current opinion on the subject.

But what were Chaucer's own beliefs concerning war? Only in his *Tale of Melibee* do we find any direct statements about war, and this *Tale,* which has for its theme that peace is better than war and legal punishment better than private vengeance, is an almost word for word translation of the thirteenth-century *Liber Consolationis et Consilii.*[92] It can be argued strongly, however, that Chaucer would not have gone to the labour of making a close translation of such an extensive work if he had not been in some sympathy with the ideas there expressed. Professor Robinson,[93] Professor Loomis,[94] and Professor Lawrence [95] all have pointed out that although to many modern readers the *Melibee* is dull and full of long-winded moralizing, to Chaucer's contemporaries the work was interesting and timely. Indeed, Professor Lawrence goes so far as to say:

. . . To men wearied of continual strife, in countries exhausted by internal struggle and foreign invasion, this parable [the *Liber Consolationis et Consilii*], written by no monkish idealist but by an active citizen, judge, and military leader, expressed the hope of something better and finer in the administration of justice and the settlement of wars. We may recoil at its prolixity, we may yawn at its trite aphorisms, we may smile at its crude allegory, but we cannot deny that it shows a wisdom and a vision of which the thirteenth century stood sadly in need. It was no less timely in the age of Chaucer. . . . How deeply the evils of war and the perversion of justice impressed Gower and Langland we know; can they have been absent from Chaucer's mind when he translated the *Melibeus*? May they not, indeed, have been one of the chief reasons why he made the translation? The allegory was popular for other reasons, of course, but we may well doubt whether it would have attained such vogue had it been merely, like thousands of other works, a Christian manual or a didactic floralegium.[96]

Hence may we not perhaps hear Chaucer's own voice in a grave moment, when in the *Tale of Melibee* the wise old man rises to speak?

"Lordynges," quod he, "ther is ful many a man that crieth 'Werre! werre!' that woot ful litel what werre amounteth./ Werre at his begynnyng hath so greet an entryng and so large, that every wight may entre whan hym liketh, and lightly fynde werre;/ but certes, what ende that shal therof bifalle, it is nat light to knowe./ For soothly, whan that werre is ones bigonne, ther is ful many a child unborn of his mooder that shal sterve yong by cause of thilke werre, or elles lyve in sorwe and dye in wrecchednesse./ And therfore, er that any werre bigynne, men moste have greet conseil and greet deliberacion." [97]

But we must not forget that Chaucer was a man of the court, and in no sense a reformer. He writes with apparent enthusiasm of the service of the Squire in "Flaundres, in Artoys, and Pycardie," a campaign which was very dubious as to motive, and which did call forth the denunciations of the reformers; [98] and there is every indication in many of his works that the poet frequently saw only the excitement, the adventure, and the pageantry of war. We cannot find in Chaucer the openly avowed pacifist we find in his friend Gower, who boldly condemns "dedly werre" as a "foule horrible vice," forbidden by both God and nature.[99]

NOTES

(The abbreviations used to designate books and articles mentioned in the Notes will be found listed alphabetically in the Bibliography, opposite the full reference. References to lines in the *Canterbury Tales* are given by fragment and line numbers only.)

1. *Chivalry* (ed. Prestage), p. 8.
2. ". . . procedant, inquit, contra infideles ad pugnam iam incipi dignam et trophaeo explendam, qui abusive privatum certamen contra fideles etiam consuescebant distendere quondam. Nunc fiant Christi milites, qui dudum existerunt raptores; nunc iure contra barbaros pugnent, qui olim adversus fratres et consanguineos dimicabant; nunc aeterna praemia mercennarii fuerunt." (*Ful. Car. Hist. Hier.*, Lib. I, cap. III, 7).
3. ". . . sed huiusmodi sallitorem oportet esse prudentem, provisorem, modestum, edoctum, pacificum, scrutatorem, pium, iustum, aequum, mundum." (*Ful. Car. Hist. Hier.*, Lib. I, cap. II, 7).
4. *Chivalry* (ed. Prestage), p. 25.
5. Gautier, pp. 31 ff.
6. Owst, *Lit. and Pulpit*, p. 332.

7. *Ibid.,* p. 338.

8. Schofield, pp. 30–38.

I am indebted to Schofield for the reference to Watriquet. The analysis of the words Watriquet and Chaucer employ is mine, however.

9. Watriquet, *Li Dit du Connestable de France,* ll. 30–33, 42–45.

10. *NED,* "Chivalry."

11. *Ibid.*

12. Gautier, pp. 131 f.

13. Héraucourt, pp. 72 f.

14. *Ibid.,* p. 69.

15. *Boece,* II, pr. 6, 27–30.

16. *Ibid.,* pr. 5, 12 ff.

17. VII 2642 (B² 3832).

18. X (I) 464–465.

19. *Chess-Book,* pp. 49 f.

20. Skeat, VI.

21. After the mortal combat with Grendel, Beowulf is eulogized as the deliverer who is *snotor ond swythferhth,* that is, "wise and brave."

22. *Chanson de Roland,* ll. 1722 ff., 1093. Gautier, as editor, states (p. 559): "Partout, comme on le voit, . . . [le mot *sage*] est opposé à *proz* et à *fols.*"

23. Héraucourt, pp. 93 f.

24. *Boece,* III, pr. 2, 72. Cf. Héraucourt, p. 246.

25. du Cange, *Gloss. Med. Lat.*

26. X (I) 415 ff. The *Parson's Tale* is a medieval sermon.

27. X (I) 432 ff.

28. Chaucer's *hors* in line 74 is plural as shown by the verb and the modifying adjective. The plural of "horse" was the same as the singular, *hors,* and this form was in general use for the plural until the seventeenth century, although *horses* also appears as early as the beginning of the thirteenth century. (*NED*)

29. *Ordre of Chyvalry,* p. 84.

30. Skeat says (V, 9) that the Knight is going on the pilgrimage "in his knightly array, only without his habergeon."

31. Druitt, pp. 156–162, and plates facing pp. 160, 162.

32. *NED,* "Fustian."

33. Manly, *Trans. Am. Phil. Assoc.,* XXXVIII, 89 ff.

34. Mandeville (ed. Warner), p. 14.

35. Mandeville (ed. Hamelius), p. 97.

36. *Ibid.,* pp. 31 f.

37. Manly, *loc. cit., passim.*

38. *Ibid.,* p. 92.

39. Watts, p. 184.

40. Manly, *loc. cit.,* p. 92.

41. Watts, pp. 184 ff.

42. *Foedera, Ad Regem Castellae, super Algezira Conquistata Gratulatoria, 1344.*

43. Manly, *loc. cit.*, p. 92.

44. I (A) 2498–2499.

45. *Foedera, Ad Regem Castellae, super Victoria, contra Mauros sub Rege Benemeren, Memoratissima, Congratulatoria, 1341.*

46. Froissart (Kervyn): VII, 93, 116, 267; IX, 429; XIV, 278; XVII, 425.

47. Froissart (Johnes), Bk. IV, Chap. XXII.

48. *Satalye* is *Attalia* with the Greek preposition ἐς, or εἰς, prefixed, as *Stamboul* is ἐς τὰν πόλιν. (Sedgwick, *RES*, II, 346.)

49. Makhairas, II, § 120, n. 1. I also draw upon my memory for the statements about modern Adalia.

50. *La Prise d'Alexandrie*, ll. 1–506.

51. *Ibid.*, p. xix.

52. *Ibid.*, ll. 5938–5943.

53. Froissart (Kervyn), XI, 231.

54. Mézières (Jorga), p. 305.

55. VII 2391–2398 (B² 3581–3588).

56. Froissart (Berners), IV, 227.

57. Manly, *loc. cit.*, p. 106.

58. Makhairas, I, § 118.

59. *La Prise d'Alexandrie*, ll. 643–658.

60. Makhairas, I, §§ 121, 122.

61. *Ibid.*, §§ 124, 125.

62. Manly (*loc. cit.*, p. 99, n. 1) and Dawkins (Makhairas, II, § 212, n. 4) both point out that Alaya (modern Alaia) was commonly known to Western Europeans of the Middle Ages as "Candelore," or as "Lescandelour"; it was on the site of the ancient city of Coracesium. Machaut, in *La Prise d'Alexandrie*, speaks of "Candelour" (ll. 3988 ff.) and "Alayas" (ll. 6957 ff.) as two distinct cities, the most conclusive evidence that Chaucer did not mean "Alaya" when he wrote "Lyeys."

63. Marco Polo (Yule), I, 16 f., n. 2.

64. *Ibid.*, p. 41.

65. *La Prise d'Alexandrie*, ll. 6957–7153.

66. Strambaldi, p. 66.

67. Froissart (Johnes), Bk. III, Chap. XXIII.

68. Mas Latrie, *Bib. de l'Ecole des Chartres*, I, 325, 502.

69. There is some difference of opinion as to what Chaucer had in mind when he speaks of the Knight's participation in expeditions in "the Grete See." Robinson (p. 754) and Skeat (V, 8) agree that "the Grete See" denotes the Mediterranean; but Warner (Mandeville, p. 211) states that the Black Sea— the *mare maurum* (*v. nigrum*)—was as frequently called *mare majus* in the Middle Ages; and Yule (Marco Polo, I, 3) states uncompromisingly that Chaucer's "Grete See" is the Black Sea. As English knights took part in wars in Hungary, and went afterwards to Constantinople (Manly, p. 105), a battle in the Black Sea is not an impossibility for Chaucer's Knight, but because of the extensive connection the poet has given the Knight with Peter of Cyprus, it seems much more likely that the "Grete See" is the Mediterranean.

70. See Walsingham, *Hist. Ang.*, I, 296, 299; Froissart (Johnes), Bk. I, Chap. CCXVIII; and Froissart (Kervyn), VI, 379 ff.

71. *La Prise d'Alexandrie*, ll. 813–886, 1060–1607.

72. Froissart (Luce—VI, 90) names Sir Richard Stury in this group.

73. Froissart (Johnes), Bk. I, Chap. CCXVIII.

74. *La Prise d'Alexandrie*, ll. 1876–1884. See also p. 279, n. 16.

75. Atiya, p. 148, n. 3, quotes from Philippe de Mézières's *Le Songe du Vieil Pèlerin* (MS, Paris, III, 338 vo.) as follows: "Tafforesse est un vaisseau de mer qui va à vingt ou à trente advirons et porte de XVI à XX chevaulx. Et a le dit vaisseau une grant porte en la poupe et ne lui fault que deux ou troys paulmes d'eaux. Et tous les fois que la dicte tafforesse en terre doit arrive contre les ennemis les gens d'armes seront montez sus les chevaulx dedans le vaisseau . . . et yront courre souldainement sus leurs ennemis. Et s'ilz sont chaciez ilz rentreront tout à cheval dedans la tafforesse malgré leurs ennemis et tantost se retrayront en mer."

76. Mézières ⟨Jorga⟩, p. 297.

77. See Atiya's account in *Crusade in the Later Middle Ages*.

78. *La Prise d'Alexandrie*, ll. 2107–3633.

79. Atiya, p. 370.

80. Cook, *Trans. Conn. Acad. Arts and Sci.*, XX, p. 209.

81. Manly, *loc. cit.*, pp. 101 f.

82. Cook, *JEGP*, XIV, 378–384. The original German for the selection concerning the table of honour (ll. 149–160) is printed by Cook as follows:

> Nach dem alten rechten
> Der maister gab daz hochmal
> Tzu Chunigezperge auf dem sal
> Mit reicher chost, wizzet daz;
> Da man der eren tisch wesaz,
> Chunrat von Chrey wesaz daz ort
> Tzu obrist mit gemainem wort,
> Wan er ez hat in manigem lant
> Wol verdient mit der hant
> Als ein edel ritter tut.
> Er hat vergozzen oft sein plut,
> Und ist im sawr worden
> In ritterleichem orden.

83. Manly, *loc. cit.*, p. 104.

84. *Ibid.*, p. 105.

85. *Ibid.*, p. 106.

86. *Ibid.*

87. *Ibid.*, p. 107.

88. *De Officio Regis*, Cap. XII.

89. *Ibid.*: Quantum ad illud sepe dixi quod licet pugnare et guerrare propter caritatem habendam ad deum et proximum eciam debellandum, et aliter non. . . .

90. Owst, *Lit. and Pulpit*, p. 332.

91. *Ibid.*, p. 412.

92. J. Burke Severs states (*Sources and Analogues*, p. 564) that Chaucer's translation "rarely departs" from a source manuscript of Renaud de Louens', a French version of Albertanus's *Liber Consolationis et Consilii*. Albertanus wrote this work in 1246. He was a learned judge, living in northern Italy (Brescia), and a man highly active in public affairs; he also wrote extensively. The *Liber Consolationis* had wide circulation: it was translated into French, German, Italian, and Dutch, and was incorporated into the fourteenth-century *Menagier de Paris* and into one edition of the *Livre du Chevalier de la Tour Landry*.

93. Robinson, p. 13.

94. *Essays in Honor of Carleton Brown*, p. 136.

95. *Ibid.*, pp. 100–110.

96. *Ibid.*, p. 109.

97. VII 1038–1042 (B² 2228–2332).

98. See above p. 10.

99. Gower, *Conf. Aman.*, Bk. III, ll. 2251–2269.

CHAPTER IV

THE YOUNG SQUIRE AND THE YEOMAN

With hym ther was his sone, a yong Squier,
A lovyere and a lusty bacheler,
With lokkes crulle as they were leyd in presse.
Of twenty yeer of age he was, I gesse.
Of his stature he was of evene lengthe,
And wonderly delyvere, and of greet strengthe.

.   .   .   .

Embrouded was he, as it were a meede
Al ful of fresshe floures, whyte and reede.
Syngynge he was, or floytynge, al the day;
He was as fressh as is the month of May.
Short was his gowne, with sleves longe and wyde.
Wel koude he sitte on hors and faire ryde.
He koude songes make and wel endite,
Juste and eek daunce, and weel purtreye and write.
So hoote he lovede that by nyghtertale
He sleep namoore than dooth a nyghtyngale.

(ll. 79–84, 89–98)

IN THE KNIGHT, Chaucer portrays the dignity of maturity in a character beloved for the ideals which he represents. In the Knight's son, Chaucer portrays the gayety and enthusiasms of youth in a character beloved for his universal appeal. To describe the Knight, the poet uses a language that is measured and of noble implications; to describe the Squire, he uses words that are swift and light and that suggest a May morning when Aurora displays "her fair fresh-quilted colours." The Squire speaks to youth in youth's language, and to those who are past youth in a language that can still be appreciated. May we not believe that the Squire is the smiling reminiscence of young Geoffrey himself? The twenty-year-old Chaucer must have had joy in high spirits, in the favour he sought and gained in

74

the eyes of probably more than one "lady swete," and in his own gay accomplishments and innocent frivolities. We have only to read Chaucer's early allegorical poetry to realize how large a part love played in his youthful consciousness, if not in his own experience,[1] and his mature realistic poetry would indicate that the older poet could at least celebrate Venus in retrospect. Chaucer's early training as a page, and later as a squire, in a royal household would give him as a young man the very habits and accomplishments with which he endows his Squire. It is more than speculation that causes us to link the young Geoffrey with this gay and charming portrait.

Under the feudal system of military service, a squire ranked next to a knight, and in the fourteenth century, squires usually acted as attendants upon particular knights.[2] When a squire was ready to graduate to knighthood in the chivalric organization, he was called a "bachelor," and often the term continued in use for a recently made, or a young, knight. Chaucer speaks, for example, of a youthful "knyght" who was a "lusty bacheler" in the court of King Arthur;[3] the poet praises the royal Cambyuskan by comparing his skill in arms to that of "any bacheler of all his hous";[4] he describes the earth-dwelling "Phebus" as the "flour of bachilrie."[5] Gower, too, writes of "a proud a lusti Bacheler" who is also a "knyght."[6]

The accomplishments and pastimes of the gay young squires of the fourteenth century are reported in numerous romances and books of instruction. Even in the twelfth century, one Robert de Ho, an Englishman,[7] wrote a French didactic poem, addressed to his son, which treats, among many subjects, of the proper education for a young man of gentle birth. Robert de Ho was not a *grand seigneur,* but a man whose rank was the same as that of Chaucer's Knight,[8] so that what he has to say is the more interesting for us when we are considering the traditional cultivation that produced the Squire. A part of the poem may be paraphrased as follows:

My son, I mean this by courtliness: that a man know chivalry, that he know how to ride and to manage his steed well, that he know how to versify, including nothing that is unnecessary, that he be a master of dogs, birds, and hunting; and above all that he be temperate in response and stable. Who has well learned these skills will win laurels everywhere.[9]

Similar instruction continues to be given to young gentlemen throughout the medieval period. In the *Romance of the Rose*, for example, the God of Love counsels the youthful Lover as follows:

> If thou shouldst know some cheerful play
> Or game to wile dull hours away,
> My counsel is, neglect it not,
> For praise and thanks may thence be got,
> And every man in time and place
> Should practise that which brings him grace.
> If lithe and strong of limb thou art,
> Fear not, but boldly act thy part,
> And canst thou well a-horseback sit,
> Prick high and low in pride of it;
> And much with ladies 'twill advance
> Thy suit, if well thou break'st a lance,
> For who in arms his own doth hold,
> Winneth acceptance manifold.
> And if a voice strong, sweet and clear
> Thou hast, and dames desire to hear
> Thee sing, seek not to make excuse,
> But straightway from thy memory loose
> Some ditty soft; and shouldst thou know
> To wake the viol's voice with bow,
> Or tune the flute, or deftly dance,
> Such things thy suit will much advance.[10]

The ability to sing and dance was an especially important accomplishment in the fourteenth century for all ladies and gentlemen and even for less well-born men and women. Chaucer himself gives ample proof of this in the great number of references he makes to song and dance in his writings,[11] and he himself as page and later as squire must have had thorough training in music, if not in the dance. Chaucer constantly attests his own knowledge of music, not only by wealth of reference, but also by the form and style of his poetry. As both Professor C. C. Olson and Manly observe, Chaucer deliberately chose to write in Machaut's musico-poetic verse technique in preference to traditional English forms.[12] The many figures of speech, drawn from the field of music, that Chaucer employs also give evidence that Chaucer was well versed in this subject and that it was a part of the life of his day.[13] It is therefore only natural to find that the poet has endowed the young Squire with ability to write both words and music for songs ("he koude songes make and wel endite"), to play the flute, and to dance.

The most common social dance of the late fourteenth century was the *carole*. In the *Romaunt of the Rose,* for example, the unmodified word *dance* translates the French *carole* (or *querole*). The movement of the carole was comparatively simple. Ladies and gentlemen alternately held each other by the hand and stepped in a circle to music. Professor Greene writes that the pattern was ordinarily

. . . three steps in movement to the left, followed by some kind of marking time in place. It was usual for the dancers to join hands, but gestures seem frequently to have been introduced which would require the clasp to be broken. The whole procedure was under the direction of a leader. It was the duty of this leader . . . to sing the *stanzas* of the song to which the carole was being danced. During the time of such singing the ring moved to the left. At the close of the stanza the entire company of dancers would respond with the refrain or burden of the song, dancing in place the while. Then, as the circle revolved again, the leader would sing the following stanza, and so on . . .[14]

Chaucer himself gives us a picture of ladies dancing a carole in the *Legend of Good Women:*

> And after that they wenten in compas,
> Daunsynge aboute this flour an esy pas,
> And songen, as it were in carole-wyse,
> This balade, which that I shal yow devyse.[15]

Chaucer's Squire again follows the social conventions of a young man of his class in that he knows how to draw ("purtraye"), in that he is proficient in horsemanship and likes to joust, and in that he is dressed in the height of fashion.

To joust was commanded as a necessary exercise for every young man who would become a knight by the thirteenth-century renowned churchman Ramon Lull in a book which he wrote as an instructive manual for squires. Caxton's translation, the *Book of the Ordre of Chyvalry,* states that aspirants to knighthood

. . . ought to take coursers to juste & to go to tournoyes / to holde open table / to hunte at hertes / at bores & other wyld bestes / For in

doynge these thynges the knyghtes exercyse them to armes / for to
mayntene thordre of knighthode / [16]

Pulpit orators of Chaucer's day, ignoring the pageantry and popularity of such military sport and the experience the squires and
knights might gain from them, spoke bitterly of the needless deaths
which resulted from these games, and of the extravagant waste of
spectacles which meant "fresh impoverishment of the needy." [17]
One homilist, and he seems to speak for all, complains that players
in the tournament—

. . . with the most lavish expenditure, with grievous blows, hard suffering and wounds . . . purchase the garments of vanity in their sport
of arms; with the greatest expenditure, I say, both of horses and of the
gifts which they bestow so plenteously on heralds and minstrels, for the
praise of men and the brief reward of vain men's applause.[18]

The fourteenth-century Robert de Brunne, in his *Handlyng Synne*,
goes so far as to say that all of the seven deadly sins are to be
found in the tournament! [19] But the pleas of the reformers seem
to have fallen on deaf, or unwilling, ears, and skill in military
games continued to be cultivated by all the gay young men of the
court.

The joust, in which Chaucer's Squire delights, was a separate
trial of skill in which one man opposed another, in contrast to the
tournament, in which a number of knights were engaged simul-
taneously. Both these pastimes were restricted to the nobility and
gentry; they were costly entertainments, and they usually took place
at coronations, at royal marriages, and upon other occasions of the
court. "One great reason," writes Strutt, "and perhaps the most
cogent of any, why the nobility of the middle ages, nay, and even
princes and kings delighted so much in the practice of tilting with
each other, is that on such occasions they made their appearance
with prodigious splendour, and had the opportunity of displaying
their accomplishments to the greatest advantage." [20]

An English chronicle of the fourteenth century, the *Brut*, describes one festive occasion, among others, as follows:

. . . and in the xij yere of King Richardes regne, he let crye and
ordeyne generalle Iustise, that is called a turnement, of lordes, knyghtis
and squiers. And these Iustes & turnement were holden at London in

Smithfelde, for alle maner of strayngers . . . ; and to hem and to alle
other was holden opon housholde and grete ffestis; and also grete yftis
were yeve to alle maner of straungers. And thay of the kinges syde were
alle of on sute: her cotis, her armyour, scheldes, & her hors & trapure,
alle was white hertis,* with crownes about her nekkis, and cheynes of
golde hangyng there up-on, and the croune hangyng lowe before the
hertis body; the which hert was the kinges lyveray that he yaf to lordes
& ladies, knyghtis and skquiers, for to know his housholde from other
peple. And at this first comyng to her Iustes, xxiiij ladies ladde these
xxiiij lordes of the Garther with cheynes of goolde . . . from the Tour
on hors bak through the cite of London yn-to Smythfelde, there the
Iustes schulde be do. . . .[21]

In the joust, the mounted combatants were armed with lances,
and the game consisted in striking the opponent upon the front of
his helmet either so as to unseat him backwards from his horse, or so
as to break the lance. The danger to both horses and riders was great,
but to invite risk in such adventures was a part of the tradition of
gallantry, and every true page and squire, with not the slightest heed
to the disapproval from the pulpit, looked forward to the time when
he might win renown in the lists,** and thus dazzle some fair lady
who would act as his tutelar "saint" for the occasion.[22] Even young
pages played at jousting with toy knights of brass which could be
run against each other in such a way that the more expert player
could "unhorse" the toy knight of his opponent.[23] With this fondness for military pastimes so ingrained, no hot-blooded squire or
young knight could be expected to count the cost in money or life,
and these games did indeed cost life very frequently. The *Brut*
describes a number of jousts which ended fatally; the youthful Earl
of Pembroke, for example, dies while learning the game:

And yn the xv yere of King Richardes regne, he hilde his Cristis-
masse yn the Maner of Wodestoke; and there the Erle of Penbroke, a
yong lorde, & tendir of age, wolde lerne to Iuste with a knight me
callid Ser Iohn Saint-Iohn, & redyn to gadir yn the park of Wodestoke;
and there this worthi Erle of Pembroke was slayn with that other
knightes spere, as he cast hit fro hym whanne he had cowped; and thus
this gode Erle made there his ende; for whose dethe the King and the
Quene made moche sorow.[24]

* *hertis*: "harts"
** *lists*: "scene of the tilting-contest"

The accident which resulted in the death of the Scottish Earl of Mar is described by the chronicler without a word of surprise or regret:

... certeyne lordes of Scotlande com yn-to Englonde to geter worschip, as by feet of armes: these were the persons: the Erle of Marre, and chalanged the Erle Marchall of Engelonde to Iuste with hym certeyn poyntes on horsbak with scharpe speris. And so thai redyn togadir, as ij worthi knyghtis & lordes, certayne cours, but not the fulle chalange that the Scottysche Erle made; for he was cast both hors and man, and ij of his rybbis brokyn with the ffalle; and so he was born out of Smythfelde, hom yn-to his Inne; and with-ynne a litil while aftirward he was caried homwarde yn a litter; & at York he deied.[25]

As has been said, Chaucer's Squire wears fine dress. How bright and modish indeed is the coat of the happy young man! Yet how the preachers of his time thundered forth against finery in attire and the immodesty of the fashionable short coats! "Man was first clad in skins of beasts, then in wool," the fourteenth-century Master Rypon of Durham begins, and then proceeds to comment vehemently on man's third (and present-day) stage in dress. He says:

Thirdly, through the more ample nourishing of carnal delight, they used garments made from plants of the earth, namely, of linen, and fourthly silken garments which are fashioned from the entrails of worms; all of which kinds of raiment are now rather for vain-glory and worldly pomp than for the necessity of nature, diversely decorated as it were in an infinite variety of ways, and assuredly most of all to excite lust alike in men as in women. In proof of which some men wear garments so short that . . . [they are indecent] . . . (et certe ut apparet ad osten- dendum mulieribus membra sua ut sic ad luxuriam provocentur) . . . And be they men or women, such as adorn themselves in their garments or by means of some other artificial decoration, to give wanton pleasure to each other, are well compared to a painted sepulchre in which lies a foul corpse, or to a dung-heap covered with a vine . . .[26]

Chaucer's Parson, too, in his harsh sermon on the Deadly Sins, holds forth on "superfluitee of clothyng, which that maketh it so deere, to harme of the peple," on the high cost of "embrowdynge," and on the scandalous "scarsnesse of clothyng" in words which are quite as strong as those used by Rypon.[27] This passage in the Par- son's Tale is more detailed than what is found in the thirteenth-cen- tury sources which Chaucer evidently used for so much of the Parson's discourse:[28] the Parson's sermon is made timely by a vehement denunciation of modish dress.

Although the Squire's coat is not actually indecorous, its short-ness sugggests the cause for the censure of the pulpit. The preachers likewise condemn the decoration and extravagance of such garments, "embrouded . . . as it were a meede" with "sleves longe and wyde." The author of the *Brut* says, for example:

In this tyme, Englisshe men . . . ordeyned and chaungyd ham every yere divers schappis of disgynges of clothing, of long large and wyde clothis, destitu and desert fram al old honeste and good usage; & another tyme schorte clothis & stret-wasted, dagged & ket, & on every side desslatered & boned, with sleves & tapets of sircotys & hodes overe longe & large, & overmuch hangynde, that if y soth schal say, they were more liche to turmentours & devels in hire clothyng & schewyng & other arraye then comen.[29]

But when has youth, or the world of fashion, paid attention to the words of the reformers? Chaucer's Squire rides a carefree way to Canterbury, and has our, as well as the poet's, indulgent approval of his gay young spirits. The Squire is "syngyng" or playing his flute ("floytyng")[30] "al the day," and this music seems to go perfectly with the handsome, red and white flowered coat and the "lokkes" which curl as elegantly as if they had been pressed by a curling-iron.[31]

The physical characteristics of Chaucer's Squire measure up to the descriptions of the youthful heroes of the romances and to the specifications of Ramon Lull. A squire must not be maimed or over-fat, the Caxton translation states, for

. . . hit shold not be honest to thordre of chyvalrye / yf she receyved a man for to bere armes whiche were entatched corrupt & not myghty / For so moche noble & hyhe is Chyvalry in hyr honour / that a squyer lame of ony membre / how wel that he be noble and ryche / & borne of noble lygnage is not dygne ne worthy to be received into thordre of chyvalrye / [32]

Our Squire is of "greet strengthe," he is built in proper proportions ("evene lengthe"),[33] he is wonderfully agile ("delyvere"),[34] and he is "as fressh as is the month of May." Physically he is indeed both "dygne" and "worthy" to be received into the Order of Chivalry.

The Squire's moral attributes are as pleasing as his person.

> Curteis he was, lowely, and servysable,
> And carf biforn his fader at the table.

(ll. 99–100)

The Squire, like the Knight, is courteous; that is, he possesses a generous and charitable consideration for others. Like the Knight, who is as meek as a maid and who has never said "vileynye" to anyone, the Squire is properly lowly. He gladly serves those to whom he owes attendance; he carves before his father at the table. To carve the roasts is one of the most frequently mentioned obligations of a squire, and carving itself was an art much prized in the Middle Ages. John Russell's fifteenth-century *Boke of Nurture* gives minute directions for the carving of venison, partridge, and so on.[35] The art had techniques as difficult to master as those of any other. Even in romances we find accounts of carving instruction given to the heroes, as for instance, to King Horn;[36] and in the late thirteenth-century French romance, *Jehan et Blonde*, there is a charming picture of a young squire, who might be brother to Chaucer's, and who neglects his carving duties because he is so deeply in love with his lord's fair daughter. Dr. Coulton has translated the story as follows:

Fair, and fairer still than I can say, was Blonde the Earl's daughter. She sat at dinner, and was served by Jehan, fair and free of body, who pained himself much to earn all men's grace by his courteous service. He waited not on his lady alone, but up and down throughout the hall; knight and lady, squire and page, groom and messenger, all he served according to their desire, and thus from all he earned good-will. He knew well to seize the moment for serving and honouring each guest, so that Blonde, the fair and shapely, found her needs none the worse supplied.

After their dinner they washed their hands, and went to play, each as he would, up in the forest or down by the river or in some other sort of pastime. Jehan went with whom he would; and, on his return, oftentimes would he go to play in the countess's bower, wherein the ladies, as it were by main force,* kept him to teach them French. He, as a courteous youth, did and said ever according to their prayer, as one who well knew how to comport himself. Well he knew all chamber-games—chess and tables ** and dice, wherewith he diverted the lady

---

* Coulton says: "This seems to be the meaning of the phrase *qui en destrece.*"
** *tables*: "backgammon"

Blonde; often said he *check* and *mate* to her. Many other games he taught her; and taught her a better French than she had known before his coming; wherefore she held him full dear. . . .

One day, as Blonde sat at table, it was for Jehan to carve before her. . . . By chance he cast his eyes on her; yet he had seen her daily these eighteen weeks past. . . . From this look such thoughts came into his head, that on his carving he thought no more. Blonde, who marked his thoughts astray, took upon her to rebuke him therefore, and bade him think on his carving without delay. Seeing then that Jehan heard her not for the moment, then spake she again, "Carve, Jehan! are you sleeping or dreaming here? I pray you, give me now to eat; of your courtesy, dream now no more." At this word Jehan heard her voice; therewith he started as one who is shaken suddenly from his sleep. He marvelled at this adventure; he seized the knife as a man in a dream, and thought to carve well and fair, but so distraught was he that he cut deep into two fingers: forth sprang the blood as he rose from table, and sad was Blonde at that sight. Jehan prayed another squire to carve before his lady, and went forthwith to his own chamber.[37]

It remains to speak of the Squire's campaigns.

> And he hadde been somtyme in chyvachie
> In Flaundres, in Artoys, and Pycardie,
> And born hym weel, as of so litel space,
> In hope to stonden in his lady grace.

(ll. 85–88)

These military expeditions are, in their own way, as Professor Tatlock points out, "as detailed and specific" as those of the Knight.[38] There were no English campaigns in Flanders between 1359, when Chaucer himself, as squire, saw service there, and 1383, and none between 1383 and 1395, but the campaign of 1383 is exactly right for the Squire. In May of that year, Henry Despenser, the militant Bishop of Norwich, upon the instigation of Pope Urban VI, led the so-called "crusade" against the French supporters of the antipope Clement, and, for political reasons, the greater part of this campaign took place in Flanders. Despenser, hoping to surprise the King of France, who was in Amiens with an army, entered Picardy for a short period (a "litel space"), and of course must have passed through Artois. This is precisely the region where the Squire has been in "chyvachie." * The campaign itself, Professor Tatlock also

---

* *chyvachie*: "cavalry raid or expedition"

suggests, might be the kind to appeal mistakenly to the Knight as a satisfactory first military venture for his young son, for the Knight is "just the sort of man to be imposed on by the ecclesiastical zeal of the bishop into thinking his cause a sacred one"! [39] But it is far more likely that Chaucer selected this campaign for the Squire because of its date: the Squire would have been of correct age in 1383 to begin his experience in actual warfare. Although we have become accustomed today to youth in our armed forces, the fourteenth century, which possessed no statutory age regulations, probably saw many more extremely young men as fighters than the twentieth sees. Edward, the Black Prince, was sixteen at Crecy, Chaucer may have been only sixteen when he saw service in Flanders, and the four sons of King John of France were respectively nineteen, seventeen, sixteen, and fourteen when they fought at Poitiers. Thus, since Chaucer's Squire is twenty when we meet him (Chaucer "guesses" [40] the Squire's age with engaging and realistic hesitation), 1383 would have found the Squire sixteen, the conventionally right age for a hero to begin his serious experience on the battlefield. It was also the right age to hope "to stonden in his lady grace," for from the time a boy became a page in the Middle Ages, there was emphasis on his selection of some lady to be his *"par amours"*. [41]

* * * * *

The gay young Squire has not the full burden of attendance on his father: Chaucer tells us that a yeoman also accompanies the Knight.

> A Yeman hadde he [42] and servantz namo
> At that tyme, for hym liste ryde so.
>
> (ll. 101–102)

It was essential that a knight travel with a squire and at least one servant to uphold the dignity of his office. The *Book of the Ordre of Chyvalry* gives instruction on this point as follows:

Election ne hors ne armures suffyse not yet to the hyghe honour whiche longeth to a knyght / but it behoveth / that there be gyven to hym a squyer & servaunt that may take hede to his horse/ [43]

In *A Lytell Geste of Robin Hode* we read

> It were grete shame, sayd Robyn
> A knyght alone to ryde,
> Without squyer, yeman or page; [44]

and Little John is assigned by his master to the position of knight's "knave," in a "yemans stede," [45] so that a good knight may not be shamed through having no attendant. A yeoman usually meant in Chaucer's time "an attendant or assistant to an official"; the modern meaning of "a small landowner" did not come into use until the fifteenth century.[46]

The Knight's Yeoman was a "forester," when not attending his master:

> A forster was he, soothly, as I gesse.
>
> (l. 117)

A forester in the Middle Ages was "an official more largely connected with hunting than with the preservation of timber, as in more recent times," writes O. F. Emerson. He continues:

Thus Manwood tells us,[47] . . . 'A forester is an officer of the king (or any other man) sworn to preserve the Vert and Venison of the forest, and attend upon the wild beast within his Bailiwick.' The name was applied first of all to the *master forester*, such as Chaucer himself was in 1398 at North Petherton Park, or to the 'forester of the Baillie' in which was the forest to be hunted. He was an important character, for the *Master of Game* explains [48] that 'the master of game should be in accordance with the master forester or parker where it should be that the king should hunt on such a day.' . . . Under him the master forester had numerous under foresters such as the Knight's yeoman in the *Prologue* to the *Canterbury Tales*, or that forester of the Physician's Tale; [49] a former poacher who had given up 'His likerousnesse and al his olde [or theves] crafte,' and for this reason, 'Can kepe a forest best of any man.' Thus *forester* (*forster*) as Chaucer used it was nearly equivalent to modern *gamekeeper*, and quite as important in the medieval hunt.[50]

Chaucer pictures his Yeoman as a sturdy individual, who takes pride in his calling.

And he was clad in cote and hood of grene.
A sheef of pecok arwes, bright and kene,
Under his belt he bar ful thriftily,
(Wel koude he dresse his takel yemanly:
His arwes drouped noght with fetheres lowe)
And in his hand he baar a myghty bowe.
A not heed hadde he, with a broun visage.
Of wodecraft wel koude he al the usage.
Upon his arm he baar a gay bracer,
And by his syde a swerd and a bokeler,
And on that oother syde a gay daggere
Harneised wel and sharp as point of spere;
A Cristopher on his brest of silver sheene.
An horn he bar, the bawdryk was of grene.

(ll. 103–116)

The Yeoman with his close cropped ("not") head, and the brown skin that attests his outdoor life, wears the Lincoln green coat of the hunter.[51] It is a loose garment belted in at the waist, reaching just below the hips, with full sleeves gathered at the wrist.[52] His hood, also green, is plain, as befits his station, and conical; it may either hug the neck, and then fall in a short cape, or it may be attached loosely to the coat.[53] The Yeoman's green costume is brightened by the sheaf of "pecok arwes" handily suspended from his belt.

Although Ascham, the sixteenth-century authority on archery, speaks slightingly of the use of peacock feathers on the shaft of arrows,—

And truly at a short butt, which some men doth use, the peacock feather doth seldom keep up the shaft either right or level it is so rough and heavy; so that many men, which have taken them up for gayness, hath laid them down for profit,[54]—

the fourteenth century prized this kind of feather for its arrows.[55] Chaucer, who knew a great deal about hunting, and who uses hunting terms "with a realism quite in keeping with that shown in so many particulars throughout his work," [56] speaks in admiration of the Yeoman's ability to "dress" his hunting gear ("takel") providently and in true professional style, and the poet takes pains to tell us specifically that the Yeoman's "arwes drouped noght with fetheres lowe." Lydgate, Chaucer's contemporary, also favours the peacock feather:

Through al the land of Albion
For fethered arwes, as I reherse can,
Goos is the best, as in comparison,
Except fetheres of pekok or of swan.[57]

And the fourteenth-century *Geste of Robin Hode* celebrates the pea-cock feathers on the arrows of the renowned bowmen of Sherwood Forest:

He purveyed hym an hondred bowes,
The strenges were y dyght,
An hondred shefe of arowes good,
And hedes burnyshed full bryght,
And every arowe an elle longe,
With pecocke well y dyght,
Inocked all with white sylver,
It was a semly syght.[58]

Chaucer does not tell us that the Yeoman's arrows were "an elle longe," but they must have been about that to be used with his "myghty bowe." English warfare had been revolutionized during Chaucer's lifetime by the introduction of the long-bow, a bow which had been employed by the Welsh archers during the reign of Ed-ward I; the six-foot long-bow, adopted in place of the cross-bow and short-bow, may be said to have become the English national weapon during the reign of Edward III. So skilful did the English soldier become with the long-bow in war, that shooting with the long-bow became a favourite national sport. The range of the long-bow (about 290 yards) was considerably greater than that of the cross-bow; furthermore, the long-bow could be discharged as rapidly as the short-bow and more rapidly than the cross-bow. Of course, to use the long-bow effectively, a man had to be tall and strong, for it was necessary that the string be drawn all the way to the right ear with strength of body, rather than strength of arm.[59] The force required to discharge the long arrow from the "myghty bowe," made it essen-tial for the bowman to wear a "bracer," or guard, about the bow-arm. The bracer, similar to bracers worn by archers today, was "made like a glove with a long leather top, covering the fore-arm nearly to the elbow, and of considerable strength and thickness." [60] Since the bracer of Chaucer's Yeoman is "gay," it must be studded with metal, or painted with bright colours.

The Yeoman is well equipped not only as game-keeper and hunter, but also as the Knight's servant, for at his side is "a swerd and a bokeler." It was the usual thing for retainers to carry swords and bucklers when in attendance.[61] A buckler was a small shield, carried in the left hand, and used to parry blows. The king in the romance of *King Alexander* had

> Fiftene thousande of foot laddes
> That sweord and boceleris hadde.[62]

The dagger worn by the Yeoman also indicates how well accoutred he is. Like every hunter he carries a dagger, and his is as "sharp as point of spere"; it is decorated and well mounted ("harneised"), the kind of weapon suitable for a knight's retainer.

We must not forget to observe that the Yeoman has with him his hunter's horn. It is supported by a green belt ("bawdryk") worn diagonally across the body from one shoulder under the other arm.[63] The horn was essential for the forester: different notes served to call hounds, to record stages of the hunt, and to indicate to strayed riders the position of the hunt.[64] In the *Book of the Duchess*, for example, Chaucer tells us how the master of the hunt,

> With a gret horn blew thre mot
> At the uncoupylynge of hys houndes;[65]

and how later, when the hounds had lost the scent, the hunt was recalled by the blowing of the signal called the "forloyn."[66]

As a final realistic touch to the Yeoman's costume, Chaucer adds the gleaming silver image of the Yeoman's patron saint. St. Christopher was not only the patron saint of foresters,[67] but of many artisan classes. He was accounted one of the most popular saints of the Middle Ages, and was especially entreated by anyone taking a journey. Statues of St. Christopher, for instance, often bore the inscription, "Whoever shall behold the image of St. Christopher shall not faint or fall on that day."[68] Chaucer's well set-up Yeoman, in wearing "a Cristopher on his brest," guards against accident while he escorts his worthy master to Canterbury.

The Yeoman is a sound and likable fellow. We must always regret that we meet him only in the *Prologue*.

NOTES

(The abbreviations used to designate books and articles mentioned in the Notes will be found listed alphabetically in the Bibliography, opposite the full reference. References to lines in the *Canterbury Tales* are given by fragment and line numbers only.)

1. The *Book of the Duchess*, the *Complaint unto Pity*, and the *Complaint to his Lady* are clear examples of this. The eagle in the *House of Fame* speaks of Chaucer as being the willing servant of love (ll. 616 ff.); and Alceste in the *Legend of Good Women* defends the poet as having frequently written in praise of love (Prologue F, ll. 414 ff.).

Gower also testifies to Chaucer's fondness for love poetry. In some of the MSS. of the *Confessio Amantis*, Venus speaks of Chaucer as "mi disciple and mi poete" and is enthusiastic in her praise of him (Bk. VIII, ll. 2941*–2957*).

2. *NED*, "Squire."
3. III (D) 882–883.
4. V (F) 24.
5. IX (H) 125.
6. Gower, *Conf. Aman.*, Bk. I, ll. 2594, 2604.
7. *Robert de Ho*, ed. Mary-Vance Young, pp. 4, 29.
8. *Ibid.*, p. 5.
9. *Robert de Ho*, ll. 1105–1116:

> Fiz, j (e) entent ce a corteisie
> Ke hom sache chevalerie,
> E qu'il sache bien chevauchier
> E bien eslessier sum destrier,
> E sache si versefier
> Ke rien ne mette sanz mestier,
> E de chiens sache la mestrie,
> Des oiseaus e de venerie,
> (E) bel partout e seit mesurable
> A respundre, e puis bien estable.
> Ki ces mestiers a bien apris,
> Plus chiers en ierts en tous pais.

10. *Rom. of the Rose*, Ellis, ll. 2275–2296. *Rom. de la Rose*, ll. 2175–2210.
11. Olson (*Spec.* XVI, 75 ff.) mentions all the pilgrims in the *General Prologue* who play musical instruments, and cites a great many instances from Chaucer's works in which the poet speaks of song or dance or both. Some of the most important references are: *Book of the Duchess*, ll. 471–485, 848–849, 1155–1158; *Legend of Good Women*, G 199–202, 1269–1275; *Troilus and Criseyde*, Bk. I, ll. 386–399, Bk. II, ll. 824–826, 880–883, Blk. III, ll. 610–614, 1716–1722, 1737–1771, Bk. V, ll. 456–462, 502–504, 575–581, 631–646; *Canterbury Tales*, I (A) 1361–1368, 1500–1512, 2197–2202, 3257–3260, 4370–4376, III (D) 259, 457–458, IV (E) 1848–1850, VI (C) 463–471, IX (H) 113–118, 267–268.

A striking parallel to the Squire in this connection is Aurelius, the young squire in the *Franklin's Tale*, who sings and dances and knows how to compose "layes, songes, compleintes, roundels, virelayes." V (F) 947 f.

12. Olson, *loc. cit.*, p. 84; Manly, *New Light*, pp. 274–277.

13. Olson (*loc. cit.*, p. 86) says that there are fifty-nine literary devices which mention music in Chaucer's works.

14. Greene, *Early Eng. Carols*, pp. xxxi f.

15. *Legend of Good Women*, G 199–202.

16. *Ordre of Chyvalry*, p. 31.

17. Owst, *Lit. and Pulpit*, p. 335.

18. *Ibid.*

19. *Handlyng Synne*, ll. 4574–4639.

20. Strutt, p. xxvii.

21. *Brut*, p. 343.

22. Strutt, pp. 125–143.

23. *Ibid.*, pp. 144–145. See also woodcut in Cutts, p. 408.

24. *Brut*, pp. 344 f.

25. *Ibid.*, p. 348.

26. Owst, *Lit. and Pulpit*, pp. 404 f. (Trans. from MS. Harl. 4894, fol. 176 b.)

27. X (I) 416–429.

28. Robinson, p. 876, n. 423–31.

29. *Brut*, pp. 296 f.

30. "Floytynge" may be read in modern English as "playing the flute" (Robinson, p. 754; Manly, *Cant. Tales*, p. 502; Skeat, V, 10). Flügel (*JEGP*, I, 125) interprets the word as "piping" or "whistling." Either interpretation gives the same light touch of gaiety, however.

31. Druitt (p. 198) writes that long and wavy hair seems to have been a fourteenth-century fashion.

32. *Ordre of Chyvalry*, pp. 63 f.

33. *NED*, "Even."

34. *Ibid.*, "Deliver."

35. *Early Eng. Meals and Man.*, pp. 24–32.

36. *King Horn*, l. 251.

37. Coulton, *Social Life*, p. 286. Coulton translates from the thirteenth-century romance *Jehan et Blonde*, or *Blonde of Oxford* (Camden Soc., 1858), ll. 371–408, 425–492.

38. Tatlock, *Dev. and Chron.*, p. 148.

39. *Ibid.* See above Notes to Chap. I, n. 47.

40. *NED*, "Guess": "In the 14th. c. the word was the usual rendering of L. *aestimare*, the influence of which probably affected some of the earlier senses. . . . to estimate . . . to conjecture." Chaucer is partciularly fond of the expression, as we are in the United States today. He uses "guess" in this sense sixty-seven times, exclusive of the use in *Rom. of the Rose* (*Concordance*).

41. Jean, little thirteen-year-old page, in the romance of *Petit Jean de Saintré*, is unmercifully teased by one of the ladies of the court because he has

not as yet fixed on any lady before whom he may lay his devotion. Cf. Coulton, *Ch. and his Eng.*, pp. 223 ff.

42. "he" refers to the Knight (Robinson, p. 754).

43. *Ordre of Chyvalry*, p. 19.

44. *Robin Hode*, I, 157.

45. *Ibid.*

46. *NED*, "Yeoman."

47. Emerson (*Rom. Rev.*, XIII, 121) is here quoting from John Manwood's *Lawes Forest*, xxi, 4.

48. *Master of Game*, ch. xxxvi as quoted by Emerson.

49. VI (C) 83.

50. Emerson, *loc. cit.*, pp. 121 f.

51. *Ibid.*, p. 141. Emerson quotes from the *Master of Game* (ch. xxxviii) as follows: "Phoebus [i.e., Gaston de Foix, the source of the *Master of Game*] sayth that they ought to be clad in greene when they hunt the Hart or Bucke. . . ." We are here reminded of another "yeman" of Chaucer's, who was also dressed in green and carried the bow and arrows of the hunter (III [D] 1380 ff.). He turned out to be, however, "a feend" from "the north contree."

52. Hartley, p. 41.

53. Fairholt, p. 113.

54. Ascham, p. 124.

55. See Skeat's note 104 (V, 11), and Miss Krappe's article in *MLN*, XLIII, 176 f.

56. Emerson, *loc. cit.*, p. 150.

57. Quoted by Manly (*Cant. Tales*, p. 503) from Lydgate's "The Horse, Goose, and Sheep," 211–214.

58. *Robin Hode*, I, 165.

59. *Ency. Brit.*, "Archery."

60. Fairholt, p. 461.

61. *Ibid.*, p. 468.

62. *King Alexander*, ll. 1189–1190.

63. *NED*, "Baldric."

64. Apsley, pp. 160 f.

65. *Book of the Duchess*, ll. 376–377.

66. *Ibid.*, l. 386.

67. Robinson, p. 754; Manly, *Cant. Tales*, p. 503.

68. *Cath. Ency.*, "Christopher, Saint."

CHAPTER V

THE PRIORESS, HER CHAPLAIN, AND HER PRIEST

Ther was also a Nonne, a Prioresse,
That of hir smylyng was ful symple and coy;

. . . .

And she was cleped madame Eglentyne.

(ll. 118–119, 121)

BECAUSE nuns in Chaucer's day were almost always drawn from the upper classes, it seems fitting that the portrait of "my lady Prioresse" should follow that of the Knight and his attendants. This gracious gentlewoman probably began life as a dowerless daughter, and, as in countless similar situations in the Middle Ages, the convent then proved to be a not unhappy solution to a perplexing economic problem. Although there were undoubtedly many nuns who entered upon their cloistered life because of a true "vocation," it would seem that a large majority did so because it was the only possible life for them.[1] Few women of the lower classes, on the other hand, had either incentive or opportunity to become nuns: they either married young, their dowry being their ability to labour, or, if they remained single, they were too valuable as workers to be spared from the household.[2] Thus we can be safe in assuming at the outset that Madame Eglentyne has an aristocratic background. The idea of "gentry" was sufficiently broad by the fourteenth century to include what is considered today upper middle class, as well as the lesser nobility, and as we examine her portrait, we shall see that in this respect she is indeed true to type.

Madame Eglentyne is not only a member of a religious order, but she is also the superior officer of her convent. She takes pains to uphold the dignity of her calling. She

92

. . . peyned hire to countrefete * cheere
Of court, and to been estatlich of manere,
And to ben holden digne of reverence.

(ll. 139–141)

Prioresses, as Miss Eileen Power tells us in her exhaustive study of the medieval nun, "enjoyed the same prestige as the lords of the neighbouring manors and some extra deference on account of their religion." [3] All this points to a characteristically medieval inconsistency: attempts were always being made to enforce stricter enclosure upon the prioresses, yet these ladies were welcomed so cordially in manor-houses and inns, and they themselves so much enjoyed their travels, that journeys without the convent walls were frequently undertaken. Accounts of mundane gayeties and of "frequent escapes to the freedom of the road are found not only at the greater houses but even at those which were small and poor," writes Miss Power. [4] It is to be expected that the Bishops would object to nuns' travelling for secular purposes, and when we remember the nature of fourteenth-century pilgrimages, we cannot be surprised that the Bishops also ruled against the religious journey. Early in the century Archbishop Melton strictly interdicted nuns from leaving their cloisters "by reason of any vow of pilgrimage which they might have taken," [5] a mandate which obviously failed of its purpose, for in the late fifteenth century, an archbishop still found it necessary to say, "that the prioresse lycence none of your susters to goe pilgremage." [6] The mere fact that Madame Eglentyne is one of the Canterbury pilgrims is the first point of satire in a portrait that is satiric, though it is also gentle and understanding.

To paint a portrait of one who illustrates "the engagingly imperfect submergence of the feminine in the ecclesiastical," [7] Chaucer employs the sharp colours of irony combined with the gold of humour and sympathy. To begin with, Madame Eglentyne is "ful symple and coy," and these words belong to the medieval romance. Every lady who is eulogized for her charms is endowed with simplicity and "coyness," the latter quality denoting modesty or a becomingly quiet demeanor. Lowes in one delightful and scholarly article collects many examples of the use of these words *simple* and *coy*, employed either separately or in conjunction with each other, to

* *countrefete:* "imitate"

describe a fair heroine's charms, and he takes his examples from such writers as Watriquet de Couvin, Deschamps, Froissart, Machaut, and Gower.[8] He points out that the stock phrase "simple and coy" sets the stage for the many nuances in the portrait of the Prioress which "readers of the fourteenth century must have been quick to gather." First there is "the exquisite incongruity of the gentle nun's self-chosen name."[9] The fourteenth century knew, for instance, "Se sist bele Eglentine (Raynaud's *Recueil de motets*) and the romance of "Bele Aiglentine et le quens Henris." In each one the lady bearing the name of Chaucer's Prioress is a beautiful, romantically worldly figure far removed from a nun. And if it be true, as Manly suggests, that Chaucer knew of a Madame Argentyn, actually a nun in 1375 at the Convent of St. Leonard's adjoining Stratford-Bow, there would be a double jest in changing Argentyn, sometimes spelled Eglinton in the records, to the Eglentyne of romance.[10] As will be later indicated, there is every reason to suppose that if Chaucer had in mind a particular convent for the Prioress, St. Leonard's was his choice.

Madame Eglentyne resembles the fair ladies of the romances not only in that she is "ful symple and coy" and that she bears the flower-like name of eglantine (or sweet-briar), but also in that she has certain physical characteristics:

> Hir nose tretys, hir eyen greye as glas,
> Hir mouth ful smal, and therto softe and reed;
> But sikerly she hadde a fair forheed;
> It was almoost a spanne brood, I trowe;
> For, hardily, she was nat undergrowe.
>
> (ll. 152–156)

Lowes calls to our attention the fact that this is the description of every heroine of romance. The Prioress's nose is shapely ("tretys"); her eyes are "greye as glas"—*greye* probably not meaning our "grey," but, rather, as Miss Muriel Kinney deduces from Chaucer's usage, "expressive mobility and brilliance," so that *greye as glas* is here very likely equivalent to a modern phrase such as "sparkling and bright as (Venetian) glass";[11] her mouth is small and soft and red; and her fair forehead which, fair or otherwise, should have been covered in the presence of the company, since Madame Eglentyne is a nun, is beautifully broad. Medieval standards of beauty

called for large, broad, and unwrinkled foreheads.[12] Lowes cites
many instances, drawn from medieval romances, in which the same
physical attractions are ascribed to the fair (and very worldly)
ladies: for example, Watriquet de Couvin speaks of a beautiful
lady's "grey" eyes (*vairs ieus*), straight nose (*nés traitis*), and
small red mouth (*vermeille bouchete*) ; [13] Froissart says that his lady
has eyes as "grey" as a falcon's (*les yeus vairs comme un faucons*),
a straight nose (*nés trettic*), and that her forehead is smooth, pol-
ished, beautiful, and well formed (*clers est ses frons / Polis, jolis et
bien fès*) ; [14] and Gower writes of his Lover in the *Confessio Amantis* as feeding upon the sight of his lady's countenance—

> He seth hire front is large and plein
> Withoute fronce of eny grein,
> He seth hire yhen lich an hevene,
> He seth hire nase strauht and evene,
> He seth hire rode upon the cheke,
> He seth hire rede lippes eke.[15]

Of course the jest lies in Chaucer's endowing someone who is a nun
with the physical characteristics of the fascinating, worldly heroine,
but there may also be implied satiric comment on the romances. We
should note, however, with Lowes, that Chaucer ends his description of the physical attributes of the Prioress with her countenance,
adding only the quiet statement that she is well-proportioned ("nat
undergrowe"). This shows remarkable restraint on the part of
Chaucer.[16] Conventions of the romance called for "anatomical cata-
logues" of a lady's charms, and Chaucer himself in the *Book of the
Duchess* lists methodically all the physical beauties of "goode, faire
White." [17] But judged by the standards of any age, the portrait of
Madame Eglentyne remains in good taste: she is always kept charm-
ingly dignified, even when the poet writes of her with sharp wit.

Madame Eglentyne has other characteristics of the ladies of
romance and of the court. Her table manners are excellent, and she
wears fine clothes and ornaments.

> At mete wel ytaught was she with alle:
> She leet no morsel from hir lippes falle,
> Ne wette hir fyngres in hir sauce depe;
> Wel koude she carie a morsel and wel kepe

That no drope ne fille upon hire brest.
In curteisie * was set ful muchel hir lest.
Hir over-lippe wyped she so clene
That in hir coppe ther was no ferthyng sene
Of grece, whan she dronken hadde hir draughte.
Ful semely after hir mete she raughte.

(ll. 127–136)

These lines are borrowed directly from the *Roman de la Rose*:

> She should behave her when at table
> In manner fit and convenable;
>
> .   .   .   .   .   .
>
> 'Tis well she take especial care
> That in the sauce her fingers ne'er
> She dip beyond the joint, nor soil
> Her lips with garlick, sops, or oil,
> Nor heap up gobbets and then charge
> Her mouth with pieces overlarge
> And only with the finger point
> Should touch the bit she'd fain anoint
> With sauce, white, yellow, brown, or green,
> And lift it towards her mouth between
> Finger and thumb with care and skill
> That she no sauce or morsel spill
> About her breast-cloth.
>   Then her cup
> She should so gracefully lift up
> Towards her mouth that not a gout
> By any chance doth fall about
> Her vesture, or for glutton rude,
> By such unseemly habitude,
> Might she be deemed.
>   Nor should she set
> Lips to her cup while food is yet
> Within her mouth.
>   And first should she
> Her other lip wipe delicately,
> Lest, having drunk, a grease-formed groat
> Were seen upon the wine to float.[18]

* *curteisie:* "good manners"

The humour here is not in the borrowing from romance, for the table manners described are merely those of polite society, but in the particular setting from which the lines are taken. For this is part of the account given by the Beldam, La Vieille, of the wiles a woman uses to attract and hold her lover. The words themselves were borrowed by Jean de Meun from Ovid's *Ars Amatoria*.[19]

As to the dress of Madame Eglentyne—

> Ful semyly hir wympul pynched was;
>
> .   .   .   .   ,
>
> Ful fetys was hir cloke, as I was war.
> Of smal coral aboute hire arm she bar
> A peire of bedes, gauded al with grene,
> And theron heng a brooch of gold ful sheene,
> On which ther was first write a crowned A,
> And after *Amor vincit omnia*.
>
> (ll. 151, 157–162)

Her wimple, or neck covering, is well pleated ("pynched"); her cloak, depicted by the artist of the Ellesmere MS., as the hooded, black cloak of the Benedictine Order, is well-shaped ("fetys"). About her arm, Madame Eglentyne wears a rosary (a "peire of bedes")[20] of small, bright red coral; the gauds of the rosary, that is, the larger and more ornamental beads placed between the decades of Ave Marias, are green, and from her rosary hangs a brooch of shining gold. The brooch is particularly noteworthy: it is an ornamental pin in the shape of a capital A surmounted by a crown; the motto *Amor vincit omnia* is etched on the face.[21] Originally this motto in Virgil's *Eclogues* concerned profane love, but the Church early adopted the motto and gave it a meaning which had to do with sacred love; by the fourteenth century, the motto was often again employed in its original sense, and we pause to wonder what the Prioress herself may have thought about the words. Lowes poses and answers the question for us as follows:

Now is it earthly love which conquers all, now heavenly; the phrase plays back and forth between the two. And it is precisely that happy ambiguity of the convention—itself the result of an earlier transfer—which makes Chaucer's use of it here . . . a master stroke. *Which of the two loves does "amor" mean to the Prioress? I do not know; but I think she thought she meant love celestial.*[22]

But whether or not Madame Eglentyne is correct in her interpretation of the motto on her gold brooch, she defies all regulations in wearing any ornament at all. The bishops of the fourteenth century were constantly forbidding nuns to wear furs, silks, rings, and brooches,[23] evidently without success. Here again we have a satiric touch to the portrait. The Prioress is not without worldly vanities, dear to a feminine heart.

In yet another conspicuous way is the Prioress shown to be the eternal feminine.

> Of smale houndes hadde she that she fedde
> With rosted flessh, or milk and wastel-breed.
> But soore wepte she if oon of hem were deed
> Or if men smoot it with a yerde smerte;
> And al was conscience and tendre herte.
>
> (ll. 146–150)

Madame Eglentyne in possessing her "smale houndes" sets aside an important rule; even ladies of the court were scolded for keeping pets, and nuns were forbidden to do so. The Knight of La Tour Landry tells the story of a lady who loved her two little dogs very much as the Prioress loves hers.

The lady had two little dogs, and she loved them so that she took great pleasure in the sight and feeding of them. And every day she had prepared for them dishes of sops of milk followed by meat. A friar chided her for this and said it was not well that dogs should be so fed and fattened while the poor people were hungry and lean. But the lady would not amend her ways. Consequently, when she was dying, two little black dogs were seen on her bed, licking her mouth. And after her death all about her mouth where the dogs had licked it was as black as coal. This is a good lesson as to why ladies should not have their pleasure in such beasts, nor give them that which might sustain the starving poor, who are God's own creatures, made in his likeness. Ladies should take as their model the good Countess of Mans who nourished ever thirty fatherless children and who was rewarded at her death by the sight of a group of cherubs—not of little black dogs straight from the infernal regions.[24]

With a heavier voice, the Dominican Bromyard preaches in the fourteenth century against the wealthy who provide for their dogs more readily than for the poor, more abundantly and more delicately too; so that, where the poor are so famished that they would greedily devour bran-bread, dogs are squeamish at the sight of wafer-bread, and spurn what is offered them, trampling it under their feet. They must be offered the daintiest flesh, the firstling and the choicest produce of every dish. If, glutted, they refuse it, then, as though they were infirm, there is a wailing over them on the part of those whose bowels yearn with pity for the afflicted.[25]

And how much more blameworthy for a nun, than for a lady of the world, to lavish comforts and affection on an animal! Yet it was common for nuns to keep their dogs and other pets, as is evident from the repeated injunctions against such practices.[26]

The Prioress not only keeps little dogs, but caters to their dainty appetites. According to the *Liber Albus*, the first grade of bread in Chaucer's day was called *demeine*, or the Lord's bread. The Prioress would never, of course, give this to an animal. Wastel-bread, the second in quality, was a fine wheat bread, probably white, and far superior to the third and fourth grade breads. We cannot imagine that it was found on any tables other than those of the well-to-do.[27] The roast meat lavished upon the "smale houndes" would be judged an extravagance by even the most lenient of fourteenth-century standards. The Prioress cannot be considered to be without fault, although today we smile indulgently over the tears she sheds, tears induced by her sympathetic feelings ("conscience") and tender heart, when anyone chastises her little dogs.

Though for the most part Chaucer sees the Prioress with kindliness and an understanding of her feminine foibles and venial weaknesses, there is a touch of sterner criticism when he says:

> But, for to speken of hire conscience,
> She was so charitable and so pitous
> She wolde wepe, if that she saugh a mous
> Kaught in a trappe, if it were deed or bledde.
>
> (ll. 142-145)

It is only thus far, Chaucer implies, that the Prioress's charity and pity are roused: it is the suffering of a mouse which calls forth her sympathy; she is not greatly concerned over the suffering of her fellow-man. This implication is later strengthened by her own *Tale* in which she tells with perfect blandness of the tortures visited upon the Jews;[28] and by the fact that when Chaucer writes of the charity of his Parson, he is explicit and clear in pointing out that here is a man who follows truly all the teachings of Christianity in loving his neighbour as himself. For Madame Eglentyne, then, the poet's *but* indicates a reservation. Despite her charm and dignity, she possesses a real imperfection not unmarked by the poet who has created her.

But is Chaucer the literal creator of his Prioress, or is she drawn from a living model? As Manly so persuasively suggests, it is quite possible, even probable, that Chaucer remembered his acquaintance with the nuns of St. Leonard's when he described Madame Eglentyne. St. Leonard's adjoining Stratford-Bow, was a Benedictine convent; it was here that Elizabeth of Hainault, sister of Queen Philippa, passed many years of her life before she died there in 1375. It is more than likely that it was to visit Elizabeth of Hainault that Prince Lionel went to Stratford in 1356.[29] If Chaucer was then a page in Prince Lionel's household as he may have been, for the Stratford journey took place but a few months before the first record of young Geoffrey appears in the same account book that notes the Stratford journey, Chaucer in all probability accompanied the royal visitors to St. Leonard's and so became acquainted with this convent at an early age. St. Leonard's was smaller and less aristocratic than the convent at Barking, but the presence of the Queen's sister at St. Leonard's must have given it greater vogue in the latter half of the fourteenth century. Certainly the bequests in Elizabeth of Hainault's will give the impression that the nuns of St. Leonard's were fashionably interested in jewels and finery. Manly's translation of this will reads in part as follows:

. . . Also I bequeath to the Chapel of the Blessed Mary my best mantle and best over-tunic of the colour of the mantle and best veil and the fillet with pearls. Also I bequeath to the altar of the convent my second-best mantle furred with grys and over-tunic of the same colour and second-best veil. . . . Also I bequeath to Sara my maid a green gown and a green tunic and a self-edged triffle and two hair-nets. Also I bequeath to Madame Argentyne, nun, a pair of 'lyntharbs.' Likewise I bequeath to Master Geoffrey, chaplain of the parish, three and a half yards of blanket. Also I bequeath to Andrew Tendale an ounce of gold. Also to Johanna Brerele a gown of tawny and a tunic of the same colour. Also I bequeath to Robert Aylmer three curtains, with a veil and two rugs and a blue gown and two bird cages. Also I bequeath to Roland Alis a pair of bedes of gold and a gold brooch [like that of Chaucer's Prioress?]; likewise to Madame Idoine, nun, a pair of gold tablets. [We should note that Idoine is as romantic a name as Eglentyne.] Also I bequeath to Madame Mary, prioress, a gold ring with two stones, a ruby and an emerald; also to Master Thomas of Woodstock a gold ring with four pearls and an emerald in the midst. Likewise I bequeath to Margaret Marshall a gold enamelled ring with cornelians. Also I bequeath to Johanna wife of John Taylor a blue tunic. Also I bequeath to Sara my maid a green casket with all the articles in it. Also I bequeath to Madame Argentyn a psalter . . .[30]

We should like to know, of course, if "Madame Argentyn" of Elizabeth's will is Chaucer's Madame Eglentyne, or if Chaucer merely borrowed her name to use for any one of the other nuns—perhaps for "Madame Mary, prioress" herself; but the records tell us nothing except that all the nuns of St. Leonard's seem to have imitated, as did Chaucer's Prioress, manners of the court in worldly adornment.

But even if the Prioress has no flesh-and-blood counterpart, Chaucer must have pictured her in his imagination as coming from St. Leonard's.

> And Frenssh she spak ful faire and fetisly,*
> After the scole of Stratford atte Bowe,
> For Frenssh of Parys was to hire unknowe.
>
> (ll. 124–126)

No other convent was at Stratford-Bow,[31] and the Prioress speaks the French she hears in her nunnery, not the French of Paris. Undoubtedly, Elizabeth of Hainault spoke French with an accent, and her sister nuns, drawn from the gentry and well-to-do merchant class, would have been content to copy the great lady. Furthermore, at what time in the history of England has the French of the average English middle class citizen not been a standing joke? Certainly this was true in Chaucer's day. As Professor Charles H. Livingston points out, supporting his statement by excerpts from the *fabliaux*: "The caricature of the Englishman in the Middle Ages was never complete in the eyes of the French without some allusion to or parody upon his incorrect and unpleasant manner of speaking French." [32] The ladies of St. Leonard's could hardly have been

* *fetisly:* "gracefully"

exceptional as far as their French was concerned; and to Chaucer, whose wife it is to be remembered came from Hainault, there must have been added humour in the familiar jibe. French was the language of the polite English world, it is true, but we may be very sure that it had a strange accent to an ear schooled in Paris! It was essential, of course, for Madame Eglentyne as a prioress to speak some sort of French, for the visiting bishops issued their injunctions in French throughout the fourteenth century.[33]

Chaucer's Prioress knows how to take proper part in the services of her convent:

> Ful weel she soong the service dyvyne,
> Entuned in hir nose ful semely.
>
> (ll. 122–123)

Miss Power writes that "the requirements seems to be that the nun should be able to take part in the daily offices in the quire for which reading and singing was essential."[34] The Prioress has been well instructed evidently in the techniques of her singing, for the notes are "entuned in hir nose ful semely." Chanting the service has always demanded a nasal quality to avoid strain on the vocal chords.

We have yet to speak of the much discussed "oath" of the Prioress:

> Hire gretteste ooth was but by Seinte Loy.
>
> (l. 120)

When we read any medieval romance, or indeed the *Canterbury Tales* themselves, we realize how common swearing was in Chaucer's day. The name of every part of God's body is taken in vain in the most casual conversations. "For Cristes sake, ne swereth nat so synfully in dismembrynge of Crist by soule, herte, bones, and body!" cries Chaucer's Parson,[35] but he is alone in his disapproval; the other Canterbury pilgrims resent his rebuke of Harry Bailly for the latter's ingeniously blasphemous expressions.[36] Nearly all the preachers, however, both orthodox and Wyclifite, inveigh against swearing and deplore the fact that it is so common. One fourteenth-century homilist says, for example, that the Third Commandment is " 'all wey brokyn a-monge lered and lewde, a-mong yeonge and old, a-monge ryche and pore, frome a litill yeonge chyld that can unnethe speke, to an olde berded man that age hath nygh be-nome his ryght

speche.' " [37] Women also are censured for their oaths by the preachers. One Latin sermon includes the following exemplum:

. . . I have heard of a woman whom in confession, the priest commanded to swear no more; to whom she answered, 'Sir, I will swear no
more, so help me God!' And he: 'Lo, thou swearest already.' 'Nay, by
God,' quoth she, 'but I will indeed abstain from henceforth.' Then said
the priest, 'But let your speech be yea, yea! no, no! as the Lord biddeth:
and that which is over and above these, is of evil.' Then said she, 'Sir,
ye say it again, and I say unto you, by the blessed Virgin and all the
saints! I will swear no more, but do your bidding, and ye shall never
hear me swear again.' So that accursed woman gave many promises, yet contradicted them in deed.[38]

No one, however, could call Madame Eglentyne "accursed" in her
swearing: she has the good taste, or better perhaps, the piety, to
refrain from the "dismembrynge of Crist," and her strongest oath is
"by Seinte Loy," a peculiarly happy choice if she is to swear at all.

The seventh-century St. Eligius, called "Eloi" or "Loy" by
French and English writers, was originally a courtier and an artist
of distinction, the founder of the great school of enamel-work that
centered at Limoges for centuries; the enormous number of *objets
d'art* attributed to the saint is witness to the fact, as Lowes has
shown, that the artist in Eligius had great popular appeal.[39] Eligius
was apparently a man of physical beauty also and a lover of personal
adornment, and when he withdrew from the world, his charm was
not forgotten; his early fame spread rapidly from Flanders and Picardy to France and England. The French poets of Chaucer's day,
notably Froissart and Machaut,[40] frequently mention "saint Eloy,"
and many hymns in both the thirteenth and fourteenth centuries are
addressed to St. Eligius. Chaucer would, of course, be aware of the
popularity of this saint, and of his courtly background; the poet's
linking of Madame Eglentyne with "Seinte Loy" was surely what
Lowes terms a "felicitous choice" and a "flash of inspiration." [41]

Chaucer's Prioress is gentle, demure, aristocratic in her worldly
and culpably indifferent outlook on life. She is the nun who remem-
bers life beyond the convent wall, and who longs sufficiently for some
of the more innocent yet nevertheless forbidden pleasures of that life
to circumvent politely her conventual restrictions. Chaucer was no
reformer in any sense, but certainly he and his audience knew what

the reformers were saying, and much of the exquisite humour of the Prioress's delicate yet penetrating portrait lies in that knowledge.

> Another Nonne with hire hadde she,
> That was hir chapeleyne, and preestes thre.
> (ll. 163–164)

No prioress of any standing would travel unattended. Miss Power writes that the superior of a convent was ordered "always to have with her one of the nuns as a companion and witness to her behaviour," and adds that it was usual for the accompanying nun to act as chaplain.[42] A "nun-chaplain" had the duties of secretary to her superior, as well as that of attendance upon the prioress, or abbess, in the choir at the great festivals where she was particularly required to hold the crosier.[43] A priest often accompanied a prioress and her attendant. That the head of the small convent at Stratford should have more than one priest with her, however, is quite absurd, according to Manly, and he suggests that since the *Canterbury Tales* is an unfinished work, it is highly probable that Chaucer himself wrote no more of the line than "That was hir chapeleyne . . .", and that "and preestes thre" was later added by an unknown scribe to fill out the line and make a conventional rhyme.[44] If only one priest accompanies the Prioress and her chaplain, we meet twenty-nine pilgrims at the Tabard, and that is the number Chaucer tells us are there. Furthermore, the will of Elizabeth of Hainault mentions "Master Geoffrey de Neunton" as "chaplain of the parish," and the document makes clear that this Master Geoffrey also served as the "nuns' priest" at St. Leonard's, with an implication that no other priest, or priests, held such office.[45] By the time Chaucer wrote the *Nun's Priest's Tale* it is clear he had in mind a single and distinctively witty cleric.

NOTES

(The abbreviations used to designate books and articles mentioned in the Notes will be found listed alphabetically in the Bibliography, opposite the full reference. References to lines in the *Canterbury Tales* are given by fragment and line numbers only.)

1. Power, *Med. Eng. Nun.*, p. 4.
2. *Ibid.*, p. 5.
3. *Ibid.*, p. 69.

4. *Ibid.,* p. 74.

5. *Ibid.,* p. 373.

6. *Ibid.,* pp. 373 ff.

7. Lowes, *Convention and Revolt,* p. 60.

8. Lowes, *Anglia,* XXXIII, 440–451.

9. *Ibid.,* p. 440.

10. Manly, *New Light,* pp. 202 ff.

11. Kinney, *Rom. Rev.,* X, 322–363. Miss Kinney observes (p. 341) that Chaucer was fond of double meanings: it is possible that the poet had in mind in writing of the Prioress two Middle English meanings for *grey,* that is, *grey* meaning the colour intermediate between black and white, and *grey* as a translation of French *vair* meaning "sparkling, bright." In the first case, Chaucer's *glas* would probably denote the muddy English glass of the fourteenth century; in the second case, *glas* would denote the clear Venetian glass of the time. As the Prioress is portrayed as possessing physical beauty, however, it seems better to interpret the poet's "eyen greye as glas" as complimentary.

Miss Kinney notes that in *Rom. of the Rose* (l. 822), *greye* translates French *vair;* and that in the same work (l. 1603), *fair and bright* paraphrases the French *ses yex vers* (pp. 357 f.). She states (p. 341) that she can find no authority for the assumption that Chaucer's *eyen greye as glas* means "blue eyes."

12. Curry, *Mid. Eng. Ideal of Beauty,* p. 42.

13. Lowes, *Anglia,* XXXIII, 441. (Watriquet, p. 24, ll. 734–736.)

14. *Ibid.* (*Poésies* of Froissart, ed. Scheler, II, 251.)

15. Gower, *Conf. Aman.,* Bk. VI, ll. 769–774. (Lowes calls attention to this reference.)

16. Lowes, *Anglia,* XXXIII, 442.

17. *Book of the Duchess,* ll. 895 ff.

18. *Rom. of the Rose,* Ellis, ll. 14093–14094, 14117–14140. *Rom. de la Rose,* ll. 13385–13386, 13408–13432.

19. Ovid, *Ars Amatoria,* III, ll. 755–756:

> Carpe cibos digitis: est quiddam gestus edendi:
> Ora nec immunda tota perungue manu.

20. Manly (*Cant. Tales,* pp. 506 f.) points out that until recently English kept some phrases in which *pair* meant more than two—a "pair of stairs," for example. He also calls attention to the original meaning of *bede,* which was "prayer"; modern *bead* is a transfer from the prayer counted to the object used for counting. Rosaries were of two kinds, long and short. The long rosaries were worn suspended about the arm, as is the Prioress's, or fastened to the girdle.

21. Miss Hammond (*Anglia,* XXX, 320) says that on the verso of the first flyleaf of the Ashmole MS. "is drawn with ink a large M-like letter, with a crown above it . . . This compound capital letter seems to be a fusion of . . . the letters of the word *Amor.*" See also Fairholt, "Brooch," where there is a drawing of such a brooch.

22. Lowes, *Convention and Revolt,* p. 66.

23. Kuhl, *PQ*, II, pp. 305 f.

24. La Tour Landry, Chap. XX.

25. Owst, *Lit. and Pulpit*, p. 327. (Translated from Bromyard's *Lamentations*.)

26. Kuhl, *loc. cit.*, p. 304.

27. On the whole subject of "bread" see the early fifteenth-century *Liber Albus*. The Riley translation refers to "The Assay of Bread" on pp. 302–306, 308–310.

28. VII 628–634 (B^2 1818–1824).

29. Manly, *New Light*, p. 206.

30. *Ibid.*, pp. 207 f.

31. *Ibid.*, p. 203.

32. Livingston, *PMLA*, XL, 217.

33. Power, *op. cit.*, p. 246.

34. *Ibid.*, p. 245.

35. X (I) 591.

36. II (B) 1163–1180.

37. Owst, *Lit. and Pulpit*, p. 416. (Quotation from MS. Bodl. 95, fol. Ib.)

38. Coulton, *Life in Mid. Ages*, III, 86–87.

39. Lowes, *Rom. Rev.*, V, 372.

40. *Ibid.*, p. 371, n. 14.

41. *Ibid.*, p. 380, n. 40.

42. Power, *op. cit.*, p. 62.

43. Furnivall, *Anglia*, IV, 238–240.

44. Manly, *Cant. Tales*, p. 508.

45. *Ibid.* See also Manly, *New Light*, pp. 207, 222–224.

CHAPTER VI

THE MONK WHO LOVED "VENERIE"

A Monk ther was, a fair for the maistrie,*
An outridere, that lovede venerie,
A manly man, to been an abbot able.

. . . .

Ther as this lord was kepere of the celle,
The reule of seint Maure or of seint Beneit,
By cause that it was old and somdel streit
This ilke Monk leet olde thynges pace,
And heeld after the newe world the space.*
He yaf nat of that text a pulled hen,
That seith that hunters ben nat hooly men,
Ne that a monk, whan he is recchelees,
Is likned til a fissh that is waterlees,—
That is to seyn, a monk out of his cloystre.
But thilke text heeld he nat worth an oystre;
And I seyde his opinion was good.
What sholde he studie and make hymselven wood,
Upon a book in cloystre alwey to poure,
Or swynken with his handes, and laboure,
As Austyn bit? How shal the world be served?
Lat Austyn have his swynk to hym reserved!
                                    (ll. 165–167, 172–188)

THE Monk, like his spiritual kinsman in the Shipman's *Tale,*

Hath of his abbot, as hym list, licence,
By cause he was a man of heigh prudence,
And eek an officer, out for to ryde.[1]

He does not hesitate to leave his cloister when it suits his pleasure, to "ride out" in his fine clothes on his glossy brown palfrey, even though his "old and somdel streit" Rule expressly forbids a monk to

* *a fair for the maistrie:* "an extremely fine one"
  the space: "meanwhile"

go outside the confines of the monastery. But Chaucer's Monk, if we
are to believe the evidence of contemporary literature, is no great
exception.

The disciplinarians of the Middle Ages all insist that two of the
most important stays to the principles of the monastic Rule are
labour and claustration.[2] St. Benedict's famous Rule (early sixth
century) states:

> Idleness is an enemy of the soul. Because this is so breathren ought
> to be occupied at specified times in manual labour . . .[3]

> The monastery . . . itself ought, if possible, to be so constructed
> as to contain within it all necessaries . . . so that there be no occasion
> for monks to wander abroad, since this is in no wise expedient for
> their souls. We wish this Rule to be read frequently in the community
> so that no brother may plead ignorance as an excuse.[4]

Labour was likewise especially emphasized by St. Augustine of Hippo
in his *De Opera Monachorum* (ca400), which became centuries
later in part the basis for the Augustinian Rule:

> . . . First then we ought to demonstrate that the blessed Apostle Paul
> willed the servants of God to work corporal works which should have
> as their end a great spiritual reward, for this purpose that they should
> need food and clothing of no man, but with their own hands should
> procure these for themselves: then, to show that those evangelical pre-
> cepts from which some cherish not only their sloth but even arrogance,
> are not contrary to the apostolical precept and example. Let us see then
> whence the Apostle came to this, that he would say, If any will not work
> neither let him eat, and what he thereupon joineth on, that from the
> very context of this lesson may appear his declared sentence. . . .

> For what these men are about, who will not do bodily work, to
> what things they give up their time, I should like to know. "To prayers,"
> say they, "and psalms and reading and the word of God." A holy life
> unquestionably, and in sweetness of Christ worthy of praise; but then,
> if from these we are not to be called off neither must we eat, nor our
> daily viands themselves be prepared, that they may be put before us
> and taken. Now if to find time for these things the servants of God at
> certain intervals of time by very infirmity are of necessity compelled,
> why do we not make account of some portions of time to be allotted also
> to the observance of apostolical precepts? . . . As for divine songs, . . .
> they can easily, even while working with their hands, say them . . .
> What . . . hinders a servant of God while working with his hands to

meditate in the law of the Lord and sing unto the Name of the Lord
Most High? . . . To come now to the Apostle; how could he find
time to work with his hands, unless for the bestowing of the word of
God he had set certain times? . . .[5]

Yet in spite of the ancient commands of St. Benedict, of St. Augustine, and of "seint Maure," Benedict's disciple, commands which
fourteenth-century monks were expected by the Church still to venerate, writer after writer reports that the monks avoid toil and wander
everywhere about the countryside.

As to claustration, Langland, Gower, and Wyclif use almost the
same words as Chaucer about a monk who, "out of his cloystre," is
"likned til a fissh that is waterlees." Langland writes:

> Gregorie the grete clerk . gart * write in bokes
> The ruele of alle religious . ryghtful and obedient.[6]
> Right as fisshes in flod . whenne hem faileth water,
> Deyen for drouthe . whenne thei drye liggen,
> Ryght so religion . roteth and sterveth,**
> That out of covent and cloistre . coveyteth to dwelle.[7]

In his *Mirour de l'Omme* Gower cites St. Augustine to the effect that
just as fish live only in water, so should monks live only in the cloister;[8] and again, in the *Vox Clamantis,* Gower says that a monk
should not be outside the cloister any more than a fish should be out
of water.[9] Wyclif, too, in a denunciation of religious orders in general,
states that the founders of cloisters say that monks "myghten no more
dwelle out ther-of than fiss myghte dwelle out of water . . ." [10]
Chaucer's Monk corresponds to the commonplace picture in that
he cares nothing for the requirements and duties of monastic life;
he is "recchelees." [11] He rides abroad, instead of labouring or study-
ing as "Austyn bit." But why should this fine gentleman, asks
Chaucer ironically, make himself mad with work or study? The
Monk has the right idea, for who indeed can serve the world, if he,
an important "lord," remains in his monastery! All very well for the
long dead "Austyn"—let all the toil be reserved for *him*! For the
living there are the delights of hunting to be enjoyed by a Monk
who loves them and does not give a "pulled hen" [12] for the text that
says that hunters are not "hooly."

* *gart:* "caused"   ** *sterveth:* "dies"

Ful many a deyntee hors had he in stable,
And whan he rood, men myghte his brydel heere
Gynglen in a whistlynge wynd als cleere
And eek as loude as dooth the chapel belle.

. . . .

. . . He was a prikasour aright:
Grehoundes he hadde as swift as fowel in flight;
Of prikyng and of huntyng for the hare
Was al his lust, for no cost wolde he spare.

. . . .

His palfrey was as broun as is a berye.
(ii. 168–171, 189–192, 207)

The Monk could hardly be expected to refrain from a pleasure in which such a large part of the secular world took delight, since he is the kind of man to disobey more important regulations. The text to which he refers so contemptuously may be the one found in the *Decretum* of Gratian. This was based on the *Breviarium in Psalmo* attributed to St. Jerome, a work which was, as O. F. Emerson points out, "familiar material in Chaucer's day":[13] "Esau was a hunter, therefore he was a sinner. And indeed we do not find in Scripture any virtuous hunter; on the other hand, we do find virtuous fishermen."[14] Professor Willard proves, however, that Chaucer need not have taken the "text" from any one source: as early as the ninth century, hunters were condemned as sinful men, and by the fourteenth century the idea was certainly a commonplace.[15]

The laity of the Middle Ages of course paid little attention to a dictum of the Church seldom, if ever, invoked against them, but a different standard of behaviour was demanded for men of religion. The hunting cleric in Chaucer's age is always censured by the reformers. One Lollard writer inveighs against such clergy as follows:

. . . Thei taken here worldly myrthe, haukynge & huntynge & othere vanytes doynge . . . the more that a curat hath of pore mennys goodis, the more comunly he wastith in costy fedynge of houndis & haukis . . .[16]

The more orthodox also make their complaints. Langland says that for many a day monks have "priked a-boute on palfrais" followed by "an hepe of houndes," giving thought only to their personal pleasure and ignoring their Rule; [17] while Gower declares:

That monk who is made keeper or seneschal of an outside office is not a good cloisterer, for to run about he must have horse and saddle and money to spend. He lives like a lord and becomes silly and vain. 'All is ours,' says such a monk in his luxurious living. . . .

For their pleasure, these wealthy monks keep falcons and hawks for river fowl, and dogs and great, fresh horses for hunting and chasing the hare. . . .[18]

If we turn to actual records, we find that only a generation or so before Chaucer's time fifteen hundred horses for hunting were stabled at Leicester Abbey.[19] Although the Chapter of the Augustinian Order which met at Leicester in 1346 decreed that hunting dogs were not to be kept by the monks, defeat of such a measure was immediately admitted by the addition of a provisory clause which stated that if hounds should be kept, they were at least to be excluded from the refectory! [20]

Chaucer's Monk, then, through his delight in hunting, is a perfect subject for satire. He is the complete hunter, the "prikasour aright": all his pleasure lies in tracking ("prikyng") and hunting the hare, for which he will spare no cost. He keeps greyhounds, as swift as birds in flight, and many valuable ("deyntee") horses; even the horse he has chosen to ride to Canterbury is a sleek and shining palfrey, as brown as a berry, and probably one of his hunters.[21] And the Monk, whose name we later learn to be Dan Piers,[22] has seen to it that his handsome mount is fittingly caparisoned for the journey: Dan Piers is the only one of Chaucer's pilgrims to have the famous "Canterbury bells" attached to his horse's bridle, those little bells which during the Middle Ages tinkled loudly on so many horses picking their muddy way along the Kentish roads, and which gave a popular name to the pink and white and mauve flowers of their exact shape that sway in summer gardens today. The artist of the Ellesmere MS. has given the Monk an aristocratic palfrey whose trappings are decorated with gilt (or gold) bells, and has shown the sporting greyhounds wearing obviously expensive blue and gold collars.

Dan Piers, however, is a subject for satire not only as an "outridere" and a hunter, but as a lover of all creature comforts.

I seigh his sleves purfiled* at the hond
With grys, and that the fyneste of a lond;
And, for to festne his hood under his chyn,
He hadde of gold ywroght a ful curious* pyn;
A love-knotte in the gretter ende ther was.
His heed was balled, that shoon as any glas,
And eek his face, as he hadde been enoynt.
He was a lord ful fat and in good poynt;
His eyen stepe, and rollynge in his heed,
That stemed as a forneys of a leed;
His bootes souple, his hors in greet estaat.
Now certeinly he was a fair prelaat;
He was nat pale as a forpyned* goost.
A fat swan loved he best of any roost.

(ll. 193–206)

One fourteenth-century homiletic writer complains that the prelates of his time feel themselves to be as far above simple curates and priests "as kynges above the comen peple." When one of these self-important and self-satisfied men of the Church rides out, his palfrey is worth a "20 or 30 pound" and is all "bihangid with glit-erynge gold as though it were an hooli hors" (the preacher is evidently familiar with sanctified horses!), while he himself is clad in "fyne scarlet or other cloth as good as that, and withynne with as good pelure as the quene hath any in hire gowne . . ." The writer disgustedly concludes, "God, for his endeles merci, make of hem [such prelates] sone an ende!" [23]

The Lollards are indefatigable in their attack upon the "gaye pellure" and "precious clothis" of the clergy, and the "delicat mete and drynk" these men demand.[24] The strictly orthodox are no less severe. Gower, for example, complains:

The monk of the present day wears a habit which is a beautiful adornment to the body, and for vain honour he is clad in a furred cloak. Let the monk be filled with consternation who makes himself handsome for the world, who wears the finest wool furred with costly grey squirrel [25] rather than a hair shirt! [26]

* purfiled: "bordered," or "trimmed"
  curious: "elaborate"
  forpyned: "wasted away"

The same complaint appears in the early fifteenth-century *Dives and Pauper:*

> To them that have the benefices and the goods of Holy Church, it longeth principally to give almesse and to have cure of the poor people. . . . Therefore these men of Holy Church that boocle their shone with boocles of silver, and use great silver harneys in their girdles and knyves, and men of Religion, monks and chanones, and such other, that . . . ride on high horses with saddles harnessed with gold and silver more pompously than lords, be strong thieves and do great sacrilege, so spending the goods of Holy Church in vanity and pride [and] in lust of the flesh, by which goods the poor should live. A lady of a thousand mark by year can pin her hood against the wind with a small pin of laton; xii for a penny. But a monk that is bounden to poverty by his profession will have an ouche or a broche of gold and silver, in value of a noble or much more.[27]

Several contemporary Political Poems, written for the common folk, denounce the monk of the times in much the same way, as, for example, the *Complaint of the Ploughman*: (The *pellican* and the *griffon* are arguing about the clergy.)

> The griffon began for to threte,
> And saied: "Of monkes canst thou ought?"
> The pellican said: "They been full grete,
> "And in this world much wo hath wrought.
> "Saint Benet, that her order brought,
> "Ne made hem never on such manere:
> "I trowe it came never in his thought,
> "That they should use so great powere.
>
> "That a man should a monke lord call,
> "Ne serve on knees, as a king;
> "He is as proud as prince in pall,
> "In meat, and drinke, and all thing.
> "Some wearen mitre and ring,
> "With double worsted well ydight,
> "With royall meat and rich drinke,
> "And rideth on a courser as a knight,
>
> "With hauke and with hounds eke,
> "With brooches or ouches on his hood.
> "Sume say no masse in all a week,

"Of deinties is her most food.
"They have lordships and bondmen;
"This is a royall religion;
"Saint Benet made never none of hem
"To have lorshipe of man ne toun.

"Now they ben queint and curious,
"With fine cloth clad, and served cleane:
"Proud, angrie, and envious;
"Mallice is much that they meane.
"In catching, craftie and covetous,
"Lordly they liven in great liking;
"This living is not religious,
"According to Benet in his living." [28]

Dan Piers is as true to type in his costume as in his habits. The trimming on his sleeves is "grys" (grey squirrel), a fur expressly forbidden to monks; [29] and the intricate love-knot of gold, which fastens his hood under his chin is the sheerest and most extravagant vanity, for any inexpensive pin would do for utilitarian purposes. The Monk's boots are highly inappropriate to his calling and are a sign of sinful worldliness: soft, unwrinkled ("souple") boots were expensive and only for the gentleman of the court. One thirteenth-century writer in criticizing the appearance of an exceedingly worldly abbot says: "He wore boots so smoothly stretched without crease, it was as if he had been born with them." [30] From the top of his shining bald head to the tips of his luxuriously shod feet, Dan Piers is certainly, as Chaucer says, "a fair prelaat." The face glistening as if it were anointed, the prominent ("stepe") eyes, rolling in his head and gleaming like a furnace under a cauldron ("stemed as a forneys of a leed"),[31] the well-fed body in good condition ("in good poynt"), so unlike that of a gaunt ascetic—all seem to express the hedonist and the Sybarite. And how natural that such a lover of pleasure and luxury should be especially fond of the delights of the table!

Dan Piers enjoys a plump swan, an expensive [32] and greatly prized dish, which he considers the best of any roast. Unquestionably the Monk belongs to that paradise of worldly monks, the Land of Cokaygne. There are to be had without toil or trouble delectable meats and drinks. The monks in Cokaygne have only to sit in their abbey, the walls of which are choicest pasties, the shingles "fluren cakes," and the pinnacles fat puddings fit for a king, to be fed by roasted geese cooked in garlic—geese which fly, still upon their spits, uttering cries of " 'gees al hote, al hot!' ", straight to the refectory tables! [33]

Chaucer's Monk is in truth a "fair for the maistrie," a "manly man," a "lord," a "prikasour aright," a "fair prelaat." He is fit to be an abbot of some great monastic house, and he has already attained the position of prior ("kepere") of some "celle," or smaller, dependent monastery.

It seems almost as if we might identify the Monk. Manly speaks of him as follows:

As to the Monk, although Chaucer completely threw over the one described in the *Prologue* and substituted for him [in the *Tales*] a gloomy and uninteresting person, who retains nothing of the original brilliant figure except the horse with its jingling bells, he seems to me real—drawn from a living model. Perhaps he was too real. Perhaps he or some powerful friend of his read the sketch in the *Prologue* and suggested to Chaucer that it was unmistakable and undesired.[34]

Miss Ramona Bressie may almost be said to support Manly's theory, for she writes to show that Chaucer might possibly have had in mind as model William de Cloune, Abbot of Leicester from 1345 until his death in 1378.[35] Miss Bressie points out that Cloune is the only "hunting monk" specified in known records, in spite of the fact that hunting monks were so very common in the fourteenth century. She cites Knighton, who says in his *Chronicon* that Cloune was " 'the most famous and notable hunter of hares among all the lords of the realm, so that the King himself [Edward III], his son Prince Edward, and many lords of the realm were bound under a yearly pension to hunt with him.' " [36] When Edward III in 1363 had three royal guests, the kings of France, Scotland, and Peter of Cyprus,[37] the park and stables at Leicester were put in order at the expense of the Crown, which indicates, indeed, that Cloune was at that time "a fair for the maistrie." John of Gaunt was yet another patron of Leicester Abbey.

Miss Bressie suggests that the fact that Leicester Abbey was a house of Augustinian Canons instead of Benedictine monks is relatively unimportant. The difference between a canon regular and a monk in the later Middle Ages was so slight that the terms were almost interchangeable.[38] Furthermore, there would have been special point to a veiled reference to Leicester Abbey for Chaucer's audience: during Richard II's reign an attempt was made to place the house under stricter rule, apparently without great success;[39] and there is at least enough of Cloune in Chaucer's Dan Piers to excite reminiscence.[40]

NOTES

(The abbreviations used to designate books and articles mentioned in the Notes will be found listed alphabetically in the Bibliography, opposite the full reference. References to lines in the *Canterbury Tales* are given by fragment and line numbers only.)

1. VII 63–65 (B[2] 1253–1255).
2. Coulton, *Med. Pan.*, p. 269.
3. *Rule of St. Benedict,* Chap. XLVIII.
4. *Ibid.,* Chap. LXVI.
5. Coulton, *Life in Mid. Ages,* IV, 33–34. (Taken from *Seventeen Short Treatises of St. Augustine*—pp. 470 ff.—as translated in the *Library of Fathers,* Oxford, 1847.)
6. Langland ascribes the comparison to the writings of Gregory I (seventh century), but Skeat remarks in his note to Langland's line (*Piers Plow.,* II, 67): "it would be no easy task to find the passage referred to." Skeat suggests a number of possible sources; but for such a commonplace, the source seems to be hardly important.
7. *Piers Plow.,* C. Passus VI. 147–152.
8. Gower, *Mirour,* ll. 20845 ff.
9. Gower, *Vox. Clam.,* Lib. IV, 281–282.
10. Matthew, p. 449.
11. There are many examples of this meaning of the word *recchelees.* Emerson (*MP,* I, 111 ff.) notes that OE *receleas* in the Corpus Gloss translates Latin *praevaricator,* a word meaning "one who violates his duty," and that the word is used in a similar sense in the Alfredian *Boethius* and in the Alfredian *Bede.* Emerson adds that the Middle English uses of the word follow those of Old English. Cf. the *Cursor Mundi:*

> I ha bene reckeles on many wys
> Anentis Crist and his servise . . .

Chaucer himself explains his meaning of *recchelees* when he writes parenthetically, "That is to seyn, a monk out of his cloystre."

12. According to Skeat (V, 21) a "pulled," or plucked, hen was of little value.
13. Emerson, *MP,* I, 106.
14. *Ibid.* Emerson quotes from the *Decreta Pars Prima,* C. XI, as follows: "Sperabo in Domino. Esau venator erat, quoniam peccator erat. Et penitus non invenimus, in Scripturis sanctis, sanctum aliquem venatorem; piscatores

invenimus sanctos." Nimrod is mentioned as well as Esau in this decretal, although not specifically in connection with the "sin" of hunting, but with tyranny and other vices. Skeat suggests (V, 21) that Chaucer had the legend of Nimrod in mind, and Flügel argues strongly (*JEGP*, I, 126–133) for the Nimrod tradition. As Willard (Texas *St. in Eng.*, 1947, pp. 209–251) points out, however, Nimrod and Esau are closely associated in both Christian and Rabbinical literature, and the mention of the one man almost implies the inclusion of the other in any context involving hunting.

15. Willard, *loc. cit.*, pp. 209–251. Willard says (pp. 224 ff.) the origin of the belief that hunting was sinful lies in the fact that *venator* originally meant "killer of beasts in an arena": the *venator* was classed with chariot racers, actors, and public women, and was considered "sinful" because he provided only delights of the flesh. This entertainer in time became confused with the hunter of game, and *venator* was so translated. Willard also points out that the tie between sin and hunting was strengthened by the Mosaic injunction, "Thou shalt not kill." (P. 242.)

16. Matthew, p. 151.

17. *Piers Plow.*, C. Passus VI. 156–161.

18. Gower, *Mirour*, ll. 20953–20966, 21044–21048.

19. Bressie, *MLN*, LIV, 483.

20. *Ibid.*, p. 481.

21. Karkeek says (p. 494): "Palfreys were commonly used for journeys, and also for hunting."

22. VII 2792 (B² 3982).

23. Owst, *Lit. and Pulpit*, pp. 283 f. (Taken from MS. Add. 41321, fols. 17–17b and 100–1.)

24. Matthew, pp. 148–149, 123.

25. Skeat says (V, 23) that *grys* (Gower's *gris*) was much prized and very expensive in the Middle Ages. He quotes from Lydgate's "Dance of Macabre" where the Cardinal regrets that

'. . . I shal never hereafter clothed be
In grise nor ermine, like unto my degree.'

26. Gower, *Mirour*, ll. 20995–20997, 21014–21019.

27. *Dives and Pauper*, Com. VII, c. 12, as quoted by Coulton, *Med. Pan.*, p. 273.

28. Wright's *Political Poems*, I, 334.

29. Coulton, *Med. Pan.*, p. 274.

30. Skeat quotes (V, 24) from Tyrwhitt, who in turn quotes from the MS. as follows: "Ocreas habebat in cruribus quasi innatae essent, sine plica porrectas."

31. *NED*, "Lead" and "Steam."

32. The cost of a swan was four times that of a pheasant and about three times that of a chicken (Bressie, *loc. cit.*, p. 488).

33. *Land of Cockaygne*, pp. 156–161.

34. Manly, *New Light*, pp. 261 f.

35. Bressie, *loc. cit.*, pp. 477–490.

36. *Ibid.*, p. 477.

37. It seems a significant fact that Peter of Cyprus, having visited Leicester Abbey when Cloune was abbot, is made the subject of one of Dan Piers's "modern" tragedies some twenty-five years later.

38. *NED*, "Canon."

39. Bressie, *loc. cit.*, p. 489. As late as 1439 there were greyhounds, "a great crowd of useless hounds," kept at Leicester Abbey.

40. Miss Bressie says (*loc. cit.*, pp. 489 f.) that if Cloune were the only "hunter of hares" honoured with the King's patronage, Chaucer's Monk "would inevitably recall" Cloune for members of court circles, and that the opulent worldliness of the Monk would be a reminder in every respect of the actual abbot.

Tatlock (*MLN*, LV, 350–54) takes issue in general with traditional views about the Monk, and in particular with points raised by Manly and by Miss Bressie. He claims that Chaucer painted the portrait without sarcasm, and that the Monk of the *Prologue* is no different from the Monk of the *Tales*. Tatlock says that the Monk is a Benedictine, and since he mentions St. Edward the Confessor in his own *Prologue* (VII 1970—B² 3160), a saint not "specially prominent" in the fourteenth century, the Monk is marked as of the Benedictine Order established at Westminster by St. Edward. Tatlock states further that no one in the Middle Ages would use the term "monk" of an Augustinian Canon, and later points out (*MLN*, LVI, 80) that Chaucer himself distinguished between "monk" and "canon." Kuhl (*MLN*, LV, 480) disagrees with Tatlock; he says that St. Edward was very well known in the fourteenth century, and that there was little or no difference between "monk" and "canon," giving evidence to support his contentions. Miss Bressie replies (*MLN*, LVI, 161–162) to Tatlock partially as follows: ". . . the Benedictines, so far as is known, enforced living in cloister,—unlike the Augustinians, who notoriously occupied the monastery manors and granges as country-residences which were colloquially known as cells, while the monk in charge was called *custos* or keeper. . . . Westminster Abbey is not known to have had any cells that were not regularly constituted priories, so that if the Monk were 'prelate' of one of them . . . his house would be his own priory, not Westminster Abbey, and, residing in his cell as his duty required, he could not be regarded as living out of cloister."

On the whole, except for the fact that Chaucer does distinguish between "canon" and "monk" in the *Tales*, Tatlock's argument should probably be disregarded.

CHAPTER VII

THE WORTHY FRIAR

A Frere ther was, a wantowne and a merye,
A lymytour, a ful solempne man.
In alle the ordres foure is noon that kan
So muchel of daliaunce and fair langage.

.   .   .   .   *

This worthy lymytour was cleped Huberd.

(ll. 208–211, 269)

THE FRIAR is one of the most strongly individualized figures
Chaucer introduces to us; he is also one of the most typical. Aside
from the Prioress, whose flower-like name may have been chosen
for her merely because it seemed appropriate, Brother Hubert is the
only one of the pilgrims at the Tabard who is named in the *General
Prologue*. Since the name is not a common one in English records of
the time,[1] and since there is nothing in "Hubert" to suggest the
Friar's nature, Chaucer's reason for naming him so early may have
been to identify this friar to the immediate audience, or to convey
some timely allusion. Hubert, wanton,[2] merry and pompous,[3] may
have been an actual man known to the poet and his friends; he is
also the perfect epitome of friars as a class.

To understand fully any friar of the fourteenth century, it is necessary for us today to turn to the beginnings of the Mendicant Orders, almost two hundred years before Chaucer's time. When
Chaucer was writing, four great orders of friars had long been established in England. The friars were at first religious men who were
dedicated to active service in the world, in contradistinction to the
monks, who were dedicated to cloistered contemplation. The Dominicans, founded by St. Dominic in Spain in the early thirteenth
century, were the first in England, coming there in the year 1221.
Because they were organized primarily to combat heresy through
preaching, the Dominicans were often called the Preaching Friars;
they were also sometimes called either Black Friars, because of their

garb, or Jacobins, because of the situation of a House of theirs in Paris on the Rue St. Jacques. The Franciscans, founded by St. Francis in Italy about the same time as the Dominicans, came to England in the year 1224. Because St. Francis placed great emphasis on humility and poverty, the Franciscans were often called the Minor Friars or Minorites; they were also sometimes called Grey Friars, because of their garb. The third Order of friars to come to England was that of the Carmelites, or White Friars, in 1245; the Carmelites laid pretentious claims to having been instituted by Elijah, but their rule was not formulated until the thirteenth century. Finally, the Augustine or Austin Friars established themselves in England some time after 1256 when they were formally organized; the Austin Friars said their true founder was the fifth-century St. Augustine of Hippo. But by the fourteenth century, any one of these four Orders differed from any other only in name and dress, for all had come to be dominated, at least in what they professed, by the ideals of St. Francis, and all were classed together as "Mendicants" because they theoretically "begged" their support from the world. The Rules of the Carmelites and Austin Friars were modelled on the Franciscan; even the powerful and learned Dominicans were now following a Rule which was in spirit like the others.[4] Consequently, the woeful and terrible descent from grace of all four Orders becomes an essentially Franciscan tragedy, and to examine the history of the Minor Friars is to examine the grievous course of all.

In the year 1209, Francesco Bernadone, a young man of frail health, forsook a life of worldly pleasure in the busy and moneyed town of Assisi, and went forth in his native Italy with a few disciples to preach among the destitute. The first months would have disheartened a lesser man, for Francis, like the Great Teacher in whose footsteps he trod, was despised, reviled, and rejected by many; but the gentleness of his soul, combined with the magnificent strength of his sincerity, soon formed a light that shone in radiance before all men. In less than a year, whole cities were hastening to hear this man, this saint who burned steadfastly with the one purpose of living in exact accordance with the teaching of Christ. The white fire of St. Francis's concentrated passion blazed across a rich and cynical world; men who were weary and dismayed caught the re-born vision of hard, yet glad, regeneration. They thronged to join the followers of this new apostle of Our Lord, an apostle whose sole armament was love of God and Man. Here was a Christianity stripped bare of the falsity and ornateness in which it had been robed by wealthy, ambitious prelate and scheming Pope: men once more might embrace humility and compassion and tread the straight highway of God.

Towards the middle of the thirteenth century, Matthew Paris, who is unbiased for his time, and who is called by Dr. Coulton "the greatest historian between the fall of Rome and the Renaissance," [5] pays this tribute to the early Franciscans:

At about this time [1206], the preachers who are called Minors . . . suddenly emerged and filled the earth. Dwelling by tens or by sevens in cities and in towns, owning nothing whatever, living according to the Gospel, preferring the utmost poverty in food and clothing, walking unshod, they showed the greatest example of humility to all men. . . . The Minors were discovered to be as much the more clear-sighted in their contemplation of heavenly matters as they were alien to earthly matters and to carnal pleasures. They keep no kind of food in reserve for themselves, in order that the spiritual poverty which thrives in their minds may be made known to all through their deeds and their way of life. [6]

Thomas of Eccleston also testifies to the excellence and simplicity of the early English Franciscans. Eccleston's *Tractate* is composed of accounts of individual friars, in which they are extolled for their piety, their holy disregard of bodily comforts, their good deeds, and their sweet humility. No complicated rules were necessary then, for the brothers possessed an inward urge to live according to the simple code formulated by St. Francis. [7] And, indeed, the earliest Rule of St. Francis was comprehended in three brief sentences: "If thou wilt be perfect, go and sell all that thou hast and give to the poor"; "Take nothing for your journey"; and "If any man will come after Me, let him deny himself, and take up his cross and follow Me." [8]

But heart-sickening decay set in with even the second generation of friars. These men had not known the inspiring founders, and so were without the burning desire to strive after the unattainable. Furthermore, the intricate realities of a sophisticated social system made absolute poverty impossible, and begging, which St. Francis had permitted only as a necessity, [9] became the exceedingly profitable business of the Order. The Rules increased in number and detail, and obedience to them ceased to be spontaneous as the letter came more and more to outweigh the spirit. Also the Pope, although St. Francis himself had sought from the Vicar of Christ only a blessing and a permission for the new Order to preach the Word of God, now observed a new army extraordinarily well adapted to be pressed into service as tax-gatherers and emissaries of Rome, and began to so employ the Mendicants.[10] As early as 1243, Matthew Paris writes in sadness:

. . . The monastic order did not hasten to destruction so quickly as their [i.e., the friars'] order, of whom, now, the brothers (twenty-four years having scarcely elapsed) had first built in England dwellings which rivalled regal palaces in height. These are they who daily expose to view their inestimable treasures in enlarging their sumptuous edifices, and erecting lofty walls, thereby impudently transgressing the limits of their original poverty, and violating the basis of their religion . . . Desirous of obtaining privileges in the courts of kings and potentates, they act the parts of councillors, chamberlains, treasurers, bridegrooms, and mediators for marriages; they are the executors of the papal extortions; in their sermons, they either are flatterers or most cutting reprovers, revealers of confessions, or imprudent accusers.[11]

The hundred years and more which were to elapse before Chaucer wrote of Brother Hubert saw no lessening of the evils that surrounded the Orders, and it is a safe generalization to say that every fourteenth-century writer who is not himself a friar attacks the Mendicants. As will presently be noted in more detail, Wyclif and his followers hurl violent invective against them in sermon, exegesis, and controversial tract; the orthodox Gower is no less vehement in what he has to say; Langland, writing for the more popular taste, boldly inveighs against the flagrant sins of the brothers; while the anonymous authors of the so-called Political Poems of the time loudly express the contempt and hatred felt by the common people for the Mendicant Orders. "These friars are truly the sons of Cain!" is the cry, for

> Nou se the sothe whedre it be swa,
> That frer Carmes come of a k.,*
> The frer Austynes come of a.,
> Frer Jacobynes of i.,

* *come of:* "derived from" (the letters *k, a, i, m* were thought of as spelling *Cain,* which to anyone in the Middle Ages had the greatest significance)

Of m. comen the frer Menours;
Thus grounded Caym thes four ordours,
That fillen the world ful of errours,
    And of ypocrisy.
Alle wyckednes that men can telle
    regnes ham among;
Ther shal no saule have rowme in helle,
    of frers ther is suche throng.[12]

And Gower, the good churchman, says, "It is useless for these evil
friars to plead the virtues of Francis when they do not follow him in
any respect. Although the brethren may differ from each other in
their dress, all are alike in neglect of their Rule." [13]

But, we may well ask, if awareness of corruption was so universal,
why did not every man arise in his wrath and refuse to tolerate these
known cheats and extortioners, these wily flatterers and despoilers
of women? Probably there are three answers of importance to this
question. First, there were undoubtedly many friars who did strive
to uphold the ideals of their founders, and thus compensated in part
for the sinful majority. We have only to call to witness the gentle
Thomas de Hales, the learned Roger Bacon, the philosophical John
Duns Scotus, and the rigorously moral Bromyard of Chaucer's own
time, to realize that not all friars were evil.[14] Second, the memory
of the great tradition of St. Francis was still alive,[15] and most men
would not bring themselves to acknowledge that the glory had
dimmed so quickly. And third, medieval man, always obsessed by the
stark fear of an eternal Hell and of a Satan agog to receive his soul,
was loath to relinquish any chance of salvation. Friars, who had once
been true guides to Heaven, might still possess some remnant of
power to point the Way. Friars, then, were suffered to walk the earth,
and there were literally thousands of them [16] in fourteenth-century
England, thousands whose guile and covetousness prompted them
to meddle everywhere in every matter. Thus Chaucer's Summoner
utters a commonplace when he says in his first sputtering anger
against Brother Hubert:

A frere wol entremette hym everemo,
Lo, goode men, a flye and eek a frere
Wol falle in every dyssh and eek mateere! [17]

Brother Hubert, however, has his own special dishes and matters in which to emulate the ubiquitous fly: he is a "lymytour." A *limiter* signified in the fourteenth century a begging friar to whom was assigned a certain district or *limit* within which he had the right, sometimes the sole right, to solicit alms.[18]

> . . . He yaf a certeyn ferme for the graunt;
> Noon of his bretheren cam ther in his haunt.[19]
>
> (ll. 252ᵃ–252ᵇ)

Chaucer's Hubert pays rent ("ferme") for the exclusive begging rights in his district. Friars who were limiters evidently found it a profitable business. The Wife of Bath casually satirizes them in her *Tale* when she says that women need no longer fear the dangers of fairy enchantment under "every bussh," for the only peril to be found there nowadays is mere dishonour by the "lymytour";[20] and Gower[21] and Langland[22] both speak in familiar disparagement of limiters. All three authors, Chaucer, Gower, and Langland, stress the limiters' immoral relations with women, and Brother Hubert is, of course, no exception. He is notorious for his seduction of the young girls of his "limit":

> He hadde maad ful many a mariage
> Of yonge wommen at his owene cost.
>
> (ll. 212–213)

The findings of the late Karl Young support those of a number of other scholars[23] in the interpretation of these two lines to mean that the Friar has found husbands or dowries for the many young women who have been his concubines. Young quotes from an unpublished memorandum of 1321, taken from the register of the bishop of Bath and Wells: a certain priest was charged with breaking a promise to provide a dowry for a girl by whom he had had two children; the priest denied the pledge but acknowledged the children; "after some wrangling," the priest agreed to the bishop's ruling that he contribute a sum of money towards the girl's suitable marriage.[24] Skeat's quotation from a sixteenth-century source is still to the point: "an holy father prior" piously thanks God that the mothers of his children have never been married women, but maidens, "the faireste cowlde be gottyn," and that he always saw to it afterwards that they were married "right well"![25]

Not only young girls, but wives, too, must guard their virtue against Hubert, who knows how to insinuate himself into every household with his gossip and flattery ("daliaunce and fair langage"), his presents and jollity.

> His typet was ay farsed* ful of knyves
> And pynnes, for to yeven faire wyves.
> And certeinly he hadde a murye note:
> Wel koude he synge and pleyen on a rote;
> Of yeddynges he baar outrely the pris.
> His nekke whit was as the flour-de-lys;
> Therto he strong was as a champioun.
>
> .   .   .   .
>
> Somwhat he lipsed, for his wantownesse,
> To make his Englissh sweete upon his tonge;
> And in his harpying, whan that he hadde songe,
> His eyen twynkled in his heed aryght,
> As doon the sterres in the frosty nyght.
>
> (ll. 233–239, 264–268)

Hubert is aware just what trinkets are dear to the feminine heart, for his "typet" is always full of them. A "typet" was a long, narrow strip of cloth, either attached at one end to the hood or sleeve, or hanging loose as a scarf; it might also be a cape with hanging ends.[26] Hubert's typet was probably of the first variety and must have been of two thicknesses since he employs it as an elongated pouch. Short knives with ornamented handles were greatly prized by women in the Middle Ages, and it was the ambition of every wife to wear a pair of them in a sheath suspended from her girdle.[27] Pins were admired by everyone; even the Prioress, as we have observed, has her "brooch of gold ful sheene," and the Monk his "ful curious pyn." If we are to believe the Political Songs, Hubert is not at all unusual in gathering together such tempting wares, for the typical friar seems to have done just that. The bitterly satiric "Song Against the Friars" speaks of this evil dealing on the part of the Mendicants as follows:

> Thai dele with purses, pynnes, and knyves,
> With gyrdles, gloves, for wenches and wyves;

* *farsed:* "stuffed"

> Bot ever bacward the husband thryves
>> Ther thai are haunted tille.*
> For when the gode man is fro hame,
> And the frere comes to oure dame,
> He spares nauther for synne ne shame,
>> That he ne dos his wille.
> If thai no helpe of houswyves had,
>> when husbandes are not inne,
> The freres welfare were ful bad,
>> for thai shuld brewe ful thynne.** 28

Simple country women were easily bemused by these glittering gifts from friars, especially if the giver possessed such fascinating accomplishments as Brother Hubert. He delights his listeners with a deeply pleasant tone ("a murye note") when he sings to the accompaniment of his "rote," a medieval stringed instrument plucked somewhat as a lute.[29] Does he not merit the prize for his "yeddynges," or popular songs? Furthermore, Hubert is a fine figure of a man: he has the strength of the athletic champion,[30] and a neck as white as the fleur-de-lys. This last detail may have been added by Chaucer either to contrast humorously with Hubert's strength, or to suggest the softness of his living.[31] Hubert's mannerism *** of lisping, "to make his Englissh sweete upon his tonge," [32] of course also attracts the women of his wide acquaintance, upon whom he looks too long with eyes that twinkle as do the stars "in the frosty nyght."

But in what glaring contrast to Hubert and others of his sort was the luminous purity of St. Francis, the ideal friar! St. Bonaventura, personal friend, disciple, and biographer of St. Francis, writes of the latter as follows:

And not only did he teach that the appetites of the body must be mortified, and its impulses bridled, but also that the outer senses, through the which death entereth into the soul, must be guarded with the utmost watchfulness. He bade that intimate intercourse with women, holding converse with them, and looking upon them—the which be unto many an occasion of falling—should be zealously shunned, declaring that by such things a weak spirit is broken, and a

---

* *ther thai are haunted tille:* "where they are accustomed to go"
** Friars would "brew thin," that is, would find little success, if housewives did not aid and abet them in the husband's absence.
*** *for his wantownesse* (l. 264): "as an affectation"

strong one ofttimes weakened. . . . He himself so turned away his eyes that they might not behold vanity after this sort that he knew the features of scarce any woman—thus he once told a companion. For he thought it was not safe to dwell on the appearance of their persons, that might either rekindle a spark in the vanquished flesh, or spot the radiance of a chaste mind. For he maintained that converse with women was a vain toy, except only for confession or the briefest instruction, such as made for salvation, and was in accord with decorum. . . . He was minded that a Gospel silence should be observed by the brethren, such as, to wit, that they should at all times diligently refrain from every idle word, as those that shall give account thereof in the Day of Judgment. But if he found any Brother prone unto vain words, he would sharply chide him, declaring a shamefast sparingness of speech to be the guard of a pure heart, and no small virtue . . .

But albeit he sought with all his might to lead the Brethren unto the austere life, yet the utmost rigour of severity pleased him not—such rigour hath no bowels of compassion, nor is flavoured with the salt of discretion. . . .[33]

Wyclif and his followers, fully aware of the spectacular difference between the early friars and those of the fourteenth century, cry out strongly against the lechery of the brethren. One Lollard writes, for example, that whenever husbands are away friars visit the house, and lead astray the wives and daughters for adulterous pleasure; friars become pedlars, bearing knives, purses, pins and girdles and such vanities—all to get the carnal love of women.[34] And the same author complains that friars spend the time which should be devoted to the service of God in "veyn songis" accompanied by the over-artificial music of the harp or guitar, in order to attract the evil love of "damyselis."[35]

Gower attacks the friars for their immoral relations with women in the higher walks of life. He says that he advises all jealous lovers to think about forbidding their wives to confess to limiters, for these Mendicants corrupt the young and beautiful among their penitents, and the husband must then pass for the father of the ill-begotten children.[36] Gower writes that the ubiquitous friar will always seek out the bed of an absent husband: the confessor becomes the seducer, the friar, who should be the messenger of God, is an emissary of the devil.[37]

Those sins of the flesh in which the Mendicants so freely indulged were combined with sins of the spirit. Here again Hubert is no exception.

> He knew the tavernes wel in every toun
> And everich hostiler and tappestere
> Bet than a lazar or a beggestere;
> For unto swich a worthy man as he
> Acorded nat, as by his facultee,
> To have with sike lazars aqueyntaunce.
> It is nat honest, it may nat avaunce,
> For to deelen with no swich poraille,
> But al with riche and selleres of vitaille.
> And over al, ther as profit sholde arise,
> Curteis he was and lowely of servyse.
>
> (ll. 240–250)

Thus from his excellent knowledge of taverns everywhere, Hubert is more familiar with the innkeeper and barmaid ("tappestere") than with any leper ("lazar") or beggarmaid ("beggestere"). Indeed, says Chaucer with fine sarcasm, it is not suitable to the profession ("facultee") of a man of such high standing that he have acquaintance with sick lepers; it is inappropriate ("nat honest") and will not further his interests to consort with such poor rabble. But with the rich and the provision dealers, in fact with anyone through whom profit to himself may result, Hubert becomes the essence of chivalry; like the Knight's son, the Friar is then "curteis" and "lowely of servyse"!

As a contrast, let us turn again to the teachings of St. Francis himself. St. Bonaventura writes:

> Furthermore, he taught, as he had learnt by revelation, that the entrance into holy Religion must be made through that saying of the Gospel, "If thou wilt be perfect, go and sell that thou hast, and give to the poor"; and accordingly he would admit none into the Order that had not dispossessed themselves, keeping absolutely naught back, both because of the saying of the Holy Gospel, and that there might be no treasure-chests laid up to cause scandal.[38]

Moreover, St. Francis sought out the sick, and made them his special care. Again St. Bonaventura says:

> From that time forth, he put on the spirit of poverty, the feeling of humility, and the love of inward godliness. For whereas aforetime

not only the company, but even the distant sight, of lepers had inspired him with violent loathing, now, for the sake of Christ Crucified—Who, saith the prophet, appeared despised and marred as a leper—and that he might fully vanquish self, he would render unto the lepers humble and kindly services in his benevolent goodness. For he would often visit their dwellings, and bestow alms upon them with a bountiful hand, and with a deep impulse of pity would kiss their hands and faces.[39]

And again:

Thence that lover of utterest humility betook himself unto the lepers, and abode among them, with all diligence serving them all for the love of God. He would bathe their feet, and bind up their sores, drawing forth the corrupt matter from their wounds, and wiping away the blood . . . .[40]

And in the *Little Flowers of St. Francis*, which is illumined by the true spirit of the saint (although it was compiled at a much later date than St. Bonaventura's *Life of St. Francis*, and is made up of "memories of memories" [41]), we find once more the same tender attitude described: "And he not only served lepers gladly, but had also ordained that the friars of his Order, as they went about the world, should serve lepers for the love of Christ, who for our sakes was willing to be accounted a leper." [42]

The Lollards, naturally, were not silent about the contemporary friars' neglect of the poor and sick who cannot "advance" them in any worldly sense; one Lollard complains, for example:

. . . freris feynen hom, as ypocritis, to kepe straytly tho gospel and povert of Crist and his apostils; and yitt thei moste contrarien to Crist and his apostils in ypocrisie, pride, and coveitise. . . . In covetise thei con nevere make an ende, . . . cryen evere after worldly godis, where Crist usid none of alle these. And thus for this stynkynge covetise thei worschippen tho fend as hor God.[43]

The orthodox Gower, again in agreement with the Wyclifites, writes:

The friars preach of poverty yet they always have an open hand to receive riches. They have perverted their Order from within by their covetousness. They wish ease, but they will not labour—in no case do they do their duty.[44]

For Brother Hubert, however, the poor have to be very poor indeed in order that he pass them by entirely; anyone who has a penny or two is a prey to his cupidity.

> Ther nas no man nowher so vertuous,
> He was the beste beggere in his hous;
> For thogh a wydwe hadde noght a sho,
> So plesaunt was his *"In principio,"*
> Yet wolde he have a ferthyng, er he went,
> His purchas was wel bettre than his rente.
> And rage he koude, as it were right a whelp.
>
> (ll. 251–257)

Thus Chaucer labels the Friar as the "beste beggere" in his Order—nowhere is any man more capable ("vertuous"). For even if a poor widow has not a shoe to her name, so pleasantly persuasive is Hubert's quotation from the Gospel that he will have a farthing from her before he goes. He has craftily selected words to recite that are held in superstitious awe by his contemporaries. *In principio* may be said to be the "title" of the first fourteen verses of the first chapter of the Gospel according to St. John, and, as Professor Robert Law points out, since the Middle Ages regarded these verses as a charm against all evils, friars probably used them as a "favourite devotion," not as a greeting, and that very likely all fourteen verses were recited.[45] Certainly it would be unlike our Brother Hubert to omit as much as a syllable of such a potently lucrative "devotion"!

Professor Law, in investigating the extent to which *In principio* was employed, quotes Tyndale as speaking in 1530 of *In principio erat verbum* as "the limiter's saying," and reminds us that the political poem, "Jacke Upland," written only a year after Chaucer's death, attacks the friars on "winning" more than they should by this magical recitation:

> For ye win more by yeare
> with *In principio,*
> than with all the rules
> that ever your patrones made.[46]

Professor Law has found several more references to *In principio* in medieval literature to support his contention that the passage from St. John was frequently adopted, especially by friars; and he calls our attention to the fact that these fourteen verses are still imporant in the modern Church.[47] No wonder that Chaucer uses the proverbial expression [48] about the Friar's illegal takings ("purchas") far exceeding his legal gains ("rente")! [49]

But the enterprising Hubert has even better means of acquiring money than by his hypocritical "devotion," his flattery and his questionable presents of "knyves and pynnes," his captivating music, and a manner which can be as playful as a puppy ("and rage he koude, as it were right a whelp") : he is licensed to hear confessions.

> Unto his ordre he was a noble post.
> Ful wel biloved and famulier was he
> With frankeleyns* over al in his contree,
> And eek with worthy wommen of the toun*;
> For he hadde power of confessioun,
> As seyde hymself, moore than a curat,
> For of his ordre he was licenciat.
> Ful swetely herde he confessioun,
> And plesaunt was his absolucioun:
> He was an esy man to yeve penaunce,
> Ther as he wiste to have a good pitaunce.
> For unto a povre ordre for to yive
> Is signe that a man is wel yshryve;
> For if he yaf, he dorste make avaunt,
> He wiste that a man was repentaunt;
> For many a man so hard is of his herte,
> He may nat wepe, al thogh hym soore smerte.
> Therfore in stede of wepynge and preyeres
> Men moote yeve silver to the povre freres.
>
> (ll. 214–232)

Hubert boasts that he has a greater right to hear confessions than a parish priest; his absolution is pleasant because wherever he knows that there is an allowance of food or a gift ("pitaunce") awaiting him, he is easy in the penance he prescribes. With bold irony, Chaucer ignores the fact that absolution is conditional on contrition, and says that to give to a "povre ordre" is a sign that one is well shriven : the gift is equivalent to repentance. Also many a sinner has

---

* *frankeleyns:* "wealthy landowners" (see Chapter X)

   worthy wommen of the toun: "respectable [or "wealthy"] women living in towns"

so hard a heart, the poet adds, that he is unable to weep no matter how contrite he may be, and silver given to the Mendicants will do as well as tears and prayers!

That friars were licensed to hear confessions was a source of much ecclesiastical controversy in the Middle Ages, and the literature of complaint and satire has much to say on the subject. A papal bull of 1281 had given to the Mendicants unrestricted freedom in preaching and in the hearing of confessions, and had led to "endless friction" and "open quarrels" between the friars and secular clergy.[50] The struggle between these two groups in the matter of confession became so pronounced, writes Dr. Owst, "that it passes into the pages of contemporary literature as a byword of the times"; [51] and he calls our attention to a manuscript of the early fourteenth century which contains a Petition to the Rectors of London against the Mendicants, accusing them of "deluding their audiences into the belief that they possess special authority to give a general absolution beyond anything in the power of an ordinary 'curate'." [52] We might set these quarrels down to nothing more than human jealousy, if the majority of the friars had been godly men and so had possessed the proper qualifications to administer one of the sacraments of the Church; but, alas, as we have seen, friars in general were obviously unfit for this spiritual office, and it was the "curates" who had right on their side.

The medieval Church, like the Church of Rome today, conceived of confession as one of the parts of the Sacrament of Penance. The effect of this sacrament is deliverance from sin, and is wrought in the soul of the penitent, "who with the necessary dispositions must perform certain actions." [53] These actions may be summed up as contrition, confession, and satisfaction. Obviously the parish priest of the fourteenth century was in a far better position to administer the Sacrament of Penance than even a good friar: such a priest knew his flock intimately, he could gauge the sincerity of the penitent and effectively assign a true act of satisfaction as a penance. Between the parish priest and some hypocritical and grasping Brother Hubert without concern for repentance or proper restitution for sin, there could be no comparison.

The bitter Lollard tract entitled "Fifty Heresies and Errors of Friars" expresses indignation against the friars in their abuse of the confessional as follows:

Also freris for pride and covetise drawen fro curatis hor office and sacramentis . . . thei cryen faste that thei haf more power in confessioun then other curatis . . .

Also freris schewen no to tho puple hor grete synnes stably as God biddes, and namely to myghty men of tho worlde, bot flatren hom and glosen and norischen hom in synne. . . . For by flatryng and fals byheestis, thei leten men lyve in hor lustis and counforten hom therinne. . . . And ensaumple men may take, how freris suffren myghty men fro yeere to yeere lif in avowtrie, in covetise, in extorsiouns doyng, and mony other synnes. . . . And thus for tho money thei sellen mennis soulis to Sathanas. . . .

And tho freris, for luf of a litel stinkynge mucke, and wilfare of hor foule bely, sparen to reprove tho cursid synne of tho puple. Ffor comynly if ther be any cursid jurour, extorsioner, or avoutrer, he wil no be schryven at his owne curat, bot go to a flatryng frere, that wil asoyle hym falsely for a litel money by yeere, thof he be not in wille to make restitucioun and leeve his cursid synne. . . .[54]

The Wyclifite author of *Pierce the Plowmans Crede*, that late fourteenth-century diatribe against the Mendicant Orders, writes that the friars are founded now by the devil to destroy faith. Through their cunning they encumber the Church, and though they profess to help the *curati*, now that they have a foothold, friars through their covetousness harm many. They do not follow Dominic, but oppress the people; they do not follow Francis, but live falsely; they consider Austin's Rule to be but an idle story. Friars purchase privileges from Rome and seek after confessions for gain only. They will look at nothing which does not net them a profit.[55]

Although some allowance must be made for Lollard exaggeration, the picture the Wyclifites give us of the friars "represents none the less a very formidable widespread impression," [56] and this is verified by the writings of two of Chaucer's contemporaries, Langland and Gower, both of them sound churchmen, as has been pointed out. Langland leaves us in no doubt as to his attitude, for example, when he says in the allegorical person of Wrath:

I (continually) grafted lying tales upon *limitors* and *lectors,* till they bear leaves of servile speech, to flatter lords with, and afterwards they blossomed abroad in (my lady's) bower to hear confessions. And now there is fallen therefrom a fruit, so that folk would much rather shew their shrifts to *them,* than shrive themselves to their own parsons. And now that the parsons have found out that the friars share (the profits of confession) with them, these *possessioners* preach (to the people) and calumniate the friars, and the friars (on the other hand) find *them* to be in fault. . . . I, Wrath, go with them, and teach them out of my books.[57]

Elsewhere Langland says that only parish priests should shrive the people, for the priests are called "curatoures" for the very reason that it is their duty to know and to heal all those in their charge, to give them penance, and to see that they "shulden be ashamed in her shrifte"; but, Langland continues, these people now run to friars for absolution, for the friars will accept a small sum of money in lieu of penance, and the rest of the money is then spent in riotous living.[58] In the last section of his great poem, Langland warns once more against the friars, for they have wickedly led the people away from their true confessors, and no longer is sin dreaded.[59]

Gower is as emphatic as Langland when he writes on this subject:

A pair of friars go together continually to the end that they may be well increased in this world. They blandish and flatter only to advance sinners. The one is named Friar Hypocrisy, and he confesses my lady; the other is named Friar Flattery, and he absolves her. Hypocrisy is chosen as confessor because he will be kind; then Flattery takes over—he does not speak of sin, for it is not his business to inquire into contrition or to make any investigation: he only asks for money, and assoils without any other penalty. Thus the friar earns his food and raiment: he has the dispensation which accords with the recompense, for he can give remission without trouble or punishment and receive in return the comforts which come from the purses of the rich.[60]

Finally, the Political Poems, always concerned with the immediate questions of the day, give vent to popular indignation against the friar-confessor. The following stanza from the "Song Against the Friars" is typical.

Thai say that thai distroye synne,
And thai mayntene men moste therinne;
For hadde a man slayn al his kynne,
    Go shryve him at a frere,
And for lesse then a payre of shone
He wyl assoil him clene and sone,

And say the synne that he has done
His saule shal never dere.
It semes sothe that men sayne of hayme
in many dyvers londe,
That that caytyfe cursed Cayme
first this order fonde.[61]

In two more ways Chaucer's Hubert represents most of the friars of his time; he is richly clad, and he meddles in secular matters which should not concern him.

In love-dayes ther koude he muchel help,
For ther he was nat lyk a cloysterer
With a thredbare cope, as is a povre scoler,
But he was lyk a maister or a pope.
Of double worstede was his semycope,
That rounded as a belle out of the presse.

(ll. 258–263)

Professor John Webster Spargo has recently made a careful study [62] of the "love-dayes," which Chaucer mentions, and through extensive research has established certain conclusions: the *love-day,* or *dies amoris,* or *jour d'amour,* was a day appointed expressly by the courts for the amicable settling out of court of specific cases, with the provision that the court in question receive the fees; [63] the assumption was that a settlement so reached would create less ill-feeling than one decided in court. Professor Spargo points out that the love-day had its beginnings in local courts where litigants, judge, and jury were all known to each other. When the love-day was transferred to larger communities, the institution became corrupt, for then general public opinion was no longer concerned with the conduct or outcome of a case, and it was easy to bring about forced, unjust settlements or else to delay action to the advantage of a powerful litigant, who could, if he had the time, suborn witnesses, and create new difficulties about the case.[64] When the love-day existed in its early, beneficial state, canon law supported the participation of the clergy as arbiters, but later, according to Professor Spargo, when the love-day became vitiated, clergy were forbidden to take part except "in the cases of the poor"—an exception which could be made a rule by anyone whose conscience allowed him to misinterpret "the poor." Professor Spargo thus draws the conclusion that

Chaucer is strongly sarcastic in mentioning the Friar's activities on love-days, for the poet implies that these love-days are between persons of substance.[65]

To emphasize further that the fourteenth-century love-day had fallen into disrepute, Professor Spargo calls attention to a proclamation of 1329 by the Mayor and Aldermen of London.[66] In the interests of the king's peace during Edward III's coming absence in France, certain prohibitions are mentioned in this document, among which are the following:

. . . And that no one of the City, of whatsoever he be, shall go out of this city, to maintain parties, such as taking seisins, or holding days of love, or making other congregations, within the City or without, in disturbance of the peace of our lord the King, or in affray of the people, and to the scandal of the City. . . .[67]

Even half a century before the *Canterbury Tales* was begun, love-days could apparently be considered scandalous.

Wyclif himself[68] writes against the love day of Chaucer's time:

. . . grete men of this world debaten, and meyntenen debatis at lovedaies; and who so may be strengere wil have his wille done, be it wrong be it right, and ellis make debate among many hundrid and thousand men and sumtyme many countres, and by sich debatynge many men holden grete houses and grete araies and grete costis.[69]

Langland tells us that Mede, the personification of Bribery, leads the law at her own evil will and "lovedayes maketh," so that men lose through her what they should gain legally;[70] and further he adds that the religious orders have now become riders and runners about the leaders of love-days;[71] the friar is now dressed as a lord and has the same bearing, although he should practise humility in every way.[72] This leads us back to Brother Hubert, who affects the apparel and the manner of a lordly prelate when he helps so wrongly on love-days.

Chaucer's Friar is not like one who remains in a cloister devoted to his vows ("cloysterer"), the poet says, nor is he clad, like a poor scholar, in a threadbare cope; instead, Hubert resembles someone who has won the Master's degree[73] or even the Pope himself, for he wears a "semycope," a short, ecclesiastical cape used as an outer garment, of expensive double-worsted. It is as full and unwrinkled as the mould of a bell.[74]

St. Francis particularly forbad his followers, meant to be the blessed meek of the earth, to wear ornate or luxurious clothing:

. . . All the brothers shall be clothed in mean garments, which are to be mended with sacks and other scraps of cloth; because God said through his Evangelist [St. Matthew IX, 8] that those who wear costly, luxurious, and soft clothing belong in kingly houses.[75]

Because of St. Francis's very clear command, the Wyclifites emphasize the friars' defiance of this rule. One Lollard writes, for instance:

. . . And so of clothing thei don agenst this reule in many maneres; for men seen that the kyng or the emperour myghtte with worschipe were a garnement of a frere for goodnesse of the cloth, and namely of suche freris as schulden most kepe povert of crist and his apostelis, as ben clepid maistris of divynyte, but verreily maistris of errour bothe in techynge and in ensaumple, and summe oone hath wast clothis and costi . . .[76]

Did Chaucer perhaps hear these very words? For Hubert in his handsome "semycope" of double-worsted is certainly garbed in the vain and costly apparel of a "Master of Error"! And again we wonder how Brother Hubert was conceived: did he spring from literature or from life?

If we think that Chaucer drew upon a specific author for some part of the Friar's portrait, we have at once a striking parallel in the *Roman de la Rose,* a work with which Chaucer was completely familiar and of which he makes frequent use. Jean de Meun's False-Seeming, although he is an allegorical figure and lacks colour when placed beside the lively Hubert, has nevertheless more in common with Chaucer's Friar than has any other character in literature. Hubert despises the poor who cannot "advance" him; False-Seeming will have only to do with those who will contribute to his worldly success or who will provide him with rich dishes. Let the parish priest take care of the really destitute, for himself he prefers acquaintance with the King of France!

                              . . . But willingly
    I leave both priests and prelates free
    Poor men and women to confess,
    Who for most part are penniless;
    But little guerdon thence were got.

    .   .   .   .   s

    The good fat sheep I bear away,
    And to the pastors leave the poor
    Lean hungry ones, who growl therefore.

    .   .   .   .

    And though I poverty pretend,
    I make of no poor man a friend.
    A hundred thousand times should I
    Prefer our good king's company.
    Yea, by our Lady! though it happed
    The poor man was with virtue capped
    In fairest wise, for when I see
    These beggars shiver wretchedly
    On dunghills, hungry, cold, and bare,
    What then?—'tis none of my affair.
    Or if unto the Hotel-Dieu
    They're carried, what! should I pursue
    Them thither? ne'er with one poor groat
    They've fed my parched and hungry throat.[77]

False-Seeming is also prudently equipped with papal authority
to hear confessions. What matter if his ready and easy shriving is
but trickery as long as he first pockets the silver?

    Good shrift I give when I confess
    (Laughing at prelates' helplessness)
    All sinners whom I hap to meet;
    No prelate dare my work defeat,
    Saving our lord the Pope alone,
    From whom this privilege was won
    For our most holy brotherhood.

    .   .   .   .

    But what care I? I'm none the worse,
    With silver have I stored my purse
    And goods have heaped; so well I've striven,
    That foolish folk have freely given

> Abundance, and I lead my life
> In ease, all undisturbed by strife . . .
>
> .   .   .   .
>
> And thus I live as pleaseth me
> By fraud, deceit, and trickery.[78]

False-Seeming, like Hubert, meddles with matters belonging to the civil courts.

> Then am I great at agencies,
> Old feuds arrange, and marriages,
> Executorships I take on me,
> And further deed of warrantry,
> Inquests as pursuivant I make,
> Whereat some honest men might quake.
> 'Tis pleasure, wherewith nought compares
> To mix in other men's affairs.[79]

And lastly False-Seeming knows how to use simple words to gain his ends, just as Hubert makes his English "sweete upon his tonge"; [80] False-Seeming is as crafty as Hubert, with the result that he, too, has a "pourchaz," or illegal income, that is better than his "rente," or legal income.[81] His French words thus give us an exact parallel to Chaucer's line.

We must observe, however, that although False-Seeming so closely resembles Chaucer's Friar in many ways, the likenesses are those that contribute to the general nature of the Friar's portrait. Both characters represent any bad Mendicant of the thirteenth or fourteenth century, although False-Seeming specifically represents Hypocrisy. But certainly, as we have seen, Hubert is strongly individualized; it appears probable that Chaucer's Friar does also represent some actual contemporary. The gap of more than five hundred years prevents any specific identification, but we can at least indicate the particular Order to which Brother Hubert is likely to have belonged.

Manly thinks it significant that both the Friar and the Summoner, who seem to have been enemies long before they arrive at the Tabard, place the scenes of their respective *Tales* in the north.[82] As each of these two pilgrims obviously tells his *Tale* to spite the other, we have reason to assume that Chaucer intended the Summoner to use the

Friar of the Canterbury pilgrimage as the "original" of the friar of his *Tale*. Now the Summoner's friar is from Holderness, a part of York-shire, and there was a Franciscan house in Beverley, the most impor-tant town in the district. Also, Holderness was familiar to Chaucer and to the court, for it was the residence of Michael de la Pole,[83] a favourite of Richard II's, and of Sir Peter Bukton.[84] "Futhermore," Manly writes, "contemporary records show that the Grey Friars of Beverley were at this time collecting money to repair and enlarge their buildings as the two friars in the tale [the *Summoner's Tale*] are represented as doing."[85] Of course this is no proof that Hubert represents one of the Beverley Franciscans, but the presumptive evi-dence is strong.

Before we take leave of Brother Hubert, we should note a matter which makes his inclusion among the Canterbury pilgrims even more timely than the fact that he typifies an extremely large group of men who were encountered everywhere. For it was in 1387, just when Chaucer may have been writing about his Friar, that the Patte-shulle affair took place.[86] The chronicler Walsingham relates that in that year, one Peter Patteshulle, who had formerly been an Austin friar and was now a Lollard priest, preached against the evil lives of his late brethren. A number of friars rushed to the defence of the Orders, and in the riots which ensued many friars were injured; whereupon the London authorities, instead of arresting the Lollards, merely rebuked them.[87] Patteshulle then wrote out his charges accus-ing the friars of every imaginable crime, and boldly affixed his state-ments on the doors of St. Paul's. Immediately certain knights, and these the famous "Lollard Knights" we have met before,[88] firmly supported Patteshulle's charges, and the affair assumed considerable importance in court circles, and hence in the political world. Chau-cer's audience must, therefore, have greeted Brother Hubert with a high degree of special interest.

Then, too, Chaucer himself may have had some personal reason for including a friar in the pilgrim company. We probably have more justification for this conjecture in relation to Brother Hubert than in relation to the other pilgrims, because of an incident in the poet's youth. Manly refers us to the words of Speght in the edition of Chaucer's works published in 1598: "Yt semethe that these lerned menne [Chaucer and Gower] were of the Inner Temple, for that manye yeres since master Buckley did see a recorde in the same howse, where Geffrye Chaucer was fined two shillinges for beating a Franciscane Fryer in fletestreate." [89] Manly gives logical reasons for accepting Speght's statement as accurate,[90] and consequently we are free to wonder if the young Geoffrey's ire, directed against a particular Franciscan, did not help to form a basis for later disapproval of friars in general. How much we should like to know why Geoffrey administered the beating!

Thus Chaucer's Hubert begins and remains for us an absorbing character. He is an individual through the arrogant strength of his personality and through his merry songs, his affected lisp, his playful manner, his white neck and his twinkling eyes; he is a type through his fine clothes and his greed, through his profligacy, his meddling, his shocking hypocrisy and his cheating of God and man. But always, whether as an individual or as a type, he is so real that we can think of him only as someone we know and despise, and in this sense he comes to us across the years as a distinct and living person.

NOTES

(The abbreviations used to designate books and articles mentioned in the Notes will be found listed alphabetically in the Bibliography, opposite the full reference. References to lines in the *Canterbury Tales* are given by fragment and line numbers only.)

1. Manly, *Cant. Tales,* p. 513, n. 269.
2. According to Robinson (p. 758, n. 208) *wantowne* can be used for "an attractive mannerism . . . [but] Chaucer's description clearly implies that the Friar was 'wanton' also in the modern sense."
3. *NED,* "Solemn."
Robinson (p. 758) and Skeat (VI, 283) both interpret the word *solempne* as "festive," but Flügel (*Anglia,* XXIV, 461) and Manly (*Cant. Tales,* p. 696) appear to agree with *NED,* and give the meaning as "haughty," or "pompous." I am unable to discover any sound basis for taking the meaning as "festive."
4. Coulton, *Five Cent. of Relig.,* II, 124 and Chap. VIII and IX *passim.*
5. *Ibid.,* p. 169.
6. *Chron. Maj.,* II, 511 f.
7. Eccleston, p. 30.
8. *Life of St. Francis,* p. 317.
9. *Ibid.,* Chap. VII.
10. *Ibid.,* pp. 319 ff.
11. *Chron. Maj.,* IV, 279 f. (Translation taken from *Matthew Paris's Eng. Hist.,* I, 475.)

12. Wright's *Political Poems*, I, 266.

13. Gower, *Vox Clam.*, Lib. IV, ll. 973–978, 1183–1186.

14. Owst, *Preaching*, p. 70. Owst says that we are compelled to believe that there still existed friars "of the noblest pattern" in fourteenth-century England.

15. *Ibid.*, pp. 55 ff.

16. One of the Lollard tracts indignantly asserts that although there were no friars at all two hundred years ago, now "ben mony thousande of freris in Englond" (Arnold, III, 400).

17. III (D) 834–836.

18. *NED*, "Limiter."

19. Robinson states (p. 1005) that lines 252 [a–b] occur only in one printed and six written manuscripts, but that they are "probably genuine, though perhaps canceled by Chaucer."

20. III (D) 872–881.

21. Gower, *Mirour*, ll. 9148, 21328.

22. *Piers Plow.*, B. Passus V. 138.

23. For example, Skeat (V, 25) and Robinson (p. 758).

24. Young, *MLN*, L, 83 ff.

25. Skeat, V, 24 f.

26. *NED*, "Tippet."

27. Brand, *Pop. Antiquities,* "Bride Knives."

28. Wright's *Political Poems*, I, 264.

29. According to Pulver (*Dict. Old Eng. Music,* "Crowd"), though we treat today as one instrument the Crowd, Rote, Cruit, and Crwth, they were distinct in the Middle Ages. The Crowd resembled the modern violin, as it was played with a bow and tended to show curved sides. The Rote, on the contrary, had parallel straight sides and a hole cut in the upper part of the body for the plucking hand. It was not played with a bow.

30. Manly notes (*Cant. Tales,* p. 512) that *champioun* has the modern meaning, and not the meaning explained "by Skeat and others as 'a professional fighter in judicial lists.'"

31. Horton (*MLN*, XLVIII, 31 ff.) calls attention to ll. 2530–2533 of Lydgate and Burgh's *Secrees of Old Philisoffres:*

> Man which is / feble of Colour
> ffor thyn avayl / looke that thou flee,
> ffor he is pleynly / tak heed unto mee,
> To lecchery dispoosed / . . .

32. Although Hubert's lisp points him out as an individual, his desire to make his English "sweete" is, according to Gower (*Mirour,* ll. 21234 f.), a typical wish of the Mendicants.

33. *Life of St. Francis,* pp. 331 f.

34. Matthew, pp. 10, 12.

35. *Ibid.*, p. 9.

36. Gower, *Mirour,* ll. 9145–9156.

37. Gower, *Vox Clam.*, Lib. IV, 835–844 and 863–886. Gower is much

more detailed and witty in his accusations than the summarized translation
indicates. He writes (ll. 877–886) as follows:

> Inter apes statuit natura quod esse notandum
> Sencio, quo poterit frater habere notam.
> Nam si pungat apis, pungenti culpa repugnat
> Amplius ut stimulum non habet ipse suum;
> Postque domi latebras tenet et non evolat ultra,
> Floribus ut campi mellificare queat.
> O deus, in simili forma si frater adulter
> Perderet inflatum, dum stimularet, acum,
> Amplius ut flores non colligat in muliere,
> Nec vagus a domibus pergat in orbe suis!

38. *Life of St. Francis,* p. 344.

39. *Ibid.,* p. 310.

40. *Ibid.,* p. 314.

41. *Ibid.* (Introduction), p. xx.

42. *Ibid.* ("The Little Flowers" is published in the same volume with
the *Life of St. Francis*), pp. 44 f.

43. Arnold, III, 373.

44. Gower, *Mirour,* ll. 21217–21226.

45. Law, *PMLA,* XXXVII, 208–215.

46. Wright's *Political Poems,* II, 23.

47. The Roman Missal appoints St. John I, 1–14 to be read as the gospel
in the most important Mass on Christmas Day; the Book of Common Prayer
appoints the same passage as the Gospel for Christmas Day; and *in principio*
appears in the *Gloria Patri* (Law, *PMLA,* XXXVII, 211).

48. J. Douglas Bruce (*MLN,* XXXIV, pp. 118 f.) states that Chaucer
very probably wrote l. 256 as a proverb, although he was undoubtedly familiar
with the identical expression in *Le Roman de la Rose*: "Meauz vaut mes
pourchaz que ma rente" (l. 11566).

49. See *MLN,* XXIII, where E. A. Greenlaw (142 ff.) and Kittredge
(200) both conclude that *purchas* means "illegal income" and *rente* means
"legal income." Greenlaw takes issue with Flügel (*Anglia,* XXIII, 233 ff.)
who interprets *rente* to mean the sum paid by the Friar to his Order for his
begging privilege; Greenlaw shows that almost invariably Chaucer uses *rente*
to mean "income." Manly states (*Cant. Tales,* p. 513) that *purchas* was a
word "often used with a suggestion of fraud."

50. *Cath. Ency.,* "Friar."

51. Owst, *Preaching,* p. 71.

52. *Ibid.,* p. 76. The manuscript of which Owst speaks is MS. Camb.
Univ. Libr. Gg. iv, 32, fo. 124 et seq. It is important to note that *curate* in
the Middle Ages meant "parish priest" and not an assistant to the priest.

53 *Cath. Ency.,* "Penance."

54. Arnold, III, 374, 376–377, 394.

55. *Pl. Crede,* ll. 460–468, 471.

56. Owst, *Preaching*, p. 89.

57. This is Skeat's translation of B. Passus V. 138–50, taken from *Piers Plow.*, II, 78. Skeat defines *lector* in this context as "lecturer, or occasional preacher," and *possessioners* as "the beneficed clergy."

58. *Piers Plow.*, B. Passus, XX. 278–282, 288–290.

59. *Ibid.*, 375–377.

60. Gower, *Mirour*, ll. 21241–21264, 21283–21288.

61. Wright's *Political Poems*, I, 266.

62. Spargo, *Spec.*, XV, 36–56.

63. Spargo has found the etymology of *love-day* to be uncertain, but he is of the opinion that the word is from OE *lufu* (meaning legal "license" or "permission"), which in turn is from the ancient Scandinavian *lof* (of the same meaning). In any event, these love-days were not carried out without expense: a number of records of costs exist (p. 52).

64. *Ibid.*, pp. 51 ff.

65. *Ibid.*, p. 55.

66. *Ibid.*, p. 51.

67. Riley, *London*, p. 173.

68. Winn, p. xxix.

69. Matthew, pp. 234 f.

70. *Piers Plow.* B. Passus III. 155–158.

71. *Ibid.*, A. Passus XI. 208–209.

72. *Ibid.*, 211–215.

73. Gower writes (*Mirour*, ll. 21493–21498) that friars, instead of practising humility, would bear the title of "mestre" to advertise their fame. But Flügel says (*Anglia*, XII, 469) that the mendicants were forbidden to receive this degree.

74. Robinson, p. 758, n. 263. And see Lowes (*Rom. Rev.*, II, 118 f.), who says the phrase is "not uncommon" in the Middle Ages, especially in fourteenth-century French: *a fons de cuve* meant "made in the form of an inverted round mould."

75. *Opuscula*, Reg. I, Cap. II.

76. Matthew, p. 50.

77. *Rom. of the Rose*, Ellis, ll. 11853–11857, 11860–11862, 11887–11900. (*Rom. de la Rose*, III, 314 f., ll. 81–85, 88–90; and ll. 11237–11253.)

78. *Ibid.*, ll. 11729–11735, 11743–11748, 11753–11754. (*Rom. de la Rose*, III, 311, ll. 3–8 ^{1}, 8 ^{5}–8 ^{14}, 8 ^{19}–8 ^{20}.)

79. *Ibid.*, ll. 12339–12346. (*Rom. de la Rose*, ll. 11679–11686.)

80. *Ibid.*, ll. 11570–11571. (*Rom. de la Rose*, ll. 11073–11074.)

81. *Ibid.*, l. 12218. (*Rom. de la Rose*, l. 11566.) See above n. 48 and n. 49.

82. Manly, *New Light*, p. 103.

83. Robinson, p. 811, n. 1710.

84. *Ibid.*, p. 979.

85. Manly, *New Light*, p. 104.

86. Trevelyan, p. 327.

87. We do not know why official action was so mild: perhaps the authorities were preoccupied with the tense political situation, for Gloucester was now in strong opposition to the Crown, or perhaps most of the authorities sympathized with Patteshulle's action.

88. Walsingham, *Hist. Ang.*, II, 157–159. Walsingham writes of the knights as follows:

> Hanc chartam de capuciatis militibus perlegentes,
> pro firmo praedicaverunt cuncta fore vera quae
> scribebantur; unde et transcripta exinde sibi
> fecerunt, ut valerent suae malitiae satisfacere
> in futurum. (p. 159)

Walsingham then lists the knights supporting the Lollards (see above p. 9); these men were Chaucer's friends.

89. Manly, *New Light*, pp. 7 f.

90. *Ibid.*, pp. 9 ff.

CHAPTER VIII

THE DIGNIFIED MERCHANT

A Marchant was ther with a forked berd,
In mottelee, and hye on horse he sat;
Upon his heed a Flaundryssh bever hat,
His bootes clasped faire and fetisly.
His resons he spak ful solempnely,
Sownynge alwey th'encrees of his wynnyng.
He wolde the see were kept for any thyng
Bitwixe Middelburgh and Orewelle.
Wel koude he in eschaunge sheeldes selle.
This worthy man ful wel his wit bisette:
Ther wiste no wight that he was in dette,
So estatly was he of his governaunce
With his bargaynes and with his chevyssaunce.
For sothe he was a worthy man with alle,
But, sooth to seyn, I noot how men hym calle.

(ll. 270–284)

To NOT A FEW of Chaucer's contemporaries this portrait of a fourteenth-century merchant-prince must have been a vividly familiar figure. Chaucer says that his elegantly attired Merchant is a worthy man, but that he does not know his name; whether this is literal fact, or a result of the poet's prudence, is hard to determine. Medieval merchants, those men engaged in the wholesale traffic of wool, hides, cloth, iron, and tin, were also the bankers and money-lenders of the nation. Chaucer might easily have had dealings with such a man and would probably have thought twice before ridiculing a merchant and then identifying him. Rich and poor, proud and humble, even the King himself, all felt the power of the men who exploited the wealth of England, and who now indirectly controlled the national purse strings. Merchants in the later Middle Ages enjoyed a social position which, for all that it was tacitly and sometimes impermanently held, exceeded that of many a noble.

In the fourteenth century, two great organizations of merchants existed: the Merchants of the Staple and the Merchant Adventurers. Each of these companies claimed to be the older; each claimed an identical record of growth and achievement. We therefore find some confusion in a consideration of these two companies today—and the confusion is increased by the fact that it was not unusual for one merchant to maintain membership in both organizations.[1]

The Merchants of the Staple, or Staplers, were chartered by the Crown and given the authority to elect their own officers and execute their own laws. Their business was primarily the export of wool, wool felts, and hides; certain towns in England and on the continent were at different times named as the only ones through which this business could be transacted, and such a town was often designated as the "Staple" since wool was the "staple," or principal article of commerce.[2] The Merchant Adventurers, or simply Adventurers, on the other hand, were English merchants resident in foreign cities, engaged in bringing into the countries where they resided the cloth made in England from English wool. The Adventurers were closely connected with the Guild of Mercers, and were originally a part of the brotherhood of St. Thomas of Canterbury; they did not formally receive their charter from the Crown until the reign of Henry IV, but as the Guild of Mercers, or as the Brotherhood of St. Thomas, they had obtained, with the Staplers, a number of privileges as organized merchants at least a century before Chaucer's time.[3] Chaucer's Merchant is thus a figure whose connections have long been traditional when we meet him, and he may be Stapler, or Adventurer, or both.

From 1384 to 1388 the wool staple was at Middleburgh, a port on the Dutch coast opposite Orwell, and Chaucer's mention of these two ports at first glance may seem to point to his Merchant as a Stapler, but when we learn that after 1384 the Adventurers made Middleburgh their headquarters,[4] we realize that Chaucer's naming of "Middelburgh and Orewelle" would be equally suitable for a member of the latter company. In any case, the Merchant would be concerned over the safety of the sea between the two ports, particularly since the French and the Flemish were planning, even attempting, at this time an invasion of England.[5]

The Merchant is typical of his class. He is anxious, as all the merchants were, that his trade route, the sea, should be guarded ("kept") at all costs ("for any thyng"). The *Libel *of English Policy,* written in 1436, exhorts England to cherish the activities of her merchants in "keeping the sea" in these words:

> The trewe processe of Englysh polycye—
> Of utterwarde* to kepe thys regne* in rest
> Of oure England, that no man may denye,
> Nere* say of soth but it is one of the best—
> Is thys, that who seith* Southe, Northe, Est,
>   and West,
> Cheryshe marchandyse, kepe th'amyralte,*
> That we bee maysteres of the narrowe see.* [6]

And records, of which more will be said when we examine the Merchant as an individual, indicate that it was not unusual for merchants to be appointed to the highly lucrative government post of "keeper," or patrol, of the English Channel.

Chaucer's Merchant is also typical in his "chevyssaunce," or lending money for a price. The problem of usury, or the taking of money beyond the sum lent, became all-important in the political economy of the later Middle Ages. As Dr. Coulton remarks, the real justification of such usury lies in "that extension of industry and trade which we call the capitalist system." [7] If the individual has the money beyond his actual personal needs, he will, in general, put that money to work buying more goods or labour; the merchants, belonging to a class which was capitalistic *per se,* asked why a charge could not therefore be made legitimately to cover the loss of potential gain to themselves when this surplus money was lent. The Church made but one reply: the lender of money received his gain in blessings and sinned against the faith if he accepted pecuniary compensation. Thus men, determined as always to seek tangible and immediate rewards, baffled by the Church's refusal to countenance civil regulation of rates of interest, set up a "black market" system of money-lending under the euphemistic name of "chevyssaunce," a term which had originally meant any kind of mercantile exchange. [8] But medieval man was never comfortable in defying the

---

* *libel*: "little book"
  utterwarde: "from foes without"   *seith*: "professes to be of"
  regne: "kingdom"   *th'amyralte*: "the admiralty"
  nere: "nor"   *the narowe see*: "the Straits of Dover"

edicts of an institution which might stand between him and eternal damnation, and perhaps no one was really complaisant about "chevyssaunce," although it was practised so widely and more or less openly.

The complaints about the acceptance of money for loans are many, as we could expect. Gower says flatly:

The Usurer, denizen of the city, retains his brokers and procurers to search out and bring to him knights, squires, and 'vavasours' who must of necessity borrow. Then on them will be practised what is now called the 'chevisance' of money. . . . Alas that the sinful creditor thus gains materially, and the poor debtor is destroyed! [9]

Langland makes despicable Avarice boast of his unethical financial dealings, among which are "chevesances," as follows:

'I have lent lordes . and ladyes my chaffare*
And ben her brocour after . and boughte it my-self.
Eschaunges and chevesances . with such chaffare I
      dele,
And lene folke that lese wol . a lyppe* at every
      noble.' * [10]

The Dominican Bromyard cries out that the usurers who in this life "used to make a penny out of a farthing, and from eleven pence make twelve," are, when they die, "in the deep lake of hell" where they have a bath "more black and foul than any bath of pitch and sulphur." [11] A fourteenth-century sermon exemplum says that although God created the clergy, knights, and labourers, the Devil created usurers and burghers! [12]

Another stock charge against merchants was fraudulent concealment of debt. Jacobus de Cessolis, in treating merchants as a social class, writes in his *Chess-Book*:

. . . to owe . . . is a shame/ & to owe and not paye is a more shame/ yf y^u be poure beware how thou borowest/ . . . it is said in the proverbes y^t hit is fraude to take/ that y^u wilt not ner maist rendre & paye agayn . . .[13]

* *chaffare*: "merchandise"
  lyppe: "part"
  noble: "florin," a gold coin worth 6s. 8d.

Gower also writes in scorn of the latter-day merchants who contract enormous debts, which they cannot repay and therefore hide, so that they may live in luxury far beyond their station.[14] Chaucer's Merchant is here again true to type: he sets his wits to work to conceal the lamentable fact that he is "in dette."

Chaucer's Merchant is also typical in that he defies the civil law and deals in foreign exchange ("in eschaunge sheeldes * selle"). The quantity of money in fourteenth-century England was insufficient for the volume of business, and to prevent the escape of bullion from the country, laws were enacted forbidding private commerce in exchange.[15] Unscrupulous merchants, however, paid little attention to these edicts, and carried on a thriving trade in foreign money. If we return to what Langland has to say about "chevesances," we observe that "eschaunges" is part of the merchandise of Avarice. Although the literature of complaint is not as vehement about illegal dealings in exchange as about usury, for the one offence was merely civil and the other also ecclesiastical, we may still be very sure that Chaucer's circle, composed as it was of many members of the court, found the allusion to "eschaunge" as telling as it was timely.

Except possibly for the "Flaundryssh bever hat" there is nothing individual in the Merchant's attire. His "mottelee" (cloth of diversified colour in a figured design) was customary in the fourteenth century and later for members of every sort of company on state occasions. Although this pilgrimage to Canterbury cannot be considered to be such an occasion, Chaucer may have inserted the "mottelee" and the sitting "hye on horse" to suggest to his audience, as Miss Rickert proposes, a state procession of officials.[16] Professor Knott writes that it is evident that the Merchants of the Staple wore a distinctive livery, for in 1367 Edward III decreed that the Staplers of Calais should be excused from all duties on cloth sent to Calais for their own and their servants' liveries.[17] The artist of the Ellesmere MS. depicts Chaucer's Merchant—with his fashionably forked "berd"—in what is probably the conventional merchant's dress of the time: his motley is one of white and blue flowers on a red ground; the boot which is visible to the reader is clasped well and

* *sheeldes:* gold coins (the French *escuz*), having the figure of a shield on one face; they were valued at half a noble—i.e., 3s. 4d.

neatly ("faire and fetisly") ; and the beaver hat, which may not be part of the livery, has a rolled brim and high crown.

But although this anonymous Merchant is typical of his class in so many ways, he is also very much of an individual. His dignified manner ("estatly . . . of his governaunce"), his solemn remarks ("resons"), which always touch upon his profits ("sownynge alwey th'encrees of his wynnyng"),[18] and his extraordinary carefulness in hiding his debts, all point to a particular merchant who existed either in Chaucer's mind or in the flesh. The recent discovery of a four-teenth-century merchant's account book makes us strongly suspect that there was a living prototype for the Merchant. The document published by Miss Rickert,[19] is "the only one of its kind thus far dis-covered." It records the affairs of one Gilbert Maghfeld, a Merchant Adventurer, particularly for the years 1390–1395, but more gen-erally for a much longer period, as the book contains many entries brought forward from other account books of Maghfeld's.

Maghfeld's career, says Miss Rickert, is similar to those of "the better-known Walworth, Philpot, and Brembre." [20] Maghfeld was immensely wealthy and a man of innumerable enterprises and posi-tions. One matter of especial interest to us is that in 1383 Maghfeld and another man became, with two "mariners," "keepers of the sea" for which they received the large sum of 2,500 marks, besides the 6s. in the pound and 2s. a tun granted to the King by Parliament and half of the fines collected for non-payment of duties.[21] That Chaucer's Merchant desires the sea to be guarded at all costs between Middleburgh and Orwell may thus be a double allusion: not only would he be concerned with the safety of his trade consignments, but he may have served as one of the patrols.

Although Maghfeld was soon removed from office as keeper of the sea after only six month's service, either through his own ineffi-ciency or through rival jealousies, he was far from being out of favour at court at the time. In 1386 he was made "customer" for Boston, and in 1388 he was made one of the customers for London. Maghfeld was still in office in London when Chaucer, as Clerk of the Works, was permitted to draw upon the customs for nearly 31 l., so the two men must have known each other. Maghfeld was several times elected alderman, and in 1392 he served as sheriff; he was obviously a man of public affairs as well as of business.[22]

It is interesting to note Miss Rickert's list of commodities in which Maghfeld dealt; he had a great variety of "bargaynes":

. . . iron, copper, gravel, lead, stones, millstones, wainscot from Prussia, boards, wood, coal, quicklime, rock alum, grain, ginger, saffron, licorice, silk, wool, skins, furs, linen, hats [perhaps from Flandders!], wines, stockfish, herring, sturgeon, salmon, pearls.[23]

But a part of Maghfeld's business that was fully as large and important as his "bargaynes" was his "chevyssaunce." It is astonishing and impressive to read the list of clients to whom Maghfeld lent money, a list which includes the names of scores of other English merchants, besides merchants of Prussia, France, Italy, and Spain. Knights, squires, government officials, and prominent clergy also came to Maghfeld for money, many of them known to Chaucer's friends and associates, and we are particularly struck by the records of money loaned to "Johan Gower Esquier" and to "Geffray Chauxcer"! [24]

Maghfeld's private life was in keeping with his position of merchant-prince. At the height of his career he had a house in Billingsgate worth, together with other property, about $4,000 a year in modern money. In his account book are recorded payments to at least six servants, to workmen for the building of a *lavour,* or washing place, in the hall (Americans are not the first to consider luxurious plumbing a necessity!), and to contractors and workmen for the building and upkeep of an expensive private wharf on the property.[25] Fourteenth-century wealth, however, could not be counted on to endure any more than the wealth of other centuries, and it is not surprising to find Maghfeld dying in bankruptcy. Must there not then have been a time in his precarious financial affairs when Maghfeld saw failure ahead, but, like Chaucer's Merchant, concealed the mounting debts? It is tempting to jump to the conclusion that Maghfeld and the Merchant of the *Canterbury Tales* are one.

Miss Rickert indicates two other points of resemblance between Maghfeld and Chaucer's Merchant. The first concerns Maghfeld's probable dealings in foreign exchange because of his numerous enterprises outside of England, although here the parallel is more general than particular; [26] the second is a reference to that highly individual beaver hat. After Richard II's quarrel with the citizens of London, there was a day of pageantry proclaimed when the King formally forgave his subjects. On that day, Maghfeld's account book records the borrowing by Thomas Newenton, one of the sheriffs, of 3s. 4d. for the purpose of buying a beaver hat. That the beaver hat was part of the sheriff's livery is made clear, [27] so that Maghfeld himself, as one of the sheriffs, must have worn such a head-covering. And since there is no record of a beaver hat as part of the livery of any merchant's company, the suggestion here is very strong that Maghfeld was the model for Chaucer's Merchant.

But as has been pointed out, Chaucer would not be imprudent enough to identify too surely the stately, well-dressed Merchant, at whom he laughs, for his pompous dignity and his "bargaynes" and "chevyssaunce" and "eschaunge." One does not satirize too specifically when writing of an important magnate to whom a large part of one's world may owe money.

NOTES

(The abbreviations used to designate books and articles mentioned in the Notes will be found listed alphabetically in the Bibliography, opposite the full reference. References to lines in the *Canterbury Tales* are given by fragment and line numbers only.)

1. Manly, *New Light,* p. 183.
2. *NED,* "Staple."
3. Lucas, *Begin. of Eng. Over. Ent., passim.*
4. Manly suggests (*New Light,* p. 198) that Chaucer's selection of Orwell might possibly be because of his connection with Ipswich, of which Orwell was the port: Chaucer's father was a native of Ipswich and owned property there. But it seems as if the fact that Orwell was opposite Middleburgh would be a more natural reason for the poet's choice.
5. *Ibid.,* p. 199.
6. Cook, *Lit. Mid. Eng. Reader,* p. 383.
7. Coulton, *Med. Pan.,* pp. 334 f.
8. *Ibid.,* pp. 335 ff.
9. Gower, *Mirour,* ll. 7225 ff.
10. *Piers Plow.,* B. Passus V. 247–250. Skeat's note on l. 249 says in part: "In an ordinance against usurers (38 Edw. III) we find that certain persons exerted themselves to maintain usury—'which kind of contract, the more subtly to deceive the people, they call . . . *chevisance,* whereas it might more truly be called *mescheaunce* (wickedness)'; Liber Albus, p. 319, and see p. 344."
11. Owst, *Lit. and Pulpit,* p. 293.
12. *Ibid.,* pp. 553 f.
13. *Chess-Book,* p. 112.

14. Gower, *Mirour,* ll. 25813 ff.

15. Flügel (*Anglia,* XXIV, 474 f.) quotes from a statute of 1350 as follows: "qe bien lise a chescun homme de chaunger or pur argent ou pur or ou argent pur argent ou pur or issint qe nul homme tiegne commune eschaunge ne rien preigne de profit pur tiel eschaunge faire sur peine de forfaiture de la monoie issint chaungee, forprises les chaungeours le Roi [*the royal exchange was created to take care of all necessary transactions in exchange*] les queux preignent profit pur tiel eschaunge solonc lordinance avant faite."

16. Rickert, *MP,* XXIV, 256.

17. Knott, *PQ,* I, 9 f.

18. *NED* quotes this line of Chaucer's to illustrate the meaning of the verb *sound*: "To have a suggestion or touch of, a tendency towards, some connexion or association with a specified thing."

19. Rickert, *loc. cit.,* pp. 111–119, 249–256.

20. *Ibid.,* p. 112.

21. *Ibid.*

22. *Ibid.,* p. 113.

23. *Ibid.,* p. 114.

24. *Ibid.,* pp. 115–118. Miss Rickert cautiously points out that we do not *know* that either the Chaucer or the Gower mentioned is the poet by that name; but we do not know of any "Geoffrey" Chaucer except the great poet; and the "esquire" after "Gower" shows that this is not John Gower, the parson, and we do not know of any other John Gower except the poet.

25. *Ibid.,* p. 252.

26. *Ibid.,* p. 114.

27. *Ibid.,* p. 249.

CHAPTER IX

THE CLERK OF OXENFORD

A Clerk ther was of Oxenford also,
That unto logyk hadde longe ygo.

. . . .

. . . he hadde geten hym yet no benefice,
Ne was so worldly for to have office.

. . . .

But al that he myghte of his freendes hente,
On bookes and on lernynge he it spente,
And bisily gan for the soules preye
Of hem that yaf hym wherwith to scoleye.

. . . .

And gladly wolde he lerne and gladly teche.
(ll. 285–286, 291–292, 299–302, 309)

HASTINGS RASHDALL, the great authority on the medieval university, say that the word *clerk* in the Middle Ages indicated a student who had received the tonsure, thereby becoming entitled to certain ecclesiastical immunities.[1] Clericality in itself, Rashdall writes, "did not necessarily imply even the lowest grade of minor orders," [2] but there were, of course, many clerks who took orders, usually for the purpose of holding a benefice.[3] The benefice, as contrasted with a secular post, may be defined as an ecclesiastical living; it demanded that the recipient be in orders, particularly in English universities, where the impoverished student was to be maintained by the authorities only until such time as he secured a living.[4] Chaucer's Clerk, then, must be at least in minor orders to be a candidate for the benefice he has not yet procured.

Since the Clerk has no benefice and is obviously poor, we might ask how he manages to support himself. A man who is later described "as coy and stille as . . . a mayde" [5] is not worldly enough nor aggressive enough to "have office"—that is, to eke out his income through secular employment. Chaucer tells us that the Clerk adds to his income by teaching, that is, by tutoring as we should say nowadays. Rashdall observes that fourteenth-century Oxford had provision for a system of tutors for the undergraduate students. The older fellows, in return for money received from individual pupils and an additional allowance from the college funds, could find means of self-support through instruction of younger fellows of the university.[6] That the Clerk also accepts monetary gifts from his friends is perhaps because of his expensive taste for books.

It seems unlikely that the Clerk is a begging scholar, although the friars had made the custom of begging comparatively respectable, as Rashdall reminds us. Sometimes the chancellor of a university even granted the mendicant scholar a license to beg; in return for what he received, the scholar was expected to pray for the souls of those who helped him.[7] But as H. S. V. Jones suggests, Chaucer writes of the dignified and zealous Clerk with such appreciation that it is scarcely possible to picture him as begging from door to door; much more probably some neighbouring prelate acts as his patron, a not unusual system at Oxford at that time.[8] The Clerk would, of course, pray for anyone who helped him, as attentively ("bisily") as if he were in the position of a begging scholar.

The Clerk is "of Oxenford," and we are interested that Chaucer has selected for this student the more prominent of the two English universities, although both institutions were familiar to him and to his audience.[9] Edward of Abingdon, Robert Grosseteste, Roger Bacon, Duns Scotus, William of Ockham, and many others had at various times invested the intellectual life of Oxford with extraordinary vitality;[10] and of course Chaucer's own contemporaries, Ralph Strode and Wyclif, made permanent contribution to Oxford greatness. Since our Clerk is of such a scholarly turn of mind it is perhaps more fitting that he should attend Oxford rather than the younger and somewhat less famous Cambridge.

The Clerk when we meet him has "unto logyk . . . longe ygo*"; this suggests that he has completed the requirements for the bachelor's degree, and is now pursuing his studies for the master's

---

* *ygo*: "betaken himself"

degree. In Chaucer's time the curriculum at Oxford still consisted of two parts: the *trivium,* which included grammar, rhetoric, and logic; and the *quadrivium,* which included music, arithmetic, geometry, astronomy, and "the three philosophies," natural, moral, and metaphysic. Four years' study were required for the bachelor's degree; and three to four more for the master's degree. If we examine the medieval curricula, we discover what a great part of those years was spent in the study of Aristotle and of logic. The following requirements, summarized by Rashdall,[11] for the bachelor's and master's degrees, although dated 1409, cannot be very different from those met by Chaucer's Clerk only twenty-five years or so before.

For B.A. (*Admissio ad lecturam alicuius libri Facultatis Artium*): Four years' study.

For *Determination,* . . .

To have disputed for at least a year as a general sophister *in Parviso.*

To have heard: Donatus, *Barbarismus*; Porphyry, *Isagoge*; Gilbert de la Porrée, *Sex Principia;* Aristotle, *Sophistici Elenchi;* Arithmetic (*Algorismus integrorum*); the method of finding Easter (*Computus ecclesiasticus*); [Joannes de Sacro Bosco], *Tractatus de Sphaera—lectionatim* in College or Hall.

The Old and New Logic, except the Boethius, *Topics,* bk. iv *cursorie* from bachelors in the public schools.

To have heard, in addition to the books already read for B.A.: . . .

Grammar.	Priscian 'in majore vel minore.' (One term.)
Rhetoric.	The *Rhetoric* of Aristotle. (Three terms.)
	Or the *Topics* of Boethius, bk. iv.
	Or Cicero, *Nova Rhetorica.*
	Or Ovid's *Metamorphoses.*
	Or 'Poetria Virgilii.' [The last three alternatives may be recent additions.]
Logic.	Aristotle, *De Interpretatione.* (Three terms.)
	Or Boethius, *Topics* (first three Books).
	Or Aristotle, *Prior Analytics,* or *Topics.*
Arithmetic.	Boethius. (One term.)
Music.	Boethius. (One term.)
Geometry.	One book of Euclid . . . [According to 'Forma' six books are required.]
	Or Alhacen. (Two terms.)
	Or Vitellio, *Perspectiva.*
Astronomy.	*Theorica Planetarum.* (Two terms.)
	Or Ptolemy, *Almagesta.*

In the three philosophies:

Natural Philosophy.	Aristotle, *Physica* or *De caelo et mundo*. (Three terms.)
	Or *De proprietatibus elementorum*, or *Meteorica*, or *De vegetabilibus et plantis*, or *De Anima*, or *De Animalibus*, or 'any of the smaller books.'
Moral Philosophy.	Aristotle, *Ethica*, or *Economica*, or *Politica*. (Three terms.)
Metaphysic Philosophy.	Aristotle, *Metaphysica*. (Two terms.)

No part of the curriculum just summarized makes for easy reading, and as we glance at it we can appreciate how long the time has been since Chaucer's Clerk first betook himself unto logic, and how much he desires, for he is a born student, to possess twenty books of Aristotle: [12]

> For hym was levere have at his beddes heed
> Twenty bookes, clad in blak or reed
> Of Aristotle and his philosophie,
> Than robes riche, or fithele,* or gay sautrie.*
> But al be that he was a philosophre,
> Yet hadde he but litel gold in cofre;
> But al that he myghte of his freendes hente,
> On books and on lernynge he it spente—
>
> .   .   .   .
>
> Of studie took he moost cure and moost heede
> Noght o word spak he moore than was neede.
> And that was seyd in forme and reverence,
> And short and quyk and ful of hy sentence;
> Sownynge in moral vertu was his speche,
> And gladly wolde he lerne and gladly teche.
>
> (ll. 293–300; 303–308)

Not for the Clerk are the pleasures of another "poure scholar," the "gentle" Nicholas of the *Miller's Tale* who also keeps his books "couched at his beddes heed," but whose tastes turn to the more commercially profitable study of "astrologye" and to gay investigations into the art of love. Nor does our pilgrim Clerk resemble the happy-go-lucky John and Aleyn of the *Reeve's Tale* who, although

---

* *fithele*: "fiddle"   *sautrie*: "psaltery"—that is, a medieval stringed instrument played as a small harp.

they are also "poure scolers," are ever "lusty for to pleye" and to take their fun where they find it. The joys of the Clerk of Oxenford are all of the mind, and his room at his college, except for the gay bindings [13] of red and black on the books he may have begun to collect, is probably austere. Rashdall writes:

The senior men had ordinary bedsteads, in connexion with which various gorgeously coloured coverlets, a 'celer and tester,' or hanging linen and curtains are sometimes mentioned. . . . There is usually a table with a few chairs or 'playne joyned stooles' or 'joyned formes.' 'A new cistern or a troughe of lead,' or 'a lead to wash with a cocke,' or 'a picher and a bolle,' are sometimes but not universally mentioned. (In some colleges there appears to have been a public lavatory in the hall.) . . . In the case of humbler scholars blankets or counterpanes appear without the sheets. The musical man had his 'lewt.' There was a chest or 'cofer' or 'canveisse' for clothes; if the occupant were a serious student there would be a 'presse' or shelves for books. In the inventories of more sporting characters, knives and swords, bows and arrows, a hatchet or a silver 'misericordia' [i.e., a dagger for giving the *coup de grace*] are more conspicuous than books.[14]

Chaucer's Clerk, who is poor, would probably buy second-hand books at reduced prices, as many students do today; it is therefore possible that he may have already completed his library of twenty volumes. On the other hand, if he wishes his books to be new, he can hardly have yet afforded them. Even though books were not as scarce in the fourteenth century as is often imagined, the supply was relatively much lower than today's, and the cost correspondingly higher. According to Mr. Wilbur Lang Schramm, who has made a study of the cost of books in Chaucer's age, very few books could be bought for less than 1*s.* a volume,[15] and at that rate the Clerk's twenty books would be far beyond his present slender means.[16] It seems more logical to suppose, however, that the Clerk has purchased used books, and so has already satisfied his desires.

For the Clerk as a type we have almost no contemporary records. As Rashdall observes, "the life of the virtuous student has no annals," [17] although he adds that the earnest students, even if a minority, must have furnished "an immense mass of real intellectual enthusiasm for the development of a university to become possible." [18] But it is not impossible to reconstruct the typical day of a genuine student, and thus gather a more vivid idea of the Clerk. He undoubtedly rises early, before five or six o'clock at the latest, and attends one or two lectures, perhaps preceded or followed by mass. His dinner hour is at ten o'clock in the morning, and dinner is probably his first meal of the day. After dinner there is a brief period for relaxation followed by another lecture, or by disputations of various kinds, or by informal catechetical classes of small numbers, the forerunner of the modern recitation,—or by study. Supper takes place at five o'clock, and in the evening, when the less studious clerks are illegally amusing themselves in gambling, in playing chess, in dancing or jumping in the halls, in playing musical instruments, in indulging in practical jokes, and in more grave breaches of the peace, the serious student reads, or—if candles are too expensive— seeks out a wealthier friend or pupil with whom he may share a light for study or teaching.[19] This serious student probably finds his principal diversion in the observance of Church festivals;[20] and sometimes he enjoys all the excitements of a journey to Canterbury. Not for him are the more earthly and more usual pleasures of Chaucer's "myrie" and exceedingly amorous clerk Absolon, who

> In twenty manere koude he trippe and daunce
> After the scole of Oxenforde tho,
> And with his legges casten to and fro,
> And pleyen songes on a smal rubible; *
> Therto he song som tyme a loud quynyble.*
> And as wel koude he pley on a giterne.* [21]

We cannot imagine that anyone who did not speak one word "moore than was neede" ever tripped and danced, or cast "his legges to and fro" as did the unregenerate Absolon. The Clerk's few words are spoken with decorum and modesty ("in forme and reverence") ; they are short and quick and full of noble meaning ("ful of hy sentence"), and they are consonant with righteousness ("sownynge in moral vertu").[22] And of course we are sure that the Clerk was never guilty of crime, although Oxford students were notorious for crimes of violence in Chaucer's day. Dr. Coulton gives us a startling picture of Oxford affrays of the period from Coroners' Rolls, a pic-

---

* *rubible*: a two-stringed instrument, played with a bow
  quynyble: one octave above the treble
  giterne: a kind of guitar

ture which will well serve to emphasize through contrast the shy, retiring nature of Chaucer's Clerk, whom the Host twits as being like a bride at the marriage feast.

. . . [The jury] say upon their oath that, on the Saturday aforesaid, after the hour of noon, the Northern clerks on the one part, and the Southern and Western clerks on the other, came to St. John's Street and Grope Lane with swords, bucklers, bows, arrows, and other arms, and there they fought together; and in that conflict Robert de Bridlington, Adam de Alderbeck, Richard de Louthby and Richard de Holwell stood together in a certain Soler [or private room] in Gutter Hall, situate in St. John's Street, shooting down through a window into Grope Lane: and there the said Robert de Bridlington with a small arrow, smote the aforesaid Henry of Holy Isle and wounded him hard by the throat, on the left side in front; and the wound was of the breadth of one inch, and in depth even unto the heart; and thus he slew him. Moreover, the aforesaid jury say that [the others above-named] incited the said Robert to shoot the same Henry dead, and to slay him, and they were consenting unto his death. . . . And in the same conflict John de Benton came with a falchion into Grope Lane and gave David de Kirkby a blow on the back of the head, six inches in length and in depth even unto the brain. At which same time came William de la Hyde and smote the aforesaid David with a sword across his right knee and leg: and at the same time came William de Astley and smote the said David under the left arm with a misericorde, and thus they slew him. Moreover, concerning the goods of the aforesaid evildoers, or those who have received them, the jury say that they know nothing.[23]

Rashdall also comments on Oxford brawls and on the medieval acceptance of such disturbances as mere commonplace events; he adds with some humour that nothing worse happened to the culprits in the majority of cases than "being compelled to go to Cambridge"! [24]

But Chaucer seriously admires the earnestness of his Clerk, and has given us a portrait of a true "philosophre"; and here the poet makes one of his rare puns,[25] for the word *philosopher* in his time could mean not only a lover and student of what we understand by "philosophy," but an alchemist as well. As it was the principal claim of the alchemists that they could transform the baser metals into gold, Chaucer's play on words becomes obvious. The Clerk has certainly no gold "in coffre," for

As leene was his hors as is a rake,
And he nas nat right fat, I undertake,
But looked holwe, and therto sobrely,
Ful thredbare was his overeste courtepy . . .

(ll. 287–290)

Again we realize that the Clerk cared more for his books and his learning in Aristotle than for "robes riche." The Ellesmere MS. depicts the Clerk in a violet academic gown with a white edging on hood, cape, and skirt; Rashdall tells us that black gowns were not prescribed until a much later date.[26] The cap is red, as are the hose; the black shoes are unfashionably square of toe. The artist of the miniature has given the Clerk a lean cheek, and an expression to match his sober demeanor. The threadbare short upper coat is not shown; but the decrepit nag which it is the Clerk's unhappy lot to ride all the way to Canterbury is faithfully presented, even to the prominent ribs, which Chaucer suggests by comparing the poor beast to a rake.

The Clerk is perhaps best summed up by Chaucer's now famous line, "And gladly wolde he lerne and gladly teche," for he is a true student, gladly sacrificing gaiety and comfort for learning, and gladly performing his tutorial duties with much more professional interest than eagerness for money. We hope that Chaucer knew such a worthy individual in actual life and that the poet was one of the "freendes" who helped this poor Oxonian "to scoleye."

NOTES

(The abbreviations used to designate books and articles mentioned in the Notes will be found listed alphabetically in the Bibliography, opposite the full reference. References to lines in the *Canterbury Tales* are given by fragment and line numbers only.)

1. Rashdall, I, 181. Rashdall rather impatiently remarks that even Savigny (the primary authority on Roman Law in the Middle Ages) "never could understand what a *clericus* meant . . . [Savigny] says that *clericus* must mean merely 'scholar.'" The *NED* ("Clerk") defines the word as used by Chaucer to mean someone "able to read and write—or, simply, a scholar." But Rashdall proves his point through quotation of the following Statute of Ferrara (Borsetti, i, 367): "Et si fieri posset, sit (Rector) qui promotus sit ad primos ordines ecclesiasticos, scilicet ad primam tonsuram et quatuor Ordines Minores et hoc quo convenitor (*lege* convenienter) Iudex competens Scholaribus fieri queat."

2. *Ibid.,* III, 393 f.

3. *Ibid.,* p. 395.

4. *Ibid.,* p. 197.

5. IV (E) 2.

6. Rashdall, III, 216.

7. *Ibid.,* pp. 406 ff.

8. Jones, *PMLA,* XXVII, 111.

9. In the *Miller's Tale* the clerk Nicholas is also from Oxford, but in the *Reeve's Tale* the clerks John and Aleyn are from Cambridge. There is every reason to suppose that Chaucer was acquainted with the locality of both universities, as Prof. Robinson reminds us. Prof. Robinson also calls attention to the fact that in 1388 the King's Council met at Oxford, and Parliament met at Cambridge (p. 790, n. 3921).

10. Rashdall, III, 238–265.

11. *Ibid.,* pp. 153 ff.

12. Chaucer's admiration for Ralph Strode, the eminent Oxford authority on logic, may have prompted him to invest the Clerk, a very much humbler man, with the same interests as Strode.

13. The 1387 inventory of the books belonging to Simon de Burley, probably one of Chaucer's friends, mentions several volumes bound in red. (Hibbard, *MLN,* XXX, 170 f. The inventory is from Brit. Mus. Add. MS. 25459, f. 206.)

Mr. Curt Bühler of the Pierpont Morgan Library, New York, calls my attention to E. P. Goldschmidt's *Gothic and Renaissance Bookbindings* (London, 1928) and G. D. Hobson's *English Binding before 1500* (Cambridge, 1929) in both of which the colours of bindings listed include brown, white, red, black, reddish yellow, blue and pink. The Clerk's desire for red or black seems conservative!

14. Rashdall, III, 417–418. Rashdall obtained this material from inventories found in *Reg. Cancell. Oxon. 1434–1469,* ed. H. E. Salter (O. H. S.).

15. Schramm, *MLN,* XLVIII, 143.

16. Schramm estimates (p. 145) the value of the Clerk's prospective library at 40 *l.* in the fourteenth century, a sum which would indeed be vast for the Clerk.

17. Rashdall, III, 441.

18. *Ibid.,* p. 442.

19. *Ibid.,* Chap. XIV *passim.*

20. *Ibid.,* p. 423. Rashdall says that even the "ideal" student in the medieval university "enjoyed an abundance of what may be called ecclesiastical dissipation." On the many days of festival there were processions, university Masses, university sermons, dinners, and distributions of money.

21. I (A) 3328–3333.

22. Robinson gives (p. 760, n. 307) *sownynge in* as equivalent to "tendency towards, consonant with," and cites five other instances of its similar use in Chaucer. He says that the expression comes from Med. Lat. *sonare in* or *ad.* Flügel (*Anglia,* XXIV, 483) agrees with Robinson.

23. Coulton, *Life in the Mid. Ages,* II, 76–77. On p. 73 Coulton says: "The . . . inquests are chosen as typical cases from the few surviving Oxford Coroners' Rolls, which are printed on pp. 150 ff. of Prof. J. E. T. Rogers' *Oxford City Documents.*" And he adds that out of 29 inquests 13 "disclose murders committed by students"! This is partly because a clerk, who enjoyed always ecclesiastical immunity, could not be hanged for his first murder. The date of the inquest from which the quotation is taken is 1314.

24. Rashdall, III, 432.

25. Robinson, p. 760, n. 297.

26. Rashdall, III, 387.

CHAPTER X

THE SERGEANT OF THE LAW AND THE FRANKLIN IN HIS COMPANY

A Sergeant of the Lawe, war and wys,

. . . .

Ther was also, ful riche of excellence.
Discreet he was and of greet reverence—
He semed swich, his wordes weren so wise.

(ll. 309, 311–313)

As MANLY remarks, it is a pity that such a colorful and distinguished member of society as the Sergeant of the Law of the *Prologue* becomes the mere Man of Law on the journey to Canterbury.[1]
A "man of law" could be any insignificant lawyer, but a sergeant
of the law was, in Chaucer's time and for nearly five hunded years
afterwards, one of a superior order of barristers, men from whom
were chosen all the Common Law judges until 1873. The title of
"sergeant"corresponds to the Latin *serviens ad legem,* or "the server
(of the king) in legal matters." [2] Manly notes that the order of
sergeants is of "immemorial antiquity"; sergeants "ranked socially
immediately after knights bachelors and took precedence of Companions of the Bath, younger sons of knights, and even younger
sons of great nobles." [3] Sergeants as members of the legal profession
"ranked immediately after the judges of the king's bench and common pleas, and took precedence of both the attorney-general and the
solicitor-general and also barons of the exchequer, except the chief."
Sergeants were not asked to remove their head-covering, or coif,[4]
even in the presence of royalty; and the king himself "in the writ
addressed to one of them uses the respectful plural *vos* instead of
the *tu* and *te* commonly used in addressing officials and other infe-
riors." [5] Furthermore, sergeants were always men of wealth, for
when a barrister became a sergeant, after a necessary sixteen years

as a barrister, the ceremony of investiture was extremely elaborate
and expensive,[6] and the gargantuan feasts always following such
ceremonies matched them in splendour and cost.[7]

The Sergeant is wary and prudent ("war and wys"). The *wys*
is not here coupled with *worthy,* and the word therefore has a much
less complimentary connotation [8] than when Chaucer uses it to describe his Knight, who is also "worthy." The reserved and stately
Sergeant, whose words are so "wise," is not, perhaps, all he would
have us think:

> Nowher so bisy a man as he ther nas,
> And yet he semed bisier than he was.
>
> (ll. 321–322)

Everyone knows the man whose self-importance exceeds any genuine
importance he may have, whose busyness is so magnified in his own
eyes that he becomes pompously overactive. Chaucer's Sergeant is
a prominent individual in his world, but he is not as "ful riche of
excellence" as he believes himself to be.

The Sergeant of the Law has very definite professional activities.
He is a lawyer who—

> . . . often hadde been at the Parvys.
>
> .   .   .   .
>
> Justice he was ful often in assise,
> By patente and by pleyn commissioun.
> For his science and for his heigh renoun,
> Of fees and robes hadde he many oon.
> So greet a purchasour was nowher noon:
> Al was fee symple to hym in effect;
> His purchasyng myghte nat been infect.
>
> .   .   .   .
>
> In termes hadde he caas and doomes alle
> That from the tyme of kyng William were falle.
> Therto he koude endite, and make a thyng,
> Ther koude no wight pynche at his writyng;
> And every statut koude he pleyn by rote.
>
> (ll. 310, 314–320, 323–327)

The traditional interpretation of *parvis* as "the enclosed area or
court in front of a building, especially of a cathedral or a church,
in some cases surrounded as a cloister with colonnades or porticoes,"

as was the parvis of St. Paul's in London, is probably the best.[9] In his study of Chaucer's Man of Law at the Parvis, Professor G. L. Frost observes that outside of Oxford no mention is found in any record of a place connected with a parvis except St. Paul's Cathedral.[10] Sergeants of the law had a close connection with St. Paul's. Dugdale, in his *Origines Juridiciales,* as Professor Frost points out, gives an account of an investiture of sergeants in the late sixteenth century in which St. Paul's is emphasized explicitly by a reference to "that old Custome" of sergeants' hearing "their Clyents cause" near a "Pillar of Pauls." Since the law is conservative, Professor Frost argues that the old custom would include the fourteenth-century practice.[11] The question has been raised, however, as to why Chaucer would specify that his Sergeant was "often" at the "Parvys" if such procedure were merely customary. To answer this objection, Professor Frost interprets the frequent appearances of Chaucer's Sergeant at the Parvis to be upon special occasions at the time of investitures, which the fourteenth-century audience would have readily understood. Dugdale says that the older sergeants at the investiture ceremonies had the duty of introducing the newly created sergeants "to their respective pillars."[12] Therefore, since sergeants were few in number (there were only a score or so when Chaucer was writing) [13] and those few infrequently selected, a sergeant who had been "often" at an investiture ceremony would be important enough for such an unusual fact about him to be noted.[14]

Chaucer's Sergeant of the Law has often been a "justice . . . in assise," both by "patente" and by "pleyn commissioun." The assize(s) were "sessions held periodically in each county of England for the purpose of administering civil and criminal justice by judges acting under certain special commissions." [15] The term "by patente" indicates that the justice "in assise" bore an open letter of appointment from the king; "by pleyn commissioun" indicates that the justice bore a letter giving him jurisdiction in all kinds of cases.[16] How these men were regarded by their contemporaries will be considered later.

But the Sergeant has justified his eminent position in one way at least, for his legal knowledge, his "science," is extraordinary. English law is, as we are aware, almost entirely a matter of precedents, and our Man of Law knows accurately ("in termes") all the cases and decisions ("caas and doomes") which have been ruled in the courts since the time of William the Conqueror. Moreover, he has memorized every existing statute word for word ("every statut koude he pleyn by rote"). The great breadth of this knowledge on the part of the Sergeant of the Law is indicated by Manly in two quotations which he gives from Maitland's *Select Pleas of the Crown*: "Almost to the extreme limit of legal memory, almost to the coronation day of Richard I extends the series of our yet extant Plea Rolls"; and, "If the judicial records of the thirteenth century were printed in a hundred volumes, those volumes would be stout." [17] Because of his vast legal knowledge and his wide reputation, Chaucer's Sergeant has received many fees and robes from his clients. Money was scarce in the Middle Ages, so "robes" (meaning whole sets of clothing)[18] were not uncommonly used as payment for professional and other services. We may be sure that Chaucer's Sergeant is the kind of man to demand prompt and full payment of every bill.

For this Canterbury-bound Sergeant is a shrewd business man as well as a noted lawyer: nowhere is there a better buyer of land or obtainer of possessions ("purchasour")[19] than he. If land is entailed, or defective in title ("infect"), he manages somehow to get around the restriction and hold it with a clear title (in "fee symple") to himself. He can write ("endite") his documents so that no one is able to find fault with them ("koude no wight pynche at his writyng"). This Man of Law is truly "war and wys"!

In this portrait, Chaucer's satire is consistently ironic: he reports in outward praise and inward condemnation the characteristics of his Sergeant which make the Sergeant of the Law a man of purely material success. But Chaucer and his contemporaries were hardly different from their descendants in their dislikes of "sharp" legal practices. Wyclif, of course, is outspoken; in one of his tracts he writes:

. . . & yit men of lawe, that schulden distroie siche falsnesse [*the abuses of lordship*] bi here offices & don eche man right & reson, meyntenen wrong for money & fees & robis, & forbaren pore men fro here right, that it is betre to hem to pursue not for here right, be it never so opyn, than to pursue & lese more catel* for disceitis of delaies and cavellacions* & evele wilis that thei usen; & thus wrong is meyntened & trewthe & right outlawid in many statis.

. . . .

* *catel*: "goods"   *cavellacions*: "cavils"

In men of lawe regneth moche gile, for thei meyntenen falsnes for wynnynge & maken lordis to meyntene wrongis, & don wrongis whanne lordis hopen to do right & plese god, & bi here coveitise & falsenesse thei purchasen londis & rentis ynowe and don many extorsions & beren don the right bothe of pore & riche, & yit thei maken it so holy in signes outward as if thei weren angelis of hevene, to colour here falsenesse & blynde the peple therby.[20]

A follower of Wyclif, in another tract, complains bitterly that evil lawyers promote quarrels, pack juries, bribe perjurers, and contrive to get lands under their own control, thus cheating the rightful heirs. The wealth of lawyers arrives too quickly to be honestly got; always lawyers oppress the poor.[21]

Langland writes of lawyers in the same vein as the Wyclifites. He speaks of "sergeants of the law" in "hoods of silk": these sergeants serve at the bar, but they will plead only for money and never for love of Christ. It is more sensible to try to measure the mist on the Malvern hills than to try to get even a mumble from a lawyer unless one first shows him money.[22] Langland also says that Simony and Civil, representing the practitioners in the civil law, and jurors at the assizes are the most intimate of all folk with Bribery herself—

Ac Symonye and Civile . and sisours of contreis
Were most pryvye with Mede . of eny men, me thoughte.[23]

And finally Langland tells us, when Piers procures from Truth his bull of pardon for mankind, the lawyers who "loth were to plede" unless they had been paid in advance have the smallest pardons.[24]

Gower also assails the unprincipled lawyers of his day. Although some men of law are praiseworthy, he says, most will plead the cause of anyone, criminal or not, who will pay them enough. The lawyers have a thousand ways of making their profit, and their victims who are weak and without defence cannot escape their clutches.[25] The lawyer plunders everywhere, and he delights in quarrels. He seeks every means to get money, and joins house to house and field to field to increase his own holdings (in other words, the lawyer is a "purchasour").[26] England is ruined by lawyers, and they themselves are outside the law. They rapidly rise from apprentice to sergeant to judge; gifts, fear, and favour have combined to make justice worthless.[27]

The ordinary preachers of the fourteenth century turn their wrath against the men of law in much the same way as do Wyclif, Langland, and Gower. In Dr. Owst's opinion the impressions which all the homilists give are threefold.[28] First it is made abundantly clear that the people are at the mercy of "a class of trained and educated specialists" who always take advantage of them. As one typical and anonymous preacher complains: "The wytty men of this worlde, as justycis, vocates and men of lawe, these men have power in length and brede and depnes upon gentylmen of myddel degre and upon pore men, theym to deme and to juge as they lyst." [29] Second, the lawyers will never plead a case unless they receive exorbitant fees; one preacher speaks for all when he says:

A man shuld ge[ve] judgement in the peple shuld be like a balaunce yeldyng to every man right. But trewly, gefts blyndeth so the jugges yghen, that thei may not see the even ryght wey in the balaunce.[30]

And another preacher adds to the common complaint by saying that the lawyers are so intent upon winning that they will take bribes from both sides! [31] Finally, the preachers say that justice is corrupted not only by bribery, but also by a sinful willingness to placate the wicked if the wicked be powerful. The men of law fear man rather than God:

By unjuste dred, on word acombers the jugges, whan an erthly man is more drad than God, othur the right. Such a jugge was Pilate, demyng Crist to dethe, dredynge, yiff that he had saved hym, that the Jewes wold have peched hym to the Emperour. And so he preferred mans drede, afore the drede of God. . . . And trewly, so many men, as I wene, verely in arbitrement, in juggement and on questes, thei preferre the drede of othur grett men in the world byfore the drede of almyghty God; nothur thei drede not to be wittyngly forsworne.[32]

Probably Chaucer's Sergeant of the Law has earned the censure of contemporary homilists on all of the usual three counts. Certainly he is a "trained and educated specialist," and such emphasis cannot have been laid on his exhaustive knowledge of common and statutory law without the implication that he sometimes uses this knowledge to very questionable advantage. Nothing explicit is stated about the Sergeant's acceptance of bribes, but we are led to believe that he has more "fees and robes" than can honestly be explained. And could such an ambitious and successful buyer of land (entailments so easily expunged!) have come by it all in a completely upright manner? The Sergeant is "discreet"; his words are carefully chosen. Does he not, perhaps, put the fear of man before the fear of God?

As to the Sergeant's appearance, when we meet him he rides—

> . . . but hoomly in a medlee cote,
> Girt with a seint of silk, with barres smale.

> (ll. 328–329)

Sergeants of the law when officially clad wore a long robe, a garment much like a cassock; a fifteenth-century manuscript shows four illuminations of sergeants wearing such robes of striped blue and green,[33] although official colours were brown and green.[34] The "medlee cote" of Chaucer's Sergeant is probably shorter than the official robe, and as we are told that it is "medlee," it is possibly a coat striped in different colours.[35] The Ellesmere MS. depicts the Sergeant in a coat of red and blue, reaching just below the knee. The girdle ("seint") of silk, not worn with the long robe, is part of the "hoomly" attire, and is omitted from the Ellesmere picture; if the artist had included an accurate representation of the Sergeant's girdle, he would have shown the narrow metal strips ("barres smale") with which it was ornamented.[36] The artist, unprompted by the poet, does show the white coif of the Sergeant. The coif was something like a skull-cap, and was tied beneath the chin; [37] it was almost a badge of office for sergeants of the law and could be worn by them even in the royal presence.

Manly has made a thorough study of the legal records for the reign of Richard II, and although they are, as he says, "unfortunately incomplete," we can be fairly certain that "they record the career of every sergeant who was as active in the practice of his profession as was the one whom Chaucer had in mind." [38] Only one of these actual sergeants meets the requirements of the Chaucer figure, Manly tells us, and that is Thomas Pynchbek. His career, sketched much more fully by Manly, [39] may be briefly summarized as follows: Pynchbek became a sergeant of the law "at least as early as 1376";

between 1376 and 1388 he "served often as justice of the assize"; he was apparently a supporter of the Gloucester faction, and so Chaucer might have felt more free to expose him to satire; numerous records indicate that Pynchbek dealt extensively in land, and he is generally represented "as acquiring the property in fee simple"; later records give evidence that the Pynchbek family became one of great wealth, and, Manly suggests it is "not without significance that the surname Pynchbek became a proverbial term for thrift." Not only does the career of Chaucer's Sergeant resemble that of the actual Pynchbek, but, again as Manly points out,[40] there exists a definite connection between the poet himself and Pynchbek. First, the Lincolnshire estates of the Pynchbek family were near the estate of Katherine Swynford, Chaucer's sister-in-law, and there is reason to believe that Chaucer's wife frequently visited her sister, so that Chaucer would have had first-hand reports of the rising wealth of the Pynchbeks; and second, there is a traditional story, probably founded on some fact, concerning a quarrel between Pynchbek and Chaucer's friend, Sir William de Beauchamp. We must not forget, either, that Chaucer's education, which was obviously that of a gentleman, probably included some study at one of the Inns of Court, where he could hardly have failed to know Pynchbek. They were about the same age.

Manly concludes his suggestion as to the identity of Chaucer's Sergeant, by calling attention to the line, "Ther koude no wight pynche at his writyng" and by posing the question as to whether or not Chaucer intended the pun.[41] It is difficult to suppose that Chaucer had no *arrière-pensée,* but in any case we can be sure that most of Chaucer's audience would have read Pynchbek's name into the line, and for them, in their not unmalicious amusement, the Sergeant of the Law could have been none other than the over-clever and somewhat dubiously rich Thomas Pynchbek of Lincolnshire.

*   *   *

The Franklin who accompanies the Sergeant of the Law is almost, if not entirely, his social equal.

A Frankeleyn was in his compaignye.

At sessiouns ther was he lord and sire;
Ful ofte tyme he was knyght of the shire.

. . . .

A shirreve hadde he been, and a contour,
Was nowher swich a worthy vavasour.

(ll. 331, 355–356, 359–360)

A "franklin" in the fourteenth century had come to mean a wealthy
landowner of the gentry class; [42] Chaucer's Franklin, in particular,
must occupy a well established and dignified position in his community because of the many public offices he has held.

The list Chaucer gives us of his Franklin's offices is impressive.
The Franklin has presided at sessions of justices of the peace ("at
sessiouns ther was he lord and sire") ; he has often been a member
of Parliament ("ful ofte tyme he was a knyght of the shire") ; [43] and
he has been a sheriff ("shirreve"), that is, an administrative officer
of the Crown, ranking next in the shire to the Lord Lieutenant,[44]
and a pleader in court ("contour").[45] Nowhere else, Chaucer sums
up, is there such a "worthy vavasour," the terms *franklin* and *vavasour* being apparently synonymous in Middle English usage.[46]

The Franklin's many specific offices make it seem probable that
Chaucer had in mind some one person for this important figure. The
detailed description of the Franklin's personal appearance and character emphasizes that impression.

Whit was his berd as is the dayesye;
Of his complexioun he was sangwyn.
Wel loved he by the morwe a sop in wyn;
To lyven in delit was evere his wone,
For he was Epicurus owene sone,
That heeld opinion that pleyn delit
Was verraily felicitee parfit.
An housholdere, and that a greet, was he;
Seint Julian he was in his contree.
His breed, his ale, was alweys after oon;
A bettre envyned man was nowher noon.
Withoute bake mete was nevere his hous
Of fissh and flessh, and that so plentevous,
It snewed in his hous of mete and drynke,
Of alle deyntees that men koude thynke.
After the sondry sesons of the yeer,

So chaunged he his mete and his soper.
Ful many a fat partrich hadde he in muwe,
And many a breem and many a luce in stuwe.
Wo was his cook but if his sauce were
Poynaunt and sharp, and redy al his geere.
His table dormant in his halle alway
Stood redy covered al the longe day.

. . . . s

An anlaas and a gipser al of silk
Heeng at his girdel, whit as morne milk.
(ll. 332–354, 357–358)

It should first be noted that the Franklin's temperament ("complexioun") is "sangwyn." The medieval physiologist classified human
beings according to four temperaments, determined by the supposed
preponderance of one or more fluids ("humours") in the individual's
body. The "sanguine" type was so named because persons belonging
to this group were thought to possess more blood than any other
fluid; they are spoken of as "hot and moist" and their characteristics are described with little variation by all medieval writers on
the subject. What the author of the *Secreta Secretorum* has to say
about this "complexioun" is therefore common knowledge for the
fourteenth century:

> The sangyne by kynde sholde lowe Ioye and laghynge, and com-
> pany of women, and moche Slepe and syngynge: he shal be hardy
> y-nowe, of good will and wythout malice: he shalbe flesshy, his com-
> plexcion shalbe lyght to hurte and to empeyre for his tendyrnesse, he
> shall have a goode stomake, good dygescion, and good delyveraunce:
> . . . he shall be fre and lyberall, of fayre semblaunt . . .[47]

Thus if Chaucer had stopped short after telling his medieval audience
that the Franklin is "sangwyn" in temperament, they would have
seen him clearly enough as a type: the man of "goode stomake"
and "good dygescion," who loves food and joy and laughter and
good companionship, and who is "fre and lyberall." But Chaucer
did not stop short; he amplified and indulged in delightful hyper-
bole, with the result that the Franklin stands distinct, and as someone who is likely to have been immediately identified by his contemporaries.

The Franklin has more than good appetite and good digestion; he is "owene sone" to Epicurus. According to *Boece,* Epicurus is said to have "juggid and establissyde that delit is the soverayn good," [48] and the Franklin has come to the conclusion that dining well offers one of the greatest joys in life. How the Franklin enjoys a "sop in wyn" in the morning! The "sop in wyn" was no frugal apple, as suggested by one scholar,[49] but must have been one of the rich, glazed "soppes" of the Middle Ages. It was made by pouring a sauce of wine, almond milk, saffron, ginger, sugar, cinnamon, cloves, and mace, over the best white bread.[50] The Franklin's bread and ale are uniformly good ("alweys after oon"), his wine cellar is the best stocked in the country ("a bettre envyned man was nowher noon"), his larders are never without baked meats and fish; indeed, as Chaucer says, it snows food and drink in the Franklin's house! And what variety there is, following "the sondry sesons of the yeer," for both dinner and supper! "Epicurus owene sone" keeps fat partridges ready at hand in a coop ("muwe"); his private fish-pond ("stuwe") on the estate is filled with bream and pike ("luce"); and woe betide the cook if the sauces for these delectable foods are insufficiently "poynaunt and sharp," or if the cooking utensils ("geere") are not in constant readiness. The Franklin as a great and hospitable "housholdere" has changed the ordinary medieval custom of setting up boards across trestles for each meal, for he has a permanent table always in position for use ("table dormant"). Truly the Franklin is "Seint Julian . . . in his contree."

St. Julian, the patron of hospitality, was one of the most popular saints of the Middle Ages, although he was indeed "more legendary than historical." [51] The *Legenda Aurea* mentions several Julians, but since Chaucer connects him elsewhere with a "bon hostel," [52] it is probable that this "Seint Julian" is the one identified as the Bishop of Le Mans who probably lived in the third century, although legend makes him one of Christ's contemporaries. The *Legenda Aurea* says of Julian:

. . . he was the same man as Simon the Leper, who was cured by Christ, and then invited him to dine at his table. . . . It may be this Saint Julian whom travellers invoke, that they may find hospitality on their journey; this would be due to the honour which was his in receiving Our Lord as his guest.[53]

Since Chaucer's Franklin is another St. Julian, we can be positive that even the fare he usually sets before his guests is suitable for a "feast." In John Russell's *Boke of Nurture,* written about the middle of the fifteenth century, the menu for "A Fest for a Franklen" is given. The first course consists of brawn with mustard, bacon and peas; beef and boiled chickens, roast goose, capon, and "custade costable," a dish of pastries stuffed with a mixture of cream, eggs, marrow, prunes, dates, and spices. The second course consists of "mortrewes," a rich stew made of meat or fish, veal, lamb, kid or rabbit, chickens or pigeons roasted, "dowcettes" or little pastries stuffed with cream, eggs, spices, and meats; "fritters," thin slices of fried bread; apples and pears if in season; bread and cheese; spiced cakes and wafers with "bragot," a drink of ale, honey, and spices; and mead.[54] Twentieth-century imaginations reel, and perhaps not all those of the fourteenth century were quite steady, when picturing this vast quantity of food. We are inclined to think of the "snowing" of meat and drink in the Franklin's house as something very like an avalanche.

Only one physical characteristic of the Franklin is mentioned by Chaucer, but that one is especially striking: his beard is as white as a daisy ("dayesye"), with his ruddy face the center.

Chaucer says almost nothing, of course, about the Franklin's dress, for he must be clad in the ordinary garb of a country gentleman. One small distinction in apparel is, however, noted by the poet: an "anlaas" and a "gipser" hang at his girdle. The "anlaas," or *anelace,* was a large hunting dagger, having a broad blade sharpened at both edges and tapering to a point;[55] the "gipser," or *gypciere,* was an ornamental purse almost always suspended from the girdle.[56]

The Franklin's "gipser" is of silk that is as "whit as morne milk"; the white of the purse would be in sharp contrast to the colour of his gown which the Ellesmere artist depicts as particoloured red and blue. That the Franklin wears both "anlaas" and "gipser" connects him still further with the gentry, for only wealthy civilians and distinguished men of law are shown to wear both dagger and purse in the monumental brasses of the fourteenth and fifteenth centuries.[57]

As has been suggested, the Franklin is so carefully individualized by Chaucer that we feel his portrait must have been created entirely from one living model. Manly has made out an excellent case for identifying him with John Bussy of Lincolnshire. The Franklin's career parallels Bussy's very closely. Bussy was "ful ofte tyme" knight of the shire, for he served in many parliaments in the reign of Richard II.[58] Bussy was also sheriff a number of times;[59] and he repeatedly "sat on commissions of the peace and other county business."[60] Furthermore, Bussy was often associated with Pynchbek and Pynchbek's friends, and Bussy lived only a few miles from Pynchbek's estates in Lincolnshire;[61] it would have been natural for Bussy, the franklin, to have accompanied his important friend Pynchbek, a sergeant of the law, on an actual pilgrimage. Manly forestalls a possible objection to identifying the Franklin with Bussy, who was called "Sir" as early as 1384, and referred to in records as "Chevalier," by re-emphasizing that "franklin" and "vavasour" both designated a member of the gentry class, and by reminding us that not all "knights" were of the same grade.[62] "The fact that Bussy was regarded by his enemies as an upstart," Manly writes, "points to his being classed as a commoner."[63]

Of course we know nothing of Bussy's personal appearance; and there is no way to discover whether or not Bussy had earned the reputation of being the St. Julian of Lincolnshire, although we do know that he was "an housholdere, and that a greet," for his estates were large [64] enough to warrant the cost and the provisioning of many a "fest for a franklen." Had Chaucer himself sat at an ever-ready "table dormant" in Bussy's Hall, and been snowed under by all that "mete and drynke"? Did he, perhaps, observe Pynchbek's acceptance of a friendship which would gain that clever sergeant of the law such pleasantly free-of-charge delights? The temptation is to reply to these questions in the affirmative even while we are aware that in reality they must remain unanswered.

NOTES

(The abbreviations used to designate books and articles mentioned in the Notes will be found listed alphabetically in the Bibliography, opposite the full reference. References to lines in the *Canterbury Tales* are given by fragment and line numbers only.)

1. Manly, *New Light*, p. 132.
2. *NED*, "Sergeant."
3. Manly, *New Light*, p. 133.

4. Skeat says (*Piers Plow.*, II, 16) that lay lawyers shaved their heads (for the tradition of the ecclesiastical, and hence tonsured, lawyer was kept alive), and wore a coif for "distinction's sake." The coif was first made of linen, but later of white silk.

5. Manly, *New Light*, pp. 133 f.

6. *Ibid.*, pp. 137 ff.

7. *Ibid.*, pp. 142 f.

8. Héraucourt, p. 93.

9. *NED*, "Parvis"; Robinson, p. 760, n. 310.

10. Frost, *MLN*, XLIV, 499.

11. *Ibid.*, pp. 499 f.

12. *Ibid.*, p. 501.

13. Robinson, p. 760.

14. Frost, *loc. cit.*, p. 501. Skeat, Robinson, and the *NED* agree in assigning the meaning "church-porch" to *parvis*. Manly inclines to the interpretation of *parvis* as the *paradisus*, or "court," at Westminster, used either as the court of the Exchequer, or for an afternoon exercise for the students of the Inns of Court. Manly says that it is "uncertain" that St. Paul's was used for lawyer-client consultation in the fourteenth century. (*Cant. Tales*, p. 518, n. 310.) Robinson points out, however, that Fortescue's text, edited by Selden —who is Manly's source for the Westminster theory—really supports the St. Paul's theory.

15. *NED*, "Assize."

16. Manly, *Cant. Tales*, p. 518.

17. *Ibid.*, p. 519.

18. *Ibid.*, p. 518.

19. *NED*, "Purchaser." Lawyers were accused of these same tactics as late as the end of the sixteenth century. Robert Greene writes in *A Notable Discovery of Coosnage* (1592): "Think you some lawyers coulde be such purchasers, if al their pleas were short, and their proceedinges iustice and conscience?"

20. Matthew, pp. 234, 237 f.

21. *Ibid.*, pp. 182 ff.

22. *Piers Plow.*, C. Passus I. 158–164. Langland speaks in great exaggeration, of course, of "hundreds" of sergeants of the law.

23. *Ibid.*, C. Passus III. 63–64.

24. *Ibid.*, C. Passus X. 43–45.

25. Gower, *Vox. Clam.*, Lib. VI, cap. I.

26. *Ibid.*, cap. II.

27. *Ibid.*, cap. III, IV. Cf. *Mirour*, ll. 24541–24559 and 24574–24588.

28. Owst, *Lit. and Pulpit*, pp. 338–349.

29. *Ibid.*, p. 341. Quoted from the English version of the *Gesta Romanorum*, p. 434.

30. *Ibid.*, p. 342. Quoted from MS. Roy. 18 B. xxiii, fol. 135.

31. *Ibid.*, p. 343.

32. *Ibid.*, p. 344. Quoted from MS. Roy. 18 B. xxiii, fol. 135.

33. Druitt, p. 224.
34. Robinson, p. 760, n. 328.
35. Manly, *Cant. Tales,* p. 519.
36. *Ibid.*
37. *NED,* "Coif."
38. Manly, *New Light,* p. 148.
39. *Ibid.,* pp. 148–154.
40. *Ibid.,* pp. 154–156.
41. *Ibid.,* p. 157. See also Tatlock, *Flügel Mem. Vol.,* pp. 228–232.
42. G. H. Gerould has amassed much evidence (*PMLA,* XLI, 262–279) to show that fourteenth-century franklins were of the gentry, although originally the word *franklin* denoted only "a free man." Gerould quotes from thirteenth-, fourteenth-, and fifteenth-century writers to prove his point. Manly and Robinson agree with Gerould, and Manly reminds us (*Cant. Tales,* p. 520, n. 340) that Thomas Chaucer, only a generation later, was a franklin, yet "he was one of the wealthiest and most powerful persons in England." Gerould says that many scholars have argued that franklins held an inferior social position because of a confusion arising from Todd's quotation in 1810 from Waterhouse's *Commentary* on Sir John Fortescue's *De Laudibus Legum Anglae.* Todd's quotation "tended to show that franklins did not belong to the gentry," and for want of better evidence, misled scholars for many years. As Gerould points out, this mistaken interpretation even appears in the *NED.*
43. A fifteenth-century statute requires that knights of the shire be "gentlemen." Gerould quotes (*loc. cit.,* p. 273) from *Statutes of the Realm,* 23 Henry VI, cap. 14, as follows: ". . . soient notablez Chivalers . . . ou autrement tielx notablez Esquiers gentils homez del Nativite dez mesmez les Counteez comme soient ablez destre Chivalers & null home destre tiel Chivaler que estoise en la degree de vadlet & desouth."
44. Robinson, p. 761, n. 359.
45. Manly states (*Cant. Tales,* p. 521, n. 359) that this is here the more likely interpretation for the word *contour,* although the word also meant "an accountant" and is so used in the *Book of the Duchess,* l. 435.
46. Gerould says (*loc. cit.,* pp. 277 f.) that *franklin* and *vavasour* are both merely descriptive words, and for this reason they appear only infrequently in state documents. His research leads him to the positive conclusion, however, that the two words are interchangeable.
47. *Secreta Secretorum,* pp. 219 f.
48. *Boece,* III, pr. 2, 88–91.
49. *N & Q,* series X, vol. 8, p. 249.
50. *Two 15th Cent. Cook Bks.,* p. 11.
51. Robinson, p. 761, n. 340. See also Butler (*Lives of the Saints,* I, 345), who assigns 250 A.D. as a probable date for this Saint Julian.
52. *House of Fame,* l. 1022.
53. *Golden Leg.,* p. 128.
54. *Early Eng. Meals and Man.,* pp. 54 f.
55. Fairholt, p. 411.

56. *Ibid.*, p. 505.

57. Druitt, pp. 188 ff. The brass of Sir William Gascoigne, Chief Justice of the King's Bench, should be particularly noted (p. 227, n. 1).

58. Manly, *New Light,* p. 162.

59. *Ibid.,* pp. 162 f.

60. *Ibid.,* p. 163.

61. *Ibid.*

62. *Ibid.,* pp. 164 ff.

63. *Ibid.,* p. 167. K. L. Wood-Legh takes issue (*Rev. Eng. St.,* IV, 145–151) with Manly's identification of the Franklin with Bussy. He argues that, for the Middle Ages, Bussy was not often enough knight of the shire to satisfy Chaucer's "ful ofte tyme." He disregards the meaning of "pleader" for *contour,* and points out that Bussy was never an "auditor." Wood-Legh suggests Stephen de Hales of Norfolkshire as a better candidate for the Franklin's prototype than Bussy. De Hales was nine times in Parliament before 1386, he was sheriff for two terms, commissioner of the peace four times, and he served as commissioner of taxes (perhaps equivalent to "contour"?). De Hales also was associated professionally with Pynchbek. But, Wood-Legh concludes, as there are so many possibilities, the Franklin may be regarded as typical. To the present writer, if there were a flesh-and-blood model, Bussy seems the best choice.

64. Manly, *New Light,* p. 163.

CHAPTER XI

THE FIVE GILDSMEN AND THEIR COOK

An Haberdasshere and a Carpenter,
A Webbe, a Dyere, and a Tapycer,—
And they were clothed alle in o lyveree
Of a solempne and a greet fraternitee.
Ful fressh and newe hir geere apiked was;
Hir knyves were chaped noght with bras
But al with silver; wroght ful clene and weel
Hire girdles and hir pouches everydeel.

(ll. 361–368)

SINCE CHAUCER'S five gildsmen are clad in one livery and yet are of different crafts, the "greet fraternitee" to which they belong must be a parish, not a craft, gild. The parish gilds had their origin in cooperative chantries.* Mr. George Unwin, the most recent authority on the medieval gild, writes:

> The extension and rebuilding of churches which were constantly going on throughout the fourteenth and fifteenth centuries in London as elsewhere were largely supported by the foundation of chantries. The feudal magnates who had held the churches in early days were replaced by wealthy drapers, fishmongers, vintners, and mercers, who not only acquired their great houses but adopted their social traditions, and who hoped to found a family in a spiritual sense by making provision for themselves, their ancestry, and their posterity.[1]

Certainly any provision these newly rich persons planned would include masses for the dead, which was such an exceedingly important part of medieval religious observance; and, as these masses came to be neglected by monks, who had been the first to perform the office, the great majority of the later foundations were in parochial, instead of monastic, churches.[2] It was natural that members of the

* *chantry*: "endowment for priest(s) to sing masses for the founder's soul"

same parish should join together to support one priest or more who would say masses for the dead of the entire group, and thus the fraternity was formed. When a member died, it was the duty of all the brethren to attend the funeral mass in livery, or pay a fine; sometimes as many as thirty additional masses for the soul of the deceased were provided by the common funds.[3] In Chaucer's time there were in London nearly fifty of these religious gilds,[4] and more than half of them required the wearing of a livery on any important occasion. The livery, Mr. Unwin tells us, was usually paid for by the members at cost price, and members were not allowed to give away or sell their livery.[5]

Besides providing masses for the dead, the parish gilds developed social and benevolent activities. The gild came to the assistance of any member in times of accident, or need, or litigation. Toulmin Smith has edited a number of ordinances of English parish gilds of 1389, the originals of which are in the Public Record Office. The ordinance of the fraternity of "good men, in the chirche of Seint Jame atte Garlekhith in Londone" is typical. The purpose is stated: "to noriche more love bytwene the bretheren and sustren of the bretherhede"; then the rules are laid down: all brethren must be of good repute, each shall pay 6s. 8d. on entry, wardens shall render the accounts yearly, a livery suit is to be worn, a yearly feast is to be held (the brethren to be taxed for this), yearly dues are to be paid, several meetings are to be held, gifts are to be solicited, ill-behaved brethren are to be expelled, no livery is to be sold within a year, attendance at a member's funeral is obligatory, quarrels between members are to be tried within the gild, weekly help is to be tendered to members who are ill or old or "enpresoned falslich by enme," and all must swear to uphold the ordinances of the gild.[6]

In Chaucer's time the gilds had become important enough politically to warrant parliamentary action being taken against them. In 1389, Parliament petitioned Richard that gildsmen be restricted in the wearing of liveries,[7] but as the King was friendly to the parish gilds the petition was unsuccessful. It must, however, have occasioned "talk," so that Chaucer's statement that his five gildsmen are dressed in shining, expensive livery is surely a topical touch.

Chaucer describes the apparel ("geere") of the five gildsmen as "fressh" and newly trimmed ("apiked"); their knives, hanging at their handsomely made and resplendent girdles ("wrought ful clene and weel") have sheaths with silver caps ("chapes"). This must have especially amused Chaucer's audience, for the ordinary tradesman or craftsman was forbidden to wear a knife ornamented with a precious metal.[8]

We should note here what crafts Chaucer selected to represent by the five members of the "solempne" and "greet" fraternity. It was not a choice made at random. Professor Kuhl, writing on "Chaucer's Burgesses," calls our attention to the fact that the five are selected from those non-victualling trades which had taken no part in the violent struggle between the non-victuallers and victuallers for the control of London, a struggle which reached its height in Parliament in 1386 when Chaucer was knight of the shire. Professor Kuhl also observes that Chaucer seems to have chosen with discretion members of craft gilds which, although neutral, had importance.[9] Miss Ann B. Fullerton takes exception to this suggestion and says that it can scarcely be believed "that Chaucer either remembered or looked up . . . the exact rank of each of the craft guilds in London." [10] But Chaucer need not have known the exact rank to have chosen crafts of obvious importance.

Haberdashers were of two kinds: dealers in small wares or what we call "notions" today, and makers of hats. In 1377, the Haberdashers had four representatives in the City Council, and this was after election by wards had gone into effect. Formerly the election was by gilds themselves. Professor Kuhl tells us that some of the Haberdashers were important enough to inherit substantially through wills and to appear in the public records.[11]

Weavers were equally important, and Professor Kuhl connects the poet's selection of this craft with his emphasis on the accomplishments of the Wife of Bath, for one of the prominent members of the Weaver's Gild in 1376 was John de Bathe.[12]

Tapicers, who wove tapestry and, sometimes, blankets,[13] and Dyers were, like the Haberdashers and Weavers, firmly established in London and their members well known.[14]

The Carpenters were incorporated in 1344 as a gild; [15] and although their members do not seem to have figured as prominently as did those of the other four gilds Chaucer mentions, there was probably some special contemporary reason, of which we are now unaware, for the poet's including a carpenter among his burgesses.

Wel semed ech of hem a fair burgeys
To sitten in a yeldehalle on a deys.
Everich, for the wisdom that he kan,
Was shaply for to been an alderman.
For catel hadde they ynogh and rente,
And eek hir wyves wolde it wel assente;
And elles certeyn were they to blame.
It is ful fair to been ycleped "madame,"
And goon to vigilies al bifore,
And have a mantel roialliche ybore.

(ll. 369–378)

Chaucer here tells us that each of the five gildsmen seems a
burgess worthy to sit on the dais in a gild hall, but as only the Mayor
and Aldermen of the Common Council sat on the dais, Professor
Kuhl suggests that Chaucer meant to imply that each "fair burgeys"
was capable of being either mayor or one of the aldermen.[16] Chaucer
himself supports this interpretation by his repetition in the lines:

Everich, for the wisdom that he kan,
Was shaply for to been an alderman.

In other words, each of the five gildsmen, because of his knowledge
and wisdom, is really made for the office of alderman.[17] The vic-
tualling companies attempted to create a "monopoly" in aldermen
throughout the latter half of the fourteenth century, and no new
aldermen were elected between 1383 and 1388. "Did Londoners
desire an infusion of new blood into the Aldermancy?" asks Professor Kuhl. "Or was Chaucer's reference a sly thrust at the Mayor's
precept of 1384?" (That is, at Brembre's ruling of that year, backed
by the King, for unlimited repetition of terms for those already in
office.) [18]

In any event, the five burgesses are "shaped" for political office,
and they possess the necessary property ("catel") and income
("rente"). Their wives will attest the fact, or be deserving of blame!
The ladies think it most delightful to be called "madame," to pre-
cede everyone at the ceremonies which were held the evenings before
the gild festivals ("vigilies"),[19] and to have their mantles carried
with them as if they were queens! [20]

Miss Fullerton suggests that since the gildsmen are setting out
on a pilgrimage to St. Thomas's shrine, their fraternity very likely

has some association with that particular saint.[21] Only one such fraternity is known in fourteenth-century London: this originated in the chapel on the Bridge and, by the time Chaucer was writing, it had amalgamated with that of the parish of St. Magnus; both groups were especially dedicated to St. Thomas of Canterbury.[22] Miss Fullerton observes that in Chaucer's time this fraternity was surrounded by considerable pomp and pageantry, and that it was apparently an organization of wealth and prestige.[23] Thus it seems likely, although we cannot of course speak with certainty, that Chaucer had in mind the parish gild of St. Magnus as the distinguished and great brotherhood to which his five craftsmen belong.

*   *   *

We regret that we do not know more of Chaucer's five burgesses and their ambitious wives and of their "greet fraternitee," but we must be content to leave them here. At least we know something about their colourful and rascally cook.[24]

> A Cook they hadde with hem for the nones*
> To boille the chiknes with the marybones,
> And poudre-marchant tart and galyngale.
> Wel koude he knowe a draughte of Londoun ale.
> He koude rooste, and sethe, and broille, and frye,
> Maken mortreux, and wel bake a pye.
> But greet harm was it, as it thoughte me,
> That on his shyne a mormal hadde he.
> For blankmanger, that made he with the beste.
>
> (ll. 379–387)

The Cook is a good *chef,* but Chaucer implies that he is also a knave given to bad living. He is thoroughly familiar with "a draughte of Londoun ale," and London ale was a particularly potent brew, as Skeat reminds us;[25] later that "stout carl," the Miller, when very drunk, lays his intoxication to "the ale of Southwerk."[26] The unsightly and telltale mormal on the Cook's shin is to be identified with *malum mortuum* of the medieval medical treatises, according to Professor Curry.[27] He points out that this malady is described by Bernardus de Gordon (who is mentioned by Chaucer in connection with the Doctor of Physic) as follows:

* *for the nones*: "for the occasion," or, perhaps, "especially skilful"

Malum mortuum is a species of scabies, which arises from corrupted natural melancholia . . . The marks of it are large pustules of a leaden or black color, scabbed, and exceedingly fetid, though suppuration and discharge do not occur; and it is frequently accompanied by a certain insensibility in the places affected. In appearance it is most unsightly, coming out on the hip-bones and *often on the shin-bones* [italics mine].[28]

Professor Curry sums up the causes of *malum mortuum,* as given by the fourteenth-century physicians, in these words: "uncleanly personal habits," "the eating of melancholic foods and the drinking of strong wines," and "disgraceful association with diseased and filthy women"; [29] and he points out that the Cook's mormal and his drinking, although they may appear at first sight to be only casually mentioned by Chaucer, are, in reality, revealing and telling statements which fully explain the actions and remarks of the Cook as he rides to Canterbury.[30]

As has been said, the vices of the Cook do not interfere with his skill in culinary art, and we are more than ever impressed by the importance and pomp of the gildsmen who have thought it necessary to their well-being to take this specialist in delicious food with them on their pilgrimage.[31] The palate of the poet himself was evidently stimulated by the tempting dishes the Cook prepares, for he says regretfully that it is "greet harm" that anyone who can cook so well should be the sort of person to be afflicted with a mormal. For how savoury are the Cook's chicken boiled with marrow bones, to be topped off, perhaps, with sharp ("tart") "poudre-marchant" in which there is a liberal seasoning of "galyngale"! "Poudre-marchant" was a combination of pulverized spices, and "galyngale" was an aromatic root of an East Indian plant. One medieval recipe for a poudre-marchant,—and the gildsmen's employee may know this very one,—calls for, among other ingredients, powdered ginger, cinnamon, and galingale, the whole to be "tempered vppe with Wyne" which would give the sharpness so much to be desired.[32] But the Cook's skill does not end with simple boiling; he knows how to roast, to "seethe," to broil, and to fry. He is a specialist in "mortreux," in pies, and in "blankmanger." "Mortreux" were either of fish or of meat; a recipe for "mortrewes of fysshe" directs that boiled chopped fish be seasoned with almond milk, sugar, and salt, "and loke that thou caste Gyngere y-now a-boue," and that the whole be covered with grated bread;[33] a recipe for "mortrewys de fleyssh" directs that finely ground boiled pork be seasoned with saffron, salt, and ginger, and combined with ale, yolks of eggs, and grated bread.[34] A "pye" is usually called a "crustade," and one recipe is as follows:

Take a cofyn* and bake hym drye; then take Marwbonys and do ther-in; thenne nym* hard yolkys of Eyroun* and grynde hem smal, and lye hem uppe* with Milke; than nym raw yolkys of Eyroun and melle* hem a-mong chikonys y-smete*, and do therinne; and yf thou luste, Smal bridys; and a-force* wyl thin comade* with Sugre or hony; than take clowys, Maces, Pepir, and Safron, and put ther-to, and salt yt; and than bake and serve forth.[35]

For the "blankmanger," which is the Cook's masterpiece and which must not be confused with modern blancmange, the recipes are more appealing to present-day palates: nearly all the recipes call for creamed fowl, usually capon, with rice, almonds, sugar, and salt, and often eggs. Chaucer's Cook is indeed highly skilled.

If we follow the Cook from the Tabard along the road to Canterbury, we find that Chaucer presents him to us with extraordinary realism. The Cook names himself, "I highte Hogge of Ware."[36] ("Hogge," or Hodge, is a nickname for Roger, and Ware is in Hertfordshire, evidently the Cook's birthplace, for he is now of London.[37]) There are later scenes of dramatic action and dialogues in which Hogge takes part. Was there really a cook named Roger of Ware whom Chaucer knew?

Mr. Earl D. Lyon writes that we have first hand information about an actual Roger de Ware, Cook, in one of the *Ward Presentments* of Chaucer's day.[38] This flesh-and-blood Roger of Ware is accused of being a common nightwalker, and he pleads guilty. Mr. Lyon points out that a "nightwalker" may be defined as "one guilty of wandering about the streets after curfew," and that the word *common* indicates that the cook in the presentment has been frequently guilty of the offence. Furthermore, in an ordinance of 1340, nightwalkers are linked with keepers of disorderly houses and thieves; it is stated that they "would sooner consort with bad char-

---

* *cofyn*: "crust"	*melle*: "mix"
nym: "take"	*y-smete*: "chopped"
eyroun: "eggs"	*a-force*: "season"
lye hem uppe: "mix"	*comade*: "mixture"

acters and disturbers of the peace than with men of good report." [39]
Certainly, as Mr. Lyon says, this all sounds very much like Chaucer's
Roger of Ware if we judge that famous *chef* by his evident bad
habits, by his behaviour on the way to Canterbury, and by the beginning of the unsavoury tale he starts to tell.

Other scholars have found references to an actual Roger of
Ware. Miss C. Jamison discovered a record of 1377 in which appears the entry, "Roger Ware of London, Cook," in a list of attorneys
in a plea of debt; and Miss Rickert calls our attention to another
entry, also found by Miss Jamison, "Roger Knyght de Ware,
Cook," as plaintiff in a case of debt.[40] If these two entries refer
to Chaucer's Cook, it is likely that Chaucer's audience were much
amused, as Miss Rickert suggests, when they heard the later line,
"This was a fair chyvachee * of a cook!" [41]—a line which concerns the Cook's drunken and far from "knightly" tumble from his
horse.

Although the individualized Roger of Ware of the *Canterbury
Tales* knows how to cook so well, he apparently reserves the proper
exercise of his art for wealthy employers who engage him privately.
He is later accused by the Host of foisting stale and tainted food
upon the plebeian frequenters of his London "shoppe." [42] In this
practice, Roger might be any cook of fourteenth-century London.
Ordinances show that medieval cook-shops in general were given
to serving foods unfit for consumption. An ordinance of 1379, for
example, says in part:

Because that the Pastelers of the City of London have heretofore baked
in pasties rabbits, geese, and garbage, not befitting, and sometimes
stinking, in deceit of the people; and also have baked beef in pasties,
and sold the same for venison, in deceit of the people; therefore, by
assent of the four Master Pastelers, and at their prayer, it is ordered and
assented to.—[Then follow the penalties to be inflicted; the penalties
are fines, or imprisonment, or both, with provision for different
amounts or terms according as the guilty person is a new or an old
offender.] [43]

Moreover, Chaucer himself thus generalizes, through the mouth of
the Pardoner, who is even more of a rascal than the Cook, on the
ways of cooks:

* *chyvachee*: "exploit (knightly) of horsemanship"

> Thise cookes, how they stampe, and streyne,
>   and grynde,
> And turnen substaunce into accident
> To fulfille al thy likerous talent! [44]

In other words, cooks so distort the real ("substaunce") that it takes on any form, smell, colour, and taste ("accident") to satisfy the desires of the greedy.

Yes, Roger Ware of London, Cook, is a drunkard and a libertine, and thoroughly dishonest in his dealings with common folk. But we who stand so safely away in time from his offensive person and his decaying foods are fascinated by the reality of a vivid portrait. Can we not hear Hogge's thickened but confident voice across the centuries, crying his wares in company with Langland's cooks and "knaves"—

> . . . "hote pyes, hote!
> Good goos and grys . go we dyne, gowe!"? [45]

NOTES

(The abbreviations used to designate books and articles mentioned in the Notes will be found listed alphabetically in the Bibliography, opposite the full reference. References to lines in the *Canterbury Tales* are given by fragment and line numbers only.)

1. Unwin, p. 112.
2. Coulton, *Five Cent. of Relig.*, I, Chap. VII and VIII *passim*.
3. Unwin, p. 118.
4. *Ibid.*, pp. 120, 367–370.
5. *Ibid.*, p. 123.
6. Toulmin Smith, pp. 3 ff.
7. *Rotuli Parliamentorum*, III, 266.
8. Skeat, V, 36.
9. Kuhl, *Trans. Wis. Acad.*, XVIII, 653.
10. Fullerton, *MLN*, LXI, 517.
11. Kuhl, *loc. cit.*, pp. 660 f.
12. *Ibid.*, p. 663.
13. *Ibid.*, p. 664.
14. *Ibid.*, p. 657.
15. Fullerton, *loc. cit.*, pp. 516 f. Kuhl states (*loc. cit.*, p. 657) that the Carpenters had no gild; Miss Fullerton quotes from Maitland, *History and Survey of London*, who cites the letters-patent of Edward III of 1344 incorporating the Carpenters.

16. Kuhl, *loc. cit.*, p. 666. Hinckley suggests also (p. 28, n. 372) that the allusion is political, and says that we should interpret *alderman* to mean "municipal magistrate"; he notes that of the Grocers' Company sixteen members were London aldermen, and reminds us that the ill-fated Nicholas Brembre of that Company twice became Mayor of London and was knighted. To be a member of a gild was often the first step towards the realization of high political ambition.

17. Kuhl, *loc. cit.*, p. 667.

18. *Ibid.*, p. 669.

19. Manly, *Cant. Tales*, p. 522, n. 376.

20. Skeat quotes (V, 37) from Speght, who says in his *Glossary*: "It was the manner in times past, upon festival evens, called *vigiliae*, for parishioners to meet in their church-houses or church-yards, and there to have a drinking-fit for the time. . . . Hither came the wives in comely manner, and they which were of the better sort had their mantles carried with them, as well for show as to keep them from cold at table."

21. Fullerton, *loc. cit.*, p. 519.

22. *Ibid.*, pp. 519 f.

23. *Ibid.*, pp. 520 f.

24. Carroll Camden contends (*PQ*, VII, 314–317) that the gildsmen are a late addition to the *General Prologue*, and hence that the pronoun *hem* in l. 379 refers to the Sergeant of the Law and the Franklin. Camden argues that the gildsmen would not have taken along a cook, for that would have been too great an expense—cooks often cost "one hundred dollars for a single night." Robinson (p. 761) characterizes Camden's conclusion as "a bold inference." Most scholars accept Chaucer's Cook as an employee of the gildsmen: it seems more likely that five members of "a solempne and a greet fraternitee," especially since they apparently belong to the *parvenu* class, and therefore feel the need of outward show, would engage an expensive private cook than would two gentlemen from Lincolnshire. If the Sergeant of the Law is Pynchbek, we have further reason for doubting that the Cook is in his employ, for Pynchbek always counted the pennies.

25. Skeat, V. 37.

26. I (A) 3140.

27. Curry, *Ch. and Med. Sci.*, p. 48.

28. Translated by Curry (*op. cit.*, p. 48).

Haldeen Braddy disagrees (*MLQ*, VII, 265–267) with Curry and says the sore is not dry but running. In support of his point Braddy quotes from Arderne (*q.v.*, pp. 52–55) who successfully treated an unnamed canon for a mormal on the leg: the sore is described by Arderne as "pusceles brounysch and clayisch"—it needs to be dried. Braddy also suggests that since mormals were sometimes cured, they were gangrenous, not cancerous.

In either case, the Cook has a sore that is extremely repellent.

29. Curry, *op. cit.*, pp. 50 f.

30. See the *Cook's Prologue* and the *Manciple's Prologue*.

31. Jusserand, (*Eng. Way. Life*, p. 116) tells how the nobility and the

higher clergy never went on a journey without a train of servants. The gildsmen are perhaps aping this custom in taking a cook with them.

32. *Two 15th Cent. Cook. Bks.*, p. 25, cvii.

33. *Ibid.*, p. 14, xliij.

34. *Ibid.*, xliiij.

35. *Ibid.*, p. 55, xxxv.

36. I (A) 4336.

37. I (A) 4325.

38. Lyon, *MLN*, LII, 491–494.

39. *Ibid.*, pp. 492 ff. (Ordinance taken from *Calendar of Plea and Mem-
oranda Rolls, 1323–1364.*)

40. Rickert, *TLS*, 1932, p. 761.

41. *Ibid.* The line is IX (H) 50.

42. See the *Cook's Prologue.*

43. Riley, *London*, p. 438.

44. VI (C) 538–540.

45. *Piers Plow.*, C. Passus I. 226–227.

CHAPTER XII

THE SHIPMAN: MASTER OF THE MAUDELAYNE

A Shipman was ther, wonynge fer by weste;
For aught I woot, he was of Dertemouthe.
He rood upon a rouncy, as he kouthe,
In a gowne of faldyng to the knee.
A daggere hangynge on a laas hadde he
Aboute his nekke, under his arm adoun.
The hoote somer hadde maad his hewe al broun;
And certeinly he was a good felawe.
Ful many a draughte of wyn had he ydrawe
Fro Burdeux-ward, whil that the chapman sleep.
Of nyce conscience took he no keep.
If that he faught, and hadde the hyer hond,
By water he sente hem hoom to every lond.
But of his craft to rekene wel his tydes,
His stremes, and his daungers hym bisides,
His herberwe, and his moone, his lodemenage,
Ther nas noon swich from Hulle to Cartage.*
Hardy he was and wys to undertake;
With many a tempest hadde his berd been shake.
He knew alle the havenes, as they were,
Fro Gootlond to the cape of Fynystere,
And every cryke in Britaigne and in Spayne.
His barge ycleped was the Maudelayne.

(ll. 388–410)

THAT Chaucer introduces us to a sea captain is significant, for, as Professor Trevelyan points out, England "seriously took to the sea" in the reign of Edward III, and from that time on the English "never ceased to be a sea-going people, to have a parliamentary commercial policy, and to be known and feared on the continent

* *Cartage*: the Spanish port of "Cartagena"

as trade rivals in all the Northern seas." [1] Maritime trade in the fourteenth century, however, was carried on under difficulties: merchantmen were in constant danger from pirates of all nationalities and from any foreign vessel that might choose to adopt piratical methods. To protect English ships and crews, and also to provide owners of attacked vessels with an opportunity for either compensation or revenge, the Crown adopted a policy of extensive issuance of commissions for privateering, so that in the latter part of the fourteenth century, even during the brief intervals of comparative peace, the armed merchantman was taken for granted. In times of open warfare, since the State maintained only a small "navy"—the "King's ships"— trading vessels and their crews were pressed into national service as fighters.[2] Consequently, life on the sea when Chaucer was writing was "a school of hardihood and daring, though scarcely one of nice morality," as Professor Trevelyan is constrained to say,[3] and Chaucer's rough and ready Shipman is representative of his class. Even the fact that the Shipman is specifically stated to be from the west country, perhaps from Dartmouth, marks him as a type—indeed, must have summed him up for the fourteenth-century audience. The men of Dartmouth, besides holding from the king a blanket privateering commission, took the lead as freebooters, and were known as such throughout England.[4]

The Shipman, then, is a type only too familiar to the contemporary public eye. But even in his patently traditional bearing and appearance he is not without his own individuality. The Shipman rides, as well as he can (the sailor on horseback was evidently a matter for jest as early as the fourteenth century); his horse is a "rouncy," clumsy, heavy-footed,[5] perhaps allotted to him by the Host or some stableman, who would read the Shipman's equestrian inexperience at a glance; his "gowne of faldying to the knee" is a strictly utilitarian costume, short enough for action on deck, and made of a coarse, durable woolen material [6] which will withstand time and weather; his dagger is ready for instant use on a cord ("laas") worn in the position of a baldric, "aboute his nekke, under his arm adoun"; and his skin is bronzed by the hot sun of summer. One can see at once that "certeinly" he is "a good felawe"! *

The Shipman is as ready to pilfer as he is to steal in larger ways, and he has many opportunities for petty thievery. He is evidently

* a good felawe: "a fine rascal"

especially fond of the wine of Bordeaux, for when he has a cargo of that on board, he helps himself to copious draughts, possibly by tapping the casks, while the accompanying merchant, the "chapman," who always travelled with his wares, snatches what rest he can in a small vessel blown about on a rough sea. Our crafty Shipman is only too well aware that he will not be detected as the thief when the casks are gauged on arrival in England: the blame for the shortage will be shifted to the merchant himself, who can so easily be accused of connivance with the pre-lading gaugers in Bordeaux in dishonest schemes to foist on his customers the partly filled casks.[7]

But stealing is only one of the Shipman's sins. He is also given to manslaughter, for if he fights and wins, he summarily drowns all his prisoners, that is, he sends them by water "hoom to every lond"; in this custom, however, the Shipman is merely following the example of his illustrious betters, for even such a chivalrous figure as Edward III is reported to have done the same. Froissart makes no adverse criticism on Edward, who, in a naval victory over the Spaniards in 1350, captured an enemy vessel and promptly cast all the crew overboard![8] What Chaucer thought of such acts is implied in his remark that of scrupulous feeling ("of nyce conscience") the Shipman takes no heed whatever.

It was essential for a captain to be an experienced master of navigation. Chaucer's Shipman has long followed his calling; many a tempest has shaken his beard,[9] and he really merits, from the point of view of professional knowledge, his position on the *Maudelayne*. He knows how to reckon the tides, he is familiar with the currents and dangers which beset the sailor, he knows the ports, he can calculate the phases of the moon, he is a master of pilotage ("lode-menage"). Indeed, as Chaucer says, there is not another such shipman from Hull to Cartagena! The Master of the *Maudelayne* is at home in all the harbours from Gotland, an island off the coast of Sweden,[10] to Cape Finisterre, even in all the inlets ("crykes") of Brittany and Spain; he is a truly brave figure of a man, and one who, "hardy and wys," knows his business through and through.

The term *barge* in the Middle Ages denoted a trading vessel of probably less than 200 tons;[11] barges in common with other ships, including men-of-war, were fitted with one mast and a square sail. A man-of-war had two cabins: one in the bows beneath a raised platform called the "fore-castle," the other in the stern beneath the "after-castle." A merchant ship, however, might have only the after-castle, or no castle at all; such a ship as the *Maudelayne* trading with distant Bordeaux would probably be fitted with an after-castle at least, especially if she were armed. In the *Mariner's Mirror,* Mr. R. Morton Nance [12] and Mr. H. H. Brindley [13] both show drawings, taken from painted glass, of medieval merchant ships. These ships have rounded, uncastled bows, and each has a deep, square stern surmounted by a castle; according to modern standards, the ships are short in proportion to their width, and they appear to be un-wieldy. Chaucer's Shipman, as navigator of such a boat, needed all his skill.

An individualizing touch in the Shipman's portrait is the name of his barge. Three records exist of a *Maudelayne* sailing from Dart-mouth in the late fourteenth century: the first in 1379 states the master to be George Cowntre; the second and third are dated 1391. The second names the master as Peter Risshenden.[14] Manly suggests that modern students have missed the significance of these records, and argues that Chaucer had a particular model in mind when he drew the portrait of the Shipman.[15] To Manly, Peter Risshenden is undoubtedly the Piers Resselden who was captain of a Dartmouth ship, possibly the *Maudelayne,* that joined forces with the famous buccaneer John Hawley in the capture in 1386 of three foreign vessels loaded with wine. Hawley maintained that these vessels were without safe conduct, but charges were brought against him of wilful treachery, and the case became a legal *cause célèbre* which lasted for eight years, a case of which few of Chaucer's friends and associates could be unaware. Furthermore, Hawley of Dartmouth had been in the public eye as a sea-fighter even before 1386, sometimes under royal license, sometimes very much on his own; he was thus notorious when Chaucer was beginning the *Canterbury Tales.*[16] Of course, as Manly points out, Hawley was too important and too wealthy a man to have been himself the prototype of Chaucer's rude Shipman,[17] but, he adds, if the poet had any actual person in mind as a model, it is almost necessary to suppose that that person was one of Hawley's men and that he was master of a real ship called the *Maudelayne.* Manly then draws the conclusion that the Shipman is more likely to be Risshenden (or Resselden) than Cowntre, because of the former's connection with the prominent court proceedings of 1386–1394 against Hawley.

Miss Margaret Galway writes persuasively of identifying Chaucer's Shipman with the Basque John Piers, a notorious seagoing rascal of the time.[18] Her argument may be briefly summarized as follows. Piers was a shipmaster; he lived in the far west of England from 1385 to 1388; the Basque sailors wore a costume similar to the Shipman's ("short mantles . . . cut at the knee");[19] Piers went on expeditions to Bordeaux; he had no "conscience" and was a bullying coward; he was an excellent navigator and had extensive actual experience along the whole coast of Spain. Miss Galway, quoting from Salzman, reasons that since no English captain is known to have sailed through the Straits of Gibraltar until fifty years after Chaucer wrote the *Prologue*, the Shipman cannot be English;[20] but she seems to lose sight of the strong possibility that the poet's "Hulle to Cartage" may be a general expression, such as our modern "pole to pole." Finally she notes that Piers at one time captured a ship called the *Magdalen;* and she points out that Chaucer, as Controller of Customs and as a citizen of London, must have known or been aware of Piers, for the latter gained considerable notoriety in the English courts.[21] The allusion to Dartmouth Miss Galway explains as ironical: Chaucer wished to say, "for all I know, the Shipman may live next door to John Hawley!"[22] In spite of Miss Galway's carefully thought out argument, however, the weight of evidence still seems to fall more heavily on the side of identifying the Shipman with Risshenden.

But it must be re-emphasized that any attempt to identify the Shipman is only speculative, and that whether or not this "good felawe," ironically speaking, was named as an individual in the fourteenth century, he was then also a thoroughly familiar typical figure. For us in the twentieth century he is paradoxical: like his fellow-pilgrim the Friar, the more individual he becomes, the more typical we realize him to be.

NOTES

(The abbreviations used to designate books and articles mentioned in the Notes will be found listed alphabetically in the Bibliography, opposite the full reference. References to lines in the *Canterbury Tales* are given by fragment and line numbers only.)

1. Trevelyan, *Eng. in Age of Wyc.*, p. 53.
2. Clowes, *The Royal Navy*, I, 146. Clowes states that in 1345, "as in

earlier times ships, seamen, soldiers, and stores were obtained by impressment, with some payment." This was true throughout the fourteenth century. (I am indebted to Professor E. V. K. Dobbie for this reference.)

3. Trevelyan, *op. cit.*, pp. 54 f.

4. Lindsay, I, 432. Lindsay reminds the reader of Walsingham's account of the raids on the French ships of war by the men of Dartmouth and Portsmouth (*Hist. Ang.*, II, 106, 128). A grateful government could scarcely do less than give Dartmouth and Portsmouth *carte blanche* to arm privately owned craft. Lindsay copies statistical records (I, 636) of the "Englishe Fleete" of 1347. Of the grand total of approximately 700 ships and 14,000 seamen, Dartmouth furnished more than any other town except Fowey in the south and Yarmouth farther north—and Fowey and Yarmouth were the fishing centers of England, and would therefore be expected to be well supplied with ships and sailors.

5. Hinckley argues (pp. 29 f.) that *rouncy* sometimes meant a "warhorse" in Middle English, and gives evidence for that meaning as well as for "nag." Karkeek, on the other hand, states (p. 457): "The word 'rouncy,' from the Mediaeval Latin *runcinus*, implies a heavy, powerful animal, either a packhorse, or such as is used for rough agricultural purposes; in neither case was it suited for the saddle nor intended for such work." Karkeek also tells us that hackneymen were reluctant to let animals for long journeys, and that "if Harry Baily acted on the principle embodied in Hobson's choice, . . . his customers had to mount whatever animal he chose to provide"—the Shipman, ignorant of the art of riding, would probably be assigned the worst horse (p. 458). It is interesting to note that the Ellesmere MS. shows the Shipman's mount to be something like a carthorse.

6. Karkeek, p. 458.

7. Salzman (Chap. XVIII) gives a full, compact description of England's importation of wine during the Middle Ages. Especially interesting is the account of the precautions taken against false measure.

8. Coulton, *Life in Mid. Ages*, II, 99 (from Bouchon's edition of Froissart, I, 284).

9. To shake or pull anyone's beard in the Middle Ages was to inflict great indignity upon the wearer (Curry, *Mid. Eng. Ideal of Beauty*, p. 36). Chaucer's words here would thus have some added humour for his contemporaries.

10. I am indebted to Professor E. V. K. Dobbie for the following statement: "The form Gootland in the Ellesmere and Hengwrt MSS. is a difficult problem. Kemp Malone (*MLR*, XX, 6) argues in favour of Jutland on the evidence of the long vowel. (Jutland is OE. Gōtland, or more probably *Geōtland, Gotland is OE. Gotland.) But the MSS. do not agree very well. El. and Hg., the two oldest MSS., have *Gootlond*; Cp. and Gg. have *Gotlond*; and La. has *Gotelonde*. (Ha.[4] has *Scotland*!) The form *Gotland* in Cp. and Gg. may point to Gotland in the Baltic. For Jutland we would expect a Chaucerian form with initial *J*, but the earliest English form with initial *J* with which I am familiar is *Juitland* in Peter Heylyn's *Cosmographie* of 1652."

Robinson (p. 762, n. 408) interprets Gootlond as "probably" meaning the island of Gotland, off the coast of Sweden.

11. Manly states (*Cant. Tales*, p. 662) that the *barge* was a ship "in size between the carrack or great ship and the ballinger or sloop." Salzman gives (pp. 228 ff.) the size of the fourteenth-century carrack as about 200 tons, but gives no figures for the smaller ships; he says it is "difficult if not impossible to discover" how the ballinger, barge, and other sailing vessels differed from each other.

12. Nance, *Mariner's Mirror*, II, 174. I am again indebted to Professor Dobbie for this reference and the one following, and, indeed, for much information about medieval ships.

13. Brindley, *Mariner's Mirror*, I, 131. (See n. 12 above.)

14. Karkeek, pp. 488 f.

15. Manly, *New Light*, pp. 169–181.

16. *Ibid.*, p. 174.

17. *Ibid.*, p. 178.

18. Galway, *MLR*, XXXIV, 497–514.

19. *Ibid.*, p. 501.

20. *Ibid.*, pp. 498 f.

21. *Ibid.*, pp. 502 ff.

22. *Ibid.*, pp. 501 f.

CHAPTER XIII

THE DOCTOR OF PHYSIC

With us ther was a Doctour of Phisik;
In al this world ne was ther noon hym lik,
To speke of phisik and of surgerye,—
.   .   .   .
He was a verray, parfit praktisour.

(ll. 411–413, 422)

CHAUCER gives no hint of irony when he describes his Knight as a "verray, parfit" member of his class, yet when the poet applies the same words to the Physician and says that there is no one like him for talking about physic and surgery, evidence points to considerable satire in the portrait. Chaucer's detailed description of the Physician's exaggerated proficiency as a fashionable medical man makes this Canterbury pilgrim too good to be true.

First, the Physician is a "doctour," that is, he has won a degree from a university or medical school after long study. The time needed in the Middle Ages to qualify for a medical degree was nearly as long as that which is needed today. For example, Oxford [1] required eight years, and Montpellier,[2] the most famous medical school of France, required nine years for the winning of a license and admission *ad practicandum*. Medieval doctors of medicine are thus to be distinguished from ordinary leeches and herbalists; the often notable skill of the latter group came only from tradition, observation, and common sense. Yet in spite of the requisite of long study for a qualified practitioner, such a man's knowledge was more nearly that of the simple leech of his own time than that of the present day physician. Medicine as a science was still very much in its infancy when Chaucer was writing. According to Mr. H. H. Bashford, English medicine in the fourteenth century was the product of four distinct factors:

. . . legendary versions of Hippocrates and Galen, derived at second-hand from their Graeco-Latin successors; a considerable infusion, from

the same source, of Mediterranean and Oriental magic, discreetly tinc-
tured with Christianity but unchanged in essence; a native contribution of the same kind, similarly Christianised and to the same extent;
and a perhaps more trustworthy botanical lore, both indigenous and
imported.[3]

Medicine of this sort may seem fantastic to us, who take for granted
the exactnesses of modern science, but the field was nevertheless wide
and required persevering study; and Chaucer's Doctor of Physic, as
the poet takes pains to point out by the list he gives of the authorities with whom his Doctor is familiar, has admirably covered the
ground.

> Wel knew he the olde Esculapius,
> And Deyscorides, and eek Rufus,
> Olde Ypocras, Haly, and Galyen,
> Serapion, Razis, and Avycen,
> Averrois, Damascien, and Constantyn,
> Bernard, and Gatesden, and Gilbertyn.
>
> (ll. 429-434)

All the medical authorities of antiquity are here: Aesculapius, Hippocrates, Dioscorides, Galienus, and the less important Rufus of
Ephesus; so are the foremost Moslem authorities, Averroes, Avicenna, Haly, Razis, Serapio, Constantinus Africanus, and Damascenus; and Chaucer has not omitted the important men of his own
nation, Bernard Gordon, Gilbertus Anglicus, and John Gaddesden.
Almost undoubtedly Chaucer drew upon Vincent of Beauvais for
this impressive list. As Miss Pauline Aiken points out, Chaucer knew
the *Speculum Majus*,[4] and in that work Vincent refers to every
medical authority mentioned anywhere by the English poet; furthermore, the *Speculum* is the only medieval work, as far as can be
discovered, which contains the complete list of authorities compiled
by Chaucer to illustrate the unusual erudition of the Doctor of
Physic.[5] The short list which appears in the *Roman de la Rose*—

> . . . Ypocras, Galien, Rasis,
> Constantins, Avicenne—[6]

must have been noted by Chaucer, but can hardly be said to be his
source since it is made up of only five of the names.

Let us briefly examine the names which are so well known to

the Doctor of Physic. "Olde Esculapius," the father of medicine, is of course a legendary figure, but he was accepted in the Middle Ages as the author of a number of medical works. "Olde Ypocras" we recognize as Hippocrates, the founder of Greek medical science, who flourished in the fifth century before the Christian era; Dioscorides (who probably wrote in the reign of Nero) was the author of the principal ancient work on pharmacology; [7] Rufus of Ephesus (100^{ca} A.D.) wrote on the names of the parts of the human body; [8] Galen, who was born in the second century after Christ, was the author of voluminous works, early translated into Latin, and was regarded by the Middle Ages as the ancient authority *par excellence* in all medical matters—it was Galen who was primarily responsible for the medieval theory of the four "elements" and the four "qualities," [9] a theory of which more will be said later.

The naming of seven Moslem authorities with whose works Chaucer's Physician is familiar, is indicative of the high regard in which the medieval medical profession held the Moslems; indeed, Galen himself entered Europe through translations of Arabic versions of his works.[10] Of those whom Chaucer lists, Avicenna, of the eleventh century, and Averroes, of the twelfth century, are probably the most eminent; both were well known by the scholars of the Middle Ages as philosophers as well as physicians. Chaucer refers again to Avicenna in the *Pardoner's Tale* as the great authority on "signes of empoisonyng." [11] As to the lesser Moslems, Haly is most likely the tenth-century Persian physician, Hali ibn el Abbas; Serapion flourished in the eleventh or twelfth century; Razis (or Rhazes) lived in Baghdad at the end of the ninth century; "Damascien" can probably be identified with Johannes Damascenus whose name was associated with Serapion; "Constantyn," or Constantinus Africanus, was a Christian monk who brought Moslem medical learning from Africa to Salerno in the eleventh century. Chaucer mentions him a second time in the *Merchant's Tale* as the author of a treatise on letuaries.[12]

The medieval physicians mentioned by Chaucer have special interest for us. Of them, Bernard Gordon is perhaps the least famous. Bernard lived at the beginning of the fourteenth century, and wrote several medical works, important in that they re-state much of the medieval learning of the day and show a real beginning in scientific experimentation.[13] Gilbertus Anglicus, who antedates

Bernard by a century, is more justly celebrated. Gilbert, who was born not long before Thomas à Becket met his death in Canterbury, was the first Englishman to acquire an international reputation in medicine. He studied at the medical school in Salerno as a young man, and spent much of his life in France. Gilbert's *Compendium* covers the whole then known field of medicine, and new matter is also added; this great work shows that, in some respects, Gilbert was well over five hundred years ahead of his time, for the *Compendium* calls attention to the contagious nature of small-pox, say that cancer can be cured only by surgery, and gives directions for a diet which resembles any vitamin-balanced one of today.[14] But "Gatesden" must have been the best known name of the three to Chaucer's audience. John Gaddesden, who has been called "the first of the fashionable physicians," [15] was born in 1280. He attended Merton College, Oxford, and later became physician to Edward II. Gaddesden had the distinction of curing a royal prince (perhaps the future Edward III?) of small-pox by wrapping the patient in "scarlet red cloths." [16] Through highly successful practice among the wealthy, and through his renowned treatise, *Rosa Medicinae*, Gaddesden became an outstanding figure in early fourteenth-century London. Even four hundred years later an English physician felt compelled to accuse his long dead rival of laying " 'baits for the Delicate, for the Ladies, for the Rich' " ! [17] Gaddesden, however, was a sound and reputable physician, though he always had an eye out, according to his own admission, for monetary gain.[18]

Chaucer's Doctor of Physic, then, with his full preparation for his profession, is no country leech, no mere barber who has picked up small surgical knowledge as an observant apprentice; and, as a superior medical man, he has the necessary thorough knowledge of "astronomye."

> For he was grounded in astronomye.
> He kepte his pacient a ful greet deel
> In houres by his magyk natureel.
> Wel koude he fortunen the ascendent
> Of his ymages for his pacient.
> He knew the cause of everich maladye,
> Were it of hoot, or coold, or moyste, or drye,
> And where they engendred, and of what humour.

. . . .

The cause yknowe, and of his harm the roote,
Anon he yaf the sike man his boote.

(ll. 414–421, 423–424)

Astronomy in the Middle Ages included the study not only of the nature and motions of the heavenly bodies, but also of what we now term "astrology." The key to man's physical well-being was thought to be contained in the mysteries of this science, and it was essential for a competent physician to know how to bring about the proper coincidence of treatment with favourable aspects of the stars and planets. In this connection, we note what John of Burgundy has to say by way of advice to other physicians, for John of Burgundy, who practised medicine in Liège in the fourteenth century and whose treatise on the Black Death had wide circulation in England, was a contemporary of Chaucer's, and may possibly be identified with none other than Sir John Mandeville of the *Travels*.[19] John of Burgundy writes:

Also alle they whos complexion contrary to the aire that is chaunged or corupte abiden hole and elles alle folke shuld corupte and dye at onys. The aire therfore so corupt and chaunged bredith and engendreth in diverse sikenes and sores. After the variauncez or diversitees of theire humours for avery worcher or every thing that werchith performeth his werke after the abilite and disposicion of the matier that he werkith ynne. And by cause that they bene but litill proued in practik and therto allefully ignorant in the sience of Astronomy the whiche science is in phisik wonder nedefull as witnessith ypocras in epidimia sua seying what phisician that ever he be and kan not astronomy no wyse man owt to putte hym in his handis for why astronomye and phisik rectifien yche other in effect and also that one science sheweth forthe many thynges hidde in the other . . . And I 40 yere and more have oftyn tymes proved in practise that a medecyn gyven contrary to the constellacion all thogh hit were both wele compownyd or medled and ordynatly wroght after the science of phisik yit it wroght nowther aftur the purpose of the worcher nor to the profite of the pacient. And when some men have gyven a medecyn laxatyf to purge downe ward the pacient hath casten it out ayene above all thogh he lothed it noght. Wherfore they that have not dronkyn of that swete drynke of Astronomye mowe putte to thise pestilentiall sores no perfite remedie for bicause that they knowe not the cause and qualite of the sikenesse they may not hele it as seith the prynce of phisik Avicenna. How schuldest thou he saith hele a sore and thou knowe not the cause.

iij canone capitulo de curis febrium. He that knowith nat the cause hit is onpossible that he hele the sikenes. The comentour also *super secundum phisicorum* seith thus A man knowith nat a thyng but if he knowe the cause both ferre and nygh. Sithen therfor the hevenly or firmamentall bodies bene of the first and primytif causes it is bihovefull to have the knowlechyng of hem for yf the first and primytif causes be onknowen we may not come to know the causes secondary. Sithen therfor the first cause bryngeth in more plentevously his effecte than doth the cause secondary as hit shewith. *primo de causis.* Therfor it shewith wele that without Astronomye litill vayleth phisik for many man is perisshed in defawte of his councelour.[20]

The question may here arise as to how seriously the really wise scientists and physicians took the matter of astrology in Chaucer's time. Henry of Lancaster, writing his *Livre de Seyntz Medicines* in 1354, has nothing whatever to say about any part played by the stars in controlling man's health.[21] Of course, Henry was not a physician, and his book is properly described as a devotional treatise; nevertheless this first Duke of Lancaster, father of Duchess Blanche, was a brilliant man of the world, and his application of the diagnosis and treatment of disease to spiritual matters must in itself be a reflection of some school of current, intelligent medical thought. To the modern reader who has the patience to dig beneath the thick overlay of mysticism, Henry's remarks on feeling the head and the pulse,[22] and on warm baths, purges, and light, nourishing food for the sick,[23] must seem eminently sensible and a far cry from the ultra elaborate astrology of Chaucer's Doctor of Physic.

Chaucer leaves us in doubt as to his own opinion. In the *Treatise on the Astrolabe,* he disclaims belief in astrology: astrology is mere "observaunces of . . . rytes of payens, in whiche my spirit hath no feith"; [24] but in the same work, he explains soberly to "lyte Lowys" the kind of "astronomy" in which he believes: the physical effect of the zodiac and the planets on man.

. . . the zodiak in hevene is ymagyned to ben a superfice contenyng a latitude of 12 degrees . . . Amiddes this celestial zodiak is ymagined a lyne which that is clepid the ecliptik lyne, under which lyne is evermo the wey of the sonne. . . . This zodiak is dividid in 12 principale divisiouns that departen the 12 signes . . . And this forseide hevenysshe zodiak is clepid the cercle of the signes, or the cercle of the bestes, for "zodia" in langage of Grek sowneth "bestes" in Latyn tunge. And in the zodiak ben the 12 signes that han names of bestes, or ellis for whan the sonne entrith into eny of tho signes he takith the propirte of suche bestes, or ellis that for the sterres that ben ther fixed ben disposid in signes of bestes or shape like bestes, or elles whan the planetes ben under thilke signes thei causen us by her influence operaciouns and effectes like to the operaciouns of bestes.

And understond also that whan an hot planete cometh into an hot signe, than encrescith his hete; and yf a planete be cold, than amenusith his coldnesse by cause of the hoote sygne. And by thys conclusioun maist thou take ensample in alle the signes, be thei moist or drie, or moeble or fixe, reknyng the qualite of the planete as I first seide. And everich of these 12 signes hath respect to a certeyn parcel of the body of a man, and hath it in governaunce; as Aries hath thin heved, and Taurus thy nekke and thy throte, Gemini thin armholes and thin armes, and so furth . . .[25]

But no matter what Chaucer himself believed, or whether the portrait of his physician is to be taken as satire or at face value, we must inquire into the nature of the Doctor's astrological skill in order to understand fully that worthy practitioner. Most of us are familiar with the twelve signs of the zodiac, which correspond roughly to the twelve months of the year; probably some of us have heard from a fortune-teller that the particular sign under which we were born is "fiery," or "earthy," or "airy," or "watery," and that our individual temperament takes on the nature of the sign. What we no longer hear is that each of the twelve signs has attached to it one or two of the four principal complexions or qualities, hot, cold, dry, moist. Libra, for example, was said to be cold and dry. The planets, which wander in and out of the signs of the zodiac, also were thought to possess individual complexions, and each sign of the zodiac to control a different part of the human body, as Chaucer makes clear to little Lewis. Thus the configuration of the heavens at the hour of anyone's birth was believed to determine his physical constitution; his "humour" might be "choleric" (hot and dry, or "fiery"), or "melancholic" (cold and dry, or "earthy"), or "sanguine"[26] (hot and moist, or "airy"), or "phlegmatic" (cold and moist, or "watery"); and was believed partly to determine the individual's predisposition to specific diseases and the most propitious moment for a cure. The problem of a cure was further complicated by the belief that it was necessary to know the positions of the stars and the planets at the time of the onset of the sickness and at the time of the physician's visit, that each of the twenty-four hours of the day came under the special influence of some planet, varying within the week, and that fixed hours of every day took dominion over the humours as well.[27] The Moon was thought to be particularly powerful at all times over the ebb and flow of the humours. In John of Burgundy's words, "without Astronomye litill vayleth phisik." Obviously this sort of medieval medical man needed to be adept in charting the skies.

Chaucer says of his Physician that he has the skill born of "magyk natureel," meaning legitimate science as opposed to black magic, or necromancy, to watch his patient carefully and to select the astrological hours which will be advantageous for recovery. Moreover, this wise Doctor knows how to "fortunen the ascendent" of talismanic images for the patient, a science, or skill, which Professor Curry calls "the very cream of all the other sciences and of philosophy," [28] and of which he gives a detailed explanation. Professor Curry's explanation may be briefly summarized as follows: it was believed that all material objects fashioned by man received the impress of the constellation reigning at their completion, and that this impress remained with an object until the object was destroyed; astrological images, if formed in the right way at the right moment, were thought to be especially imbued with the powers of the stars, and so, applied to the sick, could be used to strengthen and weaken respectively favourable and unfavourable celestial influences. These images were round discs, as a rule, made of some such metal as copper or tin or silver or gold; on one face was engraved the pictorial representation of the sign selected (for instance, if Libra were the proper sign, a balance would be pictured) as well as magic formulae, sentences from the Bible, names of other zodiacal signs, and so on, which would also be engraved on the other face—all depending upon the erudition and skill of the maker of the image.[29] To "fortunen" the ascendent, or horoscope, of an image means, then, "that the dealer in natural magic must fortune (i.e., place in a favourable position) both Luna and the lord of the ascendent, and infortune (place in unfavourable positions) the lord of the house of death and the malefic planets." [30] The "placing" constituted the engraving of the image.

But Chaucer's Doctor of Physic has other, homelier characteristics than immense learning and skill to mark him as a successful and
prominent member of his profession.

> Ful redy hadde he his apothecaries
> To sende hym drogges and his letuaries,*
> For ech of hem made oother for to wynne—
> Hir friendshipe nas nat newe to bigynne.
>
> .   .   .   .
>
> Of his diete mesurable was he,
> For it was of no superfluitee,
> But of greet norissyng and digestible.
> His studie was but litel on the Bible.
> In sangwyn and in pers he clad was al,
> Lyned with taffata and with sendal;
> And yet he was but esy of dispence;
> He kepte that he wan in pestilence.
> For gold in phisik is a cordial,
> Therefore he lovede gold in special.
>
> (ll. 425–428, 435–444)

He is astutely aware that patients are pleased by prompt efficiency,
and he has made long-standing arrangements with the apothecaries
("hir frendshipe" is not newly begun) to supply him quickly with all
the drugs and "letuaries" he may prescribe. One of the most talked
of abuses in Chaucer's time was the collusion between physician
and apothecary whereby the "sike man" was mulcted of his money
through heavy charges for prescriptions which cost little to compound. Gower, for instance, writes of the physician who will order
a medicine of the value of a mere button so that he and his "friend,"
the apothecary, who will ask the deceived patient for a florin, may
share the large excess profit.[31] It is natural, therefore, that Chaucer
includes such a jibe in his satiric portrait of the Doctor of Physic.[32]

Still another ironic touch is added to the description when
Chaucer speaks of his Doctor's study as being "but litel on the
Bible," for the physician of the time was generally considered to be
a godless man. As Professor Robinson points out, there is a great deal
of evidence that the medieval physician was regarded as agnostic,
largely because of his reliance upon Moslem medical teaching.[33]

* *letuarie*: "electuary," a medicinal powder mixed with honey or syrup.

Furthermore, the Church of the Middle Ages was in many respects hostile to medical research: clergy, for instance were discouraged from any study or practice of surgery; the Church explicitly forbade the study of practical anatomy in the universities.[34] One can easily understand how *ubi tres medici, duo athei* became a proverb.

The Doctor of Physic is represented as cautious as to his own health, for his diet is temperate ("mesurable"): he never eats too much ("it was of no superfluitee"), and what he does eat is nourishing and digestible. This fashionable physician takes care not only of his own health, but of his personal appearance as well: he is dressed from head to foot in rich cloth of blood-red and Persian blue ("in sangwyn and in pers") lined with expensive, thin silk.[35] Yet for all his expenditure for nourishing food and costly dress, the Doctor of Physic is thrifty ("esy of dispence"); he has had an especially lucrative practice during the years of pestilence,[36] and he has not frittered away the money he then acquired. As Chaucer tells us, "gold in physik," or *aurum potabile*,[37] is a sovereign remedy, so it is entirely natural that a "doctour of physik" should love gold.

Perhaps to Chaucer's contemporaries the Doctor of Physic was immediately identifiable as some prominent physician known to the court, but today we can only observe that the Doctor fits well into the picture drawn by the fourteenth-century physician, John Arderne, of what the learned and skilled medical man should be. Possibly in Arderne himself Chaucer found the living model he used in creating his Doctor. Arderne probably received his medical degree from Montpellier; during the early years of the Hundred Years' War he served as an English military surgeon; in 1370 he settled in London, and was more than likely attached in service to John of Gaunt.[38] Arderne's work, *Treatises of Fistula in Ano*, circulated widely, and hence may have been familiar to Chaucer.

After listing a number of moral qualities desirable in the good "leche," such as charity, humility, and discretion, Arderne admonishes the ideal physician of the *Treatises* to be studious and grave; he must eschew strong drink, and never be gluttonous: "be he content in strange places of metes and drinkes ther y-founden, usyng mesure in al thingis." It is the physician's duty to consider a case carefully before taking it, or before giving advice, and to have a clear understanding about the fee before any operation is performed. The physician should also be cautious in prognosis so that false hopes are not encouraged, but he is not to fill the patient with alarm; instead, he should have ready a stock of comforting "proverbes pertenyng to his crafte" and of "gode tales" that will make "the pacientes to laugh." A good bedside manner was evidently as important in the fourteenth century as it is today! The "leche" should be clean and soberly dressed, "noght likkenyng hymself in apparalyng . . . to mynistralles," but copying the dress of serious-minded clerks.[39] And of course Arderne emphasized the necessity for the physician's thorough grounding in astrological science; in this connection he names and quotes extensively from Bernard Gordon, with whom, it will be remembered, Chaucer's Doctor of Physic is also familiar.[40] The Doctor has obviously much in common with Arderne, or with Arderne's ideal: he is a learned man, skilled in the complexities of his profession, yet a man who is interested in practical efficiency; he has, like Arderne, who has a great deal to say about money in the *Treatises,* a marked fondness for gold and a decided "thriftiness"; and he is temperate in his diet of nourishing food. The Doctor's extraordinarily fine garments form a satiric contrast, however, to Arderne's theoretic statement that a physician should be dressed in the plainest possible way. Finally, the dignified and "pitous" *Tale* with which the Doctor later edifies the company bears out Arderne's advice as to the studious and grave demeanour proper to a medical man, and is in itself a "gode tale," if not the merry one with which a physician is advised to divert a patient.

One more question about the Doctor of Physic may be raised: what was Chaucer's personal attitude about physicians in general? It would have been like Chaucer to have admired some of the competent men who made medical science their specialty; on the other hand, Chaucer writes in obvious satire of all the current abuses, of which complaint was widespread, surrounding the medical profession. Hence a brief examination of this literature of complaint may throw some further light on Chaucer's own attitude.

We have already observed that Gower inveighs specifically against fraudulent "understandings" between physician and apothecary,[41] a dishonesty which is part of the larger sin of the physician's inordinate love of money. Dr. Owst quotes the fourteenth-century John of Mirfield as saying in a sermon that the layman is, with reason, "always wont to speak ill of physicians," and that the doctors of his day have three "coveted qualifications," "subtle lying, dishonourable procedure, and a boldness in killing"; their chief vice is cupidity.[42]

Many other writers emphasize the physician's greed and the incompetence of large numbers of practitioners. The anonymous author of one of the Political Songs, for example, declares that "false fisiciens" help men to die; they will swear a man is sicker than he is, just to get a larger fee; and the medicines for which they charge so heavily are not worth a leek and do more harm than good: all that these wicked men care for is "silver for to winne." [43]

Langland indicates the layman's distrust of the doctor by the remarks which Hunger makes following his rather Spartan prescription for Piers' aching stomach. "If you diet thus," Hunger promises, "I dare wager that Phisik will have to sell his furred hoods and cloak of grey fur with the gold buttons. Be glad thus to be rid of doctors . . . Many leeches are murderers, may God amend them! By their potions, they do men to death before fate so wills." [44]

Jean de Meun puts doctors in a class with lawyers in their love of gold:

> The lawyer likewise, and the leech,
> One brush hath tarred them both, for each
> Will eagerly for lucre sell
> His soul, and both deserve right well
> The gibbet. Such foul greed for gain
> The one devoureth, that he fain
> For one sick man would have two-score,
> And t'other longs that thirty more
> Were tacked to every cause he pleads;
> Nay, multiplied by tens, their needs
> Were yet unsatisfied, so bold
> Their lust and hunger is for gold.[45]

Possibly the lowest estimate of the medical profession and of astrology is to be found in Petrarch's four books of Invectives, even though the depth of this estimate has been exaggerated by some modern scholars; [46] and it is highly probable that Chaucer's opinion about physicians in general was coloured by the jibes, sincere or otherwise, of his admired "Fraunceys Petrak." Petrarch cautions against the audacity and pomp of physicians; he says they neglect medicine proper in their pursuit of dialectic, astrology, and irrelevant reading,[47] and that many seek out the sick only for sinful gain or the wicked furthering of mere experimentation. "Remember, therefore, most gracious Father," Petrarch writes in a letter to the Pope, "the epitaph of that unhappy man who ordered nothing to be inscribed upon his tomb but 'I died from a mob of physicians,' and let the memory turn your attention from that mob which like an enemy's host (now surround you)." [48] Certainly the one physician of whom Chaucer speaks in detail can be assigned to Petrarch's "mob": he is surrounded by pomp, his dependence upon astrology seems inordinate, and he does not hesitate to gain large profits even from the Pestilence. Chaucer, like Petrarch, must have esteemed some medical men, but his obvious recognition of the sins of many others has made the Doctor of Physic in the poet's mind a reflection of a class as well as of an individual.

NOTES

(The abbreviations used to designate books and articles mentioned in the Notes will be found listed alphabetically in the Bibliography, opposite the full reference. References to lines in the *Canterbury Tales* are given by fragment and line numbers only.)

1. Rashdall, III, 156.
2. *Ibid.*, II, 126, n. 6.
3. Bashford, *Nineteenth Cent.*, CIV, 238.
4. Chaucer mentions Vincent's "Estoryal Myrour" in the *Legend of Good Women* G 307.
5. Miss Aiken has admirably indicated (*PMLA*, LI, 361–369; *Spec.*, X, 281–287; *St. Phil.*, XXXIII, 40–44) Chaucer's unmistakable debt to Vincent of Beauvais in connection with Arcite's illness, Pertelote's medical knowledge, and the Summoner's malady. Miss Aiken writes (*Spec.*, X, 286 f.): "In a survey of the evidence indicating that the *Speculum Majus* of Vincent of Beauvais is the source of Chaucer's knowledge of medicine, it should be noted that every detail [which Chaucer mentions] of medical theory and practice . . . may be found in the great encyclopedia. An examination of the principal medical works known during the period, for the purpose of ascertaining whether any one of them could have supplied all the details with which the poet is familiar, yields negative results."
6. *Rom. de la Rose*, ll. 15959–15960.
7. Thorndike, I, 605 ff.
8. Morris, *Eng. Misc.*, p. 339.
9. Thorndike, I, Chap. IV *passim*. Chaucer speaks more than once of Galen as a celebrated physician: not even "Ypocras, ne Galyen" can cure the poet of insomnia (*Book of the Duchess*, l. 572); and the Parson declares that abstinence is the cure of gluttony, "as seith Galien" (X [I] 831).

10. Robin, *Old Phys. in Eng. Lit.,* p. 4. See Robinson (p. 763) for information about the Moslem physicians.

11. VI (C) 889–891.

12. IV (E) 1810–1811.

13. Thorndike II, 479 f., 492, 848, 856 f.

14. Bashford, *loc. cit.,* pp. 241 ff.

15. *Ibid.,* p. 237.

16. Jusserand, *Eng. Way. Life,* p. 180. As short a time ago as 1870, however, small-pox patients were still placed in rooms with red walls, and were "wrapped" in red cloths. My own father as a young physician in New York City was thus successfully treated when he contracted small-pox from a patient.

17. Bashford, *loc. cit.,* p. 247.

18. *Ibid.*

19. Bormans (pp. cxxxiii f.) quotes in modernized French from an early fifteenth-century chronicle (MSS. Le Fort, 2e série, t. XXVII, p. 102, in the archives of Liège) as follows (my English translation):

"In the year 1372, on November 12, there died at Liège, a man of distinguished birth, who was content to be known under the name of John of Burgundy called *à la Barbe.* He disclosed himself, however, on his deathbed to his good friend, Jean d'Outremeuse, and made the latter the executor of his estate. In truth he was called *messire Jean de Mandeville, chevalier, compte de Montfort* in England . . . He was a great student of nature, a profound philosopher and astrologer to whom was given in particular a singular knowledge of physic, for he was rarely mistaken in diagnosis."

Cholmeley writes (p. 74): "John of Burgundy is a mysterious and interesting personality. It is possible that he and Sir John Mandeville were the same person. Dr. Payne wrote to me in 1905: 'he is not mentioned, so far as I know, in the continental Histories of Medicine, and nearly all the MSS. are in English libraries.' His treatise on the Black Death of 1348 exists in many MSS., and there are numerous copies both in English and Latin in the British Museum and the Bodleian."

20. Cholmeley (pp. 72 f.) takes this quotation from Sloane MS. 3449, f. 6—*Joannis de Burgundia de Pestilentia Liber.*

21. E. J. Arnould, editor of the *Livre de Seyntz Medicines,* writes (p. vii): "Lancaster describes in great detail, and with much repetition, seven wounds or sores which afflict his soul: they are in his senses, his limbs and his heart, all infected with the poison of the seven deadly sins. . . . He requests from the Divine Physician . . . the remedies that may heal those wounds and restore him to spiritual health. Within this general scheme and alongside the ever recurring motif of the seven wounds and the seven sins, a number of illustrations stand out, borrowed from the sick-room, from everyday life, or from the author's personal experiences."

22. *Livre de Seyntz Medicines,* p. 192.

23. *Ibid.,* pp. 194, 199, 202, 203.

24. *Astrolabe,* II, 4, 63–65.

25. *Ibid.*, I, 21, 41–85.

26. See above p. 174.

27. Curry, *Ch. and Med. Sci.*, pp. 7 ff.

28. *Ibid.*, p. 20.

29. *Ibid.*, pp. 20 ff.

30. *Ibid.*, p. 23.

31. Gower, *Mirour*, ll. 25621 ff.

32. Curry (*op. cit.*, pp. 31 ff.) takes this point of view; Robinson (p. 763, n. 425) disagrees, and says that Chaucer's use of a "current joke" on the medical profession scarcely justifies Curry's opinion that Chaucer seriously accuses the Doctor of fraud.

The link with the apothecary, however, is not the only element pointing towards satire in the portrait; hence it seems unlikely that Chaucer intended his audience to look upon the Doctor as a man of principle in this respect.

33. Robinson, p. 764, n. 438.

34. Coulton gives much evidence (*Med. Pan.*, pp. 445 ff.) as to the strained relationship between theology and medicine.

35. "Taffata" and "sendal" were silks which were considered costly luxuries.

36. The years 1348, 1349, 1362, 1369, 1376.

37. Arnald of Villanova, in the latter part of the thirteenth century, writes that there is virtue in wine heated in a golden vessel or in holding a gold coin in the mouth, but that it is best to reduce the gold to a potable form (Thorndike, II, 854, quoting from De vinis, fol. 263 v.).

38. Arderne, pp. xii f.

39. *Ibid.*, pp. 4–8.

40. *Ibid.*, pp. 14–20.

41. See above n. 31 in this chapter.

42. Owst, *Lit. and Pulpit*, pp. 350 f.

43. Wright's *Political Songs*, pp. 333 f.

44. *Piers Plow.*, B. Passus VI. 259–276.

45. *Rom. of the Rose*, Ellis, ll. 5403–5414. (*Rom. de la Rose*, ll. 5091–5102.)

46. Thorndike makes the statement (III, 217) that "Petrarch's criticisms both of medical men and of astrologers have been taken rather too seriously by some of his modern expositors and biographers." He adds that many of Petrarch's esteemed friends were prominent physicians, and that Petrarch's attitude towards medicine "seems to have varied with mood, circumstance, and the person addressed" (III, 221).

47. Thorndike, III, 221.

48. Cholmeley, pp. 101 ff.

CHAPTER XIV

THE GOOD WIFE OF JUXTA BATHON

A good Wif was ther of biside Bathe.

(l. 445)

THE Wife of Bath is perhaps the best known of Chaucer's Canter-bury pilgrims, and perhaps the one about whom there is least agree-ment. To many older readers whose conventions have been estab-lished in a less outspoken age than Chaucer's the Wife seems offen-sively coarse in her freedom of speech and in her attitude toward life; to many younger readers, the Wife appears to be an uninhibited extrovert, refreshing in her lack of restraint; and to those of us who take the middle view, the Wife stands for a fascinatingly complex human being whom we like unashamedly for her forthrightness, her immense good humour, and her warm friendliness, no matter how often and how strongly we disapprove of her want of decorum. Certainly, there can be few of us today who would regret Chaucer's own interest in the richly alive Alisoun,[1] Wife of Bath, for the poet outdoes himself in painting an extraordinarily broad and mellow portrait of her. The portrait, which is fully though briefly outlined in the *General Prologue*, is filled in with all the colours of life in the *Wife of Bath's Prologue* by the medium of Dame Alisoun's own inimitable speech. A good outline, however, is by definition a good summary; and if we meet the Wife in the *General Prologue* with fourteenth-century understanding, we shall know her well from that epitomized account.

Alisoun is not, strictly speaking, "of Bathe," but "of biside Bathe." Chaucer may have meant his fourteenth-century audience to identify the Wife by this detail; but for us, the localization of the Wife's parish only serves to make her seem more actual than she would otherwise be. Manly points out that Bath in Chaucer's time was "still confined almost entirely within its ancient walls and lay in a loop of the river Avon, which surrounded it on the east and south

214

and about half the west side." Outside the north gate, Manly continues, there had sprung up "the parish of St. Michael-without-the-
Walls, or St. Michael-without-the-North-Gate—also sometimes
designated as *juxta Bathon*." This little parish was formed by two
short streets meeting at an acute angle which had the vertex at the
north gate; facing the gate was "the ancient square-towered church
of St. Michael," the very church, so Manly suggests, at the door of
which each of Alisoun's numerous matrimonial adventures began.[2]

The Wife, as befits her station in life, has an occupation in which
she is highly skilled:

> Of clooth-makyng she hadde swich an haunt *
> She passed hem of Ypres and of Gaunt.
>
> (ll. 447–448)

St. Michael-juxta-Bathon was indeed a parish largely devoted to
weaving—and "wherever the cloth industry flourished in England,
women were prominent in it." [3] But the praise heaped upon the
Wife's expertness (after all, to surpass the weavers of "Ypres" and
of "Gaunt" would be to do better than the best) is Chaucer's way
of saying that that is what Alisoun herself thinks of her own weaving; perhaps there is an ironical twist, also, to the words, for the
West country weavers, far from being the best, did not enjoy too
good a reputation.[4] One is ready to take the Wife at her own valua-
tion, however; the force of her personality pushes through the written words, and demands that one believe.

> In al the parisshe wif ne was ther noon
> That to the offrynge bifore hire sholde goon;
> And if ther dide, certeyn so wrooth was she,
> That she was out of alle charitee.
>
> (ll. 449–452)

Of course, Dame Alisoun feels that she must be first wherever
precedence is held to be valuable! And the order of precedence in
making the offering was a matter of concern in the Middle Ages.
Chaucer's Parson, for example, in speaking of the "harmes that
cometh of Pride" mentions the kind of Pride which "waiteth first
to be salewed er he wole salewe, . . . and eek he waiteth or desireth
to sitte, or elles to goon above hym in the wey, . . . or goon to

* *haunt*: "skill"

offryng biforn his neighebor"; [5] Deschamps, too, refers more than
once to this custom of allowing importance in the community to
determine the order in which the congregation went up to make
their offerings in church.[6] But the fact that Dame Alisoun is so
wrathful that she is "out of alle charitee" when someone usurps what
she considers to be her rightful place is an indication, not of conceit,
but of frank pride in achievement. Alisoun is never troubled by
false modesty!

We expect a successful and friendly woman of affairs to care
about her appearance and the impression she makes on others. The
Wife of Bath does not disappoint us in this respect.

> Hir coverchiefs ful fyne weren of ground;
> I dorste swere they weyeden ten pound
> That on a Sonday weren upon hir heed.
> Hir hosen weren of fyn scarlet reed,
> Ful streite yteyd, and shoes ful moyste and newe.
> Boold was hir face, and fair, and reed of hewe.
>
> .   .   .   .
>
> Upon an amblere esily she sat,
> Ywympled wel, and on hir heed an hat
> As brood as is a bokeler or a targe;
> A foot-mantel aboute hir hipes large,
> And on hir feet a paire of spores sharpe.
>
> (ll. 453-458, 469-473)

It is true that Dame Alisoun is conspicuously overdressed on Sun-
days, but is not this by design? Why should she not let the world
see that she is successful enough to warrant fine clothes of good
material? Her wearing of such garments stamps her as the most
prosperous woman of business in St. Michael-juxta-Bathon, and
naturally she takes pleasure "to se, and eek for to be seye" as she
later tells us with gusto in her own *Prologue*, and adds that much
usage keeps the moths from *her* beautiful scarlet apparel! [7] We need
not believe, then, that Chaucer is exaggerating when he writes of
Alisoun's ten-pound "coverchiefs" which were so finely textured
("ful fyne of ground"). The *coverchief* of the Middle Ages was a
veil-like structure which was arranged in folds over the head; [8]
the coverchief could be simple and light, or elaborate and heavy.
The Wife's scarlet hose, also part of her festival attire, are always

tightly and neatly drawn ("ful streite yteyd"), and the shoes which complete this imposing costume are of new and supple ("moyste") leather.

The Wife's dress for the pilgrimage, however, is much more sensible. True, her hat is as broad as a shield ("a bokeler or a targe"),[9] but it is firmly placed on her trimly wimpled head; and she is careful enough to wear a protective outer skirt (a "foot-mantel")[10] about her ample hips, when she rides her "amblere." An ambling horse (often called a pacer today) is one which has been taught to lift two feet together on the same side of its body, making for comfortable riding on a long journey, and is therefore precisely the mount an experienced traveller such as Alisoun would choose. And since Alisoun wears a "paire" of sharp spurs, we know she rides astride, as most women of her class did in Chaucer's time.[11]

The Wife of Bath's orderly and well set-up appearance, as has been suggested, is in keeping with the strong directness of her char-acter. She is one who has always known exactly what she wants and exactly how to get it. She desires, and has obtained importance in her community; good times with gay companions—

> In felaweshipe wel koude she laughe and carpe;*
>
> (l. 474)

a wide variety of love affairs; and, as we shall hear, the excitements and pleasures of travel. The Wife of Bath leads a systematized life for all its florid quality, and so her bold countenance, "reed of hewe," escapes being blowzy and is attractive in its vigour.

Throughout the years, Dame Alisoun has been, perhaps, most famous—or infamous—for her marital and extra-marital adven-tures:

> She was a worthy womman al hire lyve:
> Housbondes at chirche dore she hadde fyve,
> Withouten oother compaignye in youthe,—
> But therof nedith nat to speke as nowthe.*
>
> (ll. 459–462)

Chaucer's contemporaries could not have been as startled as we are by the number of Alisoun's husbands, for, as Dr. Coulton writes,

* *carp*: "talk"
* *as nowthe*: "at present"

"the extreme promptitude with which the Wife of Bath provided herself with a new husband . . . is characteristically medieval." [12] A woman of any property in the Middle Ages found it as difficult to remain single as the dowerless daughter to marry: no matter how unwilling the woman with even a few possessions might be to enter into a marriage contract, which as a rule was literally just that, a cut-and-dried bargain, some man with a covetous eye upon her worldly goods would compel her, using violent means if necessary, to marry him. If the lady were willing, as Alisoun too plainly always was, it would be unthinkable that she should remain a widow no matter how frequently she might temporarily arrive at that state. Chaucer's audience, therefore, would not have found the fact of the Wife's five husbands astonishing or intrinsically humorous, but they undoubtedly looked forward with a keen relish to hearing the details of Alisoun's management of her various consorts; [an Alisoun in any period of history is so obviously born "to han the governance" in wedded life]

[But the Alisouns of the medieval world were certainly in the minority; the lot of most women in Chaucer's time was not one of mastery or of freedom] The common sentiment that "woman is man's ruin," was backed by the firm conviction that all females were created as vastly inferior to males. [13] A woman should never strive with her husband, writes the Knight of la Tour Landry, and proceeds to tell the story of the justifiable fate of a wife who dared to place herself on an equal footing with her husband. The latter was so angered by his wife's attempts at "governaunce" that he knocked her down, thus breaking her nose so that her face was permanently "foule blemisshed." Hence, concludes the Knight of la Tour Landry, one sees that a wife ought silently to permit her husband to be the master, "for that is her worshippe." [14] We are reminded by this edifying "ensaumple" that the Wife of Bath has suffered a physical injury for a like cause—

But she was somdel deef, and that was scathe.

(l. 446)

We find out later that, after considerable provocation, Alisoun's fifth husband, the "som tyme clerk of Oxenford," in a vain effort to assert his male superiority once struck the intractable Alisoun about the ears so violently that her hearing is now impaired. [15]

[Dr. Owst suggests that the ultimate source of the Wife of Bath is the woman in the Book of Proverbs [16] who is "subtil of heart." Fourteenth-century preachers turn again and again to this passage, expanding the interpretation to meet the exigencies of a particular sermon or the homilist's fancy. Too many modern women are "foolish," the sermons say: these women lay snares to entrap men instead of chastely staying at home with their husbands, they talk too much and love gossip, they deck themselves in unseemly finery.[17] One preacher, for example, speaks of "a foolish woman, garrulous and vagrant, impatient of quiet, not able to keep her feet within the house, now she is without, now in the streets," never constant.[18] And worst of all are the women who will not submissively follow out the wishes of their husbands! [19] [But whether Dame Alisoun owes her existence in part to sermon-complaints, or whether the sermon-complaints were brought about because there were enough actual women like Alisoun to warrant the pulpit dissatisfaction, cannot be determined] As Dr. Coulton points out, "In every generation moralists noted with pain the gradual emancipation of ladies from a restraint which had always been excessive, and had often been merely theoretical." [20] Perhaps Chaucer, in creating Alisoun, drew on both homily and the actual New Woman of his day; whatever the case, his audience must have greeted Alisoun as irresistibly amusing and lifelike.

Chaucer speaks of the five husbands whom Alisoun has had "at chirche dore," a reference to a custom which has no modern counterpart. According to George Elliott Howard, the medieval York ritual, still extant, is typical of any medieval marriage service; it directs that "the ceremony takes place before the church door, . . . the man standing 'on the right of the woman and the woman on the left of the man.' " [21] The priest's duty was then to ask the banns in the mother-tongue, after which the ceremony proceeds in striking similarity to that used now in the English Church. As Howard states, the use of the vernacular is important as it indicates that the bride and groom were regarded as the real actors in the ceremony, and the priest as merely leader and teacher; perhaps this lay nature of the ceremony entirely explains why it was not performed within the church. The vernacular was probably used also so that the witnesses would understand what was being done. After the couple were married, they and the witnesses entered the church, and the priest officiated at the nuptial mass, which was, of course, sung in Latin.[22]

Aside from Dame Alisoun's fifth marriage (which she herself engineered), Alisoun's amorous adventures have had little to do with wedded bliss. In her own *Prologue* the Wife dilates upon those experiences in love she has had with "compaignye" other than dull husbands; in the *General Prologue* we note that Chaucer passes over these experiences with humorous discretion, although he subtly epitomizes and emphasizes them a few lines later by saying—

> Of remedies of love she knew per chaunce,
> For she koude of that art the olde daunce.
>
> (ll. 475–476)

The "remedies of love," which Alisoun knows so well, is an allusion to Ovid's *Remedia Amoris,* a work familiar to some at least of Chaucer's audience.[23] The jest lies, of course, in Alisoun's knowledge of the *Remedia,* rather than the *Ars Amatoria:* she knows all the rules of the game, is a figure used by Chaucer more than once.[24]

Of the Wife of Bath's interests, second in importance only to her love affairs is her fondness for travelling in gay company:

> And thries hadde she been at Jerusalem;
> She hadde passed many a straunge strem;
> At Rome she hadde been, and at Boloigne,
> In Galice at Seint Jame, and at Coloigne.
> She koude muchel of wandrynge by the weye.
> Gat-tothed was she, soothly for to seye.
>
> (ll. 463–468)

That Chaucer couples the fact that the Wife has her teeth set wide apart with her fondness for crossing "many a straunge strem" would seem to substantiate Skeat's statement that the Middle Ages interpreted this physical characteristic as a sign of much travel and of good fortune.[25] Chaucer's later allusion to the same characteristic of the Wife's,[26] however, supports Professor Curry's contention that the fourteenth-century audience might think of a gap-toothed person as "envious, irreverent, luxurious by nature, bold, deceitful, faithless, and suspicious."[27] Professor Barnouw some years ago pointed out that women who were "gap-toothed by nature" were thought in the Middle Ages "to be predestined for the office of love." [28] But are we not justified in supposing that all three "signs" were in the minds of Chaucer's contemporaries? Certainly Alisoun's flamboyant personality bears them all out.

We should expect the Wife of Bath to be particularly eager, then, to go on pilgrimages for two reasons; the pilgrimage was the most popular form of travel for pleasure, indeed, practically the only kind of such travel, and especially appealed to women who would escape from the restrictions imposed by a husband.[29] It would be like Dame Alisoun to select the most important and the liveliest of the customary pilgrimages.

Besides the Holy Land, four places in the Middle Ages were "noted as being centers of greater pilgrimage": Rome, Compostella ("in Galice"), Canterbury, and Cologne.[30] When we meet the Wife of Bath, she is on her way to Canterbury, and she has already made the other important pilgrimages. She has been three times to Jerusalem, as well as to the less important "Boloigne." Chaucer is not exaggerating when he writes that the Wife knows a good deal about "wandrynge by the weye."

As for the pilgrimage to Rome, the late fourteenth-century *Stacions of Rome* gives us an exact picture of what Chaucer's contemporaries would expect Dame Alisoun to see in the Holy City. First to be visited is the famous St. Peter's, that "feir Munstre" with its hundred altars, where an almost illimitable number of years of pardon [31] can be obtained (14,000 years' pardon for a visit on certain occasions, 12,000 on others, 406 every time one ascends and descends the steps, and so on).[32] A visit to St. Paul's, situated "foure myle" from St. Peter's, also provides a great number of years of pardon.[33] Then there are many lesser churches, each associated with pardons or special miracles. One church has before it, for instance, the stone on which St. Paul was beheaded; [34] three wells have sprung from this stone, and their waters heal the sick.[35] Miracles are wrought also by the innumerable relics to be found in Rome, such as the bones of martyrs [1300 in one church!], the two tablets of the Law of Moses, the heads of St. Peter and St. Paul "closed in a ston," garments worn by Our Lord, and many objects connected with the Crucifixion.[36] The *Stacions of Rome* publicizes the city as effectively as a modern guide-book or prospectus. Chaucer's contemporaries must have enjoyed picturing the Wife of Bath on her visit there.

The most important medieval guide-book for Compostella, the twelfth-century *Liber IIII*[48] *sancti Jacobi Apostoli*,[37] is a much graver and more scholarly work than the *Stacions of Rome,* and probably for this reason omits any account of how St. James's shrine came to be in Spain. For this interesting and popular story we must turn elsewhere. The story of the founding of the shrine at Compostella begins in the widely known *Legenda Aurea*[38] as follows:

John Beleth relates that after the apostle's [James's] death, his disciples, in fear of the Jews, placed his body in a boat at night, embarked with him, although the boat had neither rudder nor steersman, and set sail, trusting to the providence of God to determine the place of his burial. And the angels guided the boat to the shores of Galicia in Spain . . . The disciples laid the body of the apostle on a great stone, which immediately softened as if it were wax, and shaped itself into a sarcophagus fitted to his body. . . .[39]

The actual pilgrim's guide to Compostella, as has been said, is not concerned with legend; the author's object is to give as accurate a description as he can of the churches in the city, particularly of the great edifice housing the shrine of St. James. That this description was written two hundred years before Chaucer lived makes it none the less accurate for his day. The long account may be in part summarized as follows:

The city of Compostella is situated between two rivers, the Sar on the east between the Mount of Joy [modern Monte San Marcos] and the city itself, and the Sarela on the west. There are seven gates to the city; in approaching overland from France, one enters Compostella by the north gate, near which is situated the Inn of the Poor Pilgrims. At the end of the road on which that famous inn is built, there is an enclosed court, or parvis [*paradisus*], which is entered by descending nine steps. At the foot of these steps is the most beautiful fountain in the whole world, dedicated to the benefit of the St. James pilgrims. The fountain is of stone, in the form of a large bowl (indeed, it seems large enough for fifteen men to bathe in it at once with ease), and is set on a high base. At its center is a bronze heptagonal column, surmounted by four lions from whose mouths continuously gushes clear, sweet water into the basin below. Behind the fountain stretches the stone-paved parvis; there are sold scallop-shells,[40] skins of wine, shoes,[41] wallets of deerskin, purses, straps, belts, medicinal herbs and drugs, and many other articles.

Then follows a detailed description of the size of the basilica, the number of pillars and windows, the position of the various altars, and so on. The description concludes with an account of the great altar, and of the miracles performed there:

> The great altar of St. James covers the marble tomb of the saint, whose entire body is there encased, although some other churches have laid claim to relics of St. James. The body is divinely illuminated by carbuncles of paradise, blessed by soft, heavenly perfumes, adorned by the brilliance of celestial tapers, and surrounded by angels. A modest altar is directly over the sepulchre, and above this is the great altar, the facing of which is of carved gold and silver. The canopy which is over the altar is square, and rests on four beautifully proportioned columns; it is covered inside and out with paintings and designs. Three large lamps of silver are suspended before the altar.
>
> The basilica of St. James was begun in 1078 A.D., and from that day to this [from forty to fifty years later] miracles have been performed there: the sick have been healed, the blind have seen, the dumb have spoken, the deaf have heard, the lame have walked in ease, the possessed have been delivered of evil spirits. Moreover, the prayers of the faithful have been answered, their vows have been accomplished, their chains have fallen, heaven has opened to those who knocked, and the afflicted have received consolation. From everywhere come pilgrims to St. James, and all are welcomed and helped.[42]

No wonder that the enterprising Dame Alisoun, who dearly loves to travel and see marvels, has been "in Galice at Seint Jame."

Pilgrims went to Cologne primarily to visit the tomb of the Magi; the *Legenda Aurea* tells the story of how the bodies of the three kings were taken to that city.

When they had adored Jesus, the Wise Men, who had been warned in a dream that they should not return to Herod, went back another way into their country. Their bodies were discovered by Helena, the mother of Constantine, who bore them to Constantinople. At a later time, Saint Eustorgius carried them to Milan, at which place he was bishop, and laid them in the church which now belongs to our Order of Friars Preachers. But when the Emperor Henry took possession of Milan, he had the bodies of the Magi carried down the Rhine to Cologne, where the people venerate them with great devotion.[43]

We cannot picture that strong feminist, the Wife of Bath, however, as content to stop with the tomb of Gaspar, Melchoir, and Baltha-zar. Would she not have felt particular interest in the wholesale martyrdom at Cologne of the Eleven Thousand Virgins,[44] and have visited the supposed resting place of their bones?[45]

Boulogne, although not one of the places of greater pilgrimage, had considerable fame in medieval France, and Chaucer may have included it in the Wife of Bath's "wandrynge" for that reason; he may even have visited Notre-Dame-de-Boulogne-sur-mer himself as a very young man, for the Black Prince and John of Gaunt were there in 1360,[46] and as Chaucer was twice in France during that year he may either have accompanied his royal patrons on their pious excursion or been inspired by them to make the journey by himself. The early history of the shrine at Boulogne is obscured in the legends of the seventh century, but the account given by Champagnac is briefly as follows: The people of Boulogne were assembled for prayer one day in the year 633 (or 636) in a small chapel on a hill-top, when the Virgin appeared before them in a vision. Our Lady informed the faithful that an unmanned and rudderless vessel lay near the shore, and that in this vessel they would find her image as testimony of her favour. The crowd rushed to the shore, found the miraculous ship gently riding on a calm sea and bathed in heavenly radiance, and discovered therein a beautifully carved wooden image of the Queen of Heaven and two other relics; the image and the relics were immediately taken to the chapel with joy and reverence, and the great church of Notre-Dame-de-Boulogne was later erected on the same site the better to house such treasures.[47]

To picture with fourteenth-century imagination what Dame Alisoun saw in Jerusalem we can scarcely improve upon the account of pilgrimages to that city given in Mandeville's *Travels,* the guide-book which is a composite of all the other guide-books. The position of Jerusalem is described and the history of the city is briefly out-lined.[48] Then the author writes:

And yee schull undirstonde that whan men comen to Jerusalem here first pilgrymage is to the chirche of the holy Sepulcre where oure lord was buryed that is withoute the cytee on the north syde But it is now enclosed in with the toun wall. And there is a full fair chirche all Rownd and open above and covered with leed And on the west syde is a fair tour and an high for belles strongly made And in the myddes of the chirche is a tabernacle as it were a lytyll hows made with a low lytyll dore And that tabernacle is made in manere of half a compas right curiousely and richely made of gold and azure and othere riche coloures full nobelyche made And in the right syde of that tabernacle is .viij. fote long and .v. fote wyde and .xj. fote in heghte. And it is not longe sithe the sepulcre was all open that men myghten kisse it and touche it. But for pilgrymes that comen thider peyned hem to breke the ston in peces or in poudre [the fourteenth century evidently had the same troubles as the twentieth has with souvenir-hunting vandals!] therfore the Soudan hath do make a wall aboute the sepulcre that noman may towche it. But in the left syde of the wall of the tabernacle is wel the heighte of a man is a gret ston to the quantytee of a mannes hed that was of the holy sepulcre and that ston kissen the pilgrymes that comen thider. In that tabernacle ben no wyndowes but it is all made light with lampes that hangen before the sepulcre And there is a lampe that hongeth before the Sepulcre that brenneth light and on the gode Fryday it goth out be himself and on the Pasch day it lightez agayne by it self at that hour that oure lord roos fro deth to lyve.[49]

In the same manner the pilgrim is next directed to Calvary, the sacred wonders of which are minutely described. There is the white stone on which the Cross was fixed still bearing the red marks of Our Lord's blood—the same stone on which Adam's head was found after the Flood, and on which Abraham made sacrifices to God; near this stone lie the bodies of the first Crusaders. Within the mount of Calvary are the weeping pillars ("that allweys droppen water") to which Christ was bound when He was scourged; and near there, deep under the earth, St. Helena found the True Cross. (The True Cross will revive the dead if laid upon the body; the nails of the Cross, if carried in battle, will bring victory.) Mandeville then gives detailed descriptions and histories of the great number of churches in and near Jerusalem. The account of Solomon's Temple is particularly elaborate, and the prospective visitor is told that he must procure a special permit from the Sultan to see all its marvels.[50] The fact that Mandeville may not have been the author of the Travels, or that the author, whoever he was, may never have been in Jerusalem, does not here concern us: the picture of the wonders of Jerusalem was authentic for the fourteenth century, and the Wife of Bath's three visits there can be pictured accordingly.[51]

The question as to whether or not Chaucer drew on Jean de Meun's La Vieille in the *Roman de la Rose* for the portrait of the

Wife of Bath is not of great importance to us who are meeting the Wife principally in the *General Prologue*. In the Wife's own *Prologue,* a great many of the phrases assigned to La Vieille are borrowed by the English poet for his Alisoun's use,[52] but in the *General Prologue* only one parallel to what La Vieille says is found: the Wife of Bath has had "oother compaignye in youthe"—La Vieille boasts that she ignored a number of would-be lovers when she was young, for, "j'avoie autre compaignie." [53] Furthermore, as Mead so convincingly points out, the essential character of La Vieille is fundamentally different from that of Alisoun. La Vieille is old, decrepit, through with life; the Wife of Bath has still many years to live, she is vigorous and imbued with *joie de vivre*. La Vieille is morose; the Wife is good-natured, even when she is occasionally shrewish.[54] [Chaucer may have taken words from the French poem, but Dame Alisoun is straight from life.]

As a matter of interest, we must not take leave of the Wife of Bath before we have examined briefly the detailed "horoscope" Professor Curry has so learnedly cast for her.[55] [Using the data which the Wife gives in her *Prologue* (she was born at a time when Venus and Mars were in conjunction in Taurus) [56] and quoting from the medieval authorities on "astronomye," Professor Curry shows that Alisoun is the victim of her stars: Venus by herself would make Alisoun beautiful and graceful, and would provide Alisoun with a delicate complexion, but Mars distorts the figure into heaviness ("hir hipes large" come from this planet's "excessive virility"), and makes the face "reed of hewe." The Wife's voice, which through Venus alone would be sweet and well-modulated, is, because of Mars, "raised continually in vulgar jest and indelicate banter." [57]

> For certes, I am al Venerien
> In feelynge, and myn herte is Marcien,[58]

confesses Alisoun, meaning, as Professor Curry indicates, that she would like to be charming, joyous, and pleasure-loving in the most refined sense, as well as appealing to the opposite sex in a highly ladylike fashion, but that Mars has debased these characteristics into rowdiness, boisterous spirits, a fondness for questionable "wandrynge by the weye," and the unrestrained attractiveness of the "healthy and frank female animal." [59] But again, as Professor Curry says, it is unlikely that Chaucer drew the portrait of the vivid personality of the Wife of Bath from anything but life.[60] Hence the horoscope is merely an addition to the picture, and its introduction in the Wife's *Prologue* furnishes us with another of Chaucer's witty and realistic touches.

NOTES

(The abbreviations used to designate books and articles mentioned in the Notes will be found listed alphabetically in the Bibliography, opposite the full reference. References to lines in the *Canterbury Tales* are given by fragment and line numbers only.)

1. The Wife of Bath gives her own name in III (D) 320 and 804. *Alys* and *Alisoun* are both modern "Alice."

2. Manly, *New Light*, pp. 231 f.

3. Manly, *Cant. Tales*, p. 527, n. 445.

4. Manly (see note 3 above) quotes from Atton and Holland (*The King's Customs*, p. 26) in support of this statement.

5. X (I) 407.

6. In *Le Miroir de Mariage*, ll. 3289–3290, Deschamps writes—

> . . . va la plus grande
> Devant les aultres a l'offrande.

See also ll. 3316–3323, 3376–3378.

7. III (D) 552 ff.

8. Druitt, pp. 239–244, 246, 264.

The monumental brasses of Chaucer's time which show "ladies of quality" wearing the coverchief do not support Manly's statement (*New Light*, pp. 230 f.) that this head-covering "had not been 'in style' since the middle of the century."

9. A "bokeler" was synonymous with "targe" (*NED*); the Yeoman, it will be remembered, carries a bokeler, or small round shield, used to ward off blows.

10. *NED*, "Foot-mantel."

11. Manly says (*Cant. Tales*, p. 528, n. 473) that Queen Anne, wife of Richard II, introduced the side-saddle for women, and Robinson (p. 765) also makes this statement. Manly calls attention to an early fifteenth-century illumination (plate opp. p. 192 of his *Cant. Tales*) in which ladies of the court ride side-saddle. In the Ellesmere MS., in which the Wife of Bath is depicted as riding astride, the Prioress is depicted as riding side-saddle.

12. Coulton, *Ch. and his Eng.*, p. 204.

13. *Ibid.*, Chap. XVI *passim*.

14. La Tour Landry, p. 25.

15. III (D) 666 ff.

16. Proverbs, VII, 10–12.

17. Owst, *Lit. and Pulpit*, pp. 385–404 *passim*.

18. *Ibid.*, p. 385 f. (Quotation from MS. Add. 21253, fol. 45 b.)

19. *Ibid.*, p. 389. Dr. Owst writes (n. 2) that no part of the *Canterbury Tales* "illustrates better the debt of contemporary thought and literature to the pulpit" than does the *Wife of Bath's Prologue*.

And, as has been pointed out in this chapter, the Wife of Bath's portrait in the *General Prologue* is a summary of her own *Prologue*.

20. Coulton, *Ch. and his Eng.*, p. 220.

21. Howard, *Hist. Mat. Inst.*, I, 303.

22. *Ibid.*, 303–310.

Coulton suggests (*Med. Pan.*, p. 397) that since evidence in the Middle Ages was often hard to procure, "general notoriety was of extreme value" and marriage at the church door was performed to make the ceremony as public as possible and thus obtain the maximum number of witnesses. Witnesses were extremely important in marriage services.

23. Haskins writes (*Renaissance of Twelfth Cent.*, pp. 107 ff.) that the medieval vogue of Ovid was continuous down to Chaucer and later writers. All of Ovid's works were read, especially the *Metamorphoses*, the *Art of Love*, and the *Remedies of Love*.

24. See VI (C) 79 and *Troilus and Criseyde*, III, 695.

The expression was also common in the French of the time (see Langlois's note on l. 3936 of the *Rom. de la Rose*—"Qu'el set toute la vielle dance").

25. Skeat, V, 44, n. 468. I have not been able to find evidence supporting Skeat's statement that the gap-toothed person was thought to be lucky, other than the anonymous note he himself cites, a note appearing in the "Folk Lore" section of *Notes and Queries*, First Series, VI (1852), 601, which merely states that teeth set wide apart are a sign of luck. On the other hand, the belief that such teeth presage travel for those possessing them survives as a superstition even today in Kentucky (*Kentucky Superstitions*, # 865), which is proof that at least seventeenth-century England was accepting this physical characteristic to be a sign of travel; and as folk-superstition seldom springs up overnight, it seems probable that a superstition accepted in 1600 might well have its roots in 1400.

26. III (D) 603.

27. Curry, *Ch. and Med. Sci.*, p. 109.

28. Barnouw, *The Nation*, CIII, 540.

29. See above p. 27.

30. *Cath. Ency.*, "Pilgrimage."

31. A "year's pardon" meant one year less in Purgatory for the sinner.

32. *Stacions of Rome*, ll. 17–70.

33. *Ibid.*, ll. 71–92.

34. The manner in which St. Paul died is historically uncertain (*Cath. Ency.*, "Paul").

35. *Stacions of Rome*, ll. 109–116.

36. *Ibid.*, ll. 357–366.

37. *Guide du Pèlerin* (modern French translation of *Liber IIII*[us] *Sancti Jacobi Apostoli*).

38. The *Legenda Aurea,* or *Golden Legend,* had wide circulation in the Middle Ages. Chaucer himself used this work as a source for the *Second Nun's Tale.*

39. *Golden Leg.,* pp. 371 f.

40. In the thirteenth century there were here one hundred shops, or stalls, selling these shells (*Guide du Pèlerin,* p. 96, n. 3).

41. Mlle. Viellard suggests (*ibid.,* p. 97, n. 5) that these "shoes" were like the modern espadrilles.

42. *Guide du Pèlerin,* pp. 83–125.

43. *Golden Leg.,* p. 88.

44. *Ibid.,* pp. 627 ff.

45. Coulton writes (*Five Cent. of Relig.,* III, 93) that the story of the eleven martyred virgins dates from the fifth century. Then in the ninth century, some scribe drew a bar over the figure xi for emphasis, in the same way in which we sometimes underline. But the bar drawn over a number in the Middle Ages might also denote "thousands," and so some later scribe understood it in this case. "Thenceforward," remarks Coulton, "the homely original 11 stood no chance with this new 11,000"!

46. *Cath. Ency.,* "Pilgrimage"; Champagnac, I, 348.

47. Champagnac, I, 342 ff. It is interesting to note that Champagnac mentions St. Eligius (by whom, it will be remembered, the Prioress swears) as the maker of the caskets which contain the relics brought by the Virgin.

48. Mandeville (ed. Hamelius), pp. 48 f.

49. *Ibid.,* pp. 49 f.

50. *Ibid.,* pp. 50–66.

51. Henry L. Savage gives an interesting account of fourteenth-century Jerusalem seen through the eyes of Ogier, eighth baron d'Anglure. (Reprint from *The Arab Heritage,* Princeton, 1944.) The account is substantially the same as that given by Mandeville, however.

52. Fansler (*Ch. and RR,* pp. 168 f.) lists thirty-five parallels between the *Wife of Bath's Prologue* and the *Rom. de la Rose.*

53. *Rom. de la Rose,* l. 12781.

54. Mead, *PMLA,* XVI, 394 f.

55. Curry, *op. cit.,* pp. 91–118.

56. III (D) 600 ff.

57. Curry, *op. cit.,* pp. 108 f.

58. III (D) 609–610.

59. Curry, *op. cit.,* pp. 109 ff.

60. *Ibid.,* p. 117.

Manly calls our attention (*New Light,* pp. 232 ff.) to Chaucer's probable visits to the royal forest of Petherton when he acted as one of the deputy foresters; to make such visits Chaucer would have ridden through St. Michael-juxta-Bathon. Manly adds that "Alysoun" seems to be the commonest name for women in the *Ancient Deeds* of Bath—and more than one of these Alices "rejoiced in three or more husbands"!

CHAPTER XV

THE POOR PARSON AND HIS BROTHER
THE PLOWMAN

A good man was ther of religioun
And was a povre Persoun of a Toun,
But riche he was of hooly thoght and werk.
He was also a lerned man, a clerk,
That Cristes gospel trewely wolde preche;
His parisshens devoutly wolde he teche.

(ll. 477–482)

CHAUCER'S Parson, like his Knight, is an idealized conception. In it there is none of the satire which sharpens nearly all the other portraits, unless we concern ourselves with what the Parson is not. First, this good man "of religioun," no matter how poor he may be in worldly goods, is rich in "hooly thoght and werk"; he is also a "lerned man," who has studied at a university (a "clerk"),[1] and who is therefore competent to preach truly the Gospel of Christ and to teach his parishioners devoutly.

It is interesting that the fourteenth century stressed learning as so important for priests, even for those of poor parishes. One Lollard laments that "fewe curatis han the bible and exposiciouns of the gospelis, and litel studien on hem"; if all priests would study the Bible and its expositors, they would be able to teach the people truly, and "thanne schulde good lif regne, and reste and pees and charite, and synne and falsnesse putt a bak."[2] The strictly orthodox also emphasize the importance of learning. Master Rypon, a subprior of Durham about the year 1400, says, for example, that it is essential that priests possess a knowledge of the Bible in order to teach their parishioners properly;[3] and John Myrc, in his ultra-orthodox *Instructions for Parish Priests*, of the early fifteenth century, writes as follows of the necessity for priests to be learned:

God seth hymself, as wryten we fynde,
That whenne the blynde ledeth the blynde,
In to the dyche they fallen boo,
For they ne sen whare by to go.
So faren prestes now by dawe;
They beth blynde in goddes lawe,
That whenne they scholde the pepul rede
In to synne they do hem lede,
Thus they have do now fulle yore
And alle ys for defawte of lore.[4]

Chaucer's Parson, then, is unusual in possessing the learning he
should have; he is also unusual in that he is a man of true virtue:

Benygne he was, and wonder diligent,
And in adversitee ful pacient,
And swich he was ypreved ofte sithes.
Ful looth were hym to cursen for his tithes,
But rather wolde he yeven, out of doute,
Unto his povre parisshens aboute
Of his offryng and eek of his substaunce.
He koude in litel thyng have suffisaunce.
Wyd was his parisshe, and houses fer asonder,
But he ne lefte nat, for reyn ne thonder,
In siknesse nor in meschief to visite
The ferreste in his parisshe, muche and lite,
Upon his feet, and in his hand a staf.
This noble ensample to his sheep he yaf,
That first he wroghte, and afterward he taughte,
Out of the gospel he tho wordes caughte,
And this figure he added eek therto,
That if gold ruste, what shal iren do?
For if a preest be foul, on whom we truste,
No wonder is a lewed man to ruste;
And shame it is, if a prest take keep,
A shiten shepherde and a clene sheep.
Wel oghte a preest ensample for to yive,
By his clennesse, how that his sheep sholde lyve.

(ll. 483-506)

That the Parson shows himself to be patient in adversity, and
that he is benign and diligent make him, we suspect, exceptional
as a human being; but that he is "ful looth" to "cursen for his

tithes" makes him without doubt exceptional as a fourteenth-century parish priest. The medieval Church required parsons to collect tithes, in other words an "income tax" of ten per cent, from every parishioner. Dr. Coulton writes that the parish priest "might claim tithes from every kind of gain, excepting only illicit gains, such as the usurer's, the jongleur's, or the prostitute's." [5] No matter how poor a man was,—and obviously the real burden of this tax fell on the poor,—tithes were levied upon him unless he were literally destitute. The Church then had the duty to rescue him from death by starvation, thus nullifying the tax. Personal tithes were payable by "the commandment of the law of God," the Church agreed, and anyone who resisted payment was guilty of deadly sin.[6] John Myrc tells parish priests that they must teach their charges "well and speedily" how they are to pay tithes:

> Teche hem also welle and greythe
> How they schule paye here teythe:
> Of alle thynge that doth hem newe,
> They schule teythe welle and trewe,
> After the costome of that cuntraye
> Every mon hys tethynge schale paye
> Bothe of smale and of grete,
> Of schep and swyn and other nete.*
> Teythe of huyre * and of honde,*
> Goth by costome of the londe.[7]

Myrc then adds cynically that it is "an ydul thynge" to instruct the priest further as to tithing, for only the veriest fool will neglect to gather in as much money as he possibly can.[8]

Harsh punishment was meted out to those who failed to pay tithes: the transgressor was "cursed," that is, excommunicated. As the duty of pronouncing what was called the "lesser" sentence of curse fell upon the parish priest, for only a bishop was empowered to pronounce the "greater" sentence,[9] Myrc includes directions for excommunicating in his book of instructions. He begins—

> The gret [10] sentence I write here,
> That twies or thries in the yere

* *nete:* "live cattle"   *honde:* "handiwork"
  huyre: "wages"

Thou shalt pronounce, without lette,*
Whan thi parisse is togidir mette
Thou shall pronounce this idous thing,
With crosse and candell and bell knylling *
Speke oute redely fir noght thou wond,*
That all mowe the understonde.[11]

Myrc next lists the sins for which the congregation may be cursed; prominent on the list is the sin of withholding "proper tithinges." [12] Then comes the form of the excommunication proper, which the priest has been instructed to "speke oute redely," as follows:

By the aucthorite of the ffather and of the son and of the holy goost and of our lady Seynt Mary goddes moder, of hevene, and all other virgines and Seynt mighele and all other apostles and Seynt Steven and all other martires, and Seynt Nicholas and all other confessoures and of all the holy hallowen of heven; We accursen and warren and departen from all gode dedes and preres of holy chirch, and of all thes halowen, and dampne into the peyn of hell all those that have don thes articles thar we have seid bifore, till they come to amendment; We accursen hem by the auctorite of the courte of Rome, within and withoute, sleping or waking, going and sytting, stonding and riding, lying above erthe and under erthe, spekyng and crying and drynkyng; in wode, in water, in felde, in towne: acorsen hem fader and son and holy goost: accursen hem patriarkes prophetes and apostles and all godes disapules and all holy Innocentes, martieres, confessoures and virgines, monkes, canons, heremytes, prestes and clerkes that they have no part of masse ne matenes ne of none other gode praiers, but that the peynes of hell be her mede with Judas that betrayed oure lorde Jhesu Crist; and the life of hem be put oute of the boke of lyfe tyll they come to amendment and satisfaction made. fiat fiat. Amen.[13]

"Make their hearts fearful," charges Myrc, and we cannot doubt that to the simple flock in the Middle Ages excommunication was a real and terrible punishment. We are not surprised that such a benign humanitarian as Chaucer's Parson was "ful looth" to curse his poor parishioners for non-payment of a tax which must have been difficult for even the least poor of them to meet.

The followers of Wyclif, always in sympathy with the worthy

---

* *lette*: "hindrance"   *fir* [sic] *noght thou wond*: "shrink from nothing"
  knylling: "tolling"

poor, inveigh against the grave penalty imposed for non-payment of tithes. Priests who "so cruely" curse for tithes are Satan's own, they say; priests excommunicate more for "love of worldly catel" than for sin. "Yif a man be bihynde of tithes and othere offryngis and custumes maad of synful men, he schal be . . . cursed," yet he can go unpunished no matter how openly he break "the hestis of god"; the Church robs "cristene peple of goodis of fortune, of goodis of kynde and goodis of grace" by pitiless excommunication; Lollard priests will not take a benefice because they will then have to "stryve and plede and curse for tithes" and perform other sinful acts. Every day "smale curatis" are ordered to summon and to curse poor men "for noght but for coveitise"; laws are only "scharply holden" when they concern the exaction of tithes.[14]

Although warnings to pay tithes as everyone's duty came from orthodox medieval pulpits,[15] there were many of the anti-Lollard clergy who also deplored the unseemly readiness with which unprincipled priests, who cared only for collecting money, cursed for tithes. Bromyard, for example, Dr. Owst points out, unqualifiedly condemns the punishments inflicted by the bad priest for non-payment of the tax, when "rarely or never" do these priests trouble about the spiritual welfare of their parishioners.[16]

Chaucer's Parson, however, is very different from those the Lollards and Bromyard attack: not only is he reluctant to curse for tithes, but he will even give of the "offryng," or the voluntary contributions made by the congregation, and of his own meagre "substance" to his "povre parisshens." Because of his charity, he makes a truly "litel" portion suffice for his own needs. Those that are in sickness or in adversity ("meschief"), as well as those in need, are looked after by this kind, fatherly Parson, who trudges, staff in hand,[17] to the farthest reaches of his wide parish, with houses far asunder, to bring help and comfort to his flock. This very real shepherd sets a "noble ensaumple," which he has "caught" from the Gospel: [18] he first practices good works, and then teaches them ("first he wroghte, and afterward he taughte"), a maxim which Chaucer saves from triteness by a deep sincerity and by a re-emphasis in later lines:

> But Cristes loore and his apostles twelve
> He taughte, but first he folwed it hymselve.

(ll. 527–528)

Here Gower and Langland give voice to the same idea: Gower writes in close parallel to Chaucer,

Crist wroghte ferst and after tawhte; [19]

and Langland says that Do Well is to "do," Do Bet is to "teach," but Do Best is to combine action and precept.[20] There is also a French parallel to Chaucer's lines. In the late twelfth-century poem,[21] *Li Romans de Carité,* to which Kittredge calls our attention, the parish priest is exhorted to act according to his teaching. "Thou should'st do and then speak." [22] The same figure of speech which Chaucer uses is added: "if gold rusts, what will happen to iron?" [23] Furthermore, the French author speaks of the strangeness of a "foolish" shepherd and "wise" sheep, the one "soiled" in the mud and the other "clean" in the meadow,[24] which is almost exactly what Chaucer says. Kittredge also points out that Chaucer's remarks are in the same order as those of the French poem, and he suggests that both authors may have drawn from a common and now unknown source. The origin of the proverb about "rusting" gold is perhaps biblical.[25]

Chaucer's Parson fills other requirements of the ideal parish priest:

> He sette nat his benefice to hyre
> And leet his sheep encombred in the myre
> And ran to Londoun unto Seinte Poules
> To seken hym a chaunterie for soules,
> Or with a bretherhed to been withholde;
> But dwelte at hoom, and kepte wel his folde,
> So that the wolf ne made it nat myscarie;
> He was a shepherde and noght a mercenarie.
>
> (ll. 507–514)

Dr. Workman observes that absenteeism was one of the curses of the English Church in the latter part of the fourteenth century.[26] Certainly we have ample proof of this in the literature of the period. Gower, for example, in his long complaint against contemporary parish priests in the *Vox Clamantis,* has much to say about the parson who will leave his cure; [27] in the *Mirour de l'Omme,* Gower is equally stern about the same matter: these priests are always away for "covoitise." [28] Rypon and Bromyard also protest against clerical absenteeism. Rypon declares bitterly, according to Dr. Owst, that some priests "who rarely or never go near their livings, 'the more greedily exact' the fruits of them, 'so that they may live the more luxuriously in courts, universities, or cities' "; [29] Bromyard says that when once ordained, priests " 'try to be absent from their flock as much as possible . . . so much so, that they appear to have made a compact and indenture between them and the demons, to the effect that they themselves should have the wool and milk of their sheep, that is, the temporal benefits, and that the devils should have the souls of them.' " [30] The Lollards are especially vehement about absenteeism. They say that worldly priests induce rich men to found chantries so that the priest may live a "useless" life of ease away from the hard work of a parish; [31] priests will run after fat benefices, but they "wolen not goo comunly a myle for to preche the gospel"; [32] these traitors to God "haunten lordis courtis and ben occupied in worldly office and don not here cure to here parischenys . . ." [33]

Westlake points out that chantry endowments and gild appointments of priests furnished "considerable temptation" to unscrupulous priests, for by such establishments they obtained "no little profit and no very strenuous occupation." The priest who was not bound to a parish was always tempted to accept "the offering of more masses than he could conveniently say or sing"; to neglect the study which would lead to proper instruction of the people; and to pass his great amount of spare time in taverns and even less reputable haunts. [34] Westlake translates in part a letter, written in 1362 by Archbishop Simon Islip to the Bishop of London, concerning this deplorable situation, as follows:

We are certainly informed by common fame and experience that modern priests through covetousness and love of ease, not content with reasonable salaries, demand excessive pay for their labour and receive it; and do so despise labour and study pleasure that they wholly refuse to serve as parish priests in churches and chapels or to attend the cure of souls, . . . that they may live in a leisurely manner by celebrating annals for the quick and the dead. [35]

▷ Thus again Chaucer's Parson typifies the truly ideal parish priest. He does not run to "Londoun unto Seinte Poules" to answer the advertisement of some gild for a chaplain "to been withholden" (to be retained by the gild in a sinecure), but he stays "at hoom" and guards his flock. Westlake declares that St. Paul's Cathedral or its precincts was a "regular meeting-place for wardens [of gilds] who desired to hire, or priests who desired to be engaged for duties such as wardens had to offer." [36] "The priest is now a hireling ["*mercenarius*"—cf. Chaucer's use of the word *mercenarie*], and the wolf preys upon the flock," Gower laments, and gives us another parallel for Chaucer's description.[37]

Chaucer's Parson, for all his inflexible high standards for his own conduct, is kind to the repentant sinner, yet to the unrepentant he is properly severe no matter what the "estat" of the transgressor:

> And though he hooly were and vertuous,
> He was to synful men nat despitous,*
> Ne of his speche daungerous * ne digne,*
> But in his techyng discreet and benygne.
> To drawen folk to hevene by fairnesse,
> By good ensample, this was his bisynesse.
> But it were any persone obstinat,
> What so he were, of heigh or lough estat,
> Hym wolde he snybben sharply for the nonys.
> A bettre preest I trowe that nowher noon ys.
> He waited after no pompe and reverence,
> Ne maked him a spiced conscience.
>
> (ll. 515–526)

In treating all men as equal in the sight of God, Chaucer's Parson once more shows himself to be exceptional. The reformers, both orthodox and Wyclifite, all complain that the clergy fail to reprove the rich and influential, but mete out too severe penalties to the poor and obscure.[38] One Lollard tract says, for instance—

. . . thei [i.e., priests] doren not reprove men of here opyn synnes bi forme of the gospel for displeisynge of here maistris and leesynge of here salarie; for many of hem seyn thus: "I wole not displeise him of whom I have my lyvynge." a, ye blynde foolis, drede ye more to lese a morsel of mete than o poynt of charite? drede ye more to offende an erthely wrecche than god almyghtty? . . .[39]

* *despitous:* "scornful"   *daungerous:* "haughty"
  digne: "disdainful"

But our good Parson demands "no pompe and reverence," nor is he so over-concerned with fine points ("ne maked him a spiced conscience") [40] that he loses sight of important fundamentals. He is the true Christian who walks himself along the Way he teaches others to follow.

The question as to whether or not Chaucer's "good man of religioun" is a Lollard is an interesting one. Professor Loomis argues strongly in favour of the Parson's being one of Wyclif's adherents, [41] though not, of course, one of Wyclif's "poor priests." He points out that Chaucer makes a triple reference to the Gospel and Christ's teaching in writing of the Parson, and this is Wyclifite emphasis; that Chaucer also uses the Lollard shibboleth, "Christ and his apostles" in the Parson's portrait; that the Parson never denies the two direct accusations that he is a Lollard. [42] As further evidence that the Parson's characteristics are indicative of Lollardry, we should note that when Margery Kempe referred to the Gospel or inveighed against swearing she was promptly accused of being a Lollard. Also we must bear in mind that many of Chaucer's friends were prominent Lollards, and that the poet himself had had every opportunity to develop an interest at least in Wyclif's ideas. [43] Thus, in company with "oure Hooste," we may "smelle a Lollere in the wynd," and be almost certain that there is solid substance to give rise to the odour. But whatever our opinion as to that matter, [44] all of us will join Chaucer in saying, "A bettre preest . . . nowher noon ys."

* * *

The good "Persoun of a Toun" is accompanied by his brother— a man who is related to him in character as well as by blood.

> With hym ther was a Plowman, was his brother,
> That hadde ylad of dong ful many a fother; *
> A trewe swynkere * and a good was he,
> Lyvynge in pees and parfit charitee.
> God loved he best with al his hoole herte
> At alle tymes, thogh him gamed or smerte,*

---

* *fother:* "load"　　　　　　　　*swynkere:* "labourer"
　thogh him gamed or smerte: "whether it gave him joy or sorrow," or— more generally—"in all circumstances"

And thanne his neighebor right as hymselve.
He wolde thresshe, and therto dyke and delve,
For Cristes sake, for every povre wight,
Withouten hire, if it lay in his myght.
His tithes payde he ful faire and wel,
Bothe of his propre swynk and his catel.
In a tabard he rood upon a mere.

(ll. 529–541)

This portrait is another idealization into which Chaucer seems to have put genuine admiration. In writing with such warm approval of a peasant, however, the poet displays an unfashionable point of view; generally speaking, the fourteenth-century aristocrat had little good to say about the tiller of the soil.[45] Professor Gardiner Stillwell even advances the theory that Chaucer's "evident affection for the ideal peasant suggests an antagonism towards the actual peasant," since the real peasant of the day was "revolting against everything Chaucer stood for." [46] The arguments Professor Stillwell uses to support this theory supply excellent reasons why Chaucer might have had the same attitude as most of his associates; but does that prove that Chaucer did share that attitude? Professor Stillwell reminds us that the Peasants' Revolt of 1381 would still have been fresh in Chaucer's mind when the Plowman's portrait was drawn, and that Chaucer's patron, John of Gaunt, was one of the principal targets of the rebels' wrath; that whether or not he studied at the Temple, Chaucer was justice of the peace for Kent in 1385, and thus became identified with a social group antagonistic to the peasants. Hence, of the four classes who were unsympathetic to the peasants, "royal officials, lawyers, adherents of John of Gaunt, and unpopular landlords," Chaucer is known to have been a member of the first three; he was also a member of the great middle-class group of *"chivalers, citeins, and Burgeys,"* a group which had joined with the prelates and lords temporal in crying with "one voice" in the Parliament of 1381–1383 that Richard's revocation of promises made to the rebel peasants was "bien faite!" [47] Against this presumptive evidence, however, is the weight of facts. Chaucer nowhere writes contemptuously of the peasant, rather he writes in approval of him; [48] and this particular peasant, the Plowman, is linked intimately to the Parson, for whom Chaucer has unqualifiedly great admiration. It scarcely seems possible that the poet is concealing scorn or dislike in his description of the Parson's good brother. As Professor Loomis observes,[49] the Plowman is presented to us as illustrative of Chaucer's favourite text: "gentilesse" is not inherited but comes from doing "gentil dedis."

We may be fairly confident in saying, then, that Chaucer writes with true sympathy of this poor farmer [50] who has carried many a load of dung, who threshes, makes ditches, and digs. The Plowman knows his duty as well as does the allegorical plowman of Langland's poem who serves Truth always—

'Both to sowe and to sette * . the while I swynke myghte.

.   .   .   .

Bothe ysowen his sede . and sued * his bestes
With-inne and with-outen . wayted his profyt.
I dyke and I delve . I do that treuthe hoteth; *
Some tyme I sowe . and some tyme I thresche.' [51]

In the anonymous *Seneschaucie* of the late thirteenth century, a practical book on husbandry, duties of plowmen are stated thus:

The ploughmen ought to be men of intelligence, and ought to know how to sow, and how to repair broken ploughs and harrows, and to till the land well, and crop it rightly; and they ought to know also how to yoke and drive the oxen, without beating or hurting them, and they ought to forage them well, and look well after the forage that it be not stolen nor carried off; and they ought to keep them safely in meadows and several pastures, and other beasts which are found therein they ought to impound. And they and the keepers must make ditches and build and remove the earth, and ditch it so that the ground may be dry and the water drained. . . .[52]

Thus as a tiller of the soil, Chaucer's Plowman is accurately defined by the standards put forward for his class by Langland, in idealistic allegory, and by the anonymous writer, in prosaic terms: the Plowman has pride and interest in doing his duty.

The Plowman has great personal virtue. He obeys primarily (in implicit comparison to the Parson) the two commandments on which hang all the Law and Prophets: under all conditions he

* *to sette:* "to plant"   *hoteth:* "bids"
  sued: "attended"

loves God with his whole heart, and then his neighbour as himself. The Plowman lives "in pees and parfit charitee"; he will always help without charge ("withouten hire") anyone in poorer circumstances than himself. Like the Parson he has unfailing charity. The Parson is reluctant to excommunicate for non-payment of tithes; the Plowman presents the good parishioner's side of the picture, and gives his brother no cause for such "cursing." He knows that as a labourer it is his especial duty to pay his tithes 'ful faire and wel," both the tithes derived from his personal industry, his "propre swynk," and those derived from the profits on his stock (his "catel").[53] In the *Chess-Book,* Jacobus de Cessolis instructs the tiller of the soil as follows:

. . . But hit behoveth for necessite that some shold labour the erthe after the synne of adam/ for to fore er adam synned/ the erthe brought forth fruyt with out labour of handes/ but syn he synned/ hit muste nedes be labourid with the handes of men . . . And god that formed us of the erthe hath ordeyned that by the laboure of men she shold gyve nourysshyng unto alle that lyveth/ and first the labourer of the erthe ought to knowe his god that formed and made heven and erthe of nought And ought to have loyaulte and trouth in hymself/ and despise deth for to entende to his laboure And he ought to gyve thankyngis to hym that made hym And of whom he receyveth all his goodes temporall/ wherof his lyf is susteyned/ And also he is bounden to paye the dismes and tythes of alle his thynges And not as Caym dide. But as Abell dyde of the beste that he chese allway for to gyve to god and to plese hym/ For they that grucche and be grevyd in that they rendre and gyve to god the tienthes of her goodes/ they ought to be aferd and have drede that they shall falle in necessite . . .[54]

It is evident that Chaucer's Plowman is fully aware of his heavy obligation as a descendant of "Caym" to "gyve to god" the tenths of his goods, and of the fruits of his labour.

The Plowman's costume and his mount are suitable, for here is no man of humble rank aping his betters, nor the starving wretch of *Pierce the Ploughmans Crede,*[55] which presents a pitiable picture of a peasant in the late fourteenth century that is very different from Chaucer's contented Plowman. The latter's "tabard" is a durable and well-made garment proper to a self-respecting workman who knows exactly his "estaat" and his "degree," a garment resembling the smock worn by country labourers in England as late as the end of the nineteenth century, and by artists and house-wives today.[56] Chaucer's Plowman also properly rides a mare. As Karkeek says, "No person pretending to belong to the 'quality' would have mounted a mare, except under circumstances of direst necessity." [57] The Political Poem, "On the Execution of Richard Scrope, Archbishop of York," in lamenting the many indignities suffered by the Archbishop, notes that the prelate was led to his execution riding a mare.[58] It is thus eminently fitting that Chaucer's humble Plowman selects a mare for his journey to Canterbury.

That Chaucer writes with affection of his good peasant is obvious, but the figure has not quite the warm vitality of the Parson, whose light seems to shine in the real world, illuminating the way for all who observe his glowing virtue and good works.

NOTES

(The abbreviations used to designate books and articles mentioned in the Notes will be found listed alphabetically in the Bibliography, opposite the full reference. References to lines in the *Canterbury Tales* are given by fragment and line numbers only.)

1. See Chapter IX, note 1.
2. Matthew, p. 145.
3. Owst, *Preaching*, p. 28.
Master Rypon repeats many times that it is necessary for the parish priests to possess learning.
4. Myrc, ll. 1–10.
5. Coulton, *Med. Village*, p. 291.
6. *Ibid.*, p. 292 and Chap. XX, XXI *passim*.
7. Myrc, ll. 346–355.
8. *Ibid.*, ll. 356 ff.
9. Fowler, *Trans. Royal Hist. Soc.*, VIII, 114.
10. Myrc must here mean "gret" as "important," and not in any titular sense.
11. Myrc, ll. 675–682.
12. *Ibid.*, ll. 683 ff.
13. *Ibid.*, ll. 751–776.
14. Matthew, pp. 145, 150 f., 160, 245, 285. I am indebted to Flügel (*Anglia*, XXIV, 499) for these references. Tatlock (*MP*, XIV, pp. 257–268) gives similar references for Arnold's *Select English Works of John Wyclif* and for the great body of Wyclif's Latin works. More extended use is made of Tatlock's article in connection with Chaucer's Summoner (see below).
15. Owst, *Lit. and Pulpit*, pp. 365 f. (See especially p. 366, n. 1.)
16. *Ibid.*, p. 260 f.

17. Cook calls attention (*Trans. Conn. Acad. Arts and Sci.*, XXIII, 29) to four biblical parallels to "in his hand a staf": Exodus, XII, 11; I Sam. XVII, 40; II Kings IV, 29; Zechariah III, 4.

18. St. Matthew, V, 19.

19. Gower, *Conf. Aman.*, V, 1825. (The Latin gloss is *Incepit Jhesus facere et docere.*)

20. *Piers Plow.*, B. Passus XIII. 115–117. (The Latin gloss is *Qui facit et docuerit, magnus vocabitur in regno celorum.*)

Cook (see note 17 above) calls attention to this *Piers Plowman* parallel, and also to one more ancient in Bede's *Historiae Ecclesiasticae Gentis Anglorum*, where Bede says, in writing of the life of Bishop Aedan, "*cuius doctrinam id maxime commendabat omnibus, quod non aliter quam vivebat cum suis ipse docebat*" (lib. III, cap. v). The modern editors of Bede's work remark that the success of the early missionaries in England was founded on their doing what they preached (p. 226).

21. Van Hamel assigns this date, stating his reasons for so doing (*Romans de Carité*, p. clxxiv).

22. Kittredge, *MLN*, XII, 114 f.

The lines from the *Romans de Carité* are:

> . . . Prestre, tu dois issi bien faire
> Ke selonc le tien essemplaire
> Puist le gens se vie portraire.
> Prestre, tu dois faire et puis dire. . . .
>
> (st. lviii.)

23. *Romans de Carité:*

> . . . Se ors enrunge, queus ert fers? . . .
>
> (st. lxii.)

24. *Ibid.:*

> . . . Quel merveille est se merveille ai
> De fol pastour, de sage oeille?
> Chele est nete, chil se soeille,
> Chele est ou pre et chil ou tai.
>
> (st. lxxi.)

Flügel points out (*Anglia*, XXIV, 501) that the paradox of the befouled shepherd and the clean sheep has another analogue in Gower's *Vox Clam.* (III, 1063):

> Sic ovis ex maculis pastoris fit maculosa.

25. Kittredge (*loc. cit.*) says the source may be Lamentations IV, 1, as interpreted in Gregory's *Pastoral Care*.

26. Workman, II, 110.

27. Gower, *Vox. Clam.*, Lib. III, cap. xvi–xxix.

28. Gower, *Mirour*, ll. 20209–20832.

29. Owst, *Lit. and Pulpit*, p. 271. (Translated from MS. Harleian 4894, fol. 194.)

30. *Ibid.*, pp. 261 f. (Translated from Bromyard's *Summa*, "Custodia.")

31. Matthew, p. 177.

32. *Ibid.*, p. 144.

33. *Ibid.*, p. 149.

34. Westlake, pp. 45 f.

35. *Ibid.*, p. 46.

36. *Ibid.*, p. 48.

37. Gower, *Vox Clam.*, Lib. III, 81–82.

38. Owst, *Lit. and Pulpit*, pp. 255 ff.

39. Matthew, p. 171.

40. *NED*, "Spiced."

41. *Essays in Honor of Carleton Brown*, pp. 141–144.

42. II (B) 1173, 1177.

43. See above pp. 9 f.

44. Robinson thinks (p. 765) that the Parson's portrait should not be taken to represent a Lollard; that although the portrait praises some of the beliefs of the Wyclifites, and condemns certain abuses they condemned, some of the "most distinguishing beliefs" of the Lollards are omitted. (Manly agrees, *Cant. Tales*, p. 528, in substance with Robinson.) But Robinson seems to base his conclusion largely on negative evidence. Is it not more important in this case to examine what Chaucer includes, as does Loomis (see reference in n. 41 above), than what he excludes? As many times pointed out in this book, Chaucer avoids explicit references he might have made to current problems, particularly when the omitted matter is seriously controversial, and he would be unlikely here to paint his admired Parson in pronounced heretical colours. After all, as Owst comments, "it is amazing to reckon up the number of minor doctrines and ideas supposed to be characteristic of Wyclif, . . . which are nothing more nor less than pulpit commonplaces of the orthodox" (*Lit. and Pulpit*, p. 289, n. 1). In the light of Loomis's evidence, however, it is difficult to consider the Parson other than at least having strong Wyclifite sympathies.

45. Coulton states (*Med. Village*, p. 237), "In all medieval literature the peasant is very seldom noticed, and, even then, the notice is almost universally scornful." For example, Gower, in spite of what Coulton terms his "theoretical socialism," inveighs vehemently against the peasant (see particularly the *Mirour*, ll. 26425–26508). Coulton mentions *Piers Plowman* as the outstanding exception to his general statement. See also n. 55 below.

46. Stillwell, *ELH*, VI, 285.

47. *Ibid.*, pp. 285–290.

48. Horrell (*Spec.*, XIV, 82–92) argues that Chaucer used the Plowman as a symbol and gave the "lowliest" pilgrim the highest virtue. In pointing out that Chaucer does not handle the Plowman contemptuously as would many medieval writers, Horrell implies that Chaucer was greatly in sympathy with the peasants' hard lot.

Loomis speaks (*loc. cit.*, pp. 133 ff.) of Chaucer's neutral attitude in the Peasants' Revolt, an attitude he attributes to Chaucer's awareness of the right and wrong on both sides, and he says that "it is little short of amazing that . . . this poet of the court should sketch for us a representative peasant, . . . not as a loafer, a scamp, a bolshevik, a sower of class hatred, but as a model of all the social and Christian virtues."

Chaucer elsewhere praises the peasant, either directly or indirectly, as, for example, in the *Wife of Bath's Tale* (III [D] 1109 ff.); in the *Friar's Tale* (III [D] 1584 ff.); in the *Clerk's Tale* (IV [E] 204 ff.); in the *Nun's Priest's Tale* (VII 2821 ff. [B² 4011 ff.]); and in two of the short poems, *The Former Age* and *Gentilesse*.

49. *Essays in Honor of Carleton Brown*, p. 135.

50. Skeat says (V, 47, n. 529) that the Plowman is "not a hind or farm-labourer, but a poor farmer, who himself held the plough."

51. *Piers Plow.*, B. Passus V. 548, 550–553.

52. *Seneschaucie*, in *Walter of Henley's Husbandry*, p. 111.

53. Clarke (p. 40) states, quoting from Blackstone: "Tithe is 'the tenth part of the INCREASE yearly arising and renewing from the profits of lands, the stock upon lands, and the personal industry of the inhabitants.'" Clarke defines *predial tithes* as the tenths of the gains from all that grows from the earth (crops, timber, and so on); *mixt tithes* as the tenths of the gains from all that feeds upon the earth (wool, sheep, cattle, milk, and so on); and *personal tithes* as the tenths of the net gains from wages.

54. *Chess-Book*, pp. 76 f.

55. The anonymous author of *Pierce the Ploughmans Crede* gives us a grim picture of the gaunt, poverty-stricken peasant, clad only in rags, struggling in the mud of marshy fields (ll. 420–430). Coulton proves (*Ch. and his Eng.*, Chap. XX. *passim*) that the picture is not exaggerated.

56. Skeat, VI, "Tabard"; also *NED*, "Tabard."

57. Karkeek, p. 496.

58. Wright's *Political Poems*, II, 115.

CHAPTER XVI

THE MILLER, THE REEVE, AND A GENTLE MANCIPLE

HAVING idealized the Parson and the Plowman, Chaucer writes next with engaging realism of two individuals.

> Ther was also a Reve, and a Millere,
>
> (l. 542)

and of these two, the Miller is the first to concern us.

In his authoritative work, *Six Centuries of Work and Wages,* Rogers asserts that the miller was the most important lay tenant of a medieval manor. "The mill was the lord's franchise and the use of the manor mill was an obligation on the tenants," he states, and calls attention to the fact that millers are prominent in the stories and ballads of the Middle Ages. The miller is "the opulent villager, who is keen after his gains, and not over honest in the collection of them." [1] Chaucer himself illustrates these statements. In the *Reeve's Tale,* the miller Symkyn has the right to take great toll "of al the land aboute," [2] and the plot of the *Tale* turns on Symkyn's eagerness for gain and his dishonesty in his attempts to achieve it. Langland, too, speaks of the miller, and incidentally of the reeve as well, as a thief, [3] and as an ignorant rascal. [4] Certainly the character of Chaucer's Canterbury-bound Miller, who is named for us by the Host as Robin, [5] bears out the general conception.

> He was a janglere and a goliardeys,
> And that was moost of synne and harlotries.
> Wel koude he stelen corn and tollen thries;
> And yet he hadde a thombe of gold, pardee.
>
> (ll. 560–563)

Robin is an idle talker ("janglere") and a teller of indecent stories ("a goliardeys . . . that was moost of synne and harlot-

246

ries") ; [6] he well knows how to steal corn and take his toll three times, he is a perfect illustration of the proverb—"An honest miller has a golden thumb"—or, in other words, he is honest as millers go, which means that he is not honest at all.[7] Furthermore, if we follow the rules laid down by the medieval physiognomists as Professor Curry has done,[8] we find that Robin's physical make-up is in accordance with his typical character as a miller.

> The Millere was a stout carl for the nones *;
> Ful byg he was of brawn, and eek of bones.
>
> . . . .
>
> He was short-sholdred, brood, a thikke knarre *;
> Ther was no dore that he nolde heve of harre *,
> Or breke it at a rennyng with his heed.
> His berd as any sowe or fox was reed,
> And therto brood, as though it were a spade.
> Upon the cop * right of his nose he hade
> A werte, and theron stood a toft of herys,
> Reed as the brustles of a sowes erys;
> His nosethirles * blake were and wyde.
>
> . . . .
>
> His mouth as greet was as a greet forneys.
>
> (ll. 545-546, 549-557, 559)

Professor Curry quotes from such authorities as Aristotle, Rhases, and the *Secreta Secretorum* to show that a strong fellow (a "stout carl"), big of brawn and of bone, with short forearms and high shoulders ("short-sholdred"),[9] broad and thickset as to build, was expected to be "shameless, immodest, and loquacious" as well as "bold and easily angered." [10] His broad spade beard, which is as red as a sow or a fox, makes him treacherous; [11] his flaring black nostrils indicate lust and anger; [12] the wart, surmounted by the tuft of red hairs which are like the bristles in a sow's ear, signifies a person given to "shameful fornication" and violence; [13] the Miller's mouth, as large as a great furnace,—a phrase which is perhaps reminiscent of the smelting districts of Kent,[14]—shows that he is a pro-

---

* *for the nones:* "exceedingly"   *cop:* "tip"
    harre: "hinge"   *knarre:* "stout fellow"
                                     nosethirles: "nostrils"

digious babbler and liar who is given to swearing.[15] Thus there is interesting correspondence between Robin's body and spirit, a medieval "scientific" correspondence which probably made for easy understanding of him on the part of Chaucer's contemporaries.

The Miller is exceedingly strong, for no door exists that he cannot heave off its hinge, or break down by using his head as a battering ram. That such feats are no gross exaggeration has been abundantly attested: even in the present day unusually thick skulls have been used by their proud possessors in butting through heavy doors. Professor Whiting tells us, for example, that a San Francisco prize-fighter about fifty years ago not only butted through doors with his head, once through a door of heavy oak, but also fought with his head; in 1933 a certain "clown" in a New York gymnasium entertained by breaking down doors with his head.[16] Robin also shows his strength in other ways—

> . . . for over al there he cam,
> At wrastlynge he wolde have alwey the ram.
>
> (ll. 547–548)

Wrestling, which requires that the participants be strong, was one of the favourite sports of the common people in Chaucer's time. In the *Tale of Gamelyn,* an anonymous work contemporary with the *Canterbury Tales,* a wrestling match is described in detail: it is a popular event evidently, in which the prize is both a ram and a ring; [17] and in Chaucer's *Sir Thopas,* where the doughty knight is everything no knight should be, the hero is represented as winning the ram every time he wrestles.[18] A ram was the most usual and appropriate prize given to the champion wrestler, although other prizes were sometimes awarded.[19]

The glimpse Chaucer gives us of the Miller's "array" is enough to prove that here is another element in the portrait that is consistent with character.

> A swerd and bokeler bar he by his syde.
>
> . . . .
>
> A whit cote and a blew hood wered he.
> A baggepipe wel koude he blowe and sowne,
> And therwithal he broghte us out of towne.
>
> (ll. 558, 564–566)

The white coat, to be sure, is probably merely appropriate to the Miller's calling, and the blue hood only his fancy, as is also the wearing of a sword and buckler. It is fitting, however, that he plays the bagpipe,[20] as powerful lungs are needed for that instrument; the sounds Robin extracts from his bagpipe must be a perfect match for his coarse manners and his loud speech. Later on he is described as crying out "in Pilates voys," [21] that is, in a voice like that of the ranting Pilate of the mystery plays. No wonder the "piping," or stentorian trumpeting, of such a self-important fellow is employed to lead the cavalcade out of Southwark! We are reminded of Master William Thorpe's complaint that pilgrims were over-noisy with their bagpipes.[22]

It is probable that the Miller comes from Norfolk, for he and the Reeve, who is stated to be a Norfolk man, are bound together by a long standing enmity. In the *Miller's Prologue* and in the *Reeve's Prologue* it is patent that these two rascals have known each other long before their meeting at the Tabard Inn. Robin, the Miller, addresses Oswald, the Reeve, by name, and he is aware that Oswald has a wife; [23] the Reeve vulgarly calls upon the drunken Robin to hold his tongue, as if he knew exactly what story Robin is going to tell. Is it accident which prompts the Miller to give his own name to the "knave" of the duped carpenter in his *Tale*, a knave who is also "a strong carl for the nones" and able to heave doors off their hinges? [24] Or is it slyness which supplies these details? As Professor Robert A. Pratt suggests,[25] Robin may be telling a story with considerable factual background, in which both he himself and the Reeve actually figured years before. This would certainly give added point to Oswald's anger when he hears the story, for he is now an important officer on a Norfolk estate, and to be personally ridiculed by someone from out of the past would be unbearably humiliating. For now he cannot be anyone's dupe—

> Wel koude he kepe a gerner and a bynne;
> Ther was noon auditor koude on him wynne.
> Wel wiste he by the droghte and by the reyn
> The yeldynge of his seed and of his greyn.
> His lordes sheep, his neet, his dayerye,
> His swyn, his hors, his stoor, and his pultrye
> Was hoolly in this Reves governyng,
> And by his covenant yaf the rekenyng,

> Syn that his lord was twenty yeer of age.
> Ther koude no man brynge hym in arrerage.
> Ther nas baillif, ne hierde, nor oother hyne,
> That he ne knew his sleighte and his covyne;
> They were adrad of hym as of the deeth.
>
> .   .   .   .
>
> He koude bettre than his lord purchace.
> Ful riche he was astored pryvely:
> His lord wel koude he plesen subtilly,
> To yeve and lene hym of his owene good,
> And have a thank, and yet a cote and hood.
>
> (ll. 593–605, 608–612)

The office of reeve on a medieval manor farm lay theoretically between that of bailiff, who was in turn subordinate to the chief manager, or seneschal, and that of provost, but in practice the three offices often became one. The activities of Chaucer's Reeve seem to indicate that he serves as both bailiff and provost, and even as seneschal. According to the anonymous, early fourteenth-century *Seneshcaucie,* the bailiff should every morning "survey the woods, corn, meadows, and pastures, and see what damage may have been done"; he "must see that there be good watch at the granges over the threshers, and that the corn be well and cleanly threshed"; he must oversee the tillage; he must "see and command   .   .   . that the corn be well gathered and reaped evenly"; he must inspect all his lord's cattle regularly.[26] The almost contemporaneous treatise, *Hosebonderie,* speaks of the necessity of teaching bailiffs and provosts the proper way to render accounts. The bailiffs who hold court must, at the proper season, "give up their rolls to the lord or the auditor of the account that they may be able to charge by these rolls the provosts and bailiffs who must account for the purchases of the court throughout the year." [27]

So far Chaucer's Reeve follows the pattern of the model bailiff. He well knows how to keep a garner and a bin, no auditor can find errors in his accounts, he observes the dry and rainy seasons of the year so that he knows exactly when to sow and when to reap, he is in complete charge of his lord's sheep, cattle ("neet"), dairy, swine, horses, stock ("stoor"), and poultry. No one can discover that Oswald is ever in arrears, and there is no bailiff, no herdsman,

no farm labourer ("hyne"), who is in any way cunning or deceitful, that Oswald does not know about. Further, he can even make
purchases more successfully than the lord of the manor himself.
Up to this point the Reeve is apparently all he should be—"faithful
and profitable, and a good husbandman"; [28] but what about the
great fear he inspires in those who come under his jurisdiction?
They are as afraid of him as of the pestilence.[29] Moreover, Oswald
is far from honest when his own gains are concerned: he has secretly
his own barns "ful riche astored" largely through clever manipulation—he sells and lends the lord's own goods to the lord himself
(and by such craftiness Oswald is rewarded by the lord's thanks,
a gift of "a cote and hood," and considerable profit to himself).
Hosebonderie warns landlords against just such rascally bailiffs and
provosts:

> Survey your lands and tenements by true and sworn men. . . .
> Further, if your bailiffs or provosts say in their account that so many
> quarters have been sown on so many acres, go to the extent, and per-
> haps you shall find fewer acres than they have told you and more
> quarters sown than was necessary. . . .
>
> Have an inspection of account, or cause it to be made by some one
> in whom you trust, once a year, and final account at the end of the
> year. . . . For often it happens that servants and provosts by them-
> selves or by others make merchandise with their lord's money to their
> own profit and not to the profit of their lord, and that is not lawful. . . .
>
> Those who have the goods of others in their keeping ought to keep
> well four things: To love their lord and respect him, and as to making
> profits they ought to look on the business as their own, and as to out-
> lays, they ought to think that the business is another's. But there are
> few servants and provosts who keep these four things altogether, as I
> think, but there are many who have omitted the three and kept the
> fourth, and have interpreted that contrary to the right way, knowing
> well that the business is another's and not theirs, and take right and
> left where they judge best that their disloyalty will not be perceived.
> Look into your affairs often, and cause them to be reviewed . . .[30]

In Chaucer's time, if we believe the great smoke of pulpit literature betokens fire, actual reeves were still cheating both landlord
and tenant, and causing the poor to fear them. Bromyard severely
criticizes reeves and stewards, as Dr. Owst points out—" 'well do
they know how to extort a fine of five shillings for an offence involv-

ing sixpence,' " [31] and not only do they bully and fleece the poor tenants, but they do not hesitate to connive against the lord himself.[32] The fourteenth-century Dan Michel's *Ayenbite of Inwyt* also inveighs against "ontrewe reven, provos, and bedeles . . . that steleth the amendes and withdrayeth the rentes of hire lhordes . . ." [33] In short, such complaints were commonplaces, and in that respect, Chaucer's Reeve is merely typical.

The form in which the medieval bailiff, or reeve, drew up his accounts was the same, Rogers writes, no matter to what part of England it belonged, and "no manuscripts of the Middle Ages are commoner . . . or . . . better preserved." On one side of the form entries were made for receipts and expenditures; on the other, the current inventory was made.[34] Obviously accounts of this sort are difficult to check and exceedingly simple to falsify, and it is not surprising that reeves had as great a reputation for dishonesty as did millers, or that there was therefore considerable jealous rivalry between them.

"The strife between Reeve and Miller is thoroughly traditional," writes Professor Tupper, and brings out the professional nature of this enmity.[35] But is it entirely the traditional ill-will which prompts the Reeve to ride last in the train to Canterbury—

And evere he rood the hyndreste of oure route—

(l. 622)

while the Miller rides first, or does the angry distance between the two depend on something else? As has already been suggested, Chaucer's very real Robin and Oswald may have more to quarrel about than business.

The description of the Reeve's physical attributes and of his array serves, as does that of the Miller's, to mark him as an individual.

The Reve was a sclendre colerik man.
His berd was shave as ny as ever he kan;
His heer was by his erys ful round yshorn;
His top was dokked lyk a preest biforn,
Ful longe were his legges and ful lene,
Ylyk a staf, ther was no calf ysene.

. . . .

This Reve sat upon a ful good stot,
That was al pomely grey and highte Scot.
A long surcote of pers upon he hade
And by his syde he baar a rusty blade.

.   .   .   .

Tukked he was as is a frere aboute.
                    (ll. 587–592, 615–618, 621)

Professor Curry writes that although the description of Oswald's person is meager enough,

> it doubtless sufficed to indicate to the well informed men and women of the fourteenth century most of what Chaucer wanted to develop in the Reeve's character. . . . Everybody in Chaucer's time, it may be presumed, knew something about the four complexions of men, so that the artist thought it necessary to suggest only two characteristics of the choleric man in his description of the Reeve.[36]

Professor Curry then applies the "rules" of the *Secreta Secretorum* and of Lydgate and Burgh's *Secrees of Old Philosoffres*: the "colerike" man shall be lean of body (Oswald is "sclendre") ; he shall be of sharp wit, "wyse," and of good memory (Oswald has indeed a sharp wit, he is "prudent," and—although he gives no demonstration of his powers of memory—like all dishonest persons who are successful, he can seldom forget anything).[37] Furthermore, Oswald has long "pipe-stem" legs, and the physiognomists all state that the possessor of such calf-less legs is "lustful and intemperate" in his "sensual desires," [38] so that we should be prepared in the *General Prologue* to understand later the Reeve's outspoken bemoaning of his "coltes tooth" set in a too old body,[39] and his telling of a highly spiced tale of "ribaudye." [40]

The closely shaven face of the Reeve and his somewhat clerical haircut are typical of his inferior caste,[41] as are also the tucking up of his long surcote of blue-grey cloth ("pers"), as if he were a mendicant friar, and the rustiness of his sword. The Reeve's dappled grey ("pomely grey") "stot" is a sturdy animal,—probably a low-bred, undersized stallion,[42] named Scot, a name which is still used commonly for horses in Norfolk today.[43]

The most individualized features of Oswald's portrait, however, lie in his craft, his length of service, and his place of residence. Unfortunately his craft—

> In youthe he hadde lerne a good myster *;
> He was a wel good wrighte,* a carpenter—
> (ll. 613–614)

gives us no special picture today, no matter how much such a specific fact may have meant to Chaucer's contemporaries. But the Reeve's length of service (it will be remembered that the Reeve has kept the account—"yaf the rekenyng"—since his lord was twenty years old) together with his Norfolk surroundings—

> His wonyng was ful faire upon an heeth;
> With grene trees yshadwed was his place.
>
> .   .   .   .
>
> Of Northfolk was this Reve of which I telle,
> Biside a toun men clepen Baldeswelle—
> (ll. 606–607, 619–620)

serve almost to identify for us today the employer of the Reeve; in fact, if the records were complete, we could probably even identify "leve brother Osewolde" himself, for Manly has developed an excellent case for linking Chaucer's Reeve with an anonymous manager of the Norfolk estate of the Pembroke family.[44]

In Chaucer's day, the little hamlet of Baldeswelle lay partly in the manor of Foxley, which belonged to the Pembrokes. The second Earl of Pembroke came of age in 1368, and Chaucer's Reeve has held his position since his lord was twenty years old. Furthermore, Chaucer's friends were interested in the fortunes of the Pembroke estates. Upon the second Earl's death in 1375, the Crown made provision for the management of the estates, since the third Earl was then only three years old. The Countess of Norfolk was granted custody of Foxley Manor, and Sir William de Beauchamp, Chaucer's close friend, was granted the custody of the estates in Wales, with Chaucer himself as one of the two sureties. Almost immediately quarrels arose over the management of these estates. Sir William was accused of waste by the Countess of Norfolk, and was even-

---

* *myster:* "occupation"   *wrighte:* "craftsman"

tually obliged to relinquish his management of the Welsh property;
as Manly suggests, it is quite possible that Chaucer may have visited
Baldeswelle in a vain attempt to secure countercharges against the
Countess, and if so, there would be special point in his writing of
Oswald's sly skill in manipulation of accounts. In any event, however, Chaucer's friends at court "would infallibly recognize immediately his allusion to one of the manors belonging to the Pembroke
estates and would be interested in anything concerning the affairs
of so great a family." [45] And surely, the slender, choleric Reeve,
dwelling in the green-shaded place on a heath near Baldeswelle, is
too highly particularized to have existed alone in Chaucer's mind;
even today we see Oswald plain—exactly as though he were an
actual man, living in the present.

Since the Miller and the Reeve are such a perfect and vital pair,
it may at first seem illogical to allow the colourless Manciple to
intrude upon any account of them. But Chaucer himself puts the
portrait of the Manciple between those of Robin and Oswald, and
in a sense connects the Manciple with the Reeve, for the former
is, like the latter, over-shrewd in business dealings—indeed, the
Manciple's capabilities in this direction are explicitly compared to
those of the best stewards (or seneschals) in the land.[46]

> A gentil Maunciple was ther of a temple,
> Of which achatours * myghte take exemple
> For to be wise in byynge of vitaille;
> For wheither that he payde or took by taille,
> Algate he wayted so in his achaat
> That he was ay biforn and in good staat.
> Now is nat that of God a ful fair grace
> That swich a lewed mannes wit shal pace *
> The wisdom of an heep of lerned men?
> Of maistres hadde he mo than thries ten,
> That weren of lawe expert and curious,*
> Of which ther were a duszeyne in that hous
> Worthy to been stywardes of rente and lond
> Of any lord that is in Engelond,
> To make hym lyve by his propre good
> In honour dettelees (but if he were wood),

* *achatours:* "buyers" or "caterers"   *pace:* "outdo"
  curious: "skilful"

Or lyve as scarsly as hym list desire;
And able for to helpen al a shire
In any caas that myghte falle or happe;
And yet this Manciple sette hir aller cappe.

(ll. 567–586)

A manciple in the fourteenth century was, as he still is today, a buyer of provisions for a college, an Inn of Court, or the like.[47] Chaucer's Manciple is "of a temple," that is, he caters for the lawyers and students at one of the Inns of Court. Mr. J. Bruce Williamson notes two records of the reign of Edward III that give evidence that lawyers were then connected with the Temple,[48] but as all records of the Temple itself before 1501 were destroyed by fire, we are obliged to resort largely to inference regarding the Inns of Court of Chaucer's time.

The Knights Templars established the chief house of their Order in England in the early twelfth century. About fifty years later, they moved to an old manor house south of Fleet Street, a house which then became known as the New Temple, and later as the Temple. After the final suppression of the Order in the early fourteenth century, the property came into the king's hands and was leased and subleased a number of times. To the south of the Temple on the river front lay the estate of the Earl of Lancaster. According to Mr. Williamson, one theory as to how the lawyers came to take over the Temple is that the first group there merely happened to find it convenient to sublet the property from Thomas Earl of Lancaster, and that they then remained as permanent tenants, again by chance. Another theory, Mr. Williamson holds, is that about 1346 certain Apprentices of the Law migrated from the parish of St. Andrew, Holborne to the Temple and obtained from the Order of the Hospital a lease of the premises there.[49] In any case, lawyers were well established in the Temple when Chaucer was writing, and probably two societies had already taken up their quarters there. Chaucer's statements that his Manciple, is of "a temple" and that of the thirty or so "maistres" of the Manciple, more than a dozen are in "that hous" indicate, as Mr. A. R. Ingpen points out, that there were two societies—the one came to be known as the Society of the Middle Temple and the other as the Society of the Inner Temple. Judging by the numbers Chaucer mentions, we must think it probable that his Manciple is connected with the smaller of the two groups.[50] It is more than likely, Mr. Ingpen states, that there was no treasurer of either Society in the fourteenth century, but that the steward or manciple took charge of all the accounts under the nominal supervision of two benchers.[51] The duties of the steward (or manciple) were probably much the same as they were in the early sixteenth century: to stock the buttery; to attend the cook; to examine and keep account of the meat bought, and to see that there was no waste of it; to collect money from the lawyers and students who ate in Commons.[52] Thus it is plain that manciples and cooks were professionally related, and we should therefore be prepared for the quarrel which arises between Chaucer's Manciple and Cook on their way to Canterbury [53]—as Professor Tupper says, jealous antagonism between manciples and cooks was traditional.[54] But although the Manciple may conduct himself in the expected way on the journey to Canterbury, in the *General Prologue* he has the air of being an individual, even if not a particularly vital one.

For all buyers can take example from the Manciple in how to be wise in the purchasing of provisions, Chaucer writes. Whether the Manciple pays cash, or buys on credit ("by taille"), he always comes out well, and ahead of everyone else. Now, asks Chaucer with a smile, is not God good to allow an ignorant man to surpass the learned in sharp wits?

In regard to the Manciple's dealings on credit, Chaucer makes casual reference to a custom so common in his day that it merited no further comment, but which is unintelligible to us without some explanation: the tallies, which were the "charge accounts" of the Middle Ages. Mr. Hilary Jenkinson [55] has examined approximately two hundred and fifty tallies, the majority dating from the reign of Edward III. A *tally* was formed by a cut made through half the thickness of a strip of notched wood, usually at a distance of one-fourth or one-third the whole length of the strip, which was then split lengthwise down to this point. When a debt was contracted to be paid at some later date, debtor and creditor each retained one portion of the tally; at the time of payment, the creditor presented his part of the tally as proof of the amount owed, and collected from the debtor the other part—of course the two parts of the tally had to "fit" much as the pieces of the modern jig-saw puzzle must fall into place to produce a perfect picture. The notches signified the amount due; the description of the goods, the name of the seller, and so on were sometimes written, sometimes crudely scratched, on the face of the tally. The vernacular word *tally* (from *tailler*, to cut) is always Latinized. Mr. Jenkinson copies a number of inscriptions from medieval tallies, and describes the tallies in detail; one of 1388 is especially interesting to us because of the date. This tally has a very long stock, and is notched with three inverted *v*'s followed by four inverted *V*'s; the inscription reads as follows:

Horton Tallia Thome Symondes prepositi ibidem de cccc^mlx ouis [*sic*] de stauro Manerij liberatis Johanni Farwell' post [*festum Michaelis struck through*] [Mensem Septembris *interlineated*] Anno regni regis Ricardi Duodecimo videlicet de Multonibus C^m.iiij^{xx}.vj. De ouibus Matricibus Hegg' ferc' et Hurtard' Ciiij^{xx}xviij. Et de Agnis—lxxvj.[56]

Creditors would of course have a number of tallies in use at any one period, and these were kept together in bags of leather or sacking, many of which have been preserved furnished with the original drawstrings of twisted parchment.[57] The private tally, as distinguished from those used by the Exchequer, gives "widespread evidence of the activities, capabilities, and fashions of the *laicus literatus*," Mr. Jenkinson states; and he adds that the important businessman of the later Middle Ages was supplied with a commercial education of "range and finish." [58]

Not only is the Manciple extremely clever in managing his payments "by taille," but he always gets the better of his superiors ("this Manciple sette hir aller cappe"),[59] he outdoes even those who are capable of being stewards to "any lord that is in Engelond." Indeed, the Manciple can even cheat successfully those stewards who are able to make a lord live on his own income or as economically as he pleases (unless he be mad—"wood"), and who are able to help a whole county if such a situation presents itself. Does not our Manciple know how to deal with the drunken Roger of Ware by turning the latter's blind rage, which has been strengthened by traditional enmity, into pleased gratitude? [60] The Manciple is a man who can out-reeve the Reeve, and as such deserves to be coupled with the much more vital Oswald.

NOTES

(The abbreviations used to designate books and articles mentioned in the Notes will be found listed alphabetically in the Bibliography, opposite the full reference. References to lines in the *Canterbury Tales* are given by fragment and line numbers only.)

1. Rogers, pp. 65 f.
2. I (A) 3987–3988.
3. *Piers Plow.*, C. Passus III. 112–113.
4. *Ibid.*, B. Passus X. 38 ff.
5. I (A) 3129.
6. *NED* defines "goliardeys" as "one of the class of educated jesters, buffoons, and authors of loose or satirical Latin verse, who flourished chiefly in the twelfth and thirteenth centuries in Germany, France, and England"; the derivation is given as Latin *gula,* gluttony. The goliards were supposed to take their name from a certain Golias, dignified with the titles of *episcopus* and *archipoeta,* in whose name some of the verses are written. But as early as 913 *clerici ribaldi* were called *familia Goliae,* which fact seems to indicate that Manly's deduction (*MP*, V, 201–209) that the word *goliardeys* comes from the biblical character Goliath is more probable than the origin given in *NED*. J. W. Thompson (*St. Phil.*, XX, 83–98) brings evidence to show that the word *Goliard* is "anterior to the appellative Goliath," but this does not disprove necessarily Manly's findings—Manly argues merely that the word is derived from *Goliath.*
7. Skeat, V, 49, n. 563.
8. Curry, *Ch. and Med. Sci.*, pp. 79–90.
9. *Ibid.*, p. 80. Curry writes that "short-sholdred" means not only " 'short in the forearms'; it evidently has reference also to the fact that the Miller's broad, knotty shoulders are square and high-upreared . . ."
10. *Ibid.*
11. *Ibid.*, p. 82.
12. *Ibid.*, p. 85.
13. *Ibid.*, pp. 86 ff.
14. Skeat writes (V, 48, n. 559) that "the weald of Kent" was "a great smelting district" in Chaucer's time ,its wood "answering to our coal."
15. Curry, *op. cit.*, pp. 84 f.
16. Whiting, *MLN*, LII, 417–419; Wiley, *MLN*, LIII, 505–507; Utley, *MLN*, LVI, 534–536.
17. *The Tale of Gamelyn,* as included by Skeat in *The Works of Geoffrey Chaucer*, IV, ll. 172, 184, 280.
18. VII 740–741 (B² 1930–1931).
19. Strutt, p. 82.
20. *Grove's Dictionary*, "Bagpipe." "During the Middle Ages the bagpipe was largely used both in England and on the continent, and may have served as an accompaniment to the chanting in . . . religious houses." The gallery in Exeter Cathedral shows a fourteenth-century representation of it.

The bagpipe is a reed instrument, having a combination of fixed notes or "drones," with a melody or "chaunter"; it has a wind-chest or bag. In the fourteenth century the wind was always supplied from the breath of the player, and strong lungs were essential. The compass is of nine notes only, from treble G to A.

21. I (A) 3124.

22. See above Chapter II.

23. I (A) 3151, 3158.

24. I (A) 3466 ff.

25. Pratt, *MLN*, LIX, 47–49.

26. *Walter of Henley's Husbandry, Seneschaucie*, pp. 91–97.

27. *Ibid., Hosebonderie*, pp. 63, 65.

28. *Ibid.*, p. 89.

29. *Deeth* might possibly refer in l. 605 to "death" in general, but because the word is preceded by the definite article it more likely means "the pestilence."

30. *Walter of Henley's Husbandry, Hosebonderie*, pp. 7, 33, 35.

31. Owst, *Lit. and Pulpit*, p. 324. (From the *Summa*, "Acquisitio Mala.")

32. *Ibid.*, p. 325 (From the *Summa*, "Ministratio.")

33. *Ayenbite of Inwyt*, p. 37. Owst (*op. cit.*, p. 325, n. 2) calls attention to this reference.

34. Rogers, pp. 48 f.

35. Tupper, *JEGP*, XIV, 265.

36. Curry, *op. cit.*, pp. 71 f.

37. *Ibid.*, pp. 72 f.

38. *Ibid.*, pp. 74 f.

39. I (A) 3867–3898.

40. Curry says that the Reeve is "a coward at heart"—timidity was another characteristic of the man with small legs. The Reeve's having only "a litel" ire after the *Miller's Tale*, however, seems to me to be because he wishes the company to believe that the only personal element in the story is that the duped husband is, like himself, a carpenter. If Chaucer wished to imply that the story was "true," the Reeve is too wily a man, young or old, to permit the other pilgrims to observe how accurately the *fabliau* has struck home.

41. Robinson, p. 768, n. 589.

42. Karkeek, p. 495.

43. Skeat, V, 51, n. 616.

44. Manly, *New Light*, pp. 84–94.

45. *Ibid.*, p. 90.

46. *Cf.* Moffett's statement (*PQ*, IV, 213): "In Chaucer's remarks about the Maunciple is contained a hint of the qualification of the steward or seneschal of a great lord." In my opinion, Chaucer's remarks contain far more than "a hint."

47. *NED*, "Manciple."

48. Williamson, *Hist. of the Temple*, p. 88.

Manly observes (*Cant. Tales*, p. 531): "It appears that certain *apprenticii*, drawn mainly from St. George's Inn, one of the already existing law schools, first settled in some of the Temple buildings between 1322 and 1326. Later, another group, from Clifford's Inn, obtained a demise of the remaining parts and took possession of them. The first group became known as the Society of the Middle Temple; the other as the Society of the Inner Temple."

49. Williamson, *loc. cit.*, pp. 85 f.

50. Ingpen, *Mid. Temple Bench Bk.*, p. 6.

51. *Ibid.*, p. 17, n. 1.

52. Ingpen (ed), *Master Worsley's Book*, p. 182.

53. IX (H) 1–104.

54. Tupper, *JEGP*, XIV, 261–265.

55. Jenkinson, *Archaeologia*, LXXIV, 289–351.

56. *Ibid.*, p. 351.

57. *Ibid.*, p. 311.

58. *Ibid.*, p. 314.

59. Skeat says (V, 50, n. 586) that "to sette" someone's "cappe" means to get the better of or cheat someone. Cf. the Miller's statement (I [A] 3143) that he is going to tell a tale of how a clerk "hath set the wrightes cappe."

60. See the *Manciple's Prologue*.

CHAPTER XVII

THE SUMMONER WHO HAD A "FYR-REED" FACE

THE MILLER and the Reeve are dishonest customers about whom Chaucer writes in general and in particular disapprobation; he in no way condones their faults, yet he cannot be said to look upon these two "cherles" with loathing. His extreme disgust is reserved for two of the other pilgrims: there are at the Tabard, the poet says,

> A Somnour, and a Pardoner also.
>
> (l. 543)

He writes of them both with bitter destestation, but makes of them vivid pictures of fourteenth-century life.

A summoner, or "apparitor," was not a cleric but a minor official of the Church who was connected with the ecclesiastical courts. Chaucer's Summoner is a gross debauchee, whose very appearance makes the fact apparent to everyone:

> A Somonour was ther with us in that place,
> That hadde a fyr-reed cherubynnes face,
> For saucefleem he was, with eyen narwe.
> As hoot he was and lecherous as a sparwe,
> With scalled browes blake and piled berd.
> Of his visage children were aferd.
> Ther nas quyk-silver, lytarge, ne brymstoon,
> Boras, ceruce, ne oille of tartre noon;
> Ne oynement that wolde clense and byte,
> That hym myghte helpen of his whelkes white,
> Nor of the knobbes sittynge on his chekes.
> Wel loved he garleek, oynons, and eek lekes,
> And for to drynken strong wyn, reed as blood;
> Thanne wolde he speke and crie as he were wood.
>
> (ll. 623–636)

In writing of this character, Professor Curry has ably trans-
formed himself into a consulting physician and diagnostician of the
fourteenth century; [1] in true medieval fashion he has "borrowed"
from many medical authorities of the time in giving the opinion
that the Summoner is suffering from "a species of morphea known
as *gutta rosacea*, which has already been allowed to develop into
that kind of leprosy called *alopicia*." [2] Professor Curry translates
from that Constantinus Afer, who is twice mentioned by Chaucer,
first, as one of the authorities known to the Doctor of Physic,[3] and
second, as the man to whom the aged January looks as a restorer
of youth,[4] the following definition of "morphea":

Morphea is a corruption of the blood from which the skin of the body
is nourished, or it may be an affection of the intercutaneous flesh. The
general cause of it may be found in the digestive virtue . . .[5]

To define *gutta rosacea*, Professor Curry [6] quotes from a sixteenth-
century description of a "saucefleem" face; the writer says: "*Gutta
rosacea* be the Latin wordes. In Englyshe it is named a sauce fleume
face, which is a rednes about the nose and the chekes, with small
pymples: it is a prevye signe of leprousnes." The cause of the
infection is given as bad diet, a hot liver, and a "disorderynge"
of the "complexion" in youth through drunkenness and surfeiting.[7]
Arnoldus de Villa Nova, a thirteenth-century authority quoted by
Chaucer's Canon's Yeoman,[8] supplies a description of *alopicia:*

Alopicia is a species of leprosy which is produced *ex sanguine
adjusto*. This type is marked by a complete depilation of the eyebrows
and beard. The eyes of the patient become inflated (*inflantur*) and
exceedingly red. Pimples of a reddish colour appear in the face and
even on the whole body, from which runs corruption mixed with
blood . . .[9]

And John of Gaddesden, another of the Doctor of Physic's authorities, associates *gutta rosacea* with leprosy: in his instructions for
diagnosis of the latter disease, Gaddesden mentions the former, combined with falling hair, to be one of the indications.[10] Finally, according to the fourteenth-century English translation of Bartholomaeus Anglicus's *De proprietatibus rerum*,[11] leprosy comes from
"fleshlye lyking" by a contaminated woman—"and sometimes it
commeth of too hot meates, as long use of strong pepper, and of gar-

like, and of such other . . . and of uncleane wine and corrupt." [12]

Thus Professor Curry presents us with an accurate identification of the Summoner's malady. The Summoner's "sauce-fleem"
face is as fiery red as those of the cherubim, which in medieval
art were conventionally painted with faces coloured red.[13] His
gutta rosacea is the result of licentious habits, he is lecherous as a
"sparwe," [14] and he indulges in the strong, blood-red wine and
"garleek, oynons, and eek lekes," which aggravate his condition.
Already his disease has developed into a repellent form of "leprosy" as is plainly shown by his black, scaly brows and sparse
("piled") beard, and the suppurating whelks and "knobbes" on
the cheeks. Can we wonder that children are afraid of him, or that
he cries out as if he were mad, or that there are no ointments, no
quicksilver, or compound of lead ("lytarge"), or brimstone; no
borax, or white lead, or cream of tartar, that will "clense and byte"
his diseased face? [15]

Chaucer speaks of his monstrous Summoner with heavy, dis-
gusted sarcasm:

> He was a gentil harlot and a kynde;
> A bettre felawe sholde men noght fynde.
> He wolde suffre for a quart of wyn
> A good felawe to have his concubyn
> A twelf month, and excuse hym atte fulle;
> Ful prively a fynch eek koude he pulle.

> (ll. 647–652)

In other words, the poet says that no gentler and kinder rascal
("harlot") can be found—why, for a mere quart of wine he will
entirely excuse a kindred rascal for keeping a concubine a whole
year! The reason for such indulgence is plain: very privately he
indulges in the same sin himself ("a fynch eek koude he pulle"
is a medieval impolite expression meaning "he kept a concubine").[16] Here again Chaucer emphasizes one of the gravest supposed causes of the Summoner's disease.

The Summoner is also an ignorant, noisy rogue who likes to
make himself even more conspicuous than he need be.

> And whan that he wel dronken hadde the wyn,
> Thanne wolde he speke no word but Latyn.

A fewe termes hadde he, two or thre,
That he had lerned out of som decree—
No wonder is, he herde it al the day;
And eek ye knowen wel how that a jay
Kan clepen "Watte" as wel as kan the pope.
But whoso koude in oother thyng hym grope,
Thanne hadde he spent al his philosophie;
Ay *"Questio quid iuris"* wolde he crie.

.   .   .   .

A gerland hadde he set upon his heed
As greet as it were for an ale-stake.
A bokeleer hadde he maad hym of a cake.

(ll. 637–646, 666–668)

The Summoner knows a few Latin tags and parrots them in his cups; he has picked up two or three terms in the court where he serves, but he is unaware of their sense—like a jay, that can cry "Watte!" as well as a pope. The Summoner's fatuous refrain of *"Questio quid iuris"* * is meaningless to him, and his whole "philosophie" is expended in the phrase. And, to complete the picture of a debased and loud-mouthed Bacchus, the Summoner is crowned with a garland of flowers and leaves similar to the sign on the end of an "ale-stake." [17] As a shield, the Summoner bears a round, flattened loaf of bread (a "cake"). Perhaps he will consume it later with his "garleek" and many jugs of wine.

But monstrous as the Summoner may be as an individual, his calling makes him even worse. Although it is true, as Dr. L. A. Haselmayer has demonstrated, that there is little "actual historical documentation" for the corruption Chaucer shows us in the portrait of the Summoner, [18] the indictment of the office in literature is "definite and uncompromising." [19] In his study, Dr. Haselmayer gives evidence that the office of apparitor, or summoner, was one of widespread usage in fourteenth-century England, and that the most important activity of the apparitor was that which is now most commonly known: to bear a summons from the ecclesiastical court to the person cited to appear. By the end of the century the apparitor had become a kind of "criminal investigator" for bishop or archdeacon, who were the two officials commonly presiding in the ecclesiastical courts. For them the summoner nosed out evasions of

* "What is the law on this point?"

the law and any crimes which might come under Church jurisdiction; apparently his remuneration was a percentage of what he collected in fines for the courts.[20] It would seem inevitable under such a system that some apparitors would become extortioners, and there is documentary evidence that that was the case. As early as 1342, the Council of London listed and condemned in "vigorous language," as Dr. Haselmayer points out,[21] certain summoners for the crime of extortion; and a parliamentary plea, dated 1378, says in part:

And also the said Summoners make their summons to divers people for malice when they are going in their carts to the fields and elsewhere, and these extortioners impute crimes to the poor, contriving that the poor shall pay a fine which is called the *Bischope Almois;* or else the said Summoners demand that the people appear for trial twenty or more leagues from their homes, sometimes to two places on one day, to the great dis-ease, impoverishment, and oppression of the said poor Commons. It is begged that Parliament consider these great harms etc., etc.[22]

Dr. Haselmayer sums up his findings by stating that Chaucer's portrait of the Summoner is made up of a large number of what seem to be "intensely personal and distinctive details," and that we are almost compelled to assume that Chaucer has created "a character based upon an actual or a set of actual prototypes." Dr. Haselmayer feels, therefore, that "Chaucer's conception is more violent than necessary," although he states that "we are acquainted with the general status and probable degradation" of summoners in the late fourteenth century.[23] But in any case, whether Chaucer created his Summoner from personal experience with an exceptionally wicked apparitor, or from actual observation of a class corruption for which we now have an insufficient number of historical parallels, the Summoner is a figure to be recognized, his depravity startlingly vivid. This man has no redeeming feature, and perhaps the greatest of his sins is his misuse of his legitimate office. He operates always "to the great dis-ease, impoverishment, and oppression of the . . . poor Commons." For Chaucer writes of the Summoner—

> . . . if he foond owher a good felawe,
> He wolde techen him to have noon awe

In swich caas of the ercedekenes curs,
But if a mannes soule were in his purs;
For in his purs he sholde ypunysshed be.
"Purs is the ercedekenes helle," seyde he.
But wel I woot he lyed right in dede;
Of cursyng oghte ech gilty man him drede,
For curs wol slee right as assoillyng * savith,
And also war hym of a *Significavit.*
In daunger * hadde he at his owene gise
The yonge girles * of the diocise,
And knew hir conseil, and was al hir reed.

(ll. 653–665)

It will be recalled that Chaucer's good Parson is "ful looth"
to excommunicate the genuinely devout; the archdeacon whom the
Summoner serves (a case of "like master, like man"!) has no such
charitable scruples. True, the archdeacon and the Summoner are
both more than willing to forego the curse when their victims will
bribe them, and undoubtedly many of the victims feel that that
is the lesser of two great evils. An archdeacon's or a bishop's excommunication in Chaucer's time was indeed to be dreaded by the poor.

The sins for which a person could be excommunicated were
manifold; they can be roughly summarized as follows: non-payment of tithes, sacrilege and desecration, slander, arson, theft,
heresy, usury, fraud, perjury, treachery, witchcraft, and contact
with the already excommunicated.[24] As is at once apparent, these
sins are so general and all-embracing that nearly any act could be
interpreted as one of them, and the "almost illimitable power"
which was thus conferred on the entire Church hierarchy was bound
to be fantastically abused.[25] As Professor J. A. Work proves, by citing
many parish records, the "great curse" in the late fourteenth century
was being used for "frivolous and unworthy purposes," [26] and always
against the poor. Any of the rich who could be cursed with impunity
were, from all accounts, always able to buy their way out.

The procedure followed in the greater sentence of excommunication was direct. Those who had sinned or resisted the rulings of
the ecclesiastical courts (courts in which the Church as plaintiff,

* *assoillyng:* "absolution"   *yonge girles:* "young people"
  in daunger: "under his thumb"

was also judge and jury!) were excommunicated; forty days were then given each contumacious person in which to make reparation —nearly always a fine of some sort; if at the end of the forty-day period no reparation were made, the presiding bishop or arch-deacon [27] reported this fact to the Chancery, and a writ of *Signifi-cavit* (so called because that was the initial word),[28] or *de excom-municato capiendo,* was issued by the civil authorities for the arrest and imprisonment of the unfortunate victim until such time as he could meet the demands of his persecutors. As a captive would be without means of earning money while he was in prison, and as he would not have been in his predicament in the first place if he had had powerful friends, the sentence was very likely to be for life; and since the medieval prison (again, for the humble) was at best a foul dungeon, one can readily understand why a bribe at the outset—if the money could be in some way procured—was by far the better course.[29]

Mr. R. C. Fowler writes that about ten thousand writs of *Sig-nificavit* have been preserved; they date from the reign of Henry III to that of George III. Sometimes the offence is specified, but more frequently not; where the offence is specified, it is most com-monly non-payment of tithes—the sum due, in many instances, is very small.[30]

Obviously this is a system furnishing the widest possible oppor-tunity for the acquisition of illicit spoils, and Chaucer's Summoner takes full advantage of it. His business is exactly analogous to that of the gangster of modern times: he extorts money from anyone he can as "protection" against the "curse" of the ecclesiastical court. Furthermore, he does not hesitate to boast openly and arro-gantly to any rascally sympathizer that no one with funds need have any "awe" of the archdeacon's excommunication unless his soul lie in his purse, for it is really only in the purse that punishment need take place. "Purse is the archdeacon's hell," he announces brazenly. But that is not so, Chaucer suavely interposes; every guilty man should fear excommunication, for "curs wol slee" exactly as "assoillyng" will save the soul—and certainly one should beware the *Significavit.* Here, as Professor Tatlock suggests,[31] is one of Chaucer's masterpieces of noncommitment: the archdeacon's ex-communication is worth as much as his absolution—but what is either worth? And probably the fancy of Chaucer's contemporaries was as much pleased as is ours today by the poet's skill in implying scorn of avarice through what could also be discreetly interpreted as the upholding of an institution. That the man who is guilty should fear the *Significavit* is less probably written in ironic vein, although it is possible that many more writs were used merely as threats than were actually served upon delinquents, thus giving satirical point to Chaucer's advice.

Chaucer can have had no vestige of humour in mind, however, in speaking of the Summoner's control over the young people of the diocese. These young people are under the thumb of the Summoner, according to his own way ("at his owene gise")—and what way can that be but one of corruption? The Summoner knows their secrets ("conseil") and acts as their counsel ("reed").

Chaucer's Summoner further conforms to literary tradition as an apparitor. He himself expresses this tradition in so many words in the *Friar's Prologue:* "of a somonour may no good be sayd." [32] That all the defamatory statements about summoners in this *Prologue* and the following *Tale* ostensibly come from Brother Hubert, who is no saint himself, but whose blackness fades to grey beside the Summoner's, gives realism to the picture and serves to emphasize Chaucer's own opinion of the ecclesiastical process-server and his master.

Langland also holds the apparitor in contempt. At the marriage of Meed and Falsehood, summoners appear among the rogues who are the guests; [33] summoners praise Meed; [34] summoners are among those who love lechery. [35]

Distinctly popular literature, such as the political poems and songs, of course inveighs against the apparitor and his master. The "Song of the Corruptions of the Time," written as early as the thirteenth century, says:

The bishop loves a cheerful giver, and cares for neither right nor wrong if he smell a bribe. . . . Nor is there less wickedness in the archdeacon: whomever he gets in his clutches he holds—he has no mercy for the needy or the naked. [36]

The fourteenth-century "Satyre on the Consistory Courts" is entirely devoted to complaint against the procedures in the ecclesiastical courts where the peasant is tried. The poem says in part:

The poor man is brought into court and there sits an old "cherl" in black gown—more than forty men write the peasant's sins on parchment. The poor man must pay them a bribe and thank them. There sit six or seven summoners misjudging all men alike, they reach forth their roll. Herdsmen and every man's servant hate these summoners, for the whole parishes they put in pain. . . . At these courts, they only teach us trouble, and they wish us evil and worse to follow.[37]

One of the miracle plays also attacks the summoner. "The Trial of Joseph and Mary" in the Hegge Cycle (mistakenly called *Ludus Coventriae*) is preceded by a summoner's Prologue in which the summoner, having called before the court a long list of humble folk, outrageously declaims:

> A. serys god save you all
> here is a fayr pepyl in good ffay
> Good serys telle me what men me calle
> I trowe ye kan not be this day
> Yitt I walke wyde and many way
> but yet ther I come I do no good
> to reyse slawdyr [sic] is al my lay
> bakbytere is my brother of blood.
> Dede he ought come hedyr in al this day
> now wolde god that he wore here
> and be my trewth I dare wel say
> that Yf we tweyn to-gedyr a-pere
> More slawndyr we to xal a-rere
> with-in and howre thorwe-outh this town
> than evyr ther was this thowsand yere
> and ellys I shrewe you bothe up and down.[38]

The *Lanercost Chronicle,* written by a Franciscan who flourished about 1300, attacks the summoner's master through humorous anecdote:

I will here insert, for mirth's sake also, a certain piece of evidence which I learned through Lord Robert of Robertstone, knight of the king of Scotland, and which he repeated before many trustworthy witnesses at my instance. That nobleman had a manor in Annandale, in the diocese of Glasgow, that was let out on farm to the peasants; who, being dissolute by reason of their wealth, and waxing wanton after their visits to the tavern, commonly sinned in adultery or incontinence, and thus frequently filled the archdeacon's purse; for their relapses kept them almost perpetually on his roll. When, therefore, the lord of the manor demanded the rent due for the lands, they either pleaded their poverty or besought a respite; to whom this kindly and just man said: "Why do ye, more than all my other tenants, fail to pay your yearly rent? If it be too dear, I may lessen it; but if ye cannot till it, return it to me." Then one made answer jeering and laughing aloud, "Nay, my lord, the cause is not as thou sayest; but our frequent incontinence maketh us so poor that it falleth both upon ourselves and upon thee our lord." He therefore made answer: "I make this law among you, that, whosoever shall thus sin in future, he shall quit my manor forthwith." The peasants, terrified at this strict penalty, amended their transgressions, busied themselves with field-labour, and waxed beyond all expectation in wealth, while they decreased from day to day in the Archdeacon's roll. When therefore one day he enquired why he found no man of that manor upon his roll, then they told him what manner of law the lord had made; whereat he was moved to indignation and, meeting the knight on the road, he asked with lofty brow: "Who, my lord Robert, hath constituted thee Archdeacon or Official?" "Nay, no man," quoth the lord. "Yet," replied he, "thou dost exercise such an office, in restraining thy tenants by penal statutes." "Nay," quoth the knight; "for the statute that I have made is of mine own land and not of men's sins; but thou, with thy ransom for sin, hast sucked out the revenues of my farms; and now I see that thou wouldst reck little who should take the souls, if only thou couldst ever fill thy purse." With such words he silenced this exactor of crimes and lover of transgressions.[39]

The more aristocratic Gower writes in solemn disapproval of the summoners' masters, rather than of the summoners themselves; he pictures such prelates as boasting that their souls are in their purses [40] (we note a parallel to Chaucer's lines), and he elsewhere speaks of accused persons as being "twisted" in their purses.[41]

Pulpit literature abounds in similar complaints whether the zealous reformer be orthodox or Lollard; one example, quoted by Dr. Owst, suffices to show the tone of all these indictments. The homilist says:

Coveitous prelates of holy chirche . . . that setteth imposiciouns upon her sugettes, and chargeth hem wrongfulliche in her visitaciouns, and maketh hem to paye hem that hem lust, or what thei wole aske; or elles travailleth hem by sumpnynge to appere in fer stedes, and in other maner processe, til they have what thei wole. . . . Officiales and denes, that sitteth and holdeth her chapitles and concistories more for to wynne silver than for to destroye synne; but by reddour of the lawe of holy chirche—as doynge out of chirche, cursynge and otherwise—maketh poure folk that may overdoo bodiliche penaunce for her synne, or geve hem what thei wole aske. And grete men, that thei dore noght dele with, thei suffreth hem [to] slepe and deye in her owne synne, in sclaunder of holy chirche. And that thei thus taketh, thei clepeth hit "redempcioun," that is, "forbiggynge." But it is open extorcioun, or robbynge. Sompnoures and bedelles, that beth mynistres to this lawe, that procureth to do men be accused, and in other wyses greveth men by colour of her offices, to have of her good, and so robbeth the peple. . . .[42]

Thus we meet in Chaucer's Summoner a thoroughgoing rogue, strongly typical of his class in literature, if not in life, individualized through loud coarseness and a revealing malady. The Summoner is starkly alive, and he has aroused the real indignation of the author who has created him.

NOTES

(The abbreviations used to designate books and articles mentioned in the Notes will be found listed alphabetically in the Bibliography, opposite the full reference. References to lines in the *Canterbury Tales* are given by fragment and line numbers only.)

1. Curry, *Ch. and Med. Sci.*, pp. 37-47.
2. *Ibid.*, p. 38.
3. I (A) 433.
4. IV (E) 1810.
5. Curry, *op. cit.*, p. 38.
6. *Ibid.*, p. 40.
7. Boorde's *Introduction and Dyetary*, p. 101.
8. VIII (G) 1428.
9. Curry, *op. cit.*, pp. 43 f.
10. *Ibid.*, p. 42.
11. Gerald E. Se Bozar says (*JEGP*, XIX, 168 ff.) that Bartholomaeus wrote "the most popular encyclopaedia of the thirteenth century."
12. Curry, *op. cit.*, p. 45.
13. *NED*, "Cherub." These cherubim were the second order of angels of the Dionysian hierarchy; they were not of the "infant" form of modern times.
14. It was traditional to associate lecherousness with sparrows. Cf. Juvenal, *Satires*, IX, 54 where the debauchee is addressed as "Tell, you sparrow-" (*dic passer*). In the *Parliament of Fowls* (l. 351), Chaucer speaks of the sparrow as "Venus sone."
15. In connection with Chaucer's list of remedies which fail to cure the

Summoner, Curry calls attention (pp. 46 f.) to the fact that these remedies are "apparently lifted . . . directly from the medical books," and he quotes two medieval prescriptions for the cure of *gutta rosacea* which contain ingredients almost identical with the list given by Chaucer.

16. Kittredge writes (*MP*, VII, 475–477) that "to pull a finch" is not proverbial as some scholars have supposed, but is an indecent expression meaning "to have a concubine." He cites as English authority for this statement various punning remarks about birds in *Piers of Fulham* in Hartshorne's *Ancient Metrical Tales*.

17. The customary sign for a drinking place in the Middle Ages was a bush of ivy or a garland wreathed on a hoop suspended from a pole, called the ale-stake, which projected horizontally above the entrance. Skeat refers (V, 54, n. 666, 667) to the laws enacted against the length of ale-stakes exceeding seven feet (see *Liber Albus*, pp. 292, 389).

18. Haselmayer, *Spec.*, XII, 56.

19. *Ibid.*, pp. 54 f.

20. *Ibid.*, p. 50.

21. *Ibid.*, p. 54.

22. Haselmayer quotes directly from *Rotuli Parliamentorum*, III, 43. The translation is mine.

23. Haselmayer, *loc. cit.*, pp. 56 f.

24. Myrc, pp. 21–23.

25. Lea, *St. in Church Hist.*, pp. 235–531 *passim*.

26. Work, *PMLA*, XLVII, 425.

27. R. C. Fowler (*Trans. Royal Hist. Soc.*, VIII, 114) says that some deans and abbots claimed the right to use the greater excommunication.

28. The first sentence of the writ was usually: *Significavit nobis venerabilis pater N . . . quod talis . . . excommunicatus est.*

29. Tatlock, *MP*, XIV, 260 ff.

30. Fowler, *loc. cit.*, pp. 114 ff.

31. Tatlock, *loc. cit.*, p. 266.

32. III (D) 1281.

33. *Piers Plow.*, C. Passus III. 59.

34. *Ibid.*, Passus IV. 171.

35. *Ibid.*, Passus III. 187.

36. Wright's *Political Songs*, p. 32.

37. *Ibid.*, pp. 156–159.

38. "The Trial of Mary and Joseph," *Ludus Coventriae*, ll. 1–16.

39. Coulton, *Life in Mid. Ages*, III, 23–24.

40. Gower, *Mirour*, ll. 20197 ff.

41. Gower, *Vox Clam.*, Lib. III, ll. 189 ff.

42. Owst says (*Lit. and Pulpit*, p. 282) that the mention of "denes" in this excerpt suggests that even in the late fourteenth (or early fifteenth?) century the authority of the deans had not been taken over completely by the archdeacons. He adds that the mention of "denes" coupled with "officiales" may possibly mean that both were now "merely delegates of the archdeacon, presiding for him in his own court" (an *official* was such a delegate). (Quotation from MS. Harl. 45, fols. 67b–67c.)

CHAPTER XVIII

THE PARDONER OF ROUNCIVALE

ACCOMPANYING the lecherous Summoner, as Chaucer tells us,

> . . . ther rood a gentil Pardoner
> Of Rouncivale, his freend and his compeer;
> (ll. 669–670)

and the more we learn of this second scoundrel, the more fitting it seems that he should be the warm friend and companion of the first. The Pardoner sings a particular song,—

> Ful loude he soong "Come hider, love, to me!"
> This Somonour bar to hym a stiff bourdon;
> Was nevere trompe of half so greet a soun,—
> (ll. 672–674)

and although he has selected a verse which may be part of some popular ditty, the suggestion is that he has not chosen at random: he addresses the words evidently to the evil Summoner, who, far from being unresponsive to depraved and unnatural advances, trumpets forth a bass accompaniment ("bourdon" [1]) to emphasize his perverted friendship with the Pardoner. To be sure Chaucer may here be making allusion also to the generally observed connivance between many summoners and pardoners in their successful efforts to fleece the people; [2] but it seems plain that Chaucer meant the stress to fall on the personal nature of a specific relationship. Certainly Chaucer's description of the physical attributes of the Pardoner mark this figure explicitly as the kind of person we immediately suspect him to be.

> This Pardoner hadde heer as yelow as wex,
> But smothe it heeng as dooth a strike * of flex;

* *strike:* "hank"

By ounces * henge his lokkes that he hadde,
And therwith he his shuldres overspradde;
But thynne it lay, by colpons * oon and oon.
But hood, for jolitee, wered he noon,
For it was trussed up in his walet.
Hym thoughte he rood al of the newe jet *;
Dischevelee,* save his cappe, he rood al bare.
Swiche glarynge eyen hadde he as an hare.

. . . .

A voys he hadde as smal as hath a goot.
No berd hadde he, ne nevere sholde have;
As smothe it was as it were late shave.
I trowe he were a geldyng or a mare.

(ll. 675–684, 688–691)

In the same manner in which he diagnoses the Summoner's
malady, Professor Curry interprets the Pardoner's physical peculiari-
ties according to medieval scientific opinion. The Pardoner's wax-
yellow hair, which is straight as a hank of flax, and which is spread
as best it can be in thin clusters over his shoulders, indicates, according to the *Anonymi de Physiognomonia liber Latinus*, " 'an impoverished blood, lack of virility, and effeminacy of mind; and the
sparser the hair, the more cunning and deceptive is the man.' " [3]
The Pardoner's "effeminacy of mind" may perhaps be indicated
in his absurdly foppish wish to be in fashion: instead of wearing a
hood, he folds the hood up in his wallet, and goes bare-headed except
for his cap, for that he imagines to be the latest vogue.

Glaring eyes, such as the Pardoner's, are mentioned, Professor
Curry points out, in the works of Polemon, who flourished in the second century of the Christian era, and who was "the most famous
of the ancient physiognomists and perhaps the founder of the
science." [4] Polemon writes that glaring eyes "indicate a 'man given
to folly, a glutton, a libertine, and a drunkard,' " [5] and as we read
further in the *Canterbury Tales* we realize that the Pardoner amply
justifies this statement. The Middle English version of the *Secreta
Secretorum* also gives us to understand that the signs of a shameless
man are "ryght opyn eighyn and glysinynge . . ." [6]

* *by ounces:* "in thin clusters"   *jet:* "fashion" or "style"
  colpons: "cuttings" or "bundles"   *dischevelee:* "with loose hair"

As one would expect, the physiognomists have a good deal to say about such easily observed characteristics as a small, high voice and an absence of beard. The *Secreta Secretorum* states: "And tho that have the voyce hei, smale and swete and plesaunt, bene neshe [effeminate], and have lytell on manhode, and i-likenyd to women." [7] And the tenth-century physician Rasis, whose works are familiar to Chaucer's Doctor of Physic, remarks that he who has never had a beard is worse than "foolish, lustful, and presumptuous." [8] Nearly all the writers on the *eunuchus,* however, refer to Polemon, Professor Curry finds, as the ultimate authority on the subject. Polemon declares:

When the eye is wide open and, like marble, glitters or coruscates, it indicates a shameless lack of modesty. This quality of the eyes is observed in a man who is not like other men, *ut eunuchus qui tamen non castratus est, sed sine testiculis natus.* I have known, however, only one man of this kind.[9]

But whether or not Chaucer intended the Pardoner to be such a *rara avis,* medically speaking, as a *eunuchus ex nativitate* is questionable.[10] Polemon himself comments on the fact that he has known only one such man; and it is to be noted that in writing of wide open, glittering eyes, Polemon says only that the *eunuchus ex nativitate* possesses them, not that their possession marks the man as such. Consequently, Chaucer's line—"I trowe he were a geldyng or a mare"—may or may not be taken literally, for the doubt Chaucer casts on the virility of the Pardoner is perhaps voiced as a scornful jest aimed against an unfortunately effeminate man who happens also to be a libertine and a thorough rogue. There is nothing upright about the Pardoner—even his very calling is suspect.

A pardoner, sometimes called a *quaestor,* was a distinctively medieval official. He was engaged as a rule in three activities: in selling indulgences, in selling relics, and in preaching. The first two of these functions are perhaps more spectacular than the last, and they are certainly more closely connected with the word *pardoner;* they are therefore the two functions we tend to emphasize today in any study of the *quaestor,* although for the Middle Ages his preaching was equally important.[11]

Indulgence, as Jusserand explains, first meant "simply a commutation for penance," but gradually the idea of commutation disappeared and was supplanted by an entirely different theory, the theory of the "treasury."

It had indeed become obvious as the use of indulgences spread that they could no longer be justified as offering to the sinner nothing more than his choice between several sorts of penance. They were something else. A short prayer, a small gift in money, would exempt devout people from the greatest penalties and from numberless years of a possible purgatory; the one could scarcely be considered as being the equivalent of the other; how was the equilibrium established between the two scales? The answer was that the deficiency was made up by the application to the sinner of merits, not indeed his own, but merits of Christ, the Virgin, and the saints, of which there was an inexhaustible 'treasury,' the dispensation of which rested with the Pope and the clergy.[12]

Having established the theory, the Church needed officials to put it into practice, and about the beginning of the fourteenth century certain persons were authorized to give shares in the heavenly treasury to those of the faithful who repented and confessed. In return for these shares, the faithful gave money to be used for the maintenance of the Church on earth. The officials were called either *pardoners* (because of what they gave), or *quaestores* * (because of what they asked).[13]

Opportunities for dishonesty were inherent in the pardoners' calling: indulgences could be forged by anyone who chose to name himself a pardoner; or the legitimate pardoner, even if he did not turn thief and appropriate for himself the money he received, could sell his pardons without exaction of either repentance or confession on the part of the buyer, since the matter was left to the discretion of the pardoner. Furthermore, the Church herself aggravated the evils of the system. As the people became aware of this easy road to heaven, the demand for more imposing indulgences brought about a shockingly great supply: in the popular mind, indulgences must now be made to liberate from both punishment and guilt, and in that way they were issued—*a culpa et a poena*.[14] The Church made some effort to do away with this last outrage, which was subversive of the theory of sacraments, but too many avaricious officials surrounded those popes who would have recalled such flagrant

* or, *quaestuarii*

money-making devices. A facsimile of a pardon issued as a confessional letter under a bull of crusading indulgence by Sixtus IV in 1480 is printed by Lea, who writes about it as follows:

[The letter] grants to the recipient the right to choose a confessor who can absolve him from all sins, however enormous, as often as ne wishes, though those which are reserved to the pope can be absolved only once, and to grant him full remission and indulgence once during life and again at death. Then follows the formula of absolution, showing that it was customary to perform this at once, by the pardoner or one of his assistants.[15]

As Lea points out, nothing is said as to confession or contrition, the theologian's theory that God alone can pardon the *culpa* is ignored, and a highly "saleable article" is in the hands of an unscrupulous salesman.[16] If Chaucer's Pardoner is armed with such documents, it is easy to believe that his "bulles of popes and of cardynales, of patriarkes and bishopes," [17] find the ready market of which he so blatantly boasts.

The second activity of the pardoners, the selling of relics, combined naturally with the selling of indulgences; the *quaestor* became notorious for the monstrous objects he foisted on the simple as genuine sacred remains. Boniface IX, in a papal edict of 1390, charges, for example, that the pardoners always vow that they come fully authorized from Rome, yet many are nothing but vagabonds, or beggars, or secular clerks who hawk false pardons and relics, and who thus irreverently abuse that which is genuine by an infamous and hateful profit on that which is false. For a small amount these men will also pretend to absolve the wicked without any of the proper forms, they will release from vows, they will allow heretics to re-enter the Church, they will say they are able to remove excommunication. Since their power comes only from themselves, they are without restraint, and of course the money they collect remains theirs.[18]

If Boniface's grave papal complaint is added to Chaucer's words about the Pardoner as an individual, it is apparent that here is a man truly to be despised and mistrusted. Chaucer writes in irony that this undoubted rogue—

. . . streit was comen fro the court of Rome.

. . . .

A vernycle hadde he sowed upon his cappe.
His walet lay biforn hym in his lappe,
Bretful of pardoun, comen from Rome al hoot.

(ll. 671, 685–687)

Thus the Pardoner, like his flesh-and-blood brethren, claims that
he comes directly from Rome; he bears a wallet stuffed with pardons as evidence. Can one question the authenticity of pardons
when there are so many of them, "al hoot" from the *quaestorum*
oven? Moreover, the Pardoner has had the foresight to sew a
"vernycle" on his cap in further protestation that he is genuine;
he is aware that pilgrims to Rome usually bring home this token
of their journey. A vernicle was a miniature copy of the handkerchief which legend credited St. Veronica with having given to Christ
on the way to Calvary; the original handkerchief, said to be preserved in the Church of St. Peter at Rome, was thought to have
been miraculously imprinted with an image of Christ's face.[19]

Chaucer's Pardoner is also true to type in bearing false relics:

But of his craft, fro Berwyk into Ware,
Ne was ther swich another pardoner.
For in his male he hadde a pilwe-beer,
Which that he seyde was Oure Lady veyl:
He seyde he hadde a gobet of the seyl
That Seint Peter hadde, whan that he wente
Upon the see, til Jhesu Crist hym hente.
He hadde a croys of latoun ful of stones,
And in a glas he hadde pigges bones.
But with thise relikes, whan that he fond
A povre person dwellynge upon lond,
Upon a day he gat hym moore moneye
Than that the person gat in monthes tweye;
And thus, with feyned flaterye and japes,
He made the person and the peple his apes.

(ll. 692–706)

The Pardoner is a crafty scoundrel: by his tricks ("japes"), he
knows just how to flatter and fool both guileless priest and simple
flock (he makes "the person and the peple his apes"). He convinces
his victims that the worthless objects he carries are sacred—in his
bag ("male"), he says, are Our Lady's veil (in reality a mere pillow-
case, or "pilwe-beer"), a fragment ("gobet") of the sail from St.

Peter's boat, and a latten, or brass,[20] cross, studded with false [21] gems. The "pigges bones" which the Pardoner bears in a glass container will doubtless be foisted on the gullible as the holy remains of some saint. Small wonder that the Pardoner gets more money in one day, as a rule, than the honest parish priest in two months! In all England, from Berwick to Ware,[22] there is not another pardoner as clever—and to make his cheating the more successful, this trickster turns to the pulpit, for he is an exceptionally artful and practised speaker.

> But trewely to tellen atte laste,
> He was in chirche a noble ecclesiaste.
> Wel koude he rede a lessoun or a storie,
> And alderbest he song an offertorie;
> Ful wel he wiste, whan that song was songe,
> He must preche and wel affile his tonge*
> To wynne silver, as he ful wel koude;
> Therefore he song the murierly and loude.
>
> (ll. 707–714)

As has been said, preaching was a recognized activity of the pardoners,[23] although as far as we know no pardoner's sermon has been preserved. (Dr. Owst suggests that swindlers of every period refuse to commit themselves in writing!) There is not a single item about pardoners in medieval Episcopal Registers which fails to include mention of these men as preachers,[24] however; and, as Dr. Owst makes clear, Chaucer's picture of the Pardoner is as realistic in this respect as in every other.

But not only is Chaucer's Pardoner accustomed to the pulpit. He is also a skilled demagogic orator who knows exactly the kind of sermon to preach that will thoroughly fascinate his audience, which fact he later demonstrates in his own *Tale;* he knows how to read a lesson, too, or a series of lessons (a "storie"),[25]—so that suspicious minds will be closed and purses opened,—and how to capitalize on his soprano voice by singing the offertory [26] the best of all, for the offertory precedes the sermon, and the tongue must be in smooth running order for that if silver is to be won. As Chaucer concludes, in a final burst of irony, our Canterbury-bound Pardoner is truly "a noble ecclesiaste"!

* *affile his tonge:* "make his tongue smooth"

Although he writes in strong disapproval of the sins of pardoners, Chaucer is silent about the theory that gave rise to their office. Wyclif, on the other hand, sternly condemns the theory of indulgences,[27] and consequently the Lollard writers speak of even licensed pardoners as "deceitful," while the imposter is, of course, vilified by them. One Lollard, for example, says indignantly:

. . . there cometh a pardoner with stollen bullis and false relekis, grauntynge mo yeris of pardon than comen bifore domes day for gevynge of worldly catel to riche placis where is no nede . . . And this pardoner schalle telle of more power than evere crist grauntid to petir or poul or ony apostle, to drawe the almes fro pore bedrede neigheboris that ben knowen feble and pore, and to gete it to hem self and wasten it ful synfulli in ydelnesse and glotonye and lecherie . . .[28]

The orthodox reformer accepts the theory, but despises the practice. One such homilist, in enumerating different kinds of thieves, says in disgust:

Sothell [sic] theves beth the men that slyly can robbe men with many queynt sotell wordes, and with fals behestynge; and sum with fals letters and seeles, with crosses, and reliques that thei bere abowten them, and sei that thei be of seyntes bones or of holy mens clothinge, and behoteth myche mede that will offre to hem, and hire the letters of pardon, ichon of other, as a kowe or a nox that men lat to hure; the wiche thei sell all for the penny, and fo [sic] no man's mede, with many fals lesynges, as the feend here maister techeth hem, for to robbe the pore pepull sotelly of ther goodes.[29]

And an article of the Oxford Petition of 1414 states uncompromisingly:

Whereas the shameless pardoners purchase their vile traffic in farm with Simon, sell Indulgences with Gehazi, and squander their gains in disgraceful fashion with the Prodigal Son: but what is more detestable still, although not in holy orders, they preach publicly, and pretend falsely that they have full powers of absolving both living and dead alike from punishment and guilt, along with other blasphemies, by means of which they plunder and seduce the people, and in all probability drag them down with their own person to the infernal regions, by affording them frivolous hope and an audacity to commit sin: therefore, let the abuses of this pestilential sect be blotted out from the threshold of the Church.[30]

Langland mentions the wickedness of pardoners a number of times. The false pardoner is pictured as preaching "as he a prest were," showing his bull "with bisshopis seles," and absolving the people from any sin. The ignorant are gulled by him, and give him rings and brooches—alas, their gold only goes to keep gluttons, worthless fellows, and lovers of lechery.[31] Again, Langland writes, the pardoner is prominent on the list of the wicked,[32] the pardoner is the sole person to give a liar house-room,[33] and so on.

More popular literature occasionally also attacks the *quaestor*. When the preaching friar in *Pierce the Ploughmans Crede* would hold up the Augustinians to scorn, his worst accusation is that they live by "pur pardoners craft." [34] And in the early fifteenth-century political poem, the *Reply of Friar Daw Topias*, Friar Topias tells Jack Upland that the latter mistook pardoners for friars in the charge that friars "sette to ferme" the whole realm:

> I trowe thou menys the pardonystres
> of seint Thomas of Acres,
> of Antoun, or of Runcevale
> that rennen so fast aboute . . .[35]

(Here we must note Brother Topias's reference to "Runcevale," the convent from which Chaucer's Pardoner claims to come. More of this important headquarters for pardoners will be said later.) On the whole, however, the unsophisticated folk of Chaucer's day seem to have accepted the pardoner, whose sin was so much more subtle than the easily observed wrong-doings of the hypocritical friar and the blackmailing summoner. As Professor Trevelyan remarks, it was the worldly-wise who hated the pardoner with "all the force of intellectual scorn and moral indignation"; credulous, simple people received him and his "miraculous" relics gladly.[36]

Before taking leave of generalities about the pardoners, we should refer to John Heywood's *Foure P. P.*,[37] which indicates that even in the sixteenth century pardoners were still plying their dubious trade, and that literary comment on such trade was still timely. Heywood's pardoner, in the course of a liar's competition with a "poticary," a "pedler," and a "palmer," offers as a sample of his powerful ability to lie the statement that his pardons bring a soul to heaven "without any payne"; and his false relics, which he shamelessly offers to his rascally companions to kiss and to buy, are only slight exaggerations of the "relics" borne by Chaucer's Pardoner.[38]

Chaucer's Pardoner represents the only fourteenth-century fully developed portrait of an individual *quaestor;* other pictures of the pardoner condemn him as one of a class, although scholars have long pointed out the resemblance Chaucer's Pardoner bears to Jean de Meun's False-Seeming; both characters boast of their misdeeds in almost identical language.[39] But at best False-Seeming is only the personification of an unspecified class of ecclesiastic, and therefore hardly possesses the substance necessary to be a true parallel to Chaucer's painfully vivid and highly individualistic Pardoner. A much better probability for literary relationship is Boccaccio's Fra Cipolla (or "Brother Onion"), for although Fra Cipolla is not actually a pardoner, his actions proclaim him one in spirit, and there is nothing shadowy about him. The part of Boccaccio's story which concerns us may be briefly summarized as follows:

Fra Cipolla was not a scholar, but he was so excellent a talker and so ready of wit that his audiences not only admired him as a great rhetorician, but declared him to be Tully himself or maybe Quintilian. He preached in the parish church whenever he felt like it, and he always had relics to show and tell about. Once he came to a simple parish and informed the people that he had brought from Palestine one of the Angel Gabriel's feathers which had fallen from his wings in the Virgin's chamber "whenas he came to announce to her in Nazareth"! Fra Cipolla, hoping to drum up enthusiasm for contributions, promised to display this wonderful relic the next day, but when the appointed time came, he found that a practical-joker (a sophisticated stranger to the little parish) had substituted a few coals for the feather, which was in truth that of a parrot. Undismayed, and with his usual ready wit, Fra Cipolla announced to the assemblage that these coals also were relics, for they were the very ones over which St. Lawrence had been "roasted"; indeed, since St. Lawrence's Day was so near, the Lord Himself had substituted the more timely relic! [40]

But although it is possible that Chaucer borrowed from Boccaccio, it seems far more likely that he painted the richly coloured portrait of the Pardoner from life. Certainly the added fact that Chaucer takes pains to specify that this distressingly typical *quaestor* and highly individualized human being is "of Rouncivale" inclines us even more decidedly to the belief that the Pardoner must have been known to the poet and at least to some of his audience.

The name "Roncesvalles" is commonly known as the place of Roland's death while on the celebrated retreat from Spain in 778 A.D.; but Galloway states, in his *Hospital and Chapel of Saint Mary Roncevall,*[41] that Roncesvalles had become famous long before the *Song of Roland.* In very early Christian times,[42] a small religious House was established in the village of Roncesvalles, which lay at the southern end of the pass through the Western Pyrenees, a House which soon became noted in the small world of those distant centuries for its good works and its strongly independent character. The Order so established was formalized in the tenth century, and its members eventually adopted the Augustinian Rule. One of the first acts of the new organization, the Order of *Nuestra Señora de Roncesvalles,* was to found a hospice for the wayfarer.[43] This hospice and the church, reputed to be built upon the rock split by the mighty Roland, brought much added fame to the Order, partly because of the renown of the hero Roland, but more largely because the hospice and church were situated on one of the roads leading to the much visited shrine of St. James at Compostella: the twelfth-century guide-book for pilgrims to Compostella,[44] for example, speaks more than once of the hospice and church at Roncesvalles.[45]

Expansion of the Order at Roncesvalles was, of course, inevitable, and Houses were established outside of Spain, a number of them in England and Ireland. The first record of the Order in England is a letter of protection issued to them in 1229; only three years after this, the Order inherited a number of estates from William Marshall, Earl of Pembroke, among them being his houses at "Cherring." [46] Since the hospital and chapel established at Charing (known as St. Mary Roncevall) later became conspicuously connected with pardoners, the presumptive evidence is strong that Chaucer's "Rouncivale" means this particular House of the parent Order in Roncesvalles.

The records of St. Mary Roncevall for several years "consist mainly of statements of the gifts received from various important persons," Galloway writes; the House was steadily growing in wealth and power.[47] The exact position occupied by the hospital is uncertain. It probably extended from the mid-section of the present Charing Cross Railway Station in alignment with York Gate towards the present Craven Street and Northumberland Avenue.[48] Just before the beginning of the fourteenth century, a certain Brother Lupus appears in the records as preceptor of all the Houses in England and Ireland, and as prior of St. Mary Roncevall at Charing. Brother Lupus was also a papal envoy, and he was licensed to sell indulgences; from his advent as leader of the Order in England until well into the fifteenth century, the selling of indulgences was the special interest of the alien St. Mary Roncevall: [49] Brother Lupus had all too successfully demonstrated that traffic in pardons was an exceedingly profitable business.

St. Mary Roncevall reached its most prosperous days during the second quarter of the fourteenth century; after the Black Death its affairs were in much confusion. At that time, Galloway says, "the vacant benefices in the possession of the alien Houses were sought for and obtained by clergy on the spot who had influence, and there can be no doubt that . . . many of these persons were more concerned in advancing their own interests and in retaining the possessions thus secured than in guarding the rights of the Convent." [50] John of Gaunt was a patron of St. Mary Roncevall, and the fact that such an unscrupulous politician as he gave letters of introduction in 1372 to three of the Hospital's "procureurs" to noted ecclesiastics who were "to further them in their collection of alms," [51] is a strong indication that this branch of the Order was unduly interested in material gains. Scandals, particularly those arising from the sale of pardons, became more and more flagrant, with the result that in 1379 the Crown seized the buildings and lands of St. Mary Roncevall, and issued a writ "to arrest and bring before the King and Council all persons . . . proved . . . to have collected alms in the realm as Proctor of the Hospital, and converted the same to their own use." [52] It must be admitted that it was the policy of the government at this time to suppress all alien religious Orders: because of the war, the period was one of "England for the English"; but certainly the notoriety attendant upon the seizure of St. Mary Roncevall had its basis almost entirely in the behaviour of the many pardoners connected with the Order. After much litigation, the House at Charing was restored to the aliens, for the time being, in 1383, but the Order was never again free from suspicion or from accusations leveled against it for improper practice.[53] It is especially significant for our study of Chaucer's Pardoner "of Rouncivale" that in 1387 there was a particularly open scandal concerning the unauthorized sale of pardons by representatives of this Convent;[54] Chaucer, the friend of court officials to whom St. Mary Roncevall had become a source of unmitigated irritation, could scarcely have failed to place the Pardoner there.

But did Chaucer mean his audience to take "of Rouncivale" literally? Are we to accept the Pardoner as a bona fide member of the Order of *Nuestra Senora de Roncesvalles* having a cell at Charing, and hence as an Austin Canon?[55] Miss Marie Hamilton argues strongly for an affirmative answer to these questions.[56] She reasons that Chaucer's irony would be the more telling if he pictured a legitimate, clerical pardoner as guilty of all the sins of an imposter. She points out that the Pardoner's preaching and his reading of lessons indicate that he is in major orders,[57] and that the Canons Regular were the only Order whose members were "destined normally for the priesthood" and whose institution was "essentially sacerdotal." Miss Hamilton claims that the Pardoner's lack of tonsure, his defiance of certain Augustinian rules,[58] and his remark to the Wife of Bath concerning his possible marriage[59] in no way weaken the argument, for these matters can all be taken as evidence of the Pardoner's deliberate contempt for his Rule. The Pardoner may even have actually been to Rome when we meet him, for although he later boasts freely of the falsity of his relics, he does not speak of the falsity of his indulgences; and since the English of the late fourteenth century were in general opposed to papal bulls of any kind, as Miss Hamilton observes, there would again be added irony in the Pardoner's bearing genuine credentials which the company would think worthless.[60]

But whether or not the Pardoner comes in fact from St. Mary Roncevall, it is fitting that he claims to do so, and such claim removes all necessity for polite discretion. The Pardoner may properly be shown to be the scoundrel he is: a lying, avaricious, and shameless cheat, hawking his pigs' bones as relics, preaching eloquent sermons only to deceive, and openly singing love-ditties in his girlish voice to a diseased and wicked summoner.

NOTES

(The abbreviations used to designate books and articles mentioned in the Notes will be found listed alphabetically in the Bibliography, opposite the full reference. References to lines in the *Canterbury Tales* are given by fragment and line numbers only.)

1. Miss Dieckmann (*MP*, XXVI, 279–280) writes that *Fa-burden* and *Faux-bourdon* are terms given by the English and French respectively to the style of part-singing developed during the time of Chaucer. *Burdoun* was also associated with a humming or droning sound. Miss Dieckmann quotes from Charles W. Pearce, who says in *Modern Academic Counterpoint:* "Of the three singers standing before the book [in medieval part-singing], those who were chosen for the two upper parts sang their notes in the ordinary manner as they were written; but the remaining performer, chosen for the apparent *bourdon,* or lowest voice (the Cantus Firmus), possessed actually the highest voice. He therefore transposed the plainsong at sight to the octave above, and so sang it throughout."

The Summoner, who bears "a stif burdoun" to the Pardoner, however, undoubtedly possesses the genuine *bourdon,* or lowest voice.

2. Owst, *Preaching,* p. 104. See Bishop Grandisson of Exeter's *Register* (middle of fourteenth century).

3. Curry, *Ch. and Med. Sci.,* p. 58.

4. *Ibid.,* p. 57.

5. *Ibid.*

6. *Secreta Secretorum,* p. 223. (Curry calls my attention to this reference and to the one following.)

7. *Ibid.,* p. 231.

8. Curry, *op. cit.,* p. 59.

9. *Ibid.,* pp. 61 f.

10. Curry accepts the theory that Chaucer intended the Pardoner to be a "eunuch from birth." He argues that Chaucer's line, "I trowe he were a geldyng or a mare," is meant as literal fact, and he adds a number of other statements taken from the *Pardoner's Prologue* and *Tale,* to support his contention (pp. 58 f., 64 ff.). As all his points, except the one line just quoted, are outside the *General Prologue,* the details of his argument are here omitted. They are fully discussed, and scholarly objections to them are raised, in an article by G. G. Sedgewick, *MLQ,* I (1940), 431–458.

11. Owst, *op. cit.,* p. 99.

12. Jusserand, *Eng. Way. Life,* p. 311.

13. *Ibid.,* pp. 311 f.

14. Lea, *Hist. Confession and Indulgences,* III, 54–82.

15. *Ibid.,* p. 70 in note. The facsimile is in the Appendix to this volume, and is taken from the original in the White Historical Library, Cornell University. Lea transcribes (p. 70 in note) the form of absolution as follows: "Misereatur tui omnipotens deus etc. Dominus noster ihesus cristus per suam piissimam misericordiam te absolvat. Et auctoritate ejus et beatorum Petri

et pauli apostolurum ac Sanctissimi domini nostri pape michi commissa et tibi concessa, ego te absolvo a vinculo excommunicationis si incidisti et restituo te sacramentis ecclesie ac unioni et participationi fidelium. Et eadem auctoritate te absolvo ab omnibus et singulis criminibus delictis et peccatis tuis quantumcumque gravibus et enormibus. Etiam si talia forent propter que sedes apostolica consulenda esset, ac de ipsis eadem auctoritate tibi plenariam indulgentiam et remissionem confero. In nomine patris et filii et spiritus sancti Amen. Nota quod in mortis articulo adjungenda est hec formula. Si ab ista egritudine non decesseris plenarium remissionem et indulgentiam tibi eadem auctoritati in mortis articulo conferendam reservo."

16. There were, of course, some indulgences issued that carefully prescribed proper contrition and confession. Lea prints a facsimile of an indulgence issued by the council of Bâle in 1438 (see Appendix to Vol. III and p. 69), and there is a copy of an indulgence of forty days granted in favour of the hospital of St. Anthony of Vienne in the *Registrum Johannis Trefnant* (Canterbury and York Society, XX, 7) dated 1389, both of which illustrate this kind of indulgence. We can scarcely believe, however, that Chaucer's Pardoner is carrying with him any but the worst sort of catchpenny document.

17. VI (C) 342 f.

18. Jusserand, *op. cit.*, 433 ff. (Jusserand quotes the Latin bull of Boniface IX, A.D. 1390, from which I translate selections.)

19. Skeat (V, 56, n. 685) calls attention to two lines from *Piers Plow.* (B. Passus V. 530–531):

> And the vernicle bifore . for men shulde knowe,
> And se bi his signes . whom he soughte hadde.

Skeat says that the legend of the *vernicle* "was invented to explain the name."

20. Skeat, VI, "Latoun."

21. *Ibid.*, "Stoon."

22. From Berwick (in the north) to Ware (in Hertfordshire)—or, as we might say, "from the north to the south of England." It is difficult to see why Robinson finds this expression strange (p. 769, n. 692). We have many such expressions in present-day speech, where the places named are not very far apart or not strictly antipodal.

23. The Pardoner could have been licensed to preach (or have laid claim to have been) by either the Pope or a bishop (Owst, *op. cit.*, p. 101).

24. Owst says (*ibid.*, p. 99, n. 3) that the Registers refer to the pardoner as "*predicatio, officio predicandi, sermones*, etc." and that "in at least one entry pardoners are distinctly referred to as *predicatores quaestuarii.*"

25. Karl Young writes (*MLN*, XXX, 97 ff.) that "storie" is to be identified with the term *historia of liturgiology*. "The chief content of Matins is a series of psalms . . . and a series of *lectiones*," and among the meanings of *historia* is "a series of lectiones" covering a book of the Bible, or the *vita* of a saint—with or without musical accompaniment. Since Chaucer uses a vernacular term for liturgical *lectio* ("lessoun") and again for *offertorium*

("offertorie") in the same context with "storie," Young argues that the liturgical interpretation of *historia* should be taken.

26. Manly says (*Cant. Tales*, p. 537, n. 709 f.) that it is a mistake to suppose that the offertory could be for the benefit of the Pardoner, and theoretically this is true. We cannot help suspecting, however, that a person like the Pardoner would find a way in practice to help himself to at least a substantial part of the regular offering for the priest and the church.

27. Wyclif, *de Ecclesia*, pp. 549–583.

28. Matthew, p. 154.

29. Owst, *op. cit.*, pp. 109 f. (Quoted from MS. Roy. B. 18. xxiii.)

30. *Ibid.*, p. 105. (Translated from no. 39—Wilkins, *Conc.*, vol. iii, pp. 360 et seq.)

31. *Piers Plow.*, C. Passus I. 66-80.

32. *Ibid.*, B. Passus II. 108.

33. *Ibid.*, C. Passus III. 229.

34. *Pl. Crede*, l. 247.

35. Wright's *Political Poems*, II, 78 f.

36. Trevelyan, pp. 135 ff.

37. Skeat (V, 270, n. 349), perhaps mistakenly, speaks of this work as an "impudent plagiarism" from Chaucer. But in any case, the work proves that the pardoner still plied a scandalous trade.

38. Heywood, *The Foure P. P.*

39. Fansler, *Ch. and RR*, p. 165. In the *Pardoner's Prologue*, the Pardoner says, "For myn entente is nat but for to wynne . . ." (l. 403), and "I wol nat do no labour with myne handes . . ." (l. 444); in the *Roman de la Rose*, False-Seeming says, "En aquerre est toute m'entente . . ." (l. 12492), and "Sans james de mains traveillier . . ." (l. 12504).

40. *Decameron* (Sixth Day, Tenth Story), pp. 489–499.

41. Manly calls attention (*New Light*, p. 124 and *Cant. Tales*, p. 536) to this book by Sir James Galloway as "the best study of the pardoners of Rouncivale." A number of other scholars have also mentioned the book as definitive, indeed, have used it as a source—as, for example, Samuel Moore (in *MP*, XXV, 59–66), who acknowledges his debt at the beginning of his article on Chaucer's Pardoner to this "somewhat inaccessible monograph." Through the courtesy of the Columbia and Yale University Libraries, I have been able to examine Galloway's book, and I have used it as my source; consequently, a number of references which would otherwise have appeared in these notes now appear in the second part of the Bibliography under the heading "Books not referred to specifically in the Notes."

42. Bédier (*Légendes Épiques*, III, 311) takes exception to this ordinarily accepted statement; he puts the date for the founding of this House about 1130.

43. Galloway, pp. 10 ff.

44. The *Guide du Pèlerin* mentioned in connection with the Wife of Bath's journey to "Galice at Seint Jame."

45. *Guide du Pèlerin*, pp. 6(7), 26(27), 78(79).

46. Galloway, pp. 13 ff.

47. *Ibid.*, p. 17.

48. *Ibid.* p. 23.

49. *Ibid.*, p. 18.

50. *Ibid.*, pp. 24 f.

51. Manly, *New Light*, p. 126.

52. Galloway, p. 26.

53. *Ibid.*, pp. 26 f. (The Convent passed into English hands in 1414, and so flourished until its dissolution under Henry VIII.)

54. Manly, *New Light*, p. 127.

55. Cardinal Gasquet writes (*Eng. Mon. Life*, pp. 222 ff.) that "the clergy of every large church were in ancient times called *canonici*—canons—as being on the list of those who were devoted to the service of the Church. In the eighth century, Chrodegand, bishop of Metz, formed the clergy of his cathedral into a body, living in common under a rule and bound to the public recitation of the Divine Office. They were known still as canons, or those living under a rule of life like the monks . . . This common life was in time abandoned . . . and then institutions other than Cathedral Chapters became organized upon lines similar to those laid down by Chrodegand, and they became known as Canons Regular. They formed themselves generally on the so-called Rule of St. Augustine." Cardinal Gasquet states that the Augustinian, or Black (because of their black habits) Canons were very popular in England; their Order was conventual, or monastic, rather than congregational, or provincial, like the Friars [see above p. 115], yet they were not cloistered to the same extent as were the monks.

The members of the Order of *Nuestra Señora de Roncesvalles*, since they were under the Augustinian Rule, were known, in England at least, as Austin Canons, or Canons Regular.

56. Hamilton, *JEGP*, XL, 48–72.

57. Is not the Pardoner the kind of man who would not hesitate to perform any ecclesiastical function he could "get away with," quite without any regard for a right to do so? After all, he continually makes the parson and the people his "apes."

58. The Austin Canons were supposed to wear their black hoods on journeys to remind them that they were "dead" to the vanities of the world [the Pardoner expressly wishes to be in the latest style]; furthermore, cakes and ale and the singing of secular songs were forbidden these Canons. As Miss Hamilton suggests, if the Pardoner is to be considered as one of these men, the irony in the portrait is very much strengthened when we observe his behaviour on the pilgrimage.

59. III (D) 166.

60. Hamilton, *loc. cit.*, pp. 69 ff.

CHAPTER XIX

OUR HOST—AND VALE ATQUE AVE!

Greet chiere made oure Hoost us everichon,
And to the soper sette he us anon.
He served us with vitaille at the beste;
Strong was the wyn, and wel to drynke us leste.
A semely man Oure Hooste was withalle
For to han been a marchal in an halle.
A large man he was with eyen stepe—
A fairer burgeys is ther noon in Chepe—
Boold of his speche, and wys, and wel ytaught,
And of manhode hym lakkede right naught.
Eek therto he was right a myrie man,
And after soper pleyen he bigan,
And spak of myrthe amonges othere thynges,
Whan that we hadde maad our rekenynges,
And seyde thus: "Now, lordynges, trewely,
Ye been to me right welcome, hertely;
For by my trouthe, if that I shal nat lye,
I saugh nat this yeer so myrie a compaignye
Atones in this herberwe as is now.
Fayn wolde I doon yow myrthe, wiste I how.
And of a myrthe I am right now bythoght,
To doon yow ese, and it shal coste noght."

(ll. 747–768)

RILEY says in his Introduction to the *Liber Albus,* a compilation
of the London civic records made in 1419, that a medieval *hosteler*
was a person who received guests for a profit and who lodged and
fed the servants and horses of the guests as well.[1] "Oure Hooste"
who so efficiently manages the Tabard Inn, with its wide chambers
and stables, is obviously of this class, but since the Tabard lies across
London Bridge in Southwark, he is not affected by many of the
restrictions put upon hostelers in the city. We may note a few of
those restrictions, however, and speculate as to whether or not the

Host would abide by them. The London innkeeper was held responsible for the conduct of any guest lodging with him more than twenty-four hours; he was required to take charge of guests' arms whenever the carrying of arms was prohibited; he should keep guests from being abroad at night after curfew; he should charge only certain fixed prices for various commodities; he should not retail food and drink to any except bona fide guests, not make ale or bread; and so on.[2] We can well imagine that Harry Bailly, who is so named by the Cook on the way to Canterbury,[3] and who is such a substantial burgess, would willingly adhere to any of these regulations that would make for the respectability of his inn, but what he would do about prices is another matter. Complaints about the high costs in inns outside of London were numerous in the fourteenth century,[4] and the Tabard is too much in the medieval luxury class to be inexpensive. We remember that earlier in the *General Prologue* Chaucer says that the pilgrims "weren esed atte beste," and now again when we meet the Host, we learn that he serves "vitaille at the beste" as well as strong wine which pleases everyone, and that he is concerned for his guests' comfort and amusement. Certainly for such superior accommodations one must pay, and Harry Bailly is too much of an opportunist not to take full advantage of what he has to offer.

Although the extraordinarily vivid character of the Host is not fully developed before the pilgrims begin their journey to Canterbury, what is said of the Host in the *General Prologue* is not unrevealing. He is an agreeably fashioned man, large of body and extremely virile; his bright ("stepe")[5] eyes miss nothing, and seem to match his direct, sensible, and well-informed conversation. Moreover, he is thoroughly genial. Indeed, Chaucer remarks, there is not a fairer burgess in all of Cheapside than the Host, who could well have been a "marchal in an halle."

To say that a man was worthy of being a marshal in a lord's house ("in an halle") was a considerable compliment in the Middle Ages, for that office, according to a fifteenth-century Courtesy Book, was by no means lowly: the marshal is spoken of as a "Ientilman herberoure."[6] The duties of such gentlemen-hosts were exercised in their lords' absence; the marshal served as deputy for the lord.

The marshall . . . shall assigne all other men ther logynges, as well strangers as men of houshold; and also he shall assigne them bred, ale, wyne, wex, talowe, and fewell to ther logynge after the season of the yere, and ther degrees, and rekyn for it dayle and wokely as the lordes bookes be made.

Then the marshall and ussher shall dayle reken all the messes wythin the howse . . .

Also the marshall hathe poure to correcte all suche as dothe grete offences wythin the howse or wythoute, as in fightyng, oreble chydyng [!], makyng of debates, drawyng of knyves and stelynges, affrayes and suche other . . .

Also at all tymes of the day the marshall shall have his commond-mentes fullfillid in every office of the house . . .

Also at every tyme that the lorde commondyth drynke, the marshall or ussher shall warne esquyers or yeman to awayte theron, and they shall goo wyth hym and commonde it at every office . . .[7]

One can have little doubt that Chaucer's Host would acquit him-self well in such a grand position. For Harry Bailly does like to be master-of-ceremonies, and he can scarcely wait to be so appointed by the pilgrims at the Tabard. It is he who proposes the story-telling plan. "I have just now thought of a means to give you pleasure," he eagerly tells the assembled company, after he has prudently seen that they have paid their "rekenynges," and, upon hastily assuring them that his scheme will cost them nothing (for Harry Bailly's mind does run on money), he continues:

> "Ye goon to Caunterbury—God yow speede,
> The blisful martir quite yow youre meede!
> And wel I woot, as ye goon by the weye,
> Ye shapen yow to talen and to pleye;
> For trewely, confort ne myrthe is noon
> To ride by the weye doumb as a stoon;
> And therfore wol I maken yow disport,
> As I seyde erst, and doon yow som confort.
> And if yow liketh alle by oon assent
> For to stonden at my juggement,
> And for to werken as I shal yow seye,
> To-morwe, whan ye riden by the weye,
> Now, by my fader soule that is deed,
> But ye be myrie, I wol yeve yow myn heed!
> Hoold up youre hondes, withouten moore speche."

(ll. 769–783)

The pilgrims unanimously assent. Harry Bailly, who could easily be
a lord's marshal if some of his rough edges were filed down, has the
kind of presence that demands acceptance of his suggestions.

> Oure conseil was nat longe for to seche.
> Us thoughte it was noght worth to make it wys,*
> And graunted hym withouten moore avys,
> And bad him seye his voirdit as hym leste.
>
> (ll. 784–787)

The Host quickly follows up the company's ready assent by laying
his plan before them: each is to tell two tales on the way to Canterbury and two tales on the return journey; the pilgrim who acquits
himself best in the story-telling is to be awarded a supper at the
Tabard at the expense of the others.

> "Lordynges," quod he, "now herkneth for the beste;
> But taak it nought, I prey yow, in desdeyn.
> This is the poynt, to speken short and pleyn,
> That ech of yow, to shorte with oure weye,
> In this viage shal telle tales tweye
> To Caunterbury-ward, I mene it so,
> And homward he shal tellen othere two,
> Of aventures that whilom han bifalle.
> And which of yow that bereth hym best of alle,
> That is to seyn, that telleth in this caas
> Tales of best sentence and moost solaas,
> Shal have a soper at oure aller cost
> Heere in this place, sittynge by this post;
> Whan that we come agayn fro Caunterbury."
>
> (ll. 788–801)

Having prudently settled the matter of where the prize feast is to
be held, Harry Bailly then proposes himself as guide to the pilgrims
on their journey to Canterbury. Again there is no dissenting voice:
the company gladly elect him as their "governour, . . . juge and
reportour."

> "And for to make yow the moore mury,
> I wol myselven goodly with yow ryde,
> Right at myn owene cost, and be youre gyde;

* *to make it wys*: "to deliberate"

And whoso wole my juggement withseye
Shal paye al that we spenden by the weye.
And if ye vouche sauf that it be so,
Tel me anon, withouten wordes mo,
And I wol erly shape me therfore."
This thyng was graunted, and oure othes swore
With ful glad herte, and preyden hym also
That he wolde vouche sauf for to do so,
And that he wolde been oure governour,
And of our tales juge and reportour,
And sette a soper at a certeyn pris,
And we wol reuled been at his devys
In heigh and lough*; and thus by oon assent
We been acorded to his juggement.

(ll. 802–818)

Everything is now settled to Harry Bailly's satisfaction. Without further delay a night-cap of wine is fetched, and the company then retire so that all will be ready for an early start the following morning:

And therupon the wyn was fet anon;
We dronken, and to reste wente echon,
Withouten any lenger taryynge.
Amorwe, whan that day bigan to sprynge,
Up roos oure Hoost, and was oure aller cok,
And gadrede us togidre alle in a flok,
And forth we riden . . .

(ll. 819–825)

The definiteness of his plan, the clarity with which he explains who shall pay for what and what penalty shall be exacted for "whoso wole my juggement withseye," his ready assumption that the company will accept him as leader, his canniness in arranging for the prize supper to be held at his own inn, his being the first up the following morning to act as crowing cock for the other pilgrims,—all of these things express Harry Bailly, one of the most engaging and human Bonifaces who have ever lived. And since one Harry Bailly, innkeeper, did live in the actual Southwark of Chaucer's time, the statement that he and the poet's Host are one and the same can

* in heigh and lough: "in every respect"

be made, Manly holds, "with a satisfactory approach to fullness and accuracy." [8]

Manly gives a detailed account of the records in which the actual Harry Bailly's name appears. In the parliament of 1376–1377 at Westminster and of 1378–1379 at Gloucester, Henri Bailly was one of the two burgesses who represented Southwark, and we recall that Chaucer describes our Host as a "burgeys." In the Subsidy Roll for Southwark in 1380–1381 there is the following entry: " 'Henricus Bailiff, Ostyler, Christian Uxor eius—ijs.' "; and in 1380 Henry Bailly was one of the controllers of the subsidy for Southwark.[9] It is barely possible, of course, that more than one man in Southwark was named Harry Bailly, but it seems unlikely. Then, too, Chaucer's Host names his wife as "Goodelief," [10] a name which may easily be, as Manly suggests, a secondary form for the "Christian" of the 1380 document; or Christian may have died before the *General Prologue* was written and Goodelief may be a second wife, or Chaucer may have substituted a fictitious name for the Host's helpmate. The character of the lady as described by her perhaps prejudiced husband is, as Manly points out, equally at variance with either name.

Manly concludes what he has to say about Harry Bailly by mentioning three recently discovered references. In 1387 a Henry Bailly was one of the witnesses to a deed in a parish near Greenwich, where he and Chaucer may have been neighbours. In 1392, and again in 1393, the name of Henry Bailly appears in the Close Rolls as a special coroner.[11] Surely this actual man can be identified with "Oure Hooste," that irresistible master-of-ceremonies who conducts Chaucer's pilgrims on their immortal journey to Canterbury.

*   *   *

Often we are oppressed by sadness when an enthralling play comes to an end, but when the curtain falls on Chaucer's great play of men and manners, we know that this is only a temporary close to the scene, and so there is no regret. For this play cannot end, the curtain will ever rise again at our pleasure: these characters are no puppets of strings and sawdust, no figures to become stale and outmoded because they have existence only on a yellowed page,—rather they are perennially live and fresh beings, always speaking to us, no matter how often we meet them, in the vigour of newness yet in all the mellowness of familiarity. Hail and farewell, perhaps, but the farewell is a mere word before another greeting; the Canterbury pilgrims as created by Geoffrey Chaucer are a part of our very life, and never can we—or would we—take leave of them.

NOTES

(The abbreviations used to designate books and articles mentioned in the Notes will be found listed alphabetically in the Bibliography, opposite the full reference. References to lines in the *Canterbury Tales* are given by fragment and line numbers only.)

1. *Liber Albus, Mun. Gild. Lond.*, p. lv. Riley states that the difference between *hostelers* and *herbergeours* is not very clear, but that probably it consisted in the fact that the latter did not feed and lodge servants and horses.

2. *Ibid.*, pp. lvi-lviii. See also Riley, *London*, pp. 323, 340, 341, 347–348.

3. I (A) 4358.

4. Jusserand, *Eng. Way. Life*, p. 126, refers to Statutes 23 Edw. III. ch. 6 and 27 Edw. III. st. 1, ch. 3.

5. *NED*, "Steep." Two meanings are given for this word in Middle English. The one is: (2 a) "Of eyes: Projecting, prominent; staring, glaring with passion"; the other is: (2 b) "Of jewels, eyes, stars: Brilliant." Fourteenth-century quotations are given for both meanings. As the Host is an attractive figure, it seems here to be more consistent to take the second meaning. This agrees with Skeat's note (V, 58) on the line.

6. *Courtesy Book*, p. 13.

7. *Ibid.*, pp. 15, 17.

8. Manly, *New Light*, p. 78.

9. *Ibid.*, pp. 78 f.

10. VII 1894 (B² 3084). See Robinson's note (p. 851) on this line, and Manly's remarks (*op. cit.*, pp. 80 f.) concerning Miss Rickert's research. She found thirty instances of Goodelief as a fourteenth-century name for a woman.

11. Manly, *op. cit.*, p. 82.

BIBLIOGRAPHY

Abbreviations used in the Notes	Full title
Acad., XXIV	Anonymous. "Early-English Jottings," *The Academy*, XXIV (1883), 330–331.
Aiken, *PMLA*, LI	Pauline Aiken. "Arcite's Illness and Vincent of Beauvais," *Publications of the Modern Language Association*, LI (1936), 361–369.
Aiken, *Spec.*, X	Pauline Aiken. "Vincent of Beauvais and Dame Pertelote's Knowledge of Medicine," *Speculum*, X (1935), 281–287.
Aiken, *St. Phil.*, XXXIII	Pauline Aiken. "The Summoner's Malady," *Studies in Philology*, XXXIII (1936), 40–44.
Apsley	Lady Apsley. *Bridleways through History.* London, 1936.
Arderne	John Arderne. *Treatises.* Edited by D'Arcy Power. London, 1910 (E.E.T.S., *O.S.* 139).
Arnold	*Select English Works of John Wyclif.* Edited by Thomas Arnold. 3 vols. Oxford, 1871.
Ascham	Roger Ascham. *Toxophilus: The School of Shooting.* Reprinted from the Rev. Dr. Gile's edition of Ascham's whole works. London, 1866.
Atiya	Aziz Suryal Atiya. *Crusade in the Later Middle Ages.* London, 1938.
Ayenbite oʃ ınwyt	*Dan Michel's Ayenbite of Inwyt, or, Remorse of Conscience.* Edited by Richard Morris. London, 1866 (E.E.T.S., *O.S.* 23).
Barnouw, *The Nation*, CIII	A. J. Barnouw. Letter to *The Nation*, CIII (1916), 540.
Bashford, *Nineteenth Century*, CIV	H. H. Bashford, "Chaucer's Physician and his Forbears," *The Nineteenth Century*, CIV (1928), 237–248.
Bede's *Historiae*	Bedae *Historiae Ecclesiasticae Gentis Anglorum.* Edited by John E. B. Mayor and J. R. Lumby. Cambridge, 1912.
Bédier, *Légendes Épiques*	Joseph Bédier. *Les Légendes Épiques.* (Ed. 3.) Paris, 1926–1929.

Abbreviations used in the Notes	*Full title*
Beryn	*The Prologue and Tale of Beryn.* Edited by F. J. Furnivall and W. G. Stone, London, 1909 (E.E.T.S., *E.S.* 105).
Besant	Walter Besant. *London.* London, 1894.
Boorde's *Introduction and Dyetary*	*Andrew Boorde's Breuyary of Health* in *Introduction and Dyetary.* Edited by F. J. Furnivall. London, 1870 (E.E.T.S., *E.S.* 10).
Bormans	*Chronique et Geste de Jean des Preis dit D'Outre-meuse.* Introduction by Stanislas Bormans. Brussels, 1887 (Collection de chroniques Belges inédites, 7).
Bozar, *JEGP*, XIX	Gerald E. Se Bozar. "Bartholomaeus Anglicus and his Encyclopaedia," *Journal of English and Germanic Philology*, XIX (1920), 168–189.
Braddy, *MLQ*, VII	Haldeen Braddy. "The Cook's Mormal and its Cure," *Modern Language Quarterly*, VII (1946), 265–267.
Brand, *Pop. Antiquities*	John Brand, *Popular Antiquities.* Edited by W. Carew Hazlitt. London, 1905.
Bressie, *MLN*, LIV	Ramona Bressie. "A Gouvernour Wily and Wys," *Modern Language Notes*, LIV (1939), 477–490.
Bressie, *MLN*, LVI	Ramona Bressie. Note to *Modern Language Notes*, LVI (1941), 161–162.
Brindley, *Mariner's Mirror*, I	H. H. Brindley, "Mediaeval Ships in Painted Glass and on Seals," *The Mariner's Mirror*, I (1911), 129–134.
Brown	Paul Alonzo Brown. *The Development of the Legend of Thomas Becket.* Philadelphia, 1930.
Bruce, *MLN*, XXXIV	J. Douglas Bruce. Note to *Modern Language Notes*, XXXIV (1919), 118–119.
Brut	*The Brut, or the Chronicles of England.* Edited by W. D. Brie. London, 1906–1908 (E.E.T.S., *O.S.* 131, 136).
Bühler, *Rev. Eng. St.*, XIII	Curt F. Bühler. "London thow art the Flowre of Cytes All," *Review of English Studies*, XIII (1937), 1–9.
Butler, *Lives of the Saints*	Alban Butler. *The Lives of the Saints.* Ed. Herbert Thurston. New York, 1925.
Camden, *PQ*, VII	Carroll Camden, Jr. "Query on Chaucer's Burgesses," *Philological Quarterly*, VII (1928), 314–317.

Abbreviations used in the Notes	*Full title*
Cath. Ency.	*The Catholic Encyclopedia.*
Chambers	R. W. Chambers. "On the Continuity of English Prose from Alfred to More," *The Life and Death of Sᵣ Thomas More, Knight, Sometymes Lord high Chancellor of England.* London, 1932 (E.E.T.S., O.S. 186).
Champagnac	Louis de Sivry and Jean Baptiste Joseph Champagnac, *Dictionnaire des Pèlerinages Religieux.* 2 vols. Paris, 1850.
Chess-Book	*Caxton's Game and Playe of the Chesse 1474.* Reprinted from the first edition with an introduction by William E. A. Axon. London, 1883.
Chivalry (ed. Prestage)	*Chivalry.* Edited by Edgar Prestage. London, 1928.
Cholmeley	H. P. Cholmeley. *John Gaddesden and the Rosa Medicinae.* Oxford, 1912.
Chron. Hist. Cant. Cath.	*Chronological History of Canterbury Cathedral* by "G.S." Canterbury, 1883.
Chron. Maj.	Matthaei Parisiensis. *Chronica Majora.* Chronicles and Memorials of Great Britain and Ireland during the Middle Ages (Rolls Series, 57).
Clarke	Henry W. Clarke. *The History of Tithes from Abraham to Queen Victoria.* London, 1887.
Clowes	William Laird Clowes. *The Royal Navy.* Vol. I. London, 1897.
Concordance	John S. P. Tatlock and Arthur G. Kennedy. *A Concordance of the Complete Works of Geoffrey Chaucer.* Washington, 1927.
Cook, *JEGP,* XIV	A. S. Cook. "Beginning the Board in Prussia," *Journal of English and Germanic Philology,* XIV (1915), 375–384.
Cook, Lit. Mid. Eng. Reader	A. S. Cook. *A Literary Middle English Reader.* Boston, 1915.
Cook, Trans. Conn. Arts and Sci., XX	A. S. Cook. "Historical Background of Chaucer's Knight," *Transactions of the Connecticut Academy of Arts and Sciences,* XX (1916), 116–240.
Cook, Trans. Conn. Arts and Sci., XXIII	A. S. Cook. "Chaucerian Papers," *Transactions of the Connecticut Academy of Arts and Sciences,* XXIII (1919), 29.
Coulton, Ch. and His Eng.	G. G. Coulton. *Chaucer and His England.* London, 1937.

Abbreviations used in the Notes	*Full title*
Coulton, *Five Cent. of Relig.*	G. G. Coulton. *Five Centuries of Religion.* 3 vols. Cambridge, 1929–1936.
Coulton, *Hist. Assoc. Leaflet,* 95	G. G. Coulton. "The Meaning of Medieval Moneys," *Historical Association Leaflet, #95.* London, 1934.
Coulton, *Life in Mid. Ages*	G. G. Coulton. *Life in the Middle Ages.* 4 vols. Cambridge, 1928.
Coulton, *Med. Pan.*	G. G. Coulton. *Medieval Panorama.* Cambridge, 1939.
Coulton, *Med. Village*	G. G. Coulton. *The Medieval Village.* Cambridge, 1925.
Coulton, *Social Life*	G. G. Coulton. *Social Life in Britain.* Cambridge, 1918.
Courtesy Book	*A Fifteenth Century Courtesy Book.* Edited by R. W. Chambers. London, 1914 (E.E.T.S., *O.S.* 148).
Cripps-Day	Francis Henry Cripps-Day. *The Manor Farm.* London, 1931.
Curry, *Ch. and Med. Sci.*	Walter Clyde Curry. *Chaucer and the Medieval Sciences.* New York, 1926.
Curry, *Mid. Eng. Ideal of Beauty*	Walter Clyde Curry. *The Middle English Ideal of Personal Beauty.* Baltimore, 1916.
Cutts	Edward I. Cutts. *Scenes and Characters of the Middle Ages.* London, n.d.
Decameron	*The Decameron of Giovanni Boccaccio.* Translated by John Payne. New York, n.d.
Deschamps	Eustache Deschamps. *Oeuvres Complètes.* 11 vols. Paris, 1901 (Société des anciens textes français, 9).
Dict. Nat. Biog.	*Dictionary of National Biography.*
Dieckmann, *MP,* XXVI	Emma P. M. Dieckmann. "The Meaning of 'Burdoun' in Chaucer," *Modern Philology,* XXVI (1929), 279–280.
Druitt	Herbert Druitt. *A Manual of Costume as Illustrated by Monumental Brasses.* London, 1906.
du Cange, *Gloss. Med. Lat.*	Domino du Cange. *Glossarium Mediae et Infimae Latinitatis.* Paris, 1938.
Dunbar	*The Poems of William Dunbar.* Edited by W. Mackay Mackenzie. Edinburgh, 1932.
Early Eng. Meals and Man.	*Early English Meals and Manners.* Edited by Frederick J. Furnivall. London, 1868 (E.E.T.S., *O.S.* 32).

Abbreviations used in the Notes	*Full title*
Eccleston	*Tractatus Fr. Thomae vulgo dicti de* Eccleston *De Adventu Fratrum Minorum in Angliam*. Edited by Andrew G. Little. Paris, 1909 (Collection d'études et de documents, Tome VII).
Emerson, *MP,* I	Oliver Farrar Emerson. "Some of Chaucer's Lines on the Monk," *Modern Philology*, I (1903), 105–115.
Emerson, *Rom. Rev.,* XIII	Oliver Farrar Emerson. "Chaucer and Medieval Hunting," *Romanic Review*, XIII (1922), 115–150.
Ency. Brit.	*Encylopedia Britannica.* 14th edition.
Erasmus	Twenty-Two Select Colloquies out of Erasmus Roterodamus. Translated by Sir Roger L'Estrange. London, 1725.
Essays in Honor of Carleton Brown	*Essays and Studies in Honor of Carleton Brown.* New York, 1940.
Fairholt	F. W. Fairholt, *Costume in England*. London, 1846.
Fansler, *Ch. and RR*	Dean Spruill Fansler. *Chaucer and the Roman de la Rose.* New York, 1914.
Fifteenth Cent. Prose and Verse	*Fifteenth Century Prose and Verse.* Edited by A. W. Pollard. Edinburgh, 1903.
Flügel, *Anglia,* XXIV	Ewald Flügel. "Gower's Mirour de l'Omme und Chaucer's Prolog," *Anglia*, XXIV (1901), 437–508.
Flügel, *JEGP,* I	Ewald Flügel. "Some Notes on Chaucer's Prologue," *Journal of English and Germanic Philology*, I (1897), 118–135.
Foedera	*Foedera.* Collected by Thomas Rhymer. London, 1727.
Fowler, *Trans. Royal Hist. Soc.,* VIII	R. C. Fowler, "Secular Aid for Excommunication," *Transactions of the Royal Historical Society,* Third Series, VIII (1914), 113–117.
Froissart (Berners)	*The Chronicle of Froissart.* Edited and translated by Sir John Bourchier, Lord Berners. 6 vols. London, 1901.
Froissart (Johnes)	*Chronicles of England, France, Spain,* Sir John Froissart. Translated by Thomas Johnes. 2 vols. London, 1844.
Froissart (Kervyn)	Jean Froissart *Chroniques.* Edited by Kervyn de Lettenhove. 25 vols. Brussels, 1868.

Abbreviations used in the Notes	Full title
Froissart (Luce)	*Chroniques de J. Froissart*. Edited by Siméon Luce. 11 vols. Paris, 1869–1894.
Frost, *MLN*, XLIV	George L. Frost. "Chaucer's Man of Law at the Parvis," *Modern Language Notes*, XLIV (1929), 496–501.
Ful. Car. Hist. Hier.	*Fulcheri Carnotensis Historia Hierosolymitana*. Edited by Heinrich Hagenmeyer. Heidelberg, 1913.
Fullerton, *MLN*, LXI	Ann B. Fullerton. "The Five Craftsmen," *Modern Language Notes*, LXI (1946), 515–523.
Furnivall, *Anglia*, IV	F. J. Furnivall. "Chaucer's Prioress's Nun-Chaplain," *Anglia*, IV (1881), 238–240.
Galloway	James Galloway. *The Hospital and Chapel of Saint Mary Roncevall* (included in *Historical Sketches of Old Charing*). London, 1914.
Galway, *MLR*, XXXIII	Margaret Galway. "Chaucer's Sovereign Lady," *Modern Language Review*, XXXIII (1938), 145–199.
Galway, *MLR*, XXXIV	Margaret Galway. "Chaucer's Shipman in Real Life," *Modern Language Review*, XXXIV (1939), 497–514.
Galway, *MLR*, XXXVI	Margaret Galway. "Geoffrey Chaucer, J.P. and M.P.," *Modern Language Review*, XXXVI (1941), 1–36.
Gasquet, *Eng. Mon. Life*	Abbot Gasquet. *English Monastic Life*. London, 1904.
Gautier	Léon Gautier. *La Chevalerie*. Paris, 1884.
Gerould, *PMLA*, XLI	Gordon Hall Gerould. "The Social Status of Chaucer's Franklin," *Publications of the Modern Language Association*, XLI (1926), 262–279.
"Gest Hystoriale"	*The "Gest Hystoriale" of the Destruction of Troy*. Edited by George A. Panton and David Donaldson. London, 1869 and 1874 (E.E.T.S., *O.S.* 39 and 56).
Godefroy	Frederic Godefroy. *Dictionnaire de l'Ancienne Langue Française*. Paris, 1895.
Golden Leg.	*The Golden Legend of Jacobus de Voragine*. Translated by Granger Ryan and Helmut Ripperger. New York, 1941.
Gostling	William Gostling. *A Walk in and about the City of Canterbury*. Canterbury, 1825.
Gower, *Conf. Aman.* Gower, *Mirour*	*The Complete Works of John Gower: Mirour de l'Omme* (vol. I). *Confessio Amantis* (vols. II,

Abbreviations used in the Notes	*Full title*

Gower, *Vox Clam.* — III). *Vox Clamantis* (vol. IV). Edited by G. C. Macaulay. 4 vols. Oxford, 1899–1902.

Greene, *Early English Carols* — Richard Leighton Greene. *Early English Carols.* Oxford, 1935.

Greenlaw, *MLN,* XXIII — Edwin A. Greenlaw. "A Note on Chaucer's Prologue," *Modern Language Notes,* XXIII (1908), 142–144.

Grove's Dictionary — *Grove's Dictionary of Music and Musicians.* Edited by H. C. Colles. London, 1927.

Guide du Pèlerin — *Le Guide du Pèlerin de Saint-Jacques de Compostelle.* Edited (from the Latin MS.) and translated by Jeanne Viellard. Macon, 1938.

Hamilton, *JEGP,* XL — Marie P. Hamilton. "The Credentials of Chaucer's Pardoner," *Journal of English and German Philology,* XL (1941), 48–72.

Hammond, *Anglia,* XXX — Eleanor Prescott Hammond. "Ashmole 59 and Other Shirley MSS.," *Anglia,* XXX (1907), 320–348.

Hammond, *Bibliog. Manual* — Eleanor Prescott Hammond. *Chaucer, A Bibliographical Manual.* New York, 1908.

Handlyng Synne — *Roberd of Brunne's Handlyng Synne.* Edited by Frederick J. Furnivall. London, 1862 (Roxburghe Club 81).

Hankins, *MLN,* XLIX — John E. Hankins. "Chaucer and the *Pervigilium Veneris,*" *Modern Language Notes,* XLIX (1934), 80–83.

Hartley — Dorothy Hartley. *Mediaeval Costume and Life.* New York, 1931.

Haselmayer, *Spec.,* XII — Louis A. Haselmayer. "The Apparitor and Chaucer's Summoner," *Speculum,* XII (1937), 43–57.

Haskins, *Renaissance of Twelfth Cent.* — Charles Homer Haskins. *The Renaissance of the Twelfth Century.* Cambridge, Mass., 1928.

Héraucourt — Will Héraucourt. *Die Wertwelt Chaucers.* Heidelberg, 1939.

Heywood — *John Heywood Entertainer.* Edited by R. de la Bere. London, 1937.

Hinckley — Henry Barrett Hinckley. *Notes on Chaucer.* Northampton, Mass., 1907.

Historia Destructionis Troiae — Guido de Columnis. *Historia Destructionis Troiae.* Edited by Nathaniel Edward Griffin. Cambridge, Mass., 1936.

Abbreviations used in the Notes	*Full title*
Holmes, *Hist. Old French Lit.*	Urban Tigner Holmes. *A History of Old French Literature to 1300.* New York, 1938.
Horrell, *Spec.*, XIV	Joe Horrell. "Chaucer's Symbolic Plowman," *Speculum*, XIV (1939), 82–92.
Horton, *MLN,* XLVIII	Oze F. Horton. "The Neck of Chaucer's Friar," *Modern Language Notes,* XLVIII (1933), 31–34.
Howard, *Hist. Mat. Inst.*	George Elliott Howard. *A History of Matrimonial Institutions.* Vol. I. Chicago, 1904.
Hughes, ed. *Illust. Ch.'s Eng.*	*Illustrations of Chaucer's England.* Edited by Dorothy Hughes. London, 1918.
Illust. Views Met. Cath. Ch.	*Illustrative Views of the Metropolitan Cathedral Church of Canterbury* [William Woolnoth]. Canterbury, 1836.
Ingpen (ed.), *Master Worsley's Book*	*Master Worsley's Book.* Edited by Arthur Robert Ingpen. London, 1910.
Ingpen, *Mid. Temple Bench Bk.*	*The Middle Temple Bench Book.* Edited by Arthur Robert Ingpen. London, 1912.
Jenkins, *MLN,* XXXIII	T. Atkinson Jenkins, "Deschamps' Ballade to Chaucer," *Modern Language Notes,* XXXIII (1918), 266–278.
Jenkinson, *Archæologia,* LXXIV	Hilary Jenkinson. "Medieval Tallies Public and Private," *Archaeologia,* LXXIV (1925), 289–351.
Jones, *PMLA,* XXVII	H. S. V. Jones. "The Clerk of Oxenford," *Publications of the Modern Language Association,* XXVII (1912), 106–115.
Jusserand, *Eng. Way. Life*	J. J. Jusserand. *English Wayfaring Life in the Middle Ages.* Translated by Lucy Toulmin Smith. London, 1890.
Karkeek	P. Q. Karkeek. "Chaucer's Schipman and his Barge 'The Maudelayne,' with Notes on Chaucer's Horses," *Essays on Chaucer,* London, 1894 (Chaucer Society, Part V, XV).
Kentucky Superstitions	Daniel Lindsey Thomas and Lucy Blaney Thomas. *Kentucky Superstitions.* Princeton, 1920.
King Alexander	*Metrical Romances.* Edited by Henry William Weber. Vol. I. Edinburgh, 1810.
Kinney, *Rom. Rev.,* X	Muriel Kinney. "*Vair* and Related Words: A Study in Semantics," *Romanic Review,* X (1919), 322–363.

Abbreviations used in the Notes	Full title
Kittredge, *MLN*, XII	G. L. Kittredge. "Chaucer and the Roman de Carité," *Modern Language Notes*, XII (1897), 114–115.
Kittredge, *MLN*, XXIII	G. L. Kittredge. Letter to *Modern Language Notes*, XXIII (1908), 200.
Kittredge, *MP*, VII	G. L. Kittredge. "Chauceriana," *Modern Philology*, VII (1910), 475–477.
Knott, *PQ*, I	Thomas A. Knott. "Chaucer's Anonymous Merchant," *Philological Quarterly*, I (1922), 1–16.
Krappe, *MLN*, XLIII	Edith Smith Krappe. "A Note on Chaucer's Yeoman," *Modern Language Notes*, XLIII (1928), 176–177.
Kuhl, *MLN*, LV	Ernest P. Kuhl. Note to *Modern Language Notes*, LV (1940), 480.
Kuhl, *PQ*, II	Ernest P. Kuhl. "Notes on Chaucer's Prioress," *Philological Quarterly*, II (1923), 302–309.
Kuhl, *Trans. Wis. Acad.*, XVIII	Ernest P. Kuhl. "Chaucer's Burgesses," *Transactions of the Wisconsin Academy of Sciences, Arts, and Letters*, XVIII (1916), 652–675.
Land of Cokaygne	*The Land of Cokaygne, Transactions of the Philological Society*, 1858, pp. 156–161.
La Prise d'Alexandrie	Guillaume de Machaut. *La Prise d'Alexandrie*. Edited by M. L. de Mas Latrie. Geneva, 1877 (Société de l'Orient latin, 1).
La Tour Landry	The Book of the *Knight of La Tour Landry*. Edited by Thomas Wright. London, 1906 (E.E.T.S., *O.S.* 33).
Law, *PMLA*, XXXVII	Robert Adger Law. "In Principio," *Publications of the Modern Language Association*, XXXVII (1922), 208–215.
Lea, *Hist. Confession and Indulgences*	Henry Charles Lea. *A History of Auricular Confession and Indulgences in the Latin Church*. Vol. III. Philadelphia, 1896.
Lea, *St. in Church Hist.*	Henry Charles Lea. *Studies in Church History*. Philadelphia, 1883.
Liber Albus, *Mun. Gild. Lond.*	*Munimenta Gildhallae Londoniensis*, Liber Albus. Edited by Henry Thomas Riley. Rolls Series, 12 (1859).
Life of St. Francis	"The Little Flowers" and the *Life of St. Francis* with the "Mirror of Perfection." Introduction by Thomas Okey. London, 1912.

Abbreviations used in the Notes	*Full title*
Lindsay	W. S. Lindsay. *History of Merchant Shipping and Ancient Commerce.* Vol. I. London, 1874.
Littré	E. Littré, *Dictionnaire de la Langue Française.* Paris, 1873.
Livingston, *PMLA,* XL	Charles H. Livingston. "The Fabliau 'Des Deux Anglois et de l'Angel,'" *Publications of the Modern Language Association,* XL (1925), 217.
Livre de Seyntz Medicines	*Le Livre de Seyntz Medicines.* Unpublished Devotional Treatise of Henry of Lancaster. Edited by E. J. Arnould. Oxford, 1940 (Anglo-Norman Text Society, II).
Lowes, *Anglia,* XXXIII	John Livingston Lowes. "Simple and Coy," *Anglia,* XXXIII (1910), 440–451.
Lowes, *Convention and Revolt*	John Livingston Lowes. *Convention and Revolt in Poetry.* Boston, 1922.
Lowes, *Rom. Rev.,* II	John Livingston Lowes. "Illustrations of Chaucer," *Romanic Review,* II (1911), 113–128.
Lowes, *Rom. Rev.,* V	John Livingston Lowes. "The Prioress's Oath," *Romanic Review,* V (1914), 368–385.
Lucas, *Begin. of Eng. Ent.*	C. P. Lucas. *The Beginnings of English Overseas Enterprise.* Oxford, 1917.
Ludus Coventriae	*Ludus Coventriae, or The Plaie called Corpus Christi.* Edited by K. S. Block from Cotton MS. Vespasian D VIII. London, 1922 (E.E.T.S., *E.S.* 120).
Lyon, *MLN,* LII	Earl D. Lyon. "Roger de Ware, Cook," *Modern Language Notes,* LII (1937), 491–494.
Makhairas	*The Chronicle of Makhairas.* Edited by and translated by R. M. Dawkins. 2 vols. Oxford, 1932.
Mandeville (ed. Hamelius)	*Mandeville's Travels.* Edited by P. Hamelius. London, 1919 (E.E.T.S., *O.S.* 153–154).
Mandeville (ed. Warner)	*The Buke of John Maundevill.* Edited by George F. Warner. London, 1889 (Roxburghe Club 119).
Manly, *Cant. Tales*	*Canterbury Tales.* Edited by John Matthews Manly. New York, 1928.
Manly, *MP,* V	John Matthews Manly. "Familia Goliae," *Modern Philology,* V (1907), 201–209.
Manly, *New Light*	John Matthews Manly. *Some New Light on Chaucer.* New York, 1926.

Abbreviations used in the Notes	Full title
Manly, *Trans. Am. Phil. Assoc.*, XXXVIII	J. M. Manly. "A Knight ther was," *Transactions of the American Philological Association*, XXXVIII (1907), 89–107.
Marco Polo	*The Book of Ser Marco Polo*. Translated and edited by Sir Henry Yule. London, 1903.
Margery Kempe (Butler-Bowdon)	*Book of Margery Kempe*. Edited by W. Butler-Bowdon. New York, 1944.
Matthew	*The English Works of Wyclif Hitherto Unprinted*. Edited by F. D. Matthew. London, 1880 (E.E.T.S., *O.S.* 74).
Mead, *PMLA*, XVI	William E. Mead. "The Prologue of the Wife of Bath's Tale," *Publications of the Modern Language Association*, XVI (1901), 388–404.
Mézières (Jorga)	N. Jorga, *Philippe de Mézières*. Paris, 1896 (Bibliothèque de l'école des hautes études, 110).
Middelnederlandsch Woordenboek	E. Verwijs and J. Verdam. *Middelnederlandsch Woordenboek*. Amsterdam, 1899.
Moffett, *PQ*, IV	H. Y. Moffett. "Oswald the Reeve," *Philological Quarterly*, IV (1925), 208–223.
Moore, *MP*, XXV	Samuel Moore. "Chaucer's Pardoner of Rouncival," *Modern Philology*, XXV (1927), 59–66.
Morris, *Eng. Misc.*	E. E. Morris. "The Physician in Chaucer," *An English Miscellany*, pp. 338–346. Oxford, 1901.
Myrc	John Myrc. *Instructions for Parish Priests*. Edited by Edward Peacock. London, 1868 (E.E.T.S., *O.S.* 31).
Nance, *Mariner's Mirror*, II	R. Morton Nance. "A Trader and a Man of War," *The Mariner's Mirror*, II (1912), 174–176
Norman, *Surrey Arch.*, XIII	Philip Norman. "The Tabard Inn, Southwark, etc.," *Surrey Archaeological Society, Collections*, XIII (1897), 28–38.
Olson, *Spec.*, XVI	Clair C. Olson. "Chaucer and the Music of the Fourteenth Century," *Speculum*, XVI (1941), 64–91.
Oman	Charles Oman. *The History of England* (1377–1485). (Vol. IV of *The Political History of England*. Edited by William Hunt and Reginald L. Poole.) London, 1906.
Opuscula	*Opuscula Sancti Patris Francisci Assisiensis*. Edited by P. P. Collegii S. Bonaventurae. Florence, 1904.

Abbreviations used in the Notes	Full title
Ordre of Chyvalry	*The book of the Ordre of Chyvalry.* (Translated and printed by William Caxton from a French version of Ramon Lull's "Le libre del ordre de cauayleria.") Edited by Alfred T. P. Byles. London, 1926 (E.E.T.S., *O.S.* 168).
Owst, *Lit. and Pulpit*	G. R. Owst. *Literature and Pulpit in Medieval England.* Cambridge, 1933.
Owst, *Preaching*	G. R. Owst. *Preaching in Medieval England.* Cambridge, 1926.
Matthew Paris's Eng. Hist.	*Matthew Paris's English History.* Translated by J. A. Giles. Vol. I. London, 1902.
Piers Plow.	*The Vision of William concerning Piers the Plowman.* Edited by Walter W. Skeat. 2 vols. Oxford, 1886.
Pilgrim's Guide	*The Pilgrim's Guide to the Royal and Ancient City of Canterbury.* Published by the Canterbury and District Chamber of Trade, 1933.
Pl. Crede	*Pierce the Ploughmans Crede.* Edited by Walter W. Skeat. Oxford, 1906.
Pollard	A. F. Pollard. *The Evolution of Parliament.* London, 1920.
Power, *Med. Eng. Nun.*	Eileen Power. *Medieval English Nunneries c. 1275 to 1535.* Cambridge, 1922.
Pratt, *MLN,* LIX	Robert A. Pratt. "Was Robyn the Miller's Youth Misspent?" *Modern Language Notes,* LIX (1944) 47–49.
Pulver	Jeffrey Pulver. *A Dictionary of Old English Music and Musical Instruments.* London, 1923.
Rashdall	Hastings Rashdall. *The Universities of Europe in the Middle Ages.* Edited by F. M. Powicke and A. B. Emden. 3 vols. Oxford, 1936.
Registrum Johannis Trefnant	*Registrum Johannis Trefnant.* Edited by William W. Capes. London, 1916 (Canterbury and York Society, 20).
Rendel and Norman	William Rendel and Philip Norman. *The Inns of Old Southwark.* London, 1888.
Rickert, *MP,* XXIV	Edith Rickert. "Extracts from a Fourteenth-Century Account Book," *Modern Philology,* XXIV (1926), 111–119, 249–256.
Rickert, *TLS,* 1932	Edith Rickert. "Chaucer's 'Hodge of Ware,'" *Times Literary Supplement,* 1932, p. 761.

Abbreviations used in the Notes	*Full title*
Riley, *London*	*Memorials of London and London Life in the XIIIth, XIVth, and XVth Centuries.* Translated and edited by Henry Thomas Riley. London, 1868.
Robert de Ho	*Les Enseignements de Robert de Ho, Dits Enseignements Trebor.* Edited by Mary-Vance Young. Paris, 1901.
Robertson, *Arch. Cant.*, XIII	W. A. Scott Robertson. "The Tomb of Becket," *Archaeologia Cantiana*, XIII (1880), 500–516.
Robin, *Old Phys. in Eng. Lit.*	P. Ansell Robin. *The Old Physiology in English Literature.* London, 1911.
Robin Hode	*A Lytell Geste of Robin Hode with other Ancient and Modern Ballads and Songs Relating to this Celebrated Yeoman.* Edited by John Matthew Gutch. 2 vols. London, 1847.
Robinson	*The Complete Works of Geoffrey Chaucer.* Edited by F. N. Robinson. Cambridge, Mass., 1933.
Rogers	James E. Thorold Rogers. *Six Centuries of Work and Wages.* London, 1894.
Rom. de la Rose	*Le Roman de la Rose.* Edited by Ernest Langlois. 5 vols. Paris, 1920–1924 (Société des anciens textes français 71).
Rom. of the Rose (Ellis)	W. Lorris and J. Clopinel. *The Romance of the Rose.* Translated by F. S. Ellis. 3 vols. London, 1900.
Romans de Carité	Renclus de Moiliens. *Li Romans de Carité et Miserere.* Edited by A.-G. Van Hamel. Paris, 1885 (Bibliothèque de l'école des hautes études 61–62).
Rule of St. Benedict	*The Rule of Saint Benedict.* Translated by Cardinal Gasquet. London, 1936.
Salzman	L. F. Salzman. *English Trade in the Middle Ages.* Oxford, 1931.
Savage, *Arab Heritage*	Henry L. Savage. "Fourteenth Century Jerusalem and Cairo through Western Eyes." Reprinted from *The Arab Heritage.* Princeton, 1944.
Schofield	William Henry Schofield. *Chivalry in English Literature.* Cambridge, Mass., 1912.
Schramm, *MLN*, XLVIII	Wilbur Lang Schramm. "The Cost of Books in Chaucer's Time," *Modern Language Notes*, XLVIII (1933), 139–145.
Secreta Secretorum	*Three Prose Versions of the Secreta Secretorum.* Edited by Robert Steele. London, 1898 (E.E.T.S., E.S. 74).

Abbreviations used in the Notes	*Full title*
Sedgwick, *RES*, II	W. B. Sedgwick. "Satalye (Chaucer, *C. T. Prol.* 58)," *Review of English Studies*, II (1926), 346.
Skeat	*The Complete Works of Geoffrey Chaucer.* Edited by Walter W. Skeat. 7 vols. Oxford, 1894.
Sources and Analogues	*Sources and Analogues of Chaucer's Canterbury Tales.* Edited by W. F. Bryan and Germaine Dempster. Chicago, 1941.
Spargo, *Spec.*, XV	John Webster Spargo. "Chaucer's Love-Days," *Speculum,* XV (1940), 36–56.
Spurgeon	Caroline F. E. Spurgeon. *Five Hundred Years of Chaucer Criticism and Allusion.* Vol. I. Cambridge, 1925.
Stacions of Rome	*The Stacions of Rome* (Vernon MS.). Edited by Frederick J. Furnivall. London, 1867 (E.E.T.S., *O.S.* 25).
Stanley	Arthur Penrhyn Stanley. *Historical Memorials of Canterbury.* London, 1906.
U. S. Statistical Abstract	U. S. Department of Commerce. *Statistical Abstract of the United States, 1944–1945.* Sixty-Sixth Number.
Steel, *Richard II*	Anthony Steel. *Richard II.* Cambridge, 1941.
Stillwell, *ELH*, VI	Gardiner Stillwell. "Chaucer's Plowman and the Contemporary English Peasant," *English Literary History*, VI (1939), 285–290.
Stow	John Stow. *A Survey of London.* Edited by Charles Lethbridge Kingsford. 2 vols. Oxford, 1906.
Strambaldi	*Chroniques d'Amadi et de Strambaldi.* Edited by René de Mas Latrie. Paris, 1893 (Collection de documents inédits, première série, 79).
Strutt	Joseph Strutt. *The Sports and Pastimes of the People of England.* Edited by William Hone. London, 1845.
Tatlock, *Anglia,* XXXVII	John S. P. Tatlock. "Boccaccio and the Plan of Chaucer's *Canterbury Tales,*" *Anglia,* XXXVII (1913), 69–117.
Tatlock, *Dev. and Chron.*	John S. P. Tatlock. *The Development and Chronology of Chaucer's Works.* Chaucer Society, 1907 (Second Series 37).
Tatlock, *Flügel Mem. Vol.*	John S. P. Tatlock. "Puns in Chaucer," *Flügel Memorial Volume.* Stanford University, 1916.
Tatlock, *MLN*, LV	John S. P. Tatlock. "Chaucer's Monk," *Modern Language Notes,* LV (1940), 350–354.

Abbreviations used in the Notes	*Full title*
Tatlock, *MLN*, LVI	John S. P. Tatlock. Note to *Modern Language Notes*, LVI (1941), 80.
Tatlock, *MP*, XIV	John S. P. Tatlock. "Chaucer and Wyclif," *Modern Philology*, XIV (1916), 257–268.
Thompson, *St. Phil.*, XX	James Westfall Thompson. "The Origin of the Word *'Goliardi,'*" *Studies in Philology*, XX (1923), 83–98.
Thorndike	Lynn Thorndike. *A History of Magic and Experimental Science.* Vols. I, II, III. New York, 1923–1943.
Todd	Henry J. Todd. *Illustrations.* London, 1810.
Toulmin Smith	*English Gilds.* Edited by Toulmin Smith. London, 1870 (E.E.T.S., *O.S.* 40).
Trevelyan	George Macaulay Trevelyan. *England in the Age of Wycliffe.* London, 1925.
Tupper, *JEGP*, XIV	Frederick Tupper, "The Quarrels of the Canterbury Pilgrims," *Journal of English and Germanic Philology*, XIV (1915), 256–270.
Tuve, *MLN*, LII	Rosemond Tuve. "Spring in Chaucer and Before Him," *Modern Language Notes*, LII (1937), 9–16.
Tuve, *Seasons and Months*	Rosemond Tuve. *Seasons and Months.* Paris, 1933.
Two 15th Cent. Cook. Bks.	*Two Fifteenth-Century Cookery Books.* Edited by Thomas Austin. London, 1888 (E.E.T.S., *O.S.* 91).
Unwin	George Unwin. *The Gilds & Companies of London.* London, 1938.
Utley, *MLN*, LVI	Francis Lee Utley. "The Last of the Miller's Head?" *Modern Language Notes*, LVI (1941), 534–536.
Van Hamel	*Les Lamentations de Matheolus.* Edited by A.-G. Van Hamel. Paris, 1892 (Bibliothèque de l'école des hautes études 95, 96).
Walsingham, *Hist. Ang.*	Thomae Walsingham, Quondam Monachi S. Albani, *Historia Anglicana.* Edited by Henry Thomas Riley. Rolls Series 28.
Walter of Henley's Husbandry	*Walter of Henley's Husbandry: Hosebondrie, Seneschaucie, The Rules of St. Robert* (Robert Grosseteste). Edited and translated by Elizabeth Lamond. London, 1890.
Watriquet	*Dits de Watriquet de Couvin.* Edited by August Scheler. Brussels, 1868.

Abbreviations used in the Notes	*Full title*
Watts	H. E. Watts. *The Christian Recovery of Spain.* New York, 1894.
Westlake	H. F. Westlake. *The Parish Gilds of Mediaeval England.* London, 1919.
Wheatley	Henry B. Wheatley. *The Story of London.* London, 1904.
Whiting, *MLN,* LII	B. J. Whiting, "The Miller's Head," *Modern Language Notes,* LII (1937), 417–419.
Wiley, *MLN,* LIII	Audrey Nell Wiley. "The Miller's Head Again," *Modern Language Notes,* LIII (1938), 505–507.
Willard, Texas *St. in Eng.,* 1947	Rudolf Willard. "Chaucer's 'Text That Seith That Hunters Ben Nat Hooly Men,' " Texas *Studies in English,* 1947, pp. 209–251.
Williamson, *Hist. of the Temple*	J. Bruce Williamson. *The History of the Temple.* London, 1924.
Winn	Wyclif. *Select English Writings.* Edited by Herbert E. Winn. Oxford, 1929.
Wood-Legh, *Rev. Eng. St.,* IV	K. L. Wood-Legh. "The Franklin," *Review of English Studies,* IV (1928), 145–151.
Work, *PMLA,* XLVII	James A. Work. "Echoes of the Anathema in Chaucer," *Publications of the Modern Language Association,* XLVII (1932), 419–443.
Workman	Herbert B. Workman. *John Wyclif.* 2 vols. Oxford, 1926.
Wright, *Homes of Other Days*	Thomas Wright. *The Homes of Other Days,* London, 1871.
Wright's *Political Poems*	*Political Poems and Songs.* Edited by Thomas Wright. (Rolls Series, 14).
Wright's *Political Songs*	*The Political Songs of England.* Edited by Thomas Wright. London, 1839 (Camden Society, 6).
Wyclif, *de Ecclesia*	Iohannis Wyclif. *Tractatus de Ecclesia.* Edited by Iohann Loserth. London, 1886 (Wyclif Society).
Wyclif, *de Officio Regis*	Iohannis Wyclif, *Tractatus de Officio Regis.* Edited by Alfred W. Pollard and Charles Sale. London, 1887.
Young, *MLN,* XXX	Karl Young. "Chaucer and the Liturgy," *Modern Language Notes,* XXX (1915), 97–99.
Young, *MLN,* L	Karl Young. "A Note on Chaucer's Friar," *Modern Language Notes,* L (1935), 83–85.

The following books (and articles) are not referred to specifically in the Notes:

Abbot, Edwin A. *St. Thomas of Canterbury, his Death and Miracles.* London, 1898.

Actus Beati Francisci et Sociorum EJUS. Edited by Paul Sabatier. Paris, 1902.

Atton, Henry, and Henry Hurst Holland. *The King's Customs.* New York, 1908.

Book of Margery Kempe. Edited by S. B. Meech and Hope Allen. London, 1940 (E.E.T.S., *E.S.*, 212).

Boynton, Percy H. *London in English Literature.* Chicago, 1914.

Capes, W. W. *A History of the English Church in the Fourteenth and Fifteenth Centuries.* London, 1920.

Chronicle of Jocelin of Brakelond. Edited and translated by L. C. Jane. London, 1931.

Clarke, M. V. *Fourteenth Century Studies.* Oxford, 1937.

Clay, Rotha Mary. *The Mediaeval Hospitals of England.* London, 1909.

Coulton, G. G. *Medieval Scene.* Cambridge, 1930.

Coulton, G. G. *Ten Medieval Studies.* Cambridge, 1930.

Deschamps, Eustache. *Œuvres inédites.* Edited by Quex de Saint-Hilaire. Paris, 1879–1886 (Société des anciens textes français).

Earl of Derby's Expeditions. Edited by Lucy Toulmin Smith. London, 1894 (Camden Society 52).

Fortescue, Sir John. *The Governance of England.* Edited by Charles Plummer. Oxford, 1885.

Gascoigne, Thomas. *Loci e Libro Veritatum.* Edited by James E. T. Rogers. Oxford, 1881.

Green, John Richard. *A Short History of the English People.* London, 1936.

Heath, Sidney. *Pilgrim Life in the Middle Ages.* London, 1911.

Hobson, John Morrison. *Some Early and Later Houses of Pity.* London, 1926.

Huizinga, Johan. *The Waning of the Middle Ages.* Translated by F. Hopman. London, 1924.

Itineraries of William Wey. (Roxburghe Club, 76.)

Liber Albus: The White Book of the City of London. Translated by Henry Thomas Riley. London, 1861.

Looten, Chanoine. *Chaucer, ses modèles, ses sources, sa religion.* Lille, 1931.

Lunt, William Edward. *Papal Revenues in the Middle Ages.* Vol. I. New York, 1934.

Lydgate, John. *Minor Poems.* Edited by James Orchard Halliwell. London, 1840. (Percy Society, 2.)

Materials for the History of Thomas Becket. Edited by J. C. Robertson. (Rolls Series, 67.)

Riesman, David. *The Story of Medicine in the Middle Ages.* New York, 1935.

Roger, Jules. *La Vie Médicale.* Paris, 1907.

Satirical Poems and Songs on Costume. Edited by Frederick W. Fairholt. London, 1849. (Percy Society, 27.)

Sleeth, Charles R. "The Friendship of Chaucer's Summoner and Pardoner," *Modern Language Notes*, LVI (1941), 138.

Snape, R. H. *English Monastic Finances in the Later Middle Ages*. Cambridge, 1926.

Stubbs, William. *Medieval and Modern History*. Oxford, 1887.

Taylor, Henry Osborn. *The Classical Heritage of the Middle Ages*. New York, 1901.

Taylor, Henry Osborn. *The Medieval Mind*. London, 1930.

Tout, T. F. *Chapters in Mediaeval Administrative History*, Manchester, 1920–1933.

Tupper, Frederick. *Types of Society in Medieval Literature*. New York, 1926.

Utley, Francis Lee. *The Crooked Rib*. Columbus, Ohio, 1944.

Wallon, H. *Richard II*. Paris, 1864.

Ward, H. Snowden. *Canterbury Pilgrimages*. London, 1904.

Wylie, James Hamilton. *History of England under Henry Fourth*. Vol. I. London, 1884.